LIBRARY OF THE HISTORY OF IDEAS

VOLUME III

Race, Class and Gender
in Nineteenth-Century Culture

LIBRARY OF THE HISTORY OF IDEAS

ISSN 1050–1053

Series Editor: JOHN W. YOLTON

RACE, CLASS AND GENDER
IN NINETEENTH-CENTURY CULTURE

Edited by

MARYANNE CLINE HOROWITZ

UNIVERSITY OF ROCHESTER PRESS

This collection first published 1991

University of Rochester Press
200 Administration Building, University of Rochester
Rochester, New York 14627, USA
and at PO Box 9, Woodbridge, Suffolk IP12 3DF, UK

ISBN   1 878822 02 0

British Library Cataloguing-in-Publication Data
Race, class and gender in nineteenth-century culture. –
(Library of the history of ideas ; 1050–1053 ; 3)
  I. Horowitz, Maryanne Cline   II. Series
  306.09
  ISBN 1–878822–02–0

This publication is printed on acid-free paper

Printed in the United States of America

TABLE OF CONTENTS

PART THREE: SEX DIFFERENCES OR GENDER DISTINCTIONS

PART FOUR: FROM RANK TO CLASS

ACKNOWLEDGEMENTS

The articles in this volume first appeared in the *Journal of the History of Ideas* as indicated below, by volume, year and pages.

Alaya, Flavia, "Victorian Science and the 'Genius' of Woman", 38 (1977) 261–80.

Avineri, Shlomo, "Marx and Jewish Emancipation", 25 (1964) 445–50.

Cartwright, David E., "Kant, Schopenhauer, and Nietzsche on the Morality of Pity", 45 (1984) 83–98.

Cohen, Gerald A., "Bourgeois and Proletarians", 29 (1968) 211–30.

Curti, Merle, "Jane Addams on Human Nature", 22 (1961) 240–53.

Diamond, Sigmund, "Sigmund Freud, His Jewishness, and Scientific Method: The Seen and the Unseen as Evidence", 43 (1982) 613–34.

D'Elia, Donald J., "Dr. Benjamin Rush and the Negro", 30 (1969) 413–22.

Goldstein, Leslie F., "Early Feminist Themes in French Utopian Socialism: The St.-Simonians and Fourier", 43 (1982) 91–108.

Kearns, Francis E., "Margaret Fuller and the Abolition Movement", 25 (1964) 120–27.

Macpherson, C.B., "The Economic Penetration of Political Theory: Some Hypotheses", 39 (1978) 101–18.

McLaren, Angus, "Sex and Socialism: The Opposition of the French Left to Birth Control in the Nineteenth Century", 37 (1976) 475–92.

Manuel, Frank E., "From Equality to Organicism", 17 (1956) 54–69.

Paul, Diane, " 'In the Interests of Civilization': Marxist Views of Race and Culture in the Nineteenth Century", 42 (1981) 115–38.

Post, David M., "Jeffersonian Revisions of Locke: Education, Property-Rights, and Liberty", 47 (1986) 147–57.

Rather, L.J., "Disraeli, Freud, and Jewish Conspiracy Theories", 47 (1986) 111–31.

Teichgraeber, Richard, "Hegel on Property and Poverty", 38 (1977) 47–64.

Vander Zanden, James W., "The Ideology of White Supremacy", 20 (1959) 385–402.

Vorzimmer, Peter, "Darwin, Malthus, and the Theory of Natural Selection", 30 (1969) 527–42.

Wish, Harvey, "Aristotle, Plato, and the Mason-Dixon Line", 10 (1949) 254–66.

I

INTRODUCTION: RACE, CLASS, GENDER AND HUMAN UNITY

By Maryanne Cline Horowitz

From its inception in January, 1940, the *Journal of the History of Ideas* has set as one goal the study of the idea of human nature in all its variations. In the opening article "Reflections on the History of Ideas," Arthur O. Lovejoy welcomed contributions on four clusters of topics, including "appraisals of human nature" and "nationalism and racialism." At that poignant time of war in Europe following the September 1939 Nazi invasion of Poland, Lovejoy emphasized:

That the knowledge man needs most is knowledge of himself is a sufficiently old and respectable opinion; and intellectual history manifestly constitutes an indispensable, and the most considerable, part of such knowledge, in so far as any study of the past my contribute to it. At no moment, indeed, in the life of the race has the pertinency of the Delphian imperative been more tragically apparent; for it must now be plain to everyone that the gravest and most fundamental of our problems, that the question which more than any others demands answer is the question, "What's the matter with man?" (*JHI*, 1, 1, pp. 7, 8–9).

In opposition to Nazi racial policy, he highlighted the unity of the human species in the phrase "life of the race," and as in most philosophical writings before the establishment of women's studies in the 1970s, he intended "man" as a generic equivalent for *homo sapiens*, inclusive of man and woman. In the celebration of the fiftieth anniversary of the *Journal of the History of Ideas*, we bring together for unified consideration articles which fulfilled the journal's plea for investigation of "appraisals of human nature."

A precedent is *The Dictionary of the History of Ideas*, published in 1968, a collective effort of some editors of the journal and like this volume intended for the general public, which has a plethora of essays on the history of ideas of human nature. The Analytical Table of Contents lists "The history of ideas about human nature" as section two, and the Index cites numerous listings under such categories as "human nature"; "race" and "racial prejudice"; "class", "Marxism", "caste", and "capitalism"; "masculinity", "femininity", and "women". In teaching ideas about human nature in such courses as "Woman and Man in Western Thought" (retitled in the mid-1980s "Gender in Western Culture"), "Race, Class, and Gender," or the team-taught "European

Culture Core," I have found many *JHI* and *DHI* articles useful for studying the ideas of the unity and the diversity of humankind. I bring together this particular set of articles both to provide readings appropriate for college courses and for thoughtful consideration by the general public. In addition to celebrating the fiftieth anniversary of the *JHI* through the founding of the Library of the History of Ideas, this volume is intended to contribute to the recent burgeoning bibliography of books on race, class, and gender.

While the current trend is to treat together the threesome of race, class, and gender, often individual *JHI* articles have focused on only one or two of the topics. As students of the history of ideas are well aware, the re-grouping of topics, of disciplines, and of fields of knowledge is one of the major ways ideas take on new significance and impact. The classification system of this "Table of Contents" helps perceptive readers notice that the articles reverberate with one another both in their timely insights, as well as in their "period piece" blindspots. By bringing together in one volume articles on race, with articles on class, with articles on gender for the limited time period of the nineteenth century, this collection as a whole furthers the current trend of studying the overlapping stratifications of race, class, and gender in a specific historical context.

In this volume the discussion of human stratification juxtaposes with discussion of the complementary ideas of human unity and compassion; through such balance, the intent is to counteract the current trend that privileges discussion of "diversity" and "prejudice" over discussion of "unity" and "compassion." What emerges is a late twentieth-century awareness of the specific yet overlapping ideas which have legitimized and transformed the polarities and hierarchies of modern life: the collection of essays attests that although the constructs of race, gender, and class have particularized Western attitudes toward diverse human beings, philosophical and biological concepts of the unity of human nature nevertheless have endured. For example, the culminating article of Part One on "Human Nature" is a bridge to the sections which follow on "Race and Ethnicity," "Sex Differences or Gender Distinctions," and "From Rank to Class": Merle Curti's essay on "Jane Addams on Human Nature," presents as both historical and of enduring relevance one woman's optimistic idea that human, and especially feminine, compassion might resolve urban as well as international conflicts among people divided by race, ethnicity, gender, class, and nationality.

The first section on "Human Nature" begins chronologically with Frank E. Manuel's essay on "From Equality to Organicism" which contrasts the idea "all men were born free and equal" in Rousseau,

Helvétius and Condorcet, and the Declaration of the Rights of Man with the emphasis on physiological human disparities in Doctor Cabanis, the physiologist Bichat, De Bonald and Saint-Simon. The article's lack of attention to the significant contrast between Rousseau's omission of woman from the "equality of man" with Condorcet's greater inclusiveness rises to the surface in the amusing comment "it is difficult to discern natural inequalities among Rousseau's torpid savages who wake from time to time to eat an acorn or copulate with a woman." In our growing awareness of the dialectical tensions within as well as between discourses of inequality and equality, an appropriate sequel to the 1950s essay "From Equality to Organicism" is the 1980s essay of Leslie F. Goldstein in the section "Sex Differences or Gender Distinctions," which draws attention to the Saint-Simonians' espousal of social and political equality for women in contrast to their "mentor" Claude Henri de Saint-Simon.

The two middle articles in Part One are Peter Vorzimmer's "Darwin, Malthus, and the Theory of Natural Selection" and David Cartwright's "Kant, Schopenhauer, and Nietzsche on the Morality of Pity". Vorzimmer analyzes how Darwin in fall 1838 reevaluated his experiments and Lyell's *Principle of Geology* in the light of reading Malthus' *Essay on Population*. Drawing implications for animals in general from a study of the human species, Darwin gained a specific awareness that over-breeding places a survival pressure on each individual being and a general awareness of a "struggle for survival" in which to interrelate his own previously separate insights. Likewise drawing parallels between nineteenth-century practitioners of diverse disciplines, Cartwright shows Nietzsche's debt to Immanuel Kant, whom he claimed to scorn, for the notion that pity, the suffering of one person over another person's suffering, increases evil in the world. Nietzsche thus dismisses Schopenhauer's defense of the passionate participation in the plight of sufferers. Jane Addams' books, discussed in Curti's article, echo a Darwinian and Malthusian refrain in the recognition of the struggle for existence among paupers and share with Schopenhauer the mission to act upon warmhearted fellow-feeling to alleviate human suffering.

As we move on to discuss the next three sections "Race and Ethnicity," "Sex Differences or Gender Distinctions," and "From Rank to Class", the context is that in the Americas and in Europe today, the enduring stratification of society and culture—impacted by centuries of immigration patterns on both sides of the Atlantic—is a topic of current intellectual debate and public policy. In particular, expansion of the social sciences, and sociology in particular, has provided statistical data indicating that attributes a person rarely has the opportunity to choose—

race or ethnicity, gender, class or rank of one's parents or caregivers—are indicators of one's later position in society. Throughout the United States, colleges and universities are trying to bring about diversity in the population of students, faculty, and administration and a commensurate cultural diversity in their curricula. Current revision of general studies curricula, as well as of political philosophy, intellectual history, and literature courses, often includes the goal of analyzing race, gender, and class prejudices of the Western classics. Concomitantly, women's studies programs, sometimes led by and usually hospitable to both socialist feminist members who analyze the overlapping discrimination of class and gender and also women of color working in ethnic studies as well, have been trendsetters in giving theoretical and practical attention to the interplay of race, class, and gender. Consequently, the perplexing intellectual triad of "race, gender and class" has become an appealing title for interdisciplinary faculty colloquia and seminars. It is hoped that student and faculty, as well as the general public might gain historical and intellectual perspective—both hindsight and foresight—from this timely collection.

While the issue of affirmative action for Hispanic, Black, and Indian populations concerns Americans, the issue of fair policy for racial minorities (often from previous European colonies) concerns individual nations of Europe and the European Economic Community. Throughout the Western world, interest groups concerned for women's rank in society have been influencing public policy on issues such as access to birth control and abortion, availability of daycare, divorce law, access to professional schools, equal pay for equal work, pornography legislation, and sexism in advertising. In a nutshell, the issues of race/ethnicity and gender are not "invisible" or "private" as some might believe they were in the past, but are at the forefront of visible debates on public policy. This book shows that in the nineteenth century, as well, the issues were of concern to major thinkers.

There is increasing awareness that "race" or "ethnicity", "sex roles" or "gender", and "rank" or "class" are cultural constructs that mean different things in different places and change over time. The need today for a pair of words for each category is an indication of the role diverse ideas play in the conceptualization and choice of categories by which to classify individuals into groups. For example, the perception of color gradation utilized in judging "race" means that some people who would be viewed as "Black" in the United States would be viewed as "White" in Brazil. Likewise, while Nazi perceptions of Jews as an "inferior race" has roots in nineteenth-century racial theory, United States affirmative action policies view "Jews" as one of many advantaged Caucasian ethnic groups. The trend of the 1980s to replace the term "sex roles" by "gender" encourages one to not discriminate on sexuality, marital status, and sexual preference in providing societal opportunities for men and women. In distinguishing "sex," the biological distinction of male and female, from "gender," the cultural socialization of roles and character traits deemed either "masculine" or "feminine," the impact of women's studies, men's studies, and gender studies is to emphasize the historical and anthropological factors that culturally construct men and women in specific communities at specific times. The period under study, the nineteenth-century, witnessed the category "rank" replaced by the category "class" in the aftermath of the French Revolution and under the impact of Karl Marx's emphasis on class conflict as the catalyst of historical change. Still, sociologists and sociological historians studying the gradations between people based on such factors as family heritage and titles, income, and education need terms for distinguishing the hierarchy within the broad classes of proletariat and bourgeoisie.

Part Two "Race and Ethnicity" is divided into two clusters "American Questions on Race" and "Marx, Freud, and the Jewish Question." Our essayists who were not yet influenced linguistically by the emergence of the "Black is beautiful" movement of the 1960s utilized the term "Negro." Donald J. D'Elia in the late 1960s wrote of the continuing revolutionary inspiration that might be derived from Dr. Benjamin Rush's writings and activities starting in the 1770s to abolish slavery and promote the welfare of the Negro. Through historical analysis of the medical physician Rush, a signer of the Declaration of Independence who believed that the Negro possessed natural rights which society to its peril was denying, D'Elia gives renewed impetus to Enlightenment egalitarianism. Harvey Wish's "Aristotle, Plato, and the Mason-Dixon Line" is an amazing article of 1949 whose insight into the deleterious impact of Aristotle gained further corroboration through Lewis Hanke's *Aristotle and the American Indian: A Study of Race Prejudice in the Modern World*, 1959, and David Brion Davis' 1966 Pulitzer-prize-winning *The Problem of Slavery in Western Culture*. Wish shows that Aristotle's argument in the *Politics* that some are by nature slaves provided classical legitimacy to the proslavery cause of Professor Thomas R. Dew, John C. Calhoun, William J. Grayson, George Frederick Holmes, George Fitzhugh and a host of proslavery propagandists and journalists. Writing a contemporary history of the Southern mind in 1959, a time of segregationist resistance to the Supreme Court's 1954 rejection of "separate but equal," James W. Vander Zanden defines and presents the intellectual roots of the backlash White supremacist tripartite ideology that segregation is an eternal part of the natural order, that the Negro is inferior or at least "different" from the white and that the demise of segregation will lead to dire consequences including racial amalgamation. The second point receives the fullest amplification in Vander Zanden's distinguishing the theory of innate and permanent racial inferiority, from the theory that the Negro was a primitive race which might catch up to the white, from the argument that the Negro is simply different from the white. He stresses that the argument for innate and permanent racial inferiority, which he traces to seventeenth- and eighteenth-century thought, is the one most widely held among less educated Southerners, having gained recent impetus from racialist uses of Darwin, the nature-nurture controversy of the 1920s, and Anglo-Saxonism.

While *JHI* essayists on white supremacy in the U.S. take a directly contemporary approach, the *JHI* essayists on the Jewish question have focused on major authors of the nineteenth century. Shlomo Avineri tries to adjudicate between those who view Karl Marx, author of *Zur Judefrage*, as an antisemite and those who sidestep or hide the issue in their elaboration of Marxism. While recognizing Marx's acrimonious remarks on Jews and Judaism and Marx's identification of the Jews with the bourgeois society whose destruction he predicts, Avineri stresses that for Marx the test of the modernity of a state is the degree to which Jews have political and civil rights. As a liberal advocate of political emancipation, Karl Marx utilizes Jewish polemicists to dismiss the Hegelian Bauer's denial of political and civic rights to Jews. Diane Paul, taking a far-reaching survey of racism in " 'In the Interests of Civilization': Marxist Views of Race and Culture in the Nineteenth Century," stresses the wide currency of the Larmarckian assumption that acquired characteristics are heritable, the common nineteenth-century blurring of distinctions between "nations" and "races," and the outspoken stereotyping in nineteenth-century popular "scientific" books. While concluding that what Marx and Engels wrote about Negroes, Jews, the Irish, and Slavs was typical of contemporary prejudices of the day, still, her analysis of the private and public opinions of Marx and Engels airs Engels's "no Slavic people has a future," Marx's letter on the "Jewish nigger Lassalle" and Marx's insistence, despite Engels's humorous dismissal, of the soundness of Trémaux's case for the impact of soil differences on racial inferiorities. Her intent is for us to investigate further to what extent Marxist categories today contain nineteenth-century prejudices.

Freud's attitudes to Jews and Jewishness comes under scrutiny in essays by Sigmund Diamond and L. J. Rather. In "Sigmund Freud, His Jewishness, and Scientific Method: The Seen and the Unseen as Evidence," Diamond studies what Freud comments on and misses in his discussion of a popular novel *When it Was Dark*. Attesting to Freud's open ambivalence toward Judaism, he concludes that Freud's lack of comment on the antisemitism of the novel indicated that he had only pretended to have read it. L. J. Rather in "Disraeli, Freud, and Conspiracy Theories" draws parallels between Disraeli's and Freud's desires to vindicate the "Jewish race", Disraeli's espousal of a theory of an international Jewish conspiracy and Freud's creation of a society of loyal followers, and popular ridicule of both Disraeli and Freud. It is especially fascinating how the Freudian methodologies for unfolding what is hidden through detective investigation and associative remembrance permeate both these essays.

Echoing concerns of the section on "Race and Ethnicity" in the first essay in Part Three "Sex Differences or Gender Distinctions," Francis Kearns discusses "Margaret Fuller and the Abolition Movement." The essay traces Margaret Fuller's reputation as aloof to the abolition movement to a distortion in the account of Harriet Martineau. Margaret Fuller, primarily dedicated to the cause of broader educational and employment opportunities in the gender definition of women, had thorough sympathy for the anti-slavery principle but backed off from the mannerisms and excesses of abolitionists. In the rivalry between women's rights advocates and abolitionists which became evident in the 1830s, Fuller resented the abolitionists' reluctance to listen to female speakers, seat female delegates, and support women's rights, and she chose to give her time to advocating the rights of woman. Seeking origins of the contemporary movement of women's liberation in contrast to the nineteenth-century movement of women's rights, Leslie F. Goldstein analyzes utopian socialists' critiques of the oppression of the family. Ambivalent in her attitude toward the Saint-Simonians who argued for women's social and political equality on the premise of their intrinsic weakness and to Fourier who in freeing women from the sexual double standard appears to write "a socialized version of Hugh Hefner's Playboy philosophy," Goldstein draws attention to the neglected role of utopian socialists in the history of modern feminism. Also paying attention to the limitations of the French Left vis-à-vis the woman question, Angus McLaren studies "Sex and Socialism: The Opposition of the French Left to Birth Control in the Nineteenth Century." In a century of falling French birth rates, only the Malthusians openly advocated a woman's right to control her maternity. The Left, concerned to prove that their economic reforms would not lead to the disintegration of the family, argued that birth control would undermine the relationship of the sexes and was an individualistic act in contempt of the community. Only a few—not the female writers Jenny P. d'Héricourt or Juliette Lambert—explicated the links between sexual and political repression.

In "Victorian Science and the Genius of Woman," Flavia Alaya, explicitly seeking to show that feminism is a philosophic or ideological tradition, as well as a movement, documents a cleavage in feminism after Taylor and Mill which she traces to the "science" of Buckle, Spencer, Huxley, Darwin, Galton, the last of whom concluded that the genius of woman was to be incapable of genius. Their "scientific" proofs of the biological differences between men and women channelled potential feminist activity, such as Jane Addams', into benevolent work considered consistent with their sexist definition of women's domestic capacities and virtues. By the turn of the century, feminist writers such as Charlotte Perkins Gilman and Olive Shreiner, alike emphasized the preservative force of women's sexual and creative energies in the service of society. Very important is Alaya's recognition that both race relations and gendered relations suffered under the influence of nineteenth-century elite culture with its "scientific" distinctions of superior and inferior races and sexes. Today we can describe what occurred as an imposition of gender stereotypes onto allegedly "scientific" observations of the characteristics of the two sexes.

Racism and sexism vie with classism in the non-egalitarian ideologies of the nineteenth century. The title of Part Four "From Rank to Class" emphasizes the transformation of societal hierarchies from politico-economic titles to economic distinctions and the growing importance of Marx's theory of class conflict. "Jeffersonian Revisions of Locke: Education, Property-Rights, and Liberty," supports the 1980s trend of noting Jefferson's differences from Locke. David M. Post argues that Locke's theory of property as acquired by the most rational and industrious justified the divisions of social class and the government by property owners. In contrast, influenced by the Scottish moral sense philosophers, Jefferson believed in the moral capacity of human beings and viewed distinctions of class to be a product of environment. In Virginia he worked to abolish primogeniture and to enable white adult males to have the necessary property for suffrage. Progressing beyond Locke's notion that property-owners should educate their sons, Jefferson advocated the state's responsibility to educate its citizenry.

Richard Teichgraeber's "Hegel on Property and Poverty" elucidates how to Hegel private property is important as possession and use in stages in an individual's realizing of rational freedom. The common ownership of property is objectionable to Hegel since it would limit the expression of individual personality in ownership. The most serious unresolved problem in Hegel's system is not crimes against property, but lack of property, that is, poverty. Gerald A. Cohen in "Bourgeois and Proletarians" draws on Marx's teachings in *The Holy Family, The Ger-*

man Ideology, and the *Paris Manuscripts* to stress in contradiction of D.
C. Hodges the dehumanization of both capitalist and worker in a capitalist economy. The Hegelian belief that human beings express themselves
through acts of production underlies Marx's perception that both bourgeois and worker are alienated because they are not productive. Contributing to the analysis of Marx's newly discovered views on alienation,
Cohen elaborates that worker alienation takes the form of product- and
process-alienation and the worker becoming an appendage of a machine.
Unusual in its attention to owner-alienation, the essay stresses that capitalist alienation results from owning rather than producing, hoarding
rather than enjoying, consuming rather than producing. Capitalist
property is alienable, owned contingently, rather than an expression as in
medieval times of the person and family; yet while both capitalist and
worker are alienated in their own ways, only the worker has an alienation
that anticipates revolt.

The concluding essay of the volume, which highlights the power
relationships implicit in the hierarchy of class is C. B. Macpherson's
"The Economic Penetration of Political Theory: Some Hypotheses." By
economic ideas, Macpherson means possible relationships between
people as producers of material means and relationships of dependence
and control often labelled as classes within a system of production.
Previous to such penetration, Plato and Aristotle viewed the state as
having a higher purpose than the economy, and medieval society viewed
private property as a punishment for sin. From Machiavelli onward until
a turn in the West at the time of John Stuart Mill, economic relationships
became more and more a dominant feature of political theory. In the
classical liberal tradition there was an increasing tendency to view
human nature in a bourgeois mold and to express awareness of the
exploitive nature of society. John Stuart Mill departed from the trend in
rescuing human values from the market place; his downplaying of economic factors exemplifies that economic penetration of political theory
declines in liberal theory with the rise in political strength of the exploited class. Macpherson concludes that in the twentieth century the
awareness of the global strength of the working class resulted in the
increase of the economic penetration of political theory in socialist lands
with a corresponding fear and decline of economic penetration in the
West to the low point of necessitating a restoration by political theorists
themselves. Might it be too bold to suggest that the current interest in the
overlapping hierarchies of race, class, and gender and case-studies of
suffering the triple exploitation of racism, class exploitation, and sexism
is, in fact, such a restoration?

As time passes, it will be seen that these articles themselves show the impact of attitudes toward human unity, race, gender, and class of the post-World War II period—for example, an awareness of the dire consequences of nineteenth-century intellectual theories of race, for example on Jews during the Nazi era and Blacks in the contemporary United States. Likewise, these articles reflect a Western world sometimes in conflict and sometimes in dialogue between Marxist and capitalist economic systems and increasingly in practice creating amalgams between Marxist and capitalist procedures, as well as an academic world sometimes in silence and sometimes in dialogue between Marxist and non-Marxist perspectives. The task of studying the history of nineteenth-century ideas of rank or class thus contributes to late twentieth-century, increasingly multi-factored comprehension of the complexity of social stratification.

The emergence in the late 1960s and 1970s of Black studies, ethnic studies, and women's studies and in the 1980s of men's studies and gender studies marks an academic trend toward greater specificity—from studies of "man" to studies of the "diversity of the human experience." For historians of ideas, that means an increased awareness that "man" in English, in contrast to *anthropos* in Greek or *homo sapiens* in Latin is "androcentric," taking the male as the model for the human species. In analysis of a thinker's views, we now recognize the importance of clarifying to what extent the discussion of "man" or "human nature" is inclusive of the human species; increasingly, scholars take into account the social context of author and intended audience, the linguistic terminology and cultural traditions within which the author created, and his or her racial, class, and gender prejudices.

The *Journal of the History of Ideas* exemplifies the combined tasks of history and philosophy, of understanding thinkers who have preceded us and of creating ideas of value today. In the interplay between the historical task and the production of ideas, ideas written by a member of an educated elite may be useful for the disadvantaged, ideas espoused orally by a mass of people may be of value to the educated, and newcomers to a specific written or oral tradition have valuable ideas to contribute. In an ever-shrinking world of mass media, where humans share in the globe's fragile ecological and cultural resources, it is of utmost importance that valuable, constructive ideas and insights within texts written by the educated elites as well as by the less articulate—however limited the author's intended audience—be available for rejection or critique, revision or expansion, and cross-cultural synthesis by women as well as men, by the socially disadvantaged as well as the advantaged, and by individuals of all colors, creeds, and cultures. This volume, aiming to share a sample of *JHI* scholarship on the unity and the diversity of human nature with a wider general public, invites a reassessment of ideas of "human nature," encompassing the human diversity signified by "race" and "ethnicity," "sex" and "gender," and "rank" and "class" and the human unity signified by "compassion," "pity," and "humanity."

PART ONE

HUMAN NATURE

II

FROM EQUALITY TO ORGANICISM

By Frank E. Manuel

One of the crucial developments in modern intellectual history is the reversal from the eighteenth-century view of men as more or less equal, or at least similar, in nature and hence in rights, to the early nineteenth-century emphasis upon human uniqueness, diversity, dissimilarity, culminating in theories of inequality and organicism. It is the purpose of this paper to trace the transition in representative French thinkers from Rousseau and Helvétius and Condorcet through Cabanis, Bichat, de Bonald, and Saint-Simon, punctuating the novel elements introduced into the general climate of opinion.

The majority of eighteenth-century moralists derived from the Lockian postulate that differences among mature men as they were observable in society were the direct consequence of early education and the play of individual circumstances and experiences. While conceding that gross physical defects at birth might account for cases of monstrous intellectual deformity, it was an article of faith that, apart from such exceptions, all men were born free and equal and were molded into somewhat different shapes by their environment. The very posing of the question by the Dijon Academy in 1753— " What is the origin of inequality among men, and is it authorized by natural law? "—which Rousseau answered with his thunderous discourse, implied that inequality was a phenomenon in the history of man which had to justify itself and had to be explained. Though Rousseau's brief commentary on natural and unnatural inequalities, like many of his theses, could be developed in a number of contrary directions, the moral drawn by contemporaries from the total work was clear and simple: men were once equal in the state of nature and they could be at least semblances of real men in their unfortunate present social state only insofar as they remained more or less equal. Otherwise they became slaves and corrupt lackeys. This was the way revolutionaries read his writing and in this form its message was embodied in the great American and French political documents.

The eighteenth-century theorists were almost unanimous in their acceptance of the psychological principle that all men were equal in their natural faculties, hence in their capacity to receive impressions of the external world; and if they were given identical educations they would all have the same rational concepts.[1] Essentially the capacity to receive impressions was, had been, and was likely to be the same at all times and in all places among all men.

On the problem of whether men were really identical—not merely

---

[1] " Quintilian, Locke, and I say: Inequality among intellects is the result of a known cause and this cause is the difference in education." C. A. Helvétius, *De l'Homme* (1772), in *Oeuvres complètes* (Paris, 1818), II, 71.

similar—in the strength of their organs, the French followers of Locke, such as Helvétius and Condillac, came pretty close to a theory of absolute equivalence at birth, while Rousseau's distinction between natural and unnatural inequalities early in the Second Discourse seemed to imply a contradictory theory, that there were substantial natural inequalities, based on health, bodily strength, and powers of the intellect and the soul.[2] However, the overall reading of the Discourse makes it abundantly evident that even the natural inequalities are natural and significant only in the present civilized state of society. In the early scenes of the idyllic state of nature the primitive savages were not remarkably distinguished from one another in physical or mental prowess; the natural differences so striking in society were really the consequences of the corruption and decadence of a substantial portion of the human species under the vicious influences of the societal state. The process of civilization, in other words, had by now introduced inequalities at birth which originally, in the state of nature, were not there—or at least were minimal. It is difficult to discern natural inequalities among Rousseau's torpid savages who wake from time to time to eat an acorn or copulate with a woman. Thus in Rousseau one can distinguish few if any natural inequalities in the state of nature; these increase in number in the state of civilization; and soon even they are overwhelmed by the flood of inequalities which he designated as unnatural, primarily inequalities of wealth and status and power. La Nouvelle Heloïse was the century's most passionate plea for the right of all men to love, and the Contrat Social, whatever germs of absolutism recent critics have discovered in its pages, was in its day a proclamation of the principle of equality in the social state.

All philosophes were agreed in allowing men equality of natural civil rights, though they might differ about their precise definition. Few philosophes went so far as to posit equality in wealth and property as a natural and necessary form of equality. While Morelly, Brissot de Warville, and a minority of radicals did adopt the extreme view that since property did not exist in the state of nature, it was theft and had to be abolished in society,[3] the overwhelming body of opinion took the position that the maintenance of civilization required the preservation of inequalities of wealth and perhaps even of social status in order to make man who was by nature indolent sub-

[2] Jean-Jacques Rousseau, The Social Contract and Discourses, translated by G. D. H. Cole (London, 1947), 160.

[3] See especially Morelly's Code de la nature, and Brissot de Warville's Recherches philosophiques sur le droit de propriété et sur le vol considérés dans la nature et dans la société. André Lichtenberger, Le socialisme au xviii⁰ siècle (Paris, 1895) is still the classical work on this group.

mit to the discomforts of work. This was Voltaire's viewpoint in his paradoxical article on Equality in the *Philosophical Dictionary;* and this was the attitude of the economists who wrote about the new laws of true political economy. Even Voltaire, however, who was no sufferer of the pretensions of cooks and lackeys, held to the theory that " all men are equal in the possession of their natural faculties " and agreed that inequalities of wealth had probably been exaggerated in contemporary society.[4]

Condorcet made the establishment and preservation of " absolute equality," by which he meant equality in law, the heart of his *Déclaration des Droits* pamphlet published in 1789;[5] moreover, he was fully aware that his constitution might ultimately result in juridical "inequality in fact " unless society instituted measures to render men more or less equal in other respects. This is the dominant spirit of his final testament. The *Esquisse d'un tableau historique des progrès de l'esprit humain,* in which the ideology of the French eighteenth century found its climactic expression, exalted equality as the primary aspiration of the human spirit, a goal to which mankind was inevitably progressing. Though absolute equality might never be attained, the essence of progress was the movement towards a social state in which all nations on earth and all individuals within these nations approached as near as possible to a status of equality, material, moral, and intellectual.[6] If the universal " social art " properly fulfilled its function, all men would really become capable of enjoying a more or less equivalent level of prosperity, for there was no basis in nature for such extreme variations of man's estate as the condition of barbarism, of a colonial master's opulence, and of the pauperized lower classes of European civilized society.

The unique quality of genius and the problem of his rôle in society was perhaps the one disturbing element in the calm of this egalitarian conception. Condorcet and other *philosophes* before him had indeed wrestled with that anomalous—to Diderot almost demoniac—character who gave impetus to the progress of the whole species. Like the deformed monster at the other end of the scale, genius was a flagrant violation of the idea of natural equality. And yet the future ascendancy of man depended so heavily upon him, upon his creativity, his discoveries. In his commentary on Bacon's *New Atlantis,* Condorcet solved the dilemma of genius by placing

[4] F. M. A. de Voltaire, *Dictionnaire philosophique,* in *Oeuvres* (Paris, 1835), VII, 473–475.

[5] M. J. A. N. C. de Condorcet, *Déclaration des Droits,* in *Oeuvres,* published by C. O'Connor and F. Arago (Paris, 1847–1849), IX, 179–211.

[6] Condorcet, *Esquisse d'un tableau historique des progrès de l'esprit humain,* in *Oeuvres,* VI, 238.

the whole of society under the direction of the preeminent scientists.[7] Since the key to universal happiness lay in the cumulative discovery of scientific laws, laws of human behavior as well as laws of nature, the exceptional gifts of the scientist-genius had to be nurtured and his position of absolute independence safeguarded.   Beneath the scientists who were philosopher-kings all others were about equal.

Despite the apotheosis of the scientists, general equality of the human condition persists as the ultimate social end, for the new inventions and the new social laws, created by the scientists and embodied in legislation, tend to eradicate the twin plagues of misery and ignorance, universalizing rational behavior, drawing the whole of mankind up the mountain, ever closer behind the vanguard of scientists who are eternally forging ahead.   In each succeeding generation, as the mass of mankind approach nearer to equality with one another, they are simultaneously raised from one plateau of scientific and moral excellence to another.   This is the true progress of the human spirit: the virtual achievement of that equality in rationality of which men are capable.   But however pervasive the egalitarian ideal, the final reflection is inescapable that the dramatic recognition of the natural superiority of genius does leave the portals open for the antinomic idea of inequality and the construction of an élitist theory.

While the Declaration of the Rights of Man did not adopt a philosophical position on the nature of human equality and explicitly limited itself to the pronouncement that " Men are born and always continue free and equal *in respect of their rights* " [italics mine], loudly trumpeted egalitarian slogans became a vital, intrinsic part of the revolutionary myth. As the Revolution progressed many variations on the theme of natural equality were sounded.   The most notorious, perhaps, was Babeuf, who in the name of Rousseau proclaimed in his Manifesto that men had to be equal in property even as they were equal in the natural enjoyment of the sun in order to be truly free. Among the *enragés* and the lunatic fringe of Jacobinism, equality in the possession of women was included on occasion in a latitudinarian interpretation of the natural rights doctrine founded upon an affirmation of man's polygamous nature.

However sharp the divergences in tone and temper, extremists and sober citizens alike defined the issue in the same terms—how equal were men by nature and how equal should they be in society— and always resolved it in the general direction of equality.   For all the justifications of wealth and *bourgeois* declamations against the

---

[7] Condorcet, *Fragment sur l'Atlantide, ou efforts combinés de l'espèce humaine pour le progrès des sciences*, in *Oeuvres*, VI, 597–660.

sloth of the *canaille*, there was a widespread consciousness at the height of the Revolution that men were interchangeable in most of their social rôles. Property restrictions excluded some men from the status of active citizens even after the abolition of all other distinctions of class and occupation, but all men were capable of attaining that status by the acquisition of a minimal amount of property. Uniform costumes and uniform laws were imposed by the Revolution, enduring symbols of equality. The new political society offered equality of civil rights and through its educational system it was opening up the avenues of equality of opportunity. The Spartan ideal of continence made conspicuous display of wealth suspect. True Jacobins were in fact becoming more or less equal in dress, in consumption, in devotion and service to the state.

Strangely enough, the *volte-face* from an emphasis on man's potential, if not actual, equality, both of knowledge and of condition, to the acceptance of human inequality as the cornerstone of the good society, was executed in the very heat of the revolutionary turmoil.

A cogent expression of the idea of inequality can be found in a passage of a National Assembly committee report, prepared by Talleyrand, in which an analogy is drawn between a well-organized state and a great national workshop.[8] The image, which he could well have derived from any number of economists of the seventeenth and the eighteenth centuries, was doubtless nourished by the realities of English and French industrialization. The novelty lies in its incorporation into a government report on education. Men are born with a variety of different faculties, Talleyrand asserted—the Lockian concept is banished—and these diverse faculties lie dormant until the national system of education comes along and arouses them. A wise educational system takes cognizance of the differences among men and fosters the development of special faculties. The real secret of the social art is the placement of individual men in the most appropriate positions in the national workshop in accordance with their native talents.[9] The analogy of the workshop, which presumes acceptance of the Smithian idea of the division of labor, involved a new emphasis on the dissimilarities among individual men and on their natural inequalities, which it became salutary to preserve.

Within a few years after the publication of Talleyrand's report with its stress on the creation of schools and institutes for the education of specialists in all branches of knowledge, the *idéologue* scientists who took possession of French thought under the Directorate drew attention to another aspect of inequality, the broad

[8] D. Talleyrand–Périgord, *Rapport sur l'instruction publique fait au nom du comité de constitution de l'Assemblée Nationale, les 10, 11, et 19 septembre 1791* (Paris, 1791), 7–8. [9] *Ibid.,* 7.

physiological and psychological divergences among men. Their ultimate goal remained the egalitarian society unveiled by Condorcet,
but the new medicine was leading the *idéologues* to momentous
philosophical conclusions about the nature of man. The intellectual
revolution was generated not so much by the discovery of hitherto
unknown scientific data as by a new interpretation of empirical facts
which doctors and life scientists had been accumulating over the
century.

In the Years IV and V Doctor Cabanis read before the Class of
Moral and Political Sciences of the Institute a series of papers on
the interconnections between man's physical and moral being, in the
course of which he developed a complete typology of character, as
well as a series of generalizations on how men were affected by differences in sex, age, temperament, states of morbidity, regimen, and
climate. He concluded that even rational men did not behave the
same way at all stages of life, that their minds showed not minor
but substantial differences in performance when assailed by crisis in
their sexual nature, by illness, by senescence. Different men seemed
to react differently to crucial transformations in human nature during the course of the life cycle. The emphasis throughout was on
the physiological and psychological variations among men, not their
similarities, which the legislator would have to take into consideration.[10] Cabanis here modified the sensationalism of Locke, Helvétius,
and Condillac at its very source, their presupposition that in general
all human beings received identical impressions from nature. This
simply was not in accord with his experience, the Doctor found. The
differences in sensory perception among men were greater than their
similarities and gave rise to " different turns of mind and soul." [11]
The subject of inquiry was not a Condillac statue which was endowed
with the capacity to feel, but men living in different climates, men
with different native temperaments, obeying different patterns of
conduct, men subject to the exigencies of sexual change, age, and

[10] " When one compares one man with another, one sees that nature has set
up among individuals differences which are analogous to and correspond in a certain
sense to those which can be recognized among species." P. J. G. Cabanis, " De
l'influence des tempéramens sur la formation des idées et des affections morales,"
in *Mémoires de l'Institut de France*, Académie des sciences morales et politiques,
1ère série, II, 230.

[11] " But the impressions which the same objects make on us do not always have
the same degree of intensity and are not always of the same duration. Sometimes
they glide by hardly exciting our attention; sometimes they captivate it with an
irresistible force and leave behind profound traces. Surely men do not resemble
each other in their manner of feeling." Cabanis, " Considérations générales sur
l'étude de l'homme et sur les rapports de son organisation physique avec ses facultés
intellectuelles et morales," in *loc. cit.*, I, 65–66.

sickness. There was no "type common to the whole human species."

The doctors whom Cabanis quoted were dwelling upon the fact that men were born physiologically unequal, that the organs of their patients were far from being equally strong, that different patients reacted in diverse ways to the same doses of drug. The scientific study of pathological conditions of the body and Pinel's pioneer inquiries into the nature of madness, free from religious prejudice, were revealing wide disparities in human reactivity and capacity. Cabanis's psychology, anchored in the accumulation of physiological data and medical experience, cast a powerful light upon the dissimilarities among men and broke with the philosophical psychology of Helvétius and Condillac which in the previous generation had served as "scientific" underpinnings for the doctrine of equality.[12]

Since the Condorcet ideal of equality was still dominant, his friend Cabanis was studying human distinctions with the lodestar of a perfected Man before his mind's eye. The purpose of medicine as he conceived it was not restricted to curing individual ailments; its higher objective was the perfection of the species.[13] The study of natural human frailties or inferiorities should lead to their elimination through time, a feasible prospect since he firmly believed that acquired characteristics were inherited.[14] Cabanis still had an eighteenth-century faith in the extraordinary malleability of human nature and his aim in focussing upon congenital and environmental differences was not to utilize distinctions as Talleyrand wished but to narrow their range. He studied human pathology in order to make men equally healthy and rational and he trusted in the power of science to achieve the general perfection of the human species. Nonetheless, *idéologue* psychology was turning sharply away from Master Locke when it took to studying distinctions—it was a momentous departure.

The same interest in the investigation of disparities was reinforced by numerous lesser eighteenth and early nineteenth century researches in physiognomy and phrenology, divergent as were the

[12] Cabanis wrote that his admiration for Helvétius and Condillac did not prevent him from recognizing that "both of them lacked physiological knowledge, from which their works could have significantly profited." If Helvétius had known the "animal economy" better, he could not have "maintained his system of the equality of intellects." *Ibid.*, I, 63.

[13] Cabanis, "De l'influence des tempéramens, etc.," in *loc. cit.*, II, 283–284. In the same spirit Condorcet had said: "A well-directed system of education corrects the natural inequality of the faculties instead of strengthening them. . . . " *Esquisse d'un tableau historique des progrès*, etc., in *Oeuvres*, VI, 251.

[14] Cabanis believed that the inheritance of acquired characteristics applied both to "physical dispositions" and to "dispositions of the mind and propensities of the soul." "Considérations générales sur l'étude de l'homme, etc." in *ib.*, I, 93.

hypotheses of a Lavater [15] and a Gall.[16] Men were distinct from one another and their differences were written on their faces or in the convolutions of their brains. The mystical and astrological elements which sometimes were intermingled with these character studies only served to widen the breach between them and the common sense interpretation of human differences upon which Helvétius had insisted to the rigid exclusion of occult influences and vague concepts such as humors and tempers.

A key figure expressive of the new scientific attitude towards human nature was the physiologist Bichat, whose works were known throughout the civilized world at the turn of the century. In his *Physiological Researches upon Life and Death* he divided men into three physiological categories. While such classifications had been made often enough before in antiquity and in early modern times on the basis of dominant humors and temperaments, the importance of Bichat lies in the fact that his writings were picked up and read by one of the seminal social theorists of the age, Henri de Saint-Simon. And it was in the form expounded by Bichat that the physiological doctrine of inequality first penetrated social theory and became part of a new general conception of the nature of man and society.

Bichat distinguished among three major types—a trinary division has always communicated itself most readily in western society—a brain man, a sensory man, and a motor man. In each type one particular dominant faculty was capable of great development, while the other two were destined to remain feeble.[17] Bichat's vitalist theory allowed for only a given quantum of energy in each individual; and no man, with the rarest of exceptions, could develop all three major faculties to an equivalent degree. Physiologically men were born limited and restricted—either brain, or sensory, or motor—and vital energy invariably tended to channel itself into one receptacle rather than the two others.[18]

The consequences of this theory for education and human progress, if accepted as a new definition of human nature, are mani-

---

[15] The classical work of Johann Caspar Lavater (1741–1801) was his *Physiognomische Fragmente zur Befoerderung der Menschenkenntniss und Menschenliebe* (Leipzig, 1775–1778), 4 vols.

[16] Franz Joseph Gall (1758–1828) wrote *Recherches sur l'anatomie du système nerveux en général et du cerveau en particulier* (Paris, 1809).

[17] Xavier Bichat, *Physiological Researches upon Life and Death*, translated by Tobias Watkins (Philadelphia, 1809), 112–113. The work was originally published in France in the Year VIII (1799–1800).

[18] " You will seldom or never see the perfection of action in the locomotive organs co-incident with those of the brain or the senses, and on the other hand it is extremely rare to find the former very apt in their respective functions when the latter possess considerable energy in their's." *Ibid.*, 109.

fold. Cabanis had still concentrated upon the flexibility and easy educability of any human trait through laws and medicine; Bichat's iron law of physiology dictated that only one of the major capacities could and should be trained. It was the responsibility of society to identify a man's major faculty and to develop it to the uttermost limits of his capacity, to the negligence of the other two faculties, since it was futile to attempt to fashion what was not by nature educable. Perfectibility lay not in an identical Spartan education for all men, but in the stimulation of uniqueness, in specialization. This led to the conception of an organic society based upon differentiated functions.

The physiological theory of inequality merged at the turn of the century with elements which for want of a better term one must still call Romantic—the new emphasis on the "genesis" of national character as revealed by Herder, the new image of the unique personality as drawn by Goethe and Sénancour, the general climate of opinion that fostered a new sensibility for diversity and plenitude rather than universality and oneness.

The Romantic spirit became so all-pervasive that it is pointless to relate its diffusion to individual poets or philosophers. It discovered a new man with a complexity, with expansive dimensions which the popular theorists of the previous generation had not dreamed of. Man was capable of an acuteness, a variety of sensations, and an extravagance of behavior which the rationalist egalitarians of the eighteenth century would have curtly dismissed as an aberration of nature. Men can have equality in reason, particularly if, as with Turgot and Condorcet, there lies ahead the prospect of a complete mathematicization of all knowledge; but if the floodgates of emotion are opened and men become religious mystics, poet-seers, if they delve into the lower depths of their bestiality and ascend the heights of the ethereal, if they roam the world in search of new feeling in exotic lands, if they resurrect all past history to find new colors and forms of expression, the abstraction of virtuous men behaving in more or less similar fashion in accordance with the dictates of their equivalent, enlightened natures becomes a lifeless scarecrow. Romanticism cannot abide the *philosophe's* image of egalitarianism either as a description of man's inner nature or as a future ideal. The early identification of the romantic poets with the philosophical theocratic reaction was not fortuitous—they had a common abhorrence for the *philosophe's* man of universal, facile reason, so self-evident and so readily accessible to all in equal portions. The eighteenth-century *philosophe* turned his head away from the monster with repugnance; Romanticism made him its hero.

The idea of natural equality could not survive in a Romantic world of convulsion and prodigy.

The impact of the French Revolution upon the philosophical minds of Europe is the most potent political factor in the repudiation of the concept of equality. It was not necessary that the Revolution become a personal trauma, as it was for men like Saint-Simon and Fourier (both imprisoned by the Jacobins) and for the *émigrés*, to make men recoil with revulsion and fear before the bloody deeds of the Terror. The identification of the chaos and sheer destructiveness of the Revolution with the ideology of the *philosophes* had been made by Edmund Burke in the early years of the Revolution and his thesis had swept the continent. Egalitarianism had been a central proposition in the armory of the " literary cabal "; the revolutionaries had paraded *Egalité* upon their banners, the *enragés* among the *sans-culottes* had propounded doctrines and suggested conduct in the name of equality which profoundly shocked the sensibilities of Christian Europe. Equality was an explosive idea which had inflamed the Paris mobs with a violent passion and had implanted illusory hopes in the breasts of " ignorant proletarians." Equality had brought European society to the brink of annihilation. To consider the idea of equality—however it was interpreted—as a dangerous heresy was the instinctive reaction of the conservative thinkers of the continent, and its extirpation became a spiritual necessity for anti-revolutionary theorists of every stripe. Burke's invective against the levelling spirit had sounded the clarion call to battle against the " barbarous philosophy " of the equals. In 1793 when Necker in exile sat down to contemplate the meaning of the Revolution in which he had been a major actor, one of his first projects was the writing of *Réflexions philosophiques sur l'Egalité*.[19] If man wished to associate himself with the spirit of the Divine Creation, he had to mirror in the social order he established the diversities of the natural order. " Inequalities in a state of harmony, that is the rule of the universe." [20]

The concept of inequality as translated into political-religious terms by a group of traditionalists, foremost among them de Bonald and de Maistre, was a major new intellectual force in European thought. They created the image of an anthropomorphic medieval society as the last good society, in contrast with the conflict-ridden, atomistic, egalitarian eighteenth-century world whose bloody climax was the Terror. They revalued status, the virtues of the nobility, the corporations, and the jurands, and they conceived of the social

[19] These reflections were later appended to Necker's *De la Révolution Françoise* (Paris, 1797), 2 vols.   [20] *Ibid.*, II, 116.

order as an organic unity. These men were polemicists of stature and they knew how to excoriate the preachers of equality with a vehemence, a subtlety, and a philosophic universality which no Christian apologist had achieved in more than a century. The theocratic school was less absorbed in attacking the scientific validity of the idea of natural equality than in contrasting this " sterile " political conception with the Christian moral rules of behavior imposed upon one man in his relations with his " neighbor," his " fellow-man," his " likeness." De Bonald stripped the idea of equality of that sense of human dignity which it had acquired among the *philosophes* and revealed it as a naked political relationship in contradiction to the Christian commandment of brotherly love.[21]

But while the spirit of the counter-revolution gave forceful impetus to the anti-egalitarian onslaught, enemies of the abstract principle of equality had also sprung up in quarters which were far from hostile to the regime in France after Thermidor. Paradoxically enough, in the weakening of the ideal of equality there was a confluence of pressures from opposite directions, both from the atheistic doctors of the Institute—the *idéologue* scientists who were the official philosophers of the state until they were ousted by Napoleon—and from the *émigré* theocrats.

Henri de Saint-Simon was influenced by all these waves of doctrine, perhaps most of all by Condorcet, Cabanis, Bichat, and the Traditionalists—an odd assortment of antecedents for his organismic view of society rooted in the concept of natural inequalities. In Saint-Simon's doctrine the scientific élite of Condorcet, the findings of the new physiology of Bichat, the new psychology of Cabanis coalesced with an appreciation of the organic social order of the theocrats.

Saint-Simon has one underlying preconception which is identical with the outlook of the philosophical egalitarians, the conviction that the ideal forms of the good society must be congruent with what is natural in man. From a cursory reading of the physiologists, however, Saint-Simon came away with a different version of the natural: the natural was inequality. He inveighed against philosophism for its ignorance of the simple physiological facts, positive scientific facts, which had since been set forth by Cabanis and Bichat. Confirmed in the belief that physiology was the only sound foundation upon which to construct a social theory, after numerous experiments with variant schema of social classification in the final phase of his thinking he devised a plan which was a direct adapta-

[21] L. G. A. de Bonald, *Essai analytique sur les lois naturelles de l'ordre social, ou du pouvoir, du ministre, et du sujet dans la société*, third ed. (Paris, 1836), 214–215 and f. n. The work was first published in 1800.

tion of the Bichat typology.[22] There were three social functions and three mutually exclusive social classes which corresponded to the physiologist's three human types.[23] First, society needed scientists to discover positive laws which in turn could be translated into guides for social action. This scientific capacity—the brain type— which he sometimes called the Aristotelian capacity, if given free play would fulfill the mission which Condorcet had proposed for the leading scientific intellects. Bichat's motor capacity was transformed by Saint-Simon into the industrial class. In his latter days the term "industriels" was used to cover all men in whatever station in life who were engaged in production of material artifacts and their exchange. In the same category he bracketed a whole range of individuals from the director of a great industrial enterprise to its humblest manual laborer. Most of mankind, whose primary aptitude was the motor capacity, were destined to remain manual laborers, though a small élite of this class with essentially the same kind of talent would become the administrators of the temporal affairs of society—the men who organized states and directed public works and engineered vast projects for the exploitation of nature. Saint-Simon's third class, which corresponded to Bichat's sensory man, were the artists, poets, religious leaders, ethical teachers, whom he sometimes identified with the Platonic capacity. In the last years of his life, when he emphasized the religious character of his doctrine, he endowed the sensory aptitude with special worth since he considered it capable of overcoming the atomist, egotist, egalitarian propensities of the contemporary world in crisis. The men of sentiment would give the new industrial society its quality and cohesive humanitarian spirit.

The good society thus represented a harmonious association or cooperation of men fundamentally dissimilar in their most essential natures, organized in three natural classes. Together they embodied the total needs of mankind—rational scientific, manual administrative, sensory religious. The eighteenth-century *philosophes*, even when they admitted human inequalities, had still insisted upon organizing the state and society around those elements which men

---

[22] While Saint-Simon was already struggling with this conception in the brilliant, though eccentric, fragments he wrote under the Empire, the full meaning of his organic conception of man and society did not emerge until after 1819, in *L'Organisateur, Du système industriel, Catéchisme des industriels, Opinions littéraires, philosophiques et industrielles,* and the *Nouveau Christianisme.*

[23] The "immortal physiologist" Bichat was by Saint-Simon's own testimony the source of his conception of mutually exclusive capacities, a theory which in *Du système industriel* he called a law of human organization. *Oeuvres* (Paris, 1865–76), XXII, 56.

had in common, their natural equalities and relatively equal capacity for governance and the holding of public office. Saint-Simon and all later organicist doctrines which derived from him may have taken for granted some of the equal rights of the *philosophes,* but they then proceeded to fashion society out of the different clays which were the raw materials of human nature. All men were not equally capable of participating in the administration of society. The new philosopher of society approached the whole problem with the initial preconception that the physiological and psychological differences of men were the very brick and mortar of his perfect social edifice. Fourier's theory of the passions, independently developed with an almost compulsive detail and a mania for the multiplication of psychological types, is only an exaggeration of the same tendency. The order of the phalanstery is a harmony of properly distributed human beings who perform social functions in accordance with the requirements of their personality types.

If mankind were organized on the basis of Saint-Simon's—or for that matter Fourier's—natural physiological classification, conflict and frustration would in time vanish from society. Historic conflicts of previous ages had their origins in the fact that class stratifications were not natural, and were for the most part mere groupings of rival interest corps, competing for power over one another. Past history had witnessed the attempt of single classes to dominate the whole of society. This had been true even in the last relatively organic social epoch, the Middle Ages, when despite the universal veneration of Christ, the temporal and spiritual estates, nobility and clergy, were engaged in a death-struggle for the totality of power. As long as classes remained expressions of the lust for dominion, chaos would reign forever, there could be no peace and no social harmony. Under the new organic system of natural classes the lust for dominion would be transferred from men and directed against objects. With time the very nature of this power lust would undergo a metamorphosis.[24]

The presumption is overwhelming that each man seeks to express his own and not an alien nature, that he desires to live and work in the classification where he has natural endowments, be they Saint-Simon's scientific, administrative, and poetic capacities, or any one of Fourier's multifarious dominant passion types. Saint-Simon here adapted one of the major contentions of the theocrats, who steadfastly maintained that men were not driven by a passion for equality with other men of higher status or greater wealth, but

---

[24] " The desire to command men has slowly transformed itself into the desire to make and remake nature in accordance with our will." Henri de Saint-Simon, *L'Organisateur,* in *Oeuvres,* XX, 127 f. n.

really had a profound desire to remain in their own traditional occupations and to continue to express themselves in the traditional
rôles into which they were cast at birth. They wanted not equality
but the expression of their true social natures. Saint-Simon merely
translated this conception into scientific terms: men by nature desired not equality with others but the expression of their true social
natures based upon their intrinsic and immutable physiological aptitudes. The Aristotelian idea that every being seeks a fulfillment
of its essential character or nature has found an echo both in the
theocratic and in the Saint-Simonian theories. It is a dogma that
no man would be so monstrous as to desire to exercise administrative functions if he were born with a scientific capacity. At least,
no good social order would allow such an anarchic misplacement of
human talent. When a man operates in a social class to which he
does not naturally belong, he is wasting his own talents and reducing the total creative potential of humanity. Among Saint-Simon's
last words was a message to his favorite disciple that the quintessential goal of his new doctrine was the total development of human
capacities and the arrangement of the social order so that these capacities might achieve their maximum realization.[25]

In the last analysis the validity of human life in an organic
society derives not from the individual's relationship to his fellows,
but from his relationship to the society as a whole. Inequalities
of status and authority are as obvious as the physiological differences among men, but they are justified in terms of the society's total
organization and purpose. A rationale for these inequalities clearly
emerges in Saint-Simon's ideal industrial-scientific regime, where
power is transformed into function and privilege into responsibility.

Saint-Simon's formula for the organization of society aims to
eliminate the possibility of social maladjustment and friction. Within each class of aptitudes, of capacities, the course is always kept
open to talent. Here again there is the presumption that among
men with similar or identical aptitudes, superiority and excellence
will automatically be recognized without jealousy and without conflict. Saint-Simon generalized to all aptitudes the apparent un-
animity with which the foremost mathematicians, physicists, and
biologists seemed to be appreciated by men of science.

In the good society a natural élite corps (he was directly influenced by the contemporary analogy of Napoleon's *troupes
d'élite*), one with authentic, proved capacities, directed the various
classes. Leadership was not, as the doctrine of popular sovereignty
presupposed, a generalized capacity in which all men were more or

---

[25] *Notice historique*, in *Oeuvres*, I, 122.

less equal and which made it feasible and natural for offices to be elective. In the organic society, workers instinctively rendered obedience to their natural superiors, their "chiefs," in their own class.[26] The idealized image of the Napoleonic army, in which ordinary soldiers had risen to be marshals, in which rank was at least in theory the reward of merit, was a prototype for Saint-Simon's civilian class society.

Saint-Simon's anger against the nobility and the clergy, which he denounced as useless bodies of *fainéants*, was fired far less by their exclusive character than by their decadence, his awareness that in reality they had ceased to be functioning élites within the body politic. Unique excellence and attributes, what he called anomalies, in the Middle Ages had been the very basis for the constitution of élite corps such as the nobility and the clergy. The egalitarian *philosophes* had made the fatal error of proclaiming the abolition of all specialized corps merely because the existing élites in name had ceased to be élites in fact. In the Saint-Simonian world outlook, organic inequality among men, inequality in the social hierarchy, and difference of social function were natural and beneficent, wholly superior to the *égalité turque* of the Jacobin revolutionaries which was an equality of slavery beneath an omnipotent state authority.[27] Men who are born unequal in capacities require an organic society in which each is allotted a function "according to his capacity"—this is the true meaning of the famous slogan of the Saint-Simonian cult.

The organismic society, unlike the atomist egalitarian society, which functions like inanimate clockwork, requires a "vitalist" element—some pervasive emotion, feeling, or belief to give life to the organic body. Though the eighteenth century had developed the concepts of benevolence and humanity as characteristics of natural men of virtue, Saint-Simon in the romantic temper infused the idea of the love of humanity with an emotional drive which it had lacked in the minds of the *philosophes*. Love was the fluid which coursed through the body social, gave it movement and energy. In Saint-Simon's judgment the equal atoms of the eighteenth-century world view were always on the verge of strife; his ideal of love created an organic harmonious whole out of society's vital parts. Men hungered for this comfort on the morrow of a quarter of a

---

[26] The idea of the natural élite was developed by Saint-Simon in *L'Industrie* (1817), in *Oeuvres*, XVIII, 142–145. The same conception had been adumbrated earlier in the fragment entitled "Sur la capacité de l'Empéreur," in the *Introduction aux travaux scientifiques du xixe siècle* (Paris, 1808), 2 vols.

[27] Saint-Simon, *Du système industriel*, in *Oeuvres*, XXII, 17 f. n.

century of world revolution which had loosened the very bonds of the social fabric. The need for the emotionalization of relationships if society was not to fall apart and disintegrate into its discrete elements had been dramatized by Burke and de Bonald and de Maistre. Saint-Simon by his own testimony was communicating the same urgent longing of men for a society in which they could feel themselves integral parts, an organic society, as contrasted with a state in which isolated units competed and fought with one another. Egalitarianism had come to represent the eternal struggle of equals in a world of cold and brutal competition.

Talleyrand's image of the national workshop survives in Saint-Simon's writings, where the goal of the new society is maximum production through maximum utilization of individual capacities. In Saint-Simon's vision of the future golden age of plenty, the emphasis is placed upon ever more production and creation, rather than upon consumption and distribution. The banquet spread before mankind is so sumptuous that dwelling upon material rewards, so characteristic of a world of scarcity, seems to be beside the point. Saint-Simon's humanitarian doctrine thus incorporated the Condorcet principle that society could be so organized that misery and ignorance became accidents rather than the norm of human experience; [28] his theory had none of the crushing pessimism associated with later Social Darwinism, even though he too was inspired by biological analogies.

Perhaps the difference between the Saint-Simonian and the eighteenth-century conception has its crux in a new view of humanity. Instead of the man of reason as the most perfect expression of humanity towards which all men are striving, Saint-Simon thinks of man now and in the future as at once rational, activist, and religious, at once mind, will, and feeling. His ends are moral, intellectual, and physical, three major areas of human effort corresponding to the aptitudes of the artist, the scientist, and the industrialist. This is the whole man, whose being is paralleled in the organization of the healthy body social. If man is primarily a rational animal and the highest form of reason is mathematics, the Turgot-Condorcet egalitarian ideal of rational units behaving in accordance with mathematicized social rules is comprehensible. But if humanity is a composite whose various manifestations include the predominantly activist or religious as well as rationalist, the social structure, reflecting and embracing the variety and diversity of men, will be organismic, a harmony of complex, different, and essential parts.

Brandeis University.

[28] Condorcet, *Esquisse d'un tableau historique des progrès*, etc., in *Oeuvres*, VI, 238.

III

DARWIN, MALTHUS, AND THE THEORY OF NATURAL SELECTION

By Peter Vorzimmer

"The relationship between Darwin and Malthus is one of the most curious and misunderstood in the history of ideas."—Gertrude Himmelfarb *(Darwin and the Darwinian Revolution)*

Up to the present, historians have concluded their evaluations of the influence of Malthus' *Essay on Population* on Darwin's theory of natural selection along two main but opposing lines. The first of these has generally been felt to have been superseded by the second.

I. That Darwin first apprehended the basis for natural selection through his reading of Malthus. That before this time (1838) he had little or no conception of a mechanism or process for his evolutionary hypothesis.[1]

II. That the influence of Malthus on Darwin has been greatly over-rated—even by Darwin himself in his own retrospective analysis. That Darwin had clearly and explicitly described a competitive struggle for existence well before his reading of Malthus. That Malthus' contribution is limited to his striking *mathematical* exposition of principles already known to Darwin. That Darwin was impressed only by Malthus' arguments as to time, extent, and numbers involved.[2]

It is this writer's contention that, while there are elements of truth in both views, neither of them is essentially correct. Consequently, it is the purpose of this paper to offer, by way of an historical account of Darwin's life and thought during the two important years from his landing with the *Beagle* (October, 1836) to his reading of Malthus (October, 1838), an alternative view—one which, it is hoped, will retain the truth in the preceding views while demonstrating their considerable limitations.

Darwin's Activities from the Beagle to Malthus

Darwin landed with the *Beagle* at Falmouth on October 2, 1836. Between his return home to Shrewsbury two days later and the 10th of December when he decided to settle down to work in Cambridge, his time was almost equally divided between visiting family and friends and the disposing of his collections. Already the program for publishing the

[1]This view is generally shared by Nordenskjold, *The History of Biology* (1927); G. West, *Charles Darwin* (1937); Irvine, *Apes, Angels, and Victorians* (1955); Butterfield, *The Origins of Modern Science* (1957); R.A. Fisher, *The Genetical Theory of Natural Selection* (rev. ed., 1958); Gillispie, *The Edge of Objectivity* (1960); and Sirks & Zirkle, *The Evolution of Biology* (1964).

[2]This view shared by Himmelfarb, *Darwin and the Darwinian Revolution* (1959); Eiseley, *Darwin's Century* (1959); and De Beer, *Charles Darwin: A Scientific Biography* (1965).

observations made on the voyage had been laid out. The first two volumes would encompass Captain Fitz-Roy's contributions, the third had been allocated to Darwin. In this volume, Darwin was to turn his *Beagle* diary and notebooks into a publishable "Journal of Researches." Further plans—for the projected geology, zoology, and natural history of the voyage—would depend on securing governmental support. Darwin had chosen Cambridge as the place to begin his first serious writing because he felt the familiar and congenial atmosphere of his old university town would be most conducive to what he knew would be the difficult task ahead. By the time he arrived, to stay first with his former mentor Henslow, he knew that Fitz-Roy was already well underway with his part of the writing.

Darwin's letters of this period reflect certain feelings of inadequacy for this first venture into the professional arena:

I find, though I remain daily many hours at work, the progress is very slow: —it is an awful thing to say to oneself, every fool and every clever man in England, if he chooses, may make as many ill-natured remarks as he likes on this unfortunate sentence.[3]

We must remember that when he left on the *Beagle* five years before, untried and inexperienced, Darwin had just been graduated from the university. Though large segments of his long letters had been read before sessions of the Geological and Linnean societies, he had yet to publish formally anything under his own hand. Three days with the Henslows only served to underline his growing feeling of guilt over what he interpreted as two months' procrastination. On the 13th of December he moved into digs of his own to begin in earnest.

Cambridge, however, with all its friends and colleagues, proved a little too congenial. Going down to London at the beginning of January to visit Lyell and give his first paper before the Geological Society, Darwin had little progress to report. Visits, lengthy discussions in the comforts of university combination rooms, and more activities surrounding his collections allowed only snatches of his evening hours for the "Journal." By late February it had become clear to Darwin that Cambridge was too distracting. So it was was with very mixed feelings that he left to take up residence in London on the 7th of March. As austere as he felt London life would be, the fact that he had precious little to show for three months in Cambridge forced his decision. At least Lyell and a number of other scientists would be closer to hand.

On March 28, Darwin was able to report to Henslow that he was "going steadily & have already made a hole in the work." In this same month he stopped to read the fifth edition of Lyell's *Principles of Geology*, which had just appeared. In its treatment of the organic

[3]Letter from Darwin to Henslow, May 18, 1837 in *The Life and Letters of Charles Darwin* (2 vols.), ed. F. Darwin (New York, 1898), I, 254.

world, this edition was to have a far greater impact on Darwin than the first edition that had so impressed him on the voyage.

On the 3rd of May, Darwin took time off to read a second paper—on fossil mammals found in South America—to the Geological Society. The report of the Society's secretary in the *Proceedings* indicates that Darwin concluded his account by pointing out the unusual relationship between long-extinct fossil forms and the existing species found in the same area. It augured well for the young naturalist to focus on the phenomena for which he would some day propose a causal explanation.

By mid-May, Darwin wrote that he was "⅔rds through" the *Journal* and, by the end of the month, he told one correspondent that he hoped to have his manuscript off to the printers by August, with a view to its being published in November. By the last day of the month he felt he was sufficiently near completion to read his third paper to the Geological Society, and later in June, to visit Shrewsbury. On July 14, Darwin was able to tell Henslow with some confidence that he was mainly 'ornamenting' the *Journal*. It was probably not many days after this that Darwin opened his first notebook on "Transmutation of Species" (which his personal journal records he began that month). When the last proofs of the *Journal* were returned by him in September, Darwin allowed himself trips to Shrewsbury and the Isle of Wight, read a fourth paper to the geologists and then got back to the recently approved project of writing up the zoology and geology of the *Beagle* voyage.

It was not until the end of February of the following year (1838) that Darwin had any spare time for the diversions of general reading and his "species work." At this time, his journal records his having "speculated much about 'Existence of Species' and read more than usual." But March 7th sees him reading another geological paper and then going right on with the *Beagle* geology. By this time he had begun his second "transmutation" notebook, having filled the 281 smallish pages of the first. For most of the spring and summer, Darwin worked diligently on geology. The only time he allowed himself to jot down notes on transmutation was when he periodically fell ill—too ill to attack the more formalized efforts of his geological writing. Thus his journal records bouts of illness combined with "species" work from May 1–10 and June 1–23. On the 23rd of June, Darwin dropped everything to accept an invitation to do geology in Scotland.

It was when he returned from Scotland to visit and vacation with the family in Shrewsbury early in July that feelings of idleness and procrastination led him to start his third transmutation notebook. When he returned to London at the beginning of August he continued to "read a good deal of various and amusing books & paid some attention to Metaphysical subjects." On the 9th of August, he read Lyell's recently published *Elements of Geology*. This, presumably, got him back to the task of writing up his Glen Roy geologizing, which he finished in early September. But, for some reason, far broader subjects were weighting on Darwin's mind—specifically, metaphysics, religion, and transmutation. His journal records that "all September read a good deal on many subjects: thought much upon religion." Then, on September 28, he took up Malthus' *Essay on Population* (which he finished five days later) and, almost immediately, many disparate and unrelated ideas fell suddenly and dramatically into place. To better understand the impact of this event, it will be necessary to trace the development of Darwin's evolutionary ideas through this same period.

Without going into detail, it is possible to say that examples of three kinds of organic phenomena impressed Darwin on the voyage of the *Beagle*. These were *extinction, geographical distribution,* and *adaptation*. So it was that when Darwin thought in terms of possible causal explanations for such phenomena, he turned to the relevant sections of Lyell's *Principles of Geology* to see what existing accounts offered. It should be recalled that the young and inexperienced Darwin's principal education and training was in geology. So it was that his mentor Henslow presented him with a copy of the first of three volumes of the *Principles* before he left on the *Beagle*. The second volume, dealing with related biological changes, was received by him at Montevideo in late October, 1832. As his letters record, Darwin was much impressed with Lyell's account of the earth's former changes.

For Lyell, it was the ever-changing physical conditions that brought pressures to bear upon the species constituting the organic world. To exist, said Lyell, each species must maintain a functional equilibrium with its environment. As the environment changes, however, it becomes increasingly difficult, or even impossible, for this equilibrium to be maintained. Lyell saw three results from the effect of changing conditions upon species: *accommodation* (through physical alteration of the species as response to the new conditions); *migration* (through the species' avoidance of the inhospitable regions); or *extinction* (through total failure to adjust).

According to Lyell, however, accommodation by means of adaptive alteration of a species to the changing conditions, is limited in its extent. This, in turn, he saw as stemming from the basically fixed character of any and all specific forms. Since uniformitarian physical change is continuous (if not always uni-directional), it was a foregone conclusion with Lyell that the *accommodation* of any species correlative with physical change is inherently limited. Continuance of environmental change beyond that limit must necessarily precipitate either *extinction* or *migration*. For the most part, therefore, Lyell saw only a "die or move out" result from environmental change.

The Writing of the Journal (October, 1836 to July, 1837)

So it was on sitting down to deal with such subjects in his "Journal" that March, that Darwin turned once again to Lyell. He accepted the latter's conclusions as a reasonable explanation for extinction and, for the most part, many aspects of geographical distribution. This can be seen from his letters, diary, and the first edition of the *Journal of Researches*. It is from the same sources, however, that one can see Darwin's conviction that the phenomenon of *adaptation* was *not* explicable on these, or any other previously espoused, terms.

Had been greatly struck from about Month of previous March on character of S. American fossils—& species on Galapagos Archipelago. The facts origin (especially latter) of all my views.[4] . . . It was evident that such facts as these, as well as many other, could only be explained on the supposition that species gradually become modified; and the subject haunted me.[5]

Haunted, indeed, Darwin must have been struck by Lyell's firm conviction that species were limited in their capacity for adaptive change by the fixed nature of specific forms. Lyell would countenance minor accommodative change, but never that degree of genuine and permanent modification requisite for what the young Darwin had in mind. And there were no other acceptable accounts of organic change to which Darwin could turn for support, as he indicated in the very next line:

But it was especially evident that neither the action of the surrounding conditions, nor the will of the organisms could account for the innumerable cases in which organisms of every kind are beautifully adapted to their habits of life. . . . I had always been much struck by such adaptations, and until these could be explained it seemed to me almost useless to endeavour to prove by indirect evidence, that species have been modified.[6]

Thus it had been in examining more closely the detailed nature of geographical distribution that Darwin was led to see *adaptation* as the key to biological change. He had come to look upon geographical distribution as a form of adaptive containment. Adaptation was seen by him as the structural and functional relationship between the organism and its station. For this, Darwin had no causal explanation when he left the *Beagle* in October, 1836. By this fateful month of March, 1837, however, he had become aware that the most likely explanation would involve the assumption of the mutability of species.

When I was on board the *Beagle* I believed in the permanence of species, but, as far as I can remember, vague doubts occasionally flitted across my mind. On my return home in the autumn of 1836 I immediately began to pre-

---

[4]"Darwin's Journal," *Bulletin of the British Museum (Natural History)*, Historical Series, (1959), I, No. 1, 7.

[5]*Op. cit. Life and Letters*, I, p. 67.   [6]*Ibid.*

pare my journal for publication, and then saw how many facts indicated the common descent of species ... [7]

Thus the move to London from Cambridge and his renewed efforts on the *Journal*, his interest in adaptation and its causes, and his reading of the just-published fifth edition of the *Principles of Geology*, were not, for Darwin, unrelated events of that March. The re-reading of Lyell—in some ways, as it were, for the first time[8]—spurred him into speculations of his own. The fact that the *Principles* did not provide any satisfactory account of how adaptation had come about, or what the link was between adaptation and geographical distribution, led Darwin, for the first time, to a determined attempt to think out possible causal explanations of his own.

Adaptation, seen as a "fit" between organisms and their environment, was the one major subject an explanation of which Darwin was to devote himself to from March onwards. There seemed to him only two possible causal explanations: either this relationship had been created as such *in situ*, or, it had come to be as a result of *process*. For Darwin the first possibility offered no speculative challenge. Further, it was scientifically unsatisfying in that it required a *Deus ex machina* and thus precluded the possibility of a natural explanation. He opted for the second alternative.

Since he had explicitly rejected adaptive change as a *direct organic response* ("neither the action of the surrounding conditions, nor the will of the organisms"), he concluded that adaptation must be based upon naturally-occurring (i.e., non-responsive) changes of adaptive value. One thing was now abundantly clear: adaptation entailed the permanent modification of species. In coming to this conclusion, Darwin was aided—this time along more positive lines—by Lyell through the suggestion of a parallel in biologically-oriented changes to the uniformitarian geological changes.

Darwin knew that the projected means of organic change would have to be of a slow and gradual nature: gradual because the parallel geological changes—the moving standard by which adaptation was defined—were such; and because long-continued, adaptively-oriented transmutation would have to be based on the long-term accumulation of slight variations. At this point in time (Spring, 1837), Darwin is not consciously aware that both the concept of "adaptive fit" and the concept of the long-term accumulation of adaptive variation predicated by

[7]Letter from Darwin to Zacharias, 1877, quoted in *More Letters of Charles Darwin* (2 vols.), ed. F. Darwin and A. C. Seward, (New York, 1903), I, 367.

[8]The copy of the second volume of the principles received by Darwin while on the *Beagle* and containing the more relevant account of the factors influencing the *organic world*, was hardly marked by Darwin. On the other hand, Darwin's copies of the second and third volumes of the *fifth* edition (1837), containing the same account, have been considerably marked and annotated. As shall be shown below, Darwin's interest in the causes of biological change was to grow considerably *after* he returned from the voyage.

environmental change imply a process of *selection*. This is where the model of Lyell's methodology enters. Accepting the uniformitarian hypothesis, Darwin was led to look for the explanation of past changes as derivable from those changes which can be seen to be in operation at the present. Lyell, it turned out, provided not only the line of reasoning which Darwin was to follow, but also the starting point. In the opening pages of the second volume of the *Principles*, in a section entitled "Changes in Animals and Plants caused by Domestication," Lyell discussed the only empirically founded case for transmutation.

Where Lyell remained unconvinced that existing accounts had any bearing on the fixity of species, Darwin was struck by their implications. He felt that here were significant examples of the alteration of organic forms that could readily be seen in operation. Further, he believed that the changes brought about in the forms of cultivated plants and domestical animals at the hands of the breeder might provide a clue to the sources of past organic change. The effect of the cumulative selection of randomly-occurring variation might be projected into nature and its past. But presently observed selection was admittedly "artificial," involving as it did the god-like intervention of the breeder. Yet it was, for Darwin, an impressive example of transmutation through *selection*. It was enough of a start to begin the painstaking accumulation of relevant facts.

After my return to England it appeared to me that by following the example of Lyell in Geology, and by collecting all the facts which bore in any way on the variation of animals and plants under domestication and nature, some light might be thrown on the whole subject. My first note-book was opened in July, 1837. . . . I soon perceived that selection was the keystone of man's success in making useful races of animals and plants.[9]

By applying the approach of Lyell and thus projecting a presently operative source of selective modification into the past, Darwin was led to look for some natural analogue among the processes of the biological past, for the artificial selection practiced by man. Thus the question became "What is the natural counter-part of artificial selection?" And it was not long before Darwin became confident that selection was the key and had surmised that it must be something in nature which "selects." However, as Darwin himself later said, until he sat down to read Malthus, "how selection could be applied to organisms living in a state of nature remained for some time a mystery to me."[10]

We can now see the line of reasoning that led Darwin to open his first transmutation notebook and dictated the kind of facts he would record therein. *Adaptation* had suggested *transmutation*; transmutation toward an adaptive end suggested *selection*. The hypothesis had taken shape. Adaptation was the *end*, selection was the *means*, "changing conditions" were the *initiator*. But an important causal

[9]*Op. cit., More Letters*, I, 367.   [10]*Op. cit., Life and Letters*, I, 68.

mode was still missing. Until Darwin could provide a natural source of motive *force* to apply to the selective *process*, he would remain without a crucial element for his transmutation hypothesis. Nor would he be truly "convinced" of the fact of transmutation. It was at this juncture, during the spare time that he was increasingly devoting to "species work," that he resorted to the Baconian approach of wholesale fact-gathering. It had, after all, in the first few months, led him to the "key" of selection.

The first notebook must be looked upon as having been begun as a convenient gathering place for facts which bear upon transmutation.

On my return home in the autumn of 1836, I immediately began to prepare my journal for publication, and then saw how many facts indicated the common descent of species; *so that in* July, 1837, I opened a note-book to record any facts which might bear on *the question*; but I did not become convinced that species were mutable until, I think, two or three years had elapsed.[11]

The very nature of the subjects that were considered in the first notebooks bears out this view. The notebooks begin with Darwin's jottings from the literature on the basic issue of the *constancy* versus the *variability* of species. He goes on, assuming the first stages of the development of a new form, and seeks answers to some very important questions that would bear upon speciation. Will the new forms interbreed with the old? What would be the possible results from such a cross?

At first glance there is admittedly something puzzling about the subjects considered in these first notebooks. Only in a few rare instances does Darwin speculate as to how the transmutative process may have actually operated to produce existing forms. He deals principally with questions of crossing and hybridization, isolation, effects of environment, etc. This lack of speculation, or even of possible facts, bearing upon his central hypothesis of natural selection, however, soon becomes clear. Nearly every item comprising the pre-Malthus notes involves some facet of modification extracted from contemporary *observation*. The underlying approach is clear: Darwin was collecting documentation on *what had been shown* by experimental manipulation and observation of *existing* forms. If, as a biological uniformitarian,

[11]*Op. cit. More Letters,* I, 367, and *The Foundations of the Origin of Species,* ed. F. Darwin, (Cambridge 1909), 26.

Contrary to the opinion of Darwin's son, Francis, (who less than scrupulously deleted the phrase underlined in the above quotation to make his point), the existence of a "transmutation notebook" *per se* does *not* amount to an incontrovertible case for a belief in the mutability of species at that time (July, 1837). True enough, the pre-Malthus notes were more than just a set of relevant facts on the subject. But the best way to describe Darwin's view in these notes is to say that they were predicated on the very much *conditional supposition* that species were mutable. That, after all, was Darwin's "working hypothesis"—and, as such, would provide the orientation of his fact-gathering. But he was far from being *"convinced,"* nor would he have been likely to *assume* such at this time.

Darwin is to project the presently observed processes of modification into the organic past, so must he almost exclusively direct his fact-collecting along empirical lines. Further, it soon became obvious to him that any would-be critic could equally apply any presently observable limitations to his account as to what might have transpired in the past. Darwin himself was to come across many such cases. Thus the first notebooks are crammed with foreseen difficulties: the projected limit to variation; the tendency toward constancy of form seen as a natural function of generation; the tendency of new and hybrid forms to revert to original type; the assumption that old, established forms dominate over any newer ones; the problems attached to a blending inheritance. All of these had been taken from the existing scientific literature. It was obvious that Darwin was planning to construct his case for speciation in the biological past from processes and phenomena seen as acting in the present. So it was that Darwin (who thus, contrary to his son Francis and Sir Gavin De Beer, must be taken at his own word) was not, at this time, "convinced that species were mutable."

Darwin's second transmutation notebook was opened towards the end of February, 1838 and filled by the end of the following June. A significant portion of it shows Darwin on a new tack: considering the motive or causal factors which may constitute the transformative process. Once again, there is good evidence that a new reading of Lyell proved very suggestive.[12] Darwin was also picking up the threads of an earlier line of his own thought.

In an entry made during that same period (Spring, 1837) when he had been discussing extinction in the *Journal*, Darwin thought the following excerpt worth carrying over into his first transmutation notebook:

With respect to extinction we can easily see that variety of ostrich Petise may not be well adapted, and thus perish out, or on other hand like Orpheus being favourable, many might be produced by confined breeding and changing circumstances are continued and produce according to the adaptation of such circumstances, and therefore that death of species is a consequence (contrary to what would appear from America) of non-adaptation of circumstances.[13]

[12]The thirty-ninth page (probably written at the beginning of March, 1838) of the second notebook bears the following entry: "Lyells Principles must be abstracted and answered. Much might be argued what is *not* cause of destruction of large quadrupeds." ("Darwin's Notebooks on Transmutation of Species." Part VI, *Bulletin of the British Museum (Natural History)*. Historical Series, III, No. 5, 143)

Darwin's personal journal records that, in this year, the only opportunities that he had for "species work" were during those periods when he was too ill to continue his geological and zoological writing. The personal journal, together with internal evidence from the second notebook, allows the following approximation: February 25 to March 7 = pages 1 to 71; May 1 to 10 = pages 72 to 223; June 1 to 23 = pages 224 to 276.

[13]"Darwin's Notebooks on Transmutation of Species," Part I, *Bulletin of the British Museum (Natural History)*, Historical Series, (1960), II, No. 2, 46 (Notebook, 37).

Ten months later, his reading of the following passage in Lyell revives his interest in extinction and its causes:

It is unnecessary to accumulate a greater number of illustrations in order to prove that the stations of different plants and animals depend on a great complication of circumstances,—on an immense variety of relations in the state of the animate and inanimate worlds . . . the possibility of the existence of a certain species in a given locality, or of its thriving more or less therein, is determined not merely by temperature, humidity, soil, elevation, and other circumstances of the like kind, but also by the existence or non-existence, the abundance or scarcity, of a particular assemblage or other plants and animals in the same region.[14]

Back in the spring of 1837, Darwin had seen the relevance of Lyell's account for explaining extinction and had incorporated it into his own account of the subject in the *Journal*:

But granting that all such [physical] changes [leading to extinction] have been small, yet we are so profoundly ignorant concerning the physiological relations, on which the life, and even health (as shown by epidemics) of any existing species depends, that we argue with still less safety about either the life or death of any extinct kind.
One is tempted to believe in such simple relations, as variation of climate and food, or introduction of enemies, or the increased numbers of other species, as the cause of the succession of races.[15]

These, the very same conditions which Lyell saw as leading to either migration or extinction exclusively, were the very factors which Darwin would later show as constituting the motive force of the selective process. It is also interesting to note that it was after this very paragraph that Darwin, in the second edition (1845) adds (for the first time in a published work) his description of how the Malthusian struggle, added to the struggle precipitated by changing conditions, can result in not only extinction but permanent adaptive modification of species. This supports the contention that it was, to a considerable extent, Darwin's extension of Lyell's account that led him to the factors which constituted his own "Natural Selection." It was not until the spring of 1838, however, that Darwin would come to see Lyell's account of the disruption of organic equilibrium as relating to the process of change; this when he was once again grappling with the factors leading to extinction:

This multiplication of little means & bringing the mind to grapple with great effect produced is a most laborious & painful effort of the mind although this may appear an absurb saying) & will never be conquered by anyone (if he has any kind of prejudices) who just takes up & lays down the subject without long meditation. —His best chance is to have [pondered] profoundly over the *enormous difficulty of reproduction of species & certainly of de-*

---

[14]Charles Lyell, *Principles of Geology* (2nd ed. London 1833), II, 145–47.
[15]Charles Darwin, *Journal of Researches* (1st ed., 1839, New York, 1952), 211.

struction; then he will choose & firmly believe in his new faith of the lesser of the difficulties.[16]

Some pages later—written in mid-June of 1838—Darwin shows that he has begun to see how those same causes that had been seen to lead to extinction might very well bear upon adaptive transformation.

Is the *extinction & change of species* two very different considerations? . . . Does this law of duration [pertaining to different Classes of animals] apply to utter extinction or rapidity of specific change?[17]

Between the changes that destroy organic adaptation and the resultant extinction seen by Lyell, Darwin had come to see the possibility of the alternative of transmutation. In less than four months, his reading of Malthus crystallized his idea of the transformative process.

It is now possible to conclude that Darwin sat down to read Malthus' *Essay on Population*.

Aware that adaptation to existing conditions implied a permanent alteration of the original specific form.

Aware that adaptation was achieved as the result of some natural counterpart to artificial selection.

Aware that extinction and migration resulted from a loss of adaptation produced by changes in the surrounding conditions.

Unaware of the application of the struggle for existence ensuing from changing conditions to the process of natural selection.

Unaware of the struggle for existence that follows from reproductive over-production.

Unaware of the application of the struggle for existence following from over-reproduction to the process of natural selection.

Undoubtedly, as he testified himself, Darwin was "well prepared to appreciate" the contribution Malthus was to make to the development of his hypothesis.

In October [*sic*, September 28] 1838, that is, fifteen months after I had begun my systematic inquiry, I happened to read for amusement Malthus on *Population*, and being well prepared to appreciate the struggle for existence which everywhere goes on from long-continued observation of the habits of animals and plants, it at once struck me that under these circumstances favourable variations would tend to be preserved, and unfavourable ones to be destroyed. Here, then, I had at last got a theory by which to work.[18]

I came to the conclusion that selection was the principle of change from the study of domesticated productions; and then, reading Malthus, I saw at once how to apply this principle.[19]

There seems to be little disagreement as to what it was that Malthus said in the *Essay*[20] which so impressed Darwin. It was, as succinctly

[16]"Darwin's Notebooks on Transmutation of Species," Part II, *Bulletin of the British Museum (Natural History)*, Historical Series, 1960, II, No. 3, 90 (Notebook, 75). (Italics mine). [17]*Ibid.*, 110 (Notebook, 234 (Brackets and contents mine)

[18]*Op. cit., Life and Letters*, II, 68. [19]*Ibid.*, Darwin to Wallace, 1858, II, 465.

[20]Darwin read the 6th edition of Malthus' *Essay on the Principle of Population*, London, 1826.

put by Malthus on the very first page, "the constant tendency in all animated life to increase beyond the nourishment prepared for it." Accepting this and noting that in well-contained populations one does not find the anticipated rate of increase, Malthus concluded that "a strong check on population, from the difficulty of acquiring food, must constantly be in operation."

What particularly impressed Darwin was Malthus' mathematical demonstration of the results of the geometrical rate of increase of man and the arithmetical rate of increase of his available food supply. Malthus had said:

It may safely be pronounced, therefore, that population, when unchecked, goes on doubling itself every twenty-five years, or increases in a geometrical ratio.[21]

The basis for an all-pervading struggle for existence had certainly been well-laid by Malthus—and Darwin picked it up immediately. Here is Darwin's entry for September 28th, the day he began Malthus' *Essay*:

28th We ought to be far from wondering if changes in number of species from small changes in nature of locality. Even the energetic language of Decandolle does not convey the warring of the species as inference from Malthus. [Increase of brutes must be prevented solely by positive checks, excepting that famine may stop desire.]—in nature production does not increase, whilst no check prevail, but the positive check of famine & consequently death. [I do not doubt every one till he thinks deeply has assumed that increase of animals exactly proportionate to the number that can live.]

Population is increased at geometrical ratio in FAR SHORTER time than 25 years—yet until the one sentence of Malthus no one clearly perceived the great check amongst men. [Then in spring, like food used for other purposes as wheat for making brandy.—Even a *few* years plenty makes population in man increase & an *ordinary* crop causes a dearth.] Take Europe on an average every species must have same number killed year with year by parasites, by cold, &c.—even one species of hawk decreasing must affect instantaneously all the rest. [The final cause of all this wedging, must be to sort out proper structure, & adapt it to change]—to do that for form, which Malthus shows is the final effect of this populousness on the energy of man. One may say there is a force like a hundred thousand wedges trying to force every kind of adapted structure into the gaps in the oeconomy of nature or rather forming gaps by thrusting out weaker ones.[22]

It is important to note two aspects of Malthus' *Essay*. First, though he began with an allusion to a univeral capacity for over-reproduction, his argument centered almost exclusively on human populations. Sec-

[21]*Ibid.*, II, 6. This is the sentence which Darwin referred to in his notebook entry below.

[22]"Darwin's Notebooks on Transmutation of Species," Part VI, *Bulletin of the British Museum (Natural History)*, Historical Series, (1967), III, No. 5, 162–63 (Notebook, 134–35). I am indebted to Dr. Sidney Smith of St. Catharine's College, Cambridge, for his corrections to the published transcript as well as for his critical comments on this paper as a whole. (Bracketed material is Darwin's.)

ond, and relatedly, the conclusions to which Malthus arrived were quite different from those that followed in Darwin's application. Malthus' final conclusion, extrapolated from the pressures of over-population and the natural checks against it, runs very much counter to the successful adaptive accommodation that follows from them in Darwin's theory. For Malthus, the "observed facts" of the reproductive/sustenance ratio and the fact that physically contained populations did *not* increase in the numbers expected, led him to conclude with a decidedly pessimistic denial of any significant wide-spread basis for human improvement.

What is important, however, regarding Malthus' contribution to Darwin's thought at this time, is that it remained for Malthus' *Essay* to suggest to Darwin the great pressures bearing on each *individual* being and the resultant struggle among offspring of the same parents. It was because Malthus justified his argument bearing on man, by alluding to a general tendency toward over-reproduction throughout the organic world, that Darwin, unlike Lyell before him, was able to see the applicability of his argument to *all* individual organisms, and not just those species involved in prey-predator relationships.

We can now see how the pieces fell into place. The last notebook entry before Malthus was one based on Lyell, whose book Darwin had been reading during the previous six weeks. The reference to De Candolle comes directly from the pages of Lyell—those same pages in which Lyell had discussed the survival pressures on species due to changing conditions:

"All the plants of a given country," says De Condolle, in his usual spirited style, "are at war one with another. The first which establish themselves by chance in a particular spot, tend, by the mere occupany of space, to exclude other species—the greater choke the smaller, the longest livers replace those which last for a shorter period, the more prolific gradually make themselves masters of the ground, which species multiplying more slowly would otherwise fill."[23]

The next several pages of Lyell were directed to documenting the impressively large organic reproductive ratios.

So it was, upon his reading of Malthus, that Darwin became aware not only of the struggle for existence which followed from over-reproduction—and how it might be applied like "a force of a hundred thousand wedges" to adaptive selection—but also how this one factor yielding struggle related to the factors Lyell saw as producing a struggle for existence. For the first time, Darwin fully realized that Lyell's description of the struggle ensuing from changing physical conditions applied to more than just the "either/or" alternatives of migration and extinction. Such a struggle, he had now come to see, was part of the process that leads to *transmutation*.

[23]*Op. cit., Principles of Geology,* II, 136.

Lyell had not carried his investigation down from the two levels (species vs. environment, and species vs. species) he considered to that of *intra*specific or individual struggle.[24] It was Malthus' account, limited as it was to the single species of man, that brought Darwin to see that third and most important aspect of the struggle for existence— that between closely related members of the same species.

Turning now to that passage in the *Journal* written in 1845 and added just after his earlier (1837) account, in which he had employed Lyell's explanation for extinction, we see the following:

Nevertheless, if we consider the subject [of extinction] under another point of view, it will appear less perplexing. We do not steadily bear in mind, how profoundly ignorant we are of the conditions of existence of every animal; nor do we always remember, that some check is constantly preventing the too rapid increase of every organized being left in a state of nature. The supply of food, on an average, remains constant; yet the tendency in every animal to increase by propagation is geometrical; and its surprising effects have nowhere been more astonishingly shown, than in the case of the European animals run wild during the last few centuries in America. Every animal in a state of nature regularly breeds; yet in a species long established, any *great* increase in numbers is obviously impossible, and must be checked by some means. We are, nevertheless, seldom able with certainty to tell in any given species, at what period of life, or at what period of the year, or whether only at long intervals, the check falls; or, again, what is the precise nature of the check. Hence, probably it is, that we feel so little surprise at one, of two species closely allied in habits, being rare and the other abundant in the same district; or, again, that one should be abundant in one district, and another, filling the same place in the economy of nature, should be abundant in a neighboring district, differing very little in its conditions. If asked how this is, one immediately replies that it is determined by some slight differences in climate, food, or the number of enemies; yet how rarely, if ever, we can point out the precise cause and manner of action of the check! We are, therefore, driven to the conclusion, that causes generally quite inappreciable by us, determine whether a given species shall be abundant or scanty in numbers.[25]

This is as far as Darwin went in the second edition of the *Journal*, but then here he was offering only a possible explanation for extinction. Yet he knew that an adaptively oriented transformation was a most probable alternative.

Between Darwin's reading of Malthus and his first attempt to sketch his theory, there was still much to be done. It would be necessary to provide a detailed connection between survival pressures and

---

[24]The terms *intra*specific" and "individual" are here used interchangeably, as "individual" here means "between single individuals." I am aware of the difficulties and inconsistencies that arise over the terms as used here, and in the above figure, if the more sophisticated and modern view is held in mind. However, for the sake of historical clarity (but without loss of historical accuracy) I shall, for the present, ignore the modern view of these factors.

[25]Charles Darwin, *Journal of Researches* (2nd ed., 1845; New York 1957), 158.

the selection of adaptive variation. Upon putting down Malthus' work, Darwin said "I was so anxious to avoid prejudice, that I determined not for some time to write even the briefest sketch of it." The delay was not entirely due to the caution of a liberal mind. Only one entry in this third notebook after Malthus indicates Darwin's relative success in elaborating this connection. After discussing possible causes of variation, Darwin concludes:

It is absolutely necessary that some but not great difference (for every brother & sister are somewhat different) should be added to each individual before he can procreate. Then change may be effect of differences of parents, or external circumstances during life. —if the circumstances which must be external which induce change are always of one nature species is formed, if not—the changes oscillate backward & forward & are individual differences. (Hence every individual is different) (all this agrees well with my view of those forms slightly favoured getting the upper hand & forming species.)[26]

By early 1842, however, Darwin felt confident enough to write his first "Sketch." Here, after depicting the Lyellian and Malthusian aspects of struggle, he shows a better view of the connection when he concludes, "if there be the smallest differences in their structure, habits, instincts, health, etc., it will on an average tell; as conditions change a rather larger proportion will be preserved."[27] By the time of his "Essay" of 1844 the argument is clearer. The section on the "Natural Means of Selection" begins with Darwin's allusion to De Candolle's "war in nature," referring to it as "the doctrine of Malthus applied in most cases with ten-fold force."[28] That Darwin goes well beyond De Candolle and Lyell and sees the relevance to *individual* struggle is clearly shown by his statement that "each individual of each species holds its place either by its own struggle and capacity of acquiring nourishment in some period of its life, or by the struggle of its parents against and compared with other individuals of the same or different species."[29]

The contribution of Malthus' essay to Darwin's thought was both direct and indirect: direct in that it provided a principal element of the selective process—the survival pressure constantly exerted upon every organic element stemming from over-breeding; indirect in that it supplied not only an element but also an all-encompassing context through which Darwin would relate a large number of previously unconnected ideas.

At the same time the pressures described by Malthus were seen to apply universally, so they seemed also to bear on each individual. Malthus' account of a process of indefinite organic expansion, checked

[26]"Darwin's Notebooks on Transmutation of Species", Part III, *Bulletin of the British Museum (Natural History),* Historical Series, (1960), II, No. 4, 148–49 (Notebook, 175).
[27]*Op. cit., The Foundations of the Origin of Species,* ("Sketch of 1942"), 47.
[28]*Ibid.,* ("Essay of 1844"). 116.   [29]*Ibid.,* ("Essay of 1844"), 119.

only by the inherent limitations of fixed space, brought home to Darwin the idea that, not some particular part or process of nature, but nature herself was the determinant. If not all could exist, then some were fated to perish. Alternative meant selection. And so the connection between the struggle from overpopulation and a natural form of selection had been effected. This, then, became the context into which Darwin immediately fitted his concepts of variation, adaptation, and transmutation.

His understanding of adaptation allowed him to see that an environmental station was not simply and solely an empty and happenstance form of containment. He had come to see it as representing a well-delineated set of living conditions. The particular nature of a station was the standard for existence for any forms filling it. Thus, the limited and specific nature of environmental stations, plus the super-abundancy of widely-varying organic forms, must necessarily result in a selection of the adaptively oriented forms. Darwin had indeed "at last got a theory by which to work."

It would, however, be too easy to say, at this point, that the rest is "history." There were still, in fact, a number of unsolved problems. It was not until 1852, for example, that it suddenly came home to him that he had overlooked one vital facet of the process of multiple speciation. In his determined effort to prove a convincing account of how a single specific form could be transformed into a new one, he had failed to provide the explanation necessary to show how, at the end of such a process, both the original and the new species could still be co-existing. Or, alternatively, how an original form could produce more than a single new specific form. Thus it was only in the early 1850's that Darwin found a means to resolve that which he called 'the problem of divergence'.

But more conscious a part of Darwin's unresolved problems was that large body of well-documented biological phenomena, the implications of which appeared to run very much counter to the indefinite selection of individual variation. It was these with which Darwin was to wrestle, on his own from 1838 to 1858, and in the public arena from then until the time of his death.

Without doubt, however, the great watershed in the development of Darwin's evolutionary theory came with his reading of Malthus. Not only did Malthus provide a vital missing element, but it served to precipitate other, equally necessary, elements into their proper place in Darwin's thought. With but the one notable exception of 'divergence', from 1838 onwards Darwin was able to work with a clear formulation of his theory of natural selection.

It is hoped that this account will serve to put Malthus' contribution into its proper perspective and that his relationship to Darwin, while still a historical curiosity, will no longer be misunderstood.

Temple University

IV

KANT, SCHOPENHAUER, AND NIETZSCHE ON THE MORALITY OF PITY

By David E. Cartwright

Friedrich Nietzsche found little to recommend in Immanuel Kant's moral philosophy. Besides considering it to be a poorly written, unconditional statement of some basic German moral prejudices, he even warns us against the dangers of Kant as moralist.[1] Nietzsche's contemptuous attitudes toward Kant's ethical theory, however, should not mislead us. For there are some fundamental and important points of agreement between the two philosophers. Although Kant and Nietzsche maintained radically different conceptions of the will, for both the autonomy of the will is their central ethical conception. They are also equally adamant in their rejections of hedonism, utilitarianism, or any purely consequentialist theory of value. Another point of agreement concerns their attitudes toward pity. Even though Nietzsche's critique of pity displays a richness and sophistication lacking in Kant's, Kant's conception of pity plays a significant and largely unrecognized role in Nietzsche's assessment of the value of pity. While Nietzsche might not have precisely the same reasons as Kant, he would agree with him that pity is morally worthless, and is something right-thinking persons would ". . . desire to be free from."[2]

---

[1] In an especially revealing aphorism, Nietzsche states the following about Kant: "*Kant's Joke.* Kant wanted to prove, in a way that would dumbfound the common man, that the common man was right: that was the secret of this soul. He wrote against the scholars in support of popular prejudice, but for the scholars and not for the people." (*The Gay Science*, trans. Walter Kaufmann [New York, 1974], 205, section 193). In a note to this aphorism, Kaufmann claims that Nietzsche has in mind Kant's postulates of rational faith, i.e., God, freedom, and the immortality of the soul. He may also have had in mind Kant's claims in the first chapter of the *Grundlegung zur Metaphysik der Sitten* (Riga, 1785; 2nd ed. 1786), *Groundwork of the Metaphysic of Morals* (trans. H. J. Paton [New York, 1964], 71-73) that a person with sound, natural understanding possessed, if only obscurely, knowledge of moral principles which are present *a priori* in his or her reason. Because these things are recognized only obscurely, Kant argues, the ordinary person's sound moral judgments are often confused, corrupted, or misled by speculation. Thus one of his tasks in the *Groundwork* involves the analysis, clarification, and justification of the common person's moral judgments. By providing the ultimate standard for moral judgments, Kant hopes to ground firmly and formalize those things the common person at some level, already recognizes, in order to spare him or her confusion. Nietzsche's point is, however, that what Kant saw as the source of the practical principles *a priori* present in reason is nothing but the product of the moral prejudices of our Judeo-Christian culture: there is nothing, he argues, either *a priori* or reasonable about these things. Some of Nietzsche's strongest warnings against the danger of Kant as a moralist are found in the tenth and eleventh section of his *The Antichrist*, where he views Kant's moral philosophy as a continuation of theological ethics and as a recipe for decadence and nihilism.

[2] Immanuel Kant, *Critique of Practical Reason*, trans. Lewis White Beck (Indianapolis/New York, 1956), 123.

To appreciate the influence of Kant's conception of pity on Nietzsche's thought, one has only to read a note penned sometime between the end of 1886 and the spring of 1887, in which Nietzsche's debt to Kant is obvious.

Pity is a squadering of feeling, a parasite harmful to moral health, *"it cannot possibly be our duty to increase the evil in the world."* If one does good merely out of pity, it is really oneself one really does good to, and not the other. Pity does not depend upon maxims but upon affects; it is pathological [*pathologisch*]. The suffering of others infects us, pity is an infection [*Ansteckung*].[3]

In his translation of *The Will to Power,* Walter Kaufmann notes the obviously Kantian terminology employed by Nietzsche, e.g., "maxims," "pathological." What Kaufmann fails to note is the source of the utilitarian argument Nietzsche puts in quotation marks. Nietzsche is quoting with approval part of an argument Kant advanced against pity. In the second part of his *Methaphysics of Morals,* Kant argues that we cannot have a duty to feel pity because

... if another person suffers and I let myself (through my imagination) also become infected [*anstecken lasse*] by his pain, which I still cannot remedy, then two people suffer, although the evil (in nature) affects only the one. But *it cannot possibly be a duty to increase the evils of the world* or, therefore to do good from pity [*Mitleid*]. . . .[4]

Like Kant, Nietzsche objects to pity because it is not dianoetic, i.e., it is pathological. He even goes so far as to adopt a model of pity suggested by Kant.[5] Pity is conceived as a contagious and unwelcomed transmission of pain from the recipient of pity to the agent. Nietzsche also echos the Kantian observation that acting from pity is indulging one's inclinations, viz., it is oneself that one really benefits.

[3] Friedrich Nietzsche, *The Will to Power*, trans. Walter Kaufmann and R. J. Hollingdale (New York, 1967), 199, Section 368. The underscoring is mine. In his translation of *The Will to Power*, Kaufmann places the time of composition of this note as between the years 1883-1888. Giorgio Colli and Mazzino Montinari provide the time as between the end of 1886 and the spring of 1887. This note from Nietzsche's *Nachlass* occurs within a draft for his *Der Wille zur Macht: Versuch einer Umwerthung aller Werthe,* in the first chapter, *"Die Metaphysiker,"* of the second book, *"Herkunft der Werthe."* See *Nietzsche Werke* (Berlin, 1971), Vol. VIII, Part I, 276.

[4] Immanuel Kant, *The Metaphysical Principles of Virtue,* trans. James Ellington (Indianapolis/New York, 1964), Section 34. The underscoring is mine. The German for the underscored statement in both the Kant and Nietzsche quotes reads the same, *"es kenn aber unmöglich Pflicht sein, die Übel in der Welt zu vermehren,"* except that Nietzsche omits, without note, the contextually superfluous *aber* of Kant's original. Nietzsche also has this statement set in quotation marks.

[5] This psychological model of pity is also found in both David Hume and Benedict De Spinoza. Hume considers pity to be a secondary affection; one which arises out of sympathy. Sympathy, for Hume, is primarily a principle which explains how opinions, sentiments, and emotions can be transferred from one individual, or group of individuals, to another individual. He views pity as the communication or transferral of the suffering,

Pity, seen as an imposed transmission of suffering, becomes the basis for several of Nietzsche's criticisms of this emotion. In various points in his writings he raises this model of pity as an intuitive objection against the value of pity, e.g., ". . . [pity] increases suffering throughout the world,"[6] ". . . pity makes suffering contagious [*ansteckend*]."[7] Nietzsche's point, of course, is that anything which increases unnecessary suffering is undesirable. Nietzsche uses this view of pity as the basis for one of his most interesting observations concerning this passion.

Observe children who whine and scream so that they are pitied and, hence, wait for the moment when their condition is noticed; live with the sick and mentally oppressed, and ask yourself if the eloquent laments and whimperings, which display their misfortunes, basically have as their aim the harm of those present. Pity . . . is a consolation for the weak and suffering because through it they recognize that they still *have one power*, despite all their weakness, the *power of hurting others*. The unfortunate gains a type of pleasure in this feeling of superiority, of which the expression of pity makes him conscious; his imagination is exalted. He is still important enough to cause pain in the world.[8]

Nietzsche's notion that certain seekers after pity employ their misery to hurt, and thus to feel their power over others is predicated on Kant's

---

pain, or misery of the recipient of pity to the pitier via the associative laws of the imagination which converts an idea of the recipient's pain into an impression of this pain itself. Through pity, then, an agent experiences the recipient's pain see Hume's *A Treatise of Human Nature* [2 vols., 1839-40]; rpt. (London, 1960), 316-319, 369. Spinoza also characterizes pity as involving the agent's suffering. He claims that the agent suffers either because he or she loves the recipient, and that whatever painfully affects the recipient also affects the agent painfully, or the agent imitates the suffering of the recipient. Because the experience of pity involves pain and suffering, Spinoza, unlike Hume, who viewed sympathetic functions simply as the medium of moral judgements, also argues that pity itself is bad (see Spinoza's *Ethics* in *The Works of Spinoza*, Vol. 2, trans. R. H. Elwes [New York, 1955], Part III. Props. XXIII-XXVI, XVIII, and Part IV, Prop. L, proof and note). Nietzsche was aware of both Kant's and Spinoza's negative assessment of the value of pity. He mentions both, along with Plato and La Rochefoucald, as agreeing with his claim that pity is morally worthless (see the fifth section of his Preface to *On the Genealogy of Morals*). I will refer to this psychological model of pity as a Kantian model or conception not to ascribe any originality to Kant. Rather, I will do so to stress that this is how it probably appeared to Nietzsche. Nietzsche might not have been familiar with Hume's analysis of pity, and he seems to ignore Spinoza's, except for his claim that Spinoza also views pity as a morally worthless emotion. For a critical analysis of this psychological model of pity, see Philip Mercer's *Sympathy and Ethics* (London, 1972), 20-35, and Max Scheler's *The Nature of Sympathy*, trans. Peter Heath (Hamden, 1973), 14-18, 138-39.

[6] Friedrich Nietzsche, *Morgenröthe* in *Nietzsche Werke*, ed. Giorgio Colli and Mazzino Montinari (Berlin, 1971), Vol. V, part 1, section 134, 136, my translation. R. J. Hollingdale has recently translated this work as *Daybreak* (Cambridge, 1982).

[7] Friedrich Nietzsche, *The Antichrist*, in *The Portable Nietzsche*, trans. Walter Kaufmann (New York, 1968), section 7.

[8] Friedrich Nietzsche, *Menschliches, Allzumenschliches* I in *Nietzsche Werke*, Vol. IV, part 2, section 50, my translation.

analysis of pity. They feel superior to the pitiers because they exercise their power ⌐r control over them by simply being pitied.[9] The neurotics feel their power by causing anyone who pities them to suffer.

Hence we find that Nietzsche adopts and scores some critical points by employing the Kantian line. There is a danger for the pitier, Nietzsche claims, not simply because of the suffering involved in this emotion, but also because of the susceptibility of the pitier to the manipulation and control by those pitied. This susceptibility to the control and manipulation by others suggests two other important Kantian themes, the loss of one's self-control vs. autonomy and the irrational and involuntary nature of emotions such as pity. Both Nietzsche and Kant maintain that one of the problems with pity is that it usurps the agent's autonomy. Nietzsche argues that in being manipulated and controlled by the recipient of pity, an agent may lose autonomy in two ways. The agent is made to suffer, and this is something that most people find undesirable, and, since pity for someone is usually conative, the agent may act to help the recipient escape his or her suffering, and this may be something the agent would usually not want to do. While the agent is not exactly out of control, Nietzsche's point is that in pity the agent loses self-control by being controlled by someone else.

The notion of self-control is the basic idea behind Kant's conception of autonomy. Kant argued that to be autonomous it was necessary for agents to be free from external forces which compel their behavior. This sort of negative freedom, he argued, was not sufficient for autonomy, however. An autonomous will must also have ". . . the property . . . of being a law to itself."[10] Kant held that autonomous agents act from their own conceptions; their actions are ascribed to causal factors whose origins are, in some way, identified with their rational natures. In other words, autonomous agents are self-controlling because they determine their own actions. In pity, nevertheless, autonomy is usurped because it, like any emotion, is initiated by factors external to the agent, factors that overwhelm or "infect" the agent.

This Kantian theme is evidenced in the following note in which Nietzsche discusses the relationship between the emotions and reason:

A higher stage [than following one's feelings] is to overcome even this pressure within us and to perform a heroic act not on impulse—but coldly, *raisonnable,* without being overwhelmed by stormy feelings of pleasure—the same applied to compassion [*Mitleid*]: it must first be habitually sifted by reason; otherwise it is just as dangerous as any other affect.[11]

[9] The Kantian concept of pity as contagious suffering is employed more directly elsewhere in Nietzsche's writings, e.g., "he suffers—and his vanity wants him to suffer only with others, to feel pity;" ". . . to feel pity and . . . double this woe." See Nietzsche's *Beyond Good and Evil*, trans. Walter Kaufmann (New York, 1966), sections 222 and 30.

[10] Kant, *Groundwork*, 97.

[11] Nietzsche, *Will to Power*, section 928. There is another significant difference between Kant and Nietzsche concerning the value of the emotions in general. In section 34 of

Here we find the idea that emotional behavior is nonrational and involuntary. The passions are stormy; they overwhelm us. He appears to adopt the Kantian suggestion that one should act from reason and not from mere inclination. There is, however, a significant departure from Kantian theory. Nietzsche does not conceive of autonomy as implying the denial or suppression of one's emotions. He avoids the separation of reason from emotion, a bifurcation associated with Kant. Nietzsche does not advocate the denial or suppression of our emotions or inclinations as springs or motives of our actions. Rather, he advocates the focusing, controlling, and directing of these forces for specific aims. Like Schopenhauer, Nietzsche thought that our passions, desires, needs, and

---

the *Principles of Virtue*, Kant details *Mitfreude* as the opposite of *Mitleid*. *Mitfreude* (rejoicing with another) involves the passive transferral of another's joy (*Freude*) as *Mitleid* involves the passive transferral of another's pain (*Leiden*). They have, however, the same ethical status because they both are sensible feelings, i.e., things we passively experience, things which happen to us, things we suffer. In other words, like all emotions, *Mitfreude* and *Mitleid* are pathological. They do not belong to us as autonomous agents. Consequently, Kant argues that both types of feelings are morally worthless and are things we cannot be obligated to have. Nietzsche also details *Mitfreude* as the polar of *Mitleid*. He does not, however, consider *Mitfreude* to be morally worthless. Nietzsche argues that *Mitfreude* is desirable, e.g., "I want to teach . . . what is understood by so few today, least of all by these preachers of pity: *to share not suffering but joy [Mitfreude]*." (*The Gay Science*, Section 338) Nietzsche thus believes that certain emotions can be valuable and desirable even though they are pathological.

It should be mentioned, however, that Kant takes a more liberal view concerning the ethical significance of the emotions in the *Principles of Virtue* than he does in the *Groundwork* or the *Critique of Practical Reason*. His view becomes more liberal in the sense that he details a way in which we can control certain of our emotions. This enables him to claim that we have a general duty to cultivate our sympathetic feelings (*teilnehmende Empfindung*) and that active sympathy (*tätige Teilnehmung*) is a duty. (*Principles of Virtue*, Section 34) These things are duties in the sense that they are natural dispositions which are under our control, and which can be based on moral principles, e.g., one ought to develop those natural dispositions which are helpful to morality. While I cannot help feeling either *Mitleid* or *Mitfreude* in certain situations—this is a function of one's emotional constitution—Kant claims that one can choose to expose or not expose oneself to situations in which they are elicited, e.g., It is a duty not to shun sickrooms or prisons and so on in order to avoid the pain of compassion [*Mitgefühl*], which one may not be able to resist. For this feeling, though painful, nevertheless is one of the impulses placed in us by nature for effecting what the representation of duty might not accomplish by itself." (*Principles of Virtue*, Section 35).

This type of active sympathy, then, disposes us to do what is prescribed by duty—say, helping others—and this may later facilitate our doing our duty simply because it is our duty. In this sense, some of our emotional dispositions were viewed by Kant as having ethical dimensions, namely, those which are servicable to morality (in section 17 of the *Principles of Virtue*, the cultivation of these dispositions is classified as a duty to oneself). Nietzsche also attributes a conditional value to "*Mitgefühl*" (fellow feelings—a literal "feeling with another"). *Mitgefühl* is desirable when one has it with a noble feeling or worthy individual. It is undesirable when one has it with a vulgar feeling or unworthy individual. See his *Beyond Good and Evil*, Section 284 and *Will to Power*, Sections 864, 1020.

wants are the true motors of our actions. The problem is that these drives and forces often lack direction; they are impulsive and steer us blindly. Reason or our intellect is used to direct, shape, make efficient, and provide the means to satisfy our deepest needs. Furthermore, Nietzsche considered these drives, passions, and needs as uniquely constituting our personalities. By sifting our passions, refining, and guiding them by our rational abilities, we become more aware of our authentic nature, for reason and passion are both essential to realizing our individual personalities.

We have seen that pity can usurp agents' autonomy by placing them under the control of the persons pitied. This was one of the dangers Nietzsche saw in pity. He also detailed a parallel problem for the recipients of pity. Pity can become a surreptitious way through which agents gain control over recipients whose autonomy is threatened by pitiers:

> When we see someone suffer, we like to exploit this opportunity to take possession of him; those who become his benefactors and pity him, for example, do this and call the lust for a new possession "love."[12]

The autonomy of sufferers is in an especially vulnerable position. People usually suffer because they are unable to relieve their own misery. Suffering is typically a sufficient reason for the agent to do something to relieve it. When we lament our woes, vocalize our misery, often we are announcing our inability to care for ourselves. We seek the assistance of others. Pitiers are more than happy to give this assistance. Some pitiers, Nietzsche argued, may actively seek individuals to pity in order to heighten their own feelings of superiority and/or to gain control of the sufferer. The pitiers increase their feelings of superiority by doing for others things that they cannot do for themselves, and then by conceiving of their actions as virtuous. They gain control over others by benefiting them. The recipients become indebted to their benefactors and being in their debt is also being subject to their control. The pitier can even accentuate this sense of debt by not allowing recipients to satisfy their desire to repay it, e.g., "you do not owe me a thing." The control can become less subtle, however. The pitiers can even make the recipients completely dependent on their help by engendering within them the idea that they are helpless and need the help of others to live a minimally normal life.[13]

---

[12] Friedrich Nietzsche, *The Gay Science*, section 14.

[13] This was one of Nietzsche's points in his analysis of social decadence and individual decline. Societies or cultures in which pity is praised, promoted, or deemed desirable, are viewed as instances of "weak" cultures or societies. They are societies in which everyone is dependent on everyone else. Nietzsche argued that these societies reflect a lack of individual self-confidence and the inability for individuals to provide for themselves. Consequently, autonomy is sacrificed, the distance between individuals is obscured, and pity is praised in these societies because the members of this society have a low opinion of themselves which is engendered in them either by tradition or collective

By augmenting some Kantian themes, Nietzsche has revealed some of the insidious aspects of a reputedly benevolent passion. Kant, however, was also familiar with the darker side of pity. In addition to the utilitarian argument against pity, Kant has the following to say about pity:

... but it cannot possibly be a duty to increase the evils of the world or, therefore, to do good from pity; for this would be an insulting kind of beneficence, expressing the sort of benevolence one has for an unworthy person. Such benevolence is called soft-heartedness and should not occur at all among human beings, who are not to boast of their worthiness to be happy.[14]

Kant maintains that the recipients of pity are insulted by being humiliated. Their suffering announces their inability to overcome their own problems; for individuals usually only tolerate misery when they cannot relieve it. By seeing that others suffer, pitiers realize that the sufferers cannot help themselves. This is one of the reasons that pitiers feel compelled to help. When pitiers offer help, the recipients may be embarrassed by the pitier's knowledge of their inability to help themselves. They feel as if an inadequacy or character flaw is exposed which may be a blow to their pride and self-respect. This offer of help may be viewed as an even greater insult, if the recipients believe that they can take care of their own problems, or they may be humiliated by realizing that their welfare is contingent upon another's generosity. Because of the great potential of pity for insulting and/or humiliating the recipient, Kant advocates that we conceal such motives.

We acknowledge ourselves obligated to be beneficient to a poor man. But this kindness also involves a dependence of his welfare upon my generosity, which humiliates [erniedrigt] him. Therefore, it is a duty to spare the recipient such humiliation and to preserve his self-respect by treating this beneficence either as a mere debt that is owed him, or a small favor.[15]

As we have seen, Kant also had something to say about those who indulge their pity. He claimed that the benevolence associated with pity reveals softheartedness, and that it is unworthy of human beings, who should not brag about their worthiness to be happy. Although what Kant means by these claims is far from perspicuous, it seems he had something like the following in mind. The German noun *Barmherzigkeit,* "softheartedness," also means "charity" or "mercy." Kant considers the help given from pity to be a form of charity—something sufferers have no right to, and something pitiers are not obligated to provide. The help given out of pity, then, is something which is not owned, and, thus, depends on the pitiers' generosity. Pitiers boast or brag about their wor-

---

experience, e.g., they are currently having, or have had, a hard go at life, or they suspect that they will face difficult times, etc. It is interesting to note that Nietzsche's analysis of individuals often parallels his analysis of cultures. In this regard, he recalls Plato.

[14] Kant, *Principles of Virtue,* Section 34.   [15] Kant, *Principles of Virtue,* Section 23.

thiness to be happy by indulging their pity. They do not conceal their motives, even if it humiliates sufferers. They flaunt their pity with the excuse that they deserve to do whatever makes them happy, and they become happy by satisfying their inclinations to help out of pity. Help is given even if it does humiliate or insult the sufferers; for, in these cases, the agents' happiness becomes more important than the recipients' dignity.

Nietzsche develops similar themes. In *Morgenröthe* he writes that "Pitying is equivalent to despising [*Verachten*],"[16] and ". . . [there is] something humiliating [*Erniedrigendes*] in suffering and in pity something elevating and giving of superiority. . . ."[17] These dynamics of pity are amplified in the famous section "On Pitying" in the second part of *Thus Spoke Zarathustra,* where Zarathustra announces that God died out of his pity for human beings.[18] Zarathustra speaks thus: "Having seen the sufferer suffer, I was ashamed for the sake of his shame; and when I helped him, I transgressed grievously against his pride."[19] Zarathustra's shame has two sources. By observing another's misery, and displaying pity, he has shamed the other. The other is humiliated: Zarathustra is ashamed at that. His sense of shame, then, is intensified by actually helping the sufferer; for this is a blow to the recipient's pride. Nietzsche does not consider Zarathustra's sensitivity to the misfortune of others to be the correct response, although it is clear that he views Zarathustra's shame as preferable to the behavior of the merciful (*Barmherzig*), who ". . . feel blessed in their pity."[20]

For Nietzsche the best attitude towards sufferers is one devoid of pity. To be no longer susceptible to this emotion is considered a highly desirable state. But if one cannot overcome this emotion, like Kant, Nietzsche proposes that one does not allow others to know that they are pitied, e.g., "If I must pity, at least I do not want it known; and if I do pity, it is preferably from a distance."[21] While this may not spare the pitier the shame which results from observing another's misery, it does spare sufferers the humiliation of knowing that they are pitied. In this way some of their dignity is preserved. They do not realize that they are treated as contemptible beings, beings incapable of dealing with their problems. If one cannot refrain from offering help, Nietzsche maintains, one should help under the pretext that sufferers are really helping themselves: "Strangers . . . and the poor may themselves pluck the fruit from my tree: that will cause them less shame."[22] The illusion that sufferers

---

[16] Nietzsche, *Morgenröthe*, Section 135, my translation.

[17] Nietzsche, *Morgenröthe*, Section 138, my translation.

[18] Compare this with *Zarathustra*, Part IV, "Retired," 373, where the old pope claims that God choked "on his all-too-great pity."

[19] Nietzsche, *Thus Spoke Zarathustra*, in *The Portable Nietzsche*, trans. Walter Kaufmann (New York, 1968), Part I, "On the Pitying," 201.

[20] *Ibid.*, Part I, "On the Pitying," 200.   [21] *Ibid.*

[22] *Ibid.*, Part I, "On the Pitying," 201.

are helping themselves saves them the humiliation and shame resulting from the reputed benevolence of pity. By doing this, of course, the pitier is also less likely to promote the idea among sufferers that they are weak and helpless. In the same manner, this strategy can save the pitier from the false feelings of superiority which can result from pity. One recognizes that benefiting sufferers is not a great expression of one's power; for sufferers are in an especially vulnerable position, and, as such, are "easy prey."[23] It is far more difficult to benefit one who is relatively well-off, Nietzsche observes.

Nietzsche also provides other reasons for concealing one's pity. There are more immediate and practical dangers for pitiers than being controlled by sufferers or being deluded by false feelings of superiority. This is suggested by his claim that God died out of sacrificial pity for humans, which connotes several things, e.g., Christ's crucifixion, human suffering being too great of a burden for even a god to bear, etc. These allusions suggest that the pathology of pity involves two types of danger for pitiers. Pity may lead one to perform actions which entail undesirable forms of self-sacrifice, and/or pity may just wear one out—the suffering of others undermines one's own health. Nietzsche, however, indicates a danger to pitiers other than self-sacrifice or illness, i.e., one which is not a direct consequence of the experience of pity or of an agent's action itself. The "ugliest man" tells Zarathustra that he murdered God out of revenge;

But he had to die: he saw with eyes that saw everything; he saw man's depths and ultimate grounds, all his concealed disgrace and ugliness. His pity knew no shame: he crawled into my dirtiest nooks. This most curious, overobtrusive, overpitying, one had to die. He always saw me: on such a witness I wanted to have revenge or not live myself. The god who saw everything, *even man*—this god had to die! Man cannot bear it that such a witness should live.[24]

Although this passage recalls Nietzsche's analysis of cultural nihilism and certain of his polemics against Christianity, at a simpler level it explores another danger faced by pitiers. Because being pitied subjects individuals to shame and humilitation, this loss of dignity may prompt others to take revenge on those who pity them.

Kant's influence on Nietzsche is shown by his adoption of the Kantian view of pity, Nietzsche's use of some of his arguments against pity, the employment of Kantian terminology, a similar appreciation of the dynamics of the undesirable dimensions of a putatively desirable emotion, and the parallels between their substitutions for this dangerous passion. I would like to highlight one last aspect of Kantian influence, although the connection between Kant and Nietzsche may appear tenuous. Against Schopenhauer, Nietzsche makes two appeals to Kant. The first appeal is direct and obvious, while the second is less obvious. Against

[23] Nietzsche, *Gay Science*, Section 13.
[24] Nietzsche, *Thus Spoke Zarathustra*, in *The Portable Nietzsche*, trans. Walter Kaufmann (New York, 1968), Part I, "On the Pitying," 201.

Schopenhauer's belief that pity or compassion for the suffering of sentient beings was the basis for actions having moral worth, Nietzsche evokes Kant:

He [Kant] teaches expressly that we must be insensitive to the suffering of others, if our good deeds are to be said to have moral worth—what Schopenhauer very furiously, as one will understand, calls the Kantian bad taste.[25]

Again, then, Nietzsche appears to advocate a passionless involvement in the plight of others against Schopenhauer's passionate participation in their plight.

Schopenhauer, however, viewed Kant's assessment of the ethical significance of pity or compassion as displaying more than "bad taste." It manifested an attitude which is totally repugnant to anyone possessing genuine moral sensitivity. Kant's insistence that a right-thinking person desires to be free from "Even the feelings of sympathy [*Gefühl des Mitleids*] and warmhearted fellow-feeling [*weichherzigen Teilnehmung*] . . . and subject only to law-giving reasons,"[26] demonstrates moral pedantry at its worst. If one were granted these desires, Schopenhauer argues, the only thing which would soften the heart of an insensitive doer of good, besides other self-interested concerns, ". . . can never be anything (if he has no secondary motives) but a slavish fear of the gods, no matter whether he calls his fetish 'categorical imperative' or 'Fitzlipuzli'. For what except fear could move a hard heart."[27] Principles or rules, abstract ethical recipes, Schopenhauer thought, are totally worthless as guides for human conduct. Just as the knowledge of aesthetical rules and principles cannot make a person an artist, the knowledge of moral principles cannot make one a good human being. Schopenhauer believed that both aesthetic and moral dispositions were a function of one's character and personality over which one has no power to change. One either has the innate type of character which chooses the correct type of actions and is susceptible to the right sorts of motives, or one does not. If one does not, no amount of ethical instruction can affect any profound change in one's character or behavior.[28]

[25] Nietzsche, *Morgenröthe*, Section 132, my translation. This passage also shows how poorly Nietzsche understood Kant on the assessment of actions having moral worth. Kant never argued that insensitivity to the suffering of others was either a necessary or sufficient condition for an action to have moral worth. Kant's claim was that sensitivity or inclination had nothing to do with whether an action had moral worth. What counted, according to Kant, was whether the motive of the action was respect for the moral law or not. If it was, the action had moral worth, if not, it lacked moral worth. Thus Kant left the question of sensitivity open. I could perform an action having moral worth, and be deeply affected by another's suffering, just as long as my motive was respect for the moral law and not anything resulting from this sensitivity. See Kant's *Groundwork*, 65-71.

[26] Kant, *Critique of Practical Reason*, 123.

[27] Arthur Schopenhauer, *On the Basis of Morality*, trans. E. F. J. Payne (Indianapolis/New York, 1965), 66.   [28] *Ibid.*, 187-98.

The emptiness of Kantian ethics, Schopenhauer maintained, is also apparent when one considers its form and construction. It is a degenerate form of theological morals since it denies the central features which provide any meaning for this type of ethical theory, namely, a divine will which prescribes rules, rights, obligations, and accordingly, metes out rewards or punishments. It is only within this context, he argues, that Kant's key moral concepts, "duty," "law," "obligation," "command," and "reverence," obtain significance. Kant, however, in the *Critique of Pure Reason,* put an end to these types of transcendental theses, Schopenhauer points out. By retaining these concepts outside of this context, they become meaningless: ". . . [when] separated from the theological hypothesis from which they came, these concepts lose all meaning."[29] To call them "unconditional," to locate their meaning *a priori* in pure reason, as being applicable to all rational beings, is only to reemphasize that they are absolutely groundless. Even the notion of the categorical imperative and the idea that one can act solely out of the motive to do one's duty are empty words; this is, as Schopenhauer emphasizes, what Kant vaguely recognized: "Kant himself says, it was doubtful if at any time an action had been determined purely through it [a desire solely to do one's duty]: I say, it is completely certain that there has not, since these are empty words behind which nothing remains which could actually move a person [to act]."[30]

To avoid the pitfalls of Kant's moral philosophy, Schopenhauer proposed a different approach and project for the moral philosopher. Instead of analyzing concepts, instructing human behavior, prescribing principles and procedures,

. . . the purpose of ethics is to indicate, explain, and trace to its ultimate ground the extremely varied behavior of man from a moral point of view. Therefore there is no other way for discovering the foundation of ethics than the empirical, namely, to investigate whether there are generally any actions to which we must attribute *genuine moral worth.* Such will be actions of voluntary justice, pure philanthropy, and real magnanimity. These are then to be regarded as a given phenomenon that we have to explain correctly, that is, trace to its true grounds. Consequently, we have to indicate the peculiar motive that moves man to actions of this kind, a kind specifically different from any other. This motive together with the susceptibility to it will be the ultimate ground of morality, and a knowledge of it will be the foundation of morals. This is the humble path to which I direct ethics; it contains no construction a priori, no absolute legislation for all rational beings *in abstracto.* [31]

All human actions, Schopenhauer maintained, can be attributed to three fundamental motives, or various combinations of these incentives. These motives are: the desire for one's own well-being (egoism); the desire

---

[29] *Ibid.,* 55.
[30] Arthur Schopenhauer, *Der handschriftliche Nachlass,* Vol. 3, ed. Arthur Hübscher (Frankfurt am Main, 1970) 474, my translation.   [31] Schopenhauer, *Basis,* 130.

for another's misfortune or misery (malice); and the desire for another's well-being (compassion).[32] By examining types of actions to which we ascribe moral worth—actions like voluntary justice and loving-kindness—he concludes that neither egoism nor malice are their motives. Egoism, he argues, cannot confer moral worth on actions because the ethical significance of any action lies only "in reference to others." Schopenhauer views egoistic actions as being neither morally good nor bad. Malicious actions, on the other hand, may not be egoistic, but are morally bad because they characteristically aim at the suffering of others. This leads Schopenhauer to conclude that "the absence of all egoistic motivation is . . . *the criterion of an action of moral worth*," and that these types of actions are also free from any desire to harm others.[33] Compassion, he argues, is the only motive which satisfies this negative criterion. In other words, compassion becomes the criterion for the ascription of moral worth to any actions, i.e., ". . . only insofar as an action has sprung from compassion does it have moral value; and every action resulting from any other motive had none."[34] To provide some positive content to this claim, Schopenhauer argues that the virtues of justice (*Gerechtigkeit*) and philanthropy (*Menschenliebe*) are derived from compassion. Because he believes that these are the cardinal virtues, that all virtues "follow practically and may be derived theoretically" from them, he thinks that this will show how all virtues stem from compassion or pity (*Mitleid*).[35]

By limiting ethics to the description of the actual motives out of which human beings perform actions to which we must ascribe moral worth, Schopenhauer believed that he avoids the empty, pedantic formalism of Kantian moral philosophy. Nietzsche, however, while being more sympathetic towards Schopenhauer's methodology than Kant's, believed the projects of both philosophers were equally flawed. In their own ways, both were like most moralists who ". . . accept the morality esteemed by the people as holy and true and only attempt to systematize it, i.e., they hang their gown of science around it."[36] The only difference

---

[32] See Schopenhauer, *Basis*, 145. In the second volume of his *The World as Will and Representation*, trans. E. F. J. Payne (New York, 1966), 607, Schopenhauer, indicates that there is a fourth ultimate motive of human conduct, i.e., a desire for "one's own misfortune or woe." Schopenhauer claims that he did not consider this motive in *Basis* because it was written in the spirit of philosophical ethics prevailing in Protestant Europe, and, as such, was beyond the scope of the question posed by the Royal Danish Society for Scientific Studies, for which *Basis* was written. From his own criterion, however, Schopenhauer could have argued that this motive cannot confer moral worth on an action because the ethical significance of an action lies only in its reference to others. Schopenhauer's analysis of human actions also suffers from his failure to consider the respective value of actions which result from jointly compelling or mixed motives.

[33] Schopenhauer, *Basis*, 140.   [34] *Ibid.*, 144.   [35] *Ibid.*, 148.

[36] Nietzsche, *Morgenröthe*, 457 (Summer, 1880) my translation. In the Kritische Gesamtausgabe of *Nietzsche Werke* edited by Colli and Montinari, *Morgenröthe*, is published with Nietzsche's notes from 1880 to Spring, 1881. These notes are identified by the year of composition.

between Kant and Schopenhauer, Nietzsche argues, is that they adopt different means to glorify and absolutize conventional morality. Kant did this through his *a priori* constructions, while Schopenhauer performed the same task through *a posteriori* descriptions.

Nietzsche was particularly amused by the pretenses of Schopenhauer's methodology. Not only does he believe that he ". . . knows what specifically constitutes morality,"[37] his claim that pity was ". . . the source of all and each past and future moral action . . ."[38] showed that he lacked any sense of history, e.g., "that the history of all phenomena of morality could be simplified in the way Schopenhauer believed—namely, so that pity is discovered as the root of all moral impulse hitherto—only a thinker denuded of all historical instinct . . . could have attained to this degree of absurdity and naivete."[39] Had Schopenhauer possessed any insight into the history of morality, Nietzsche argues, he would have discovered that the taste for pity was a relatively modern phenomenon, one that has not been shared by other cultures and moralities.[40] Both the Stoics and the Epicureans, he notes, found no place for pity among their tables of value. Indeed, in noble-class morality, and among those of discriminating taste, pity is viewed as either a weakness or danger, "as with the Greeks, as an unhealthy, periodical affect from whose danger one could take temporary, voluntary release."[41]

Schopenhauer's lack of historical sense was equally balanced by a lack of psychological acumen, Nietzsche observes. Pity is both "imperfectly observed" and "poorly described" by Schopenhauer."[42] In order to fantasize about pity as he does, Nietzsche argues, ". . . one must not be acquainted with it from experience."[43] If Schopenhauer had correctly analyzed pity, Nietzsche maintains, he would never have described it as a simple, unselfish desire for another's well-being, which results from the experience of another's pain and misfortune. The passion to which we refer to by the term "pity," he claims, has depth and obscurities which are hidden by such superficial descriptions.

Against Schopenhauer, Nietzsche emphasizes the complex psychological underpinnings and the diversity of drives and affections which may constitute the passsion we call "pity." It is within this context Nietzsche makes a second appeal to Kant, although it may be better

---

[37] *Ibid.*, Section 132, my translation.   [38] *Ibid.*, Section 133, my translation.

[39] Nietzsche, *Will to Power*, Section 366.

[40] See Nietzsche, *On the Genealogy of Morals*, trans. Walter Kaufmann (New York, 1969), Preface, Section 5, and *Twilight of the Idols*, "Skirmishes of an Untimely Man," Section 37, in *The Portable Nietzsche*, 540. It is interesting to note that both Nietzsche and Schopenhauer considered Kant's ethics to be a thinly disguised form of theological ethics. Nietzsche, however, as *Twilight*, Section 37 suggests, also considered Schopenhauer's ethics to be a continuation of theological ethics.

[41] Nietzsche, *Morgenröthe*, Section 134, my translation.

[42] *Ibid.*, Section 133, my translation.   [43] *Ibid.*, 385 (Spring, 1880), my translation.

described as a point of agreement. In a well-known passage from the *Groundwork of the Metaphysic of Morals*, Kant suggests that motives are epistemically opaque. In this passage Kant says that we can never know our motives with certainty, and therefore we cannot know whether there has ever been an action having moral worth. Thus Kant thought it was possible that an action we believed was performed out of respect for the moral law may have been performed out of self-love or some other inclination.[44] That Nietzsche subscribed to the thesis that motives are epistemically opaque can be seen in the following criticism of Schopenhauer:

Another's calamity offends us; it would convince us of our impotence, perhaps our cowardliness, if we could do nothing to help him; or in itself it brings a diminution of our honor in the eyes of others or ourselves. Or the misfortune and suffering of others indicate to us our own danger, and already as signs of human peril and frailty, they could painfully affect us. We repulse this sort of pain and offense and requite it through an action of pity, which can be a subtle form of self-defense or revenge.[45]

Part of what Nietzsche is doing is offering a set of alternative explanations of an action which apparently has as its end the well-being of another, and has this end because of another's misery. This type of action is paradigmatic of an action to which Schopenhauer would ascribe compassion or pity as its motive.[46] Nietzsche's point is that we cannot be sure of the motivation of this type of action. Not only do alternative explanations of this type of action carry equal explanatory force, any one or more of these alternative explanations could pick out the actual motive or motives underlying an action which we would, from an uncritical and naive point of view, attribute to pity. For all we know, Nietzsche suggests, it might be that honor, fear, self-defense, or revenge moved us to help the sufferer even though we believe that some desire solely for the other's well-being moved us to help. Human nature, Nietzsche argues, has depths and obscurities which makes it extremely difficult, if not impossible, to

[44] See Kant, *Groundwork*, 74-75.

[45] Nietzsche, *Morgenröthe*, Section 133, my translation.

[46] Both Schopenhauer and Nietzsche employ the same German noun *Mitleid* in their works. *Mitleid* has been rendered by various translators as "sympathy," "compassion," or "pity." Sympathy, compassion, and *Mitleid* have analogous etymological structures in Greek, Latin, and German, conveying the notion of "suffering with another, e.g., *sympatheia*, Greek, *syn*, with *Pathos*, 'suffering', 'passion'; *Mitleid*, German, *mit*, with plus *Leiden*, 'to suffer'; and *compassio*, Latin, *com*, with *pati*, 'to suffer'. Pity, however, has a different etymological structure, viz, it is from the Latin *pius*, 'pious'. I would argue that despite having an analogous etymological structure, sympathy is a poor translation of *Mitleid* since sympathy involves an ability to participate in any of another's emotional states, not just painful ones. On the other hand, I would claim that either pity, despite its disanalogous structure, or compassion are the proper translation of *Mitleid*. I would be inclined to argue that what Schopenhauer referred to as *Mitleid* is compassion, while what Nietzsche referred to as *Mitleid* is pity, and that pity is different from

specify the drives and urges from which our actions stem. Insofar as Schopenhauer fails to appreciate this, Nietzsche considers his views naive and unconvincing.

Nietzsche, however, took Kant's thesis more seriously than Kant. While Kant recognizes the possibility that we cannot be certain about our actual motives, he then proceeds to develop an ethical theory in which it is important to determine our motives. After all, for Kant, only actions which result from one's respect for the moral law are actions having moral worth, and only characters who act from this motive are characters having a good will. Nietzsche takes Kant's opacity thesis, extends and revitalizes it, and uses it to challenge any type of ethical theory which determines the moral worth of characters and actions according to intentions and motives. Seen in this light, Nietzsche's criticism of Schopenhauer's ethics applies with equal force to Kant's. Our inner world, our self-conscious experiences, Nietzsche suggests, are subject to the same sort of interpretation and structuralization as the outer world, the world of our senses. Thus Nietzsche speaks of a phenomenalism of our inner world, one which parallels the phenomenalism of the outer world:

I maintain the phenomenality of the inner world, too: everything of which we become conscious is arranged, simplified, schematized, interpreted through and through—the actual process of inner "perception," the causal connection between thoughts, desires, between subject and object, are absolutely hidden from us—and are perhaps purely imaginary. The "apparent inner world" is governed by just the same forms and procedures as the "outer" world. We never encounter "facts." [47]

If we are to rely on introspection or self-consciousness to discover our motives and intentions, Nietzsche contends, we are involved in a process

---

compassion. The main reason I say this is that the emotion referred to by Schopenhauer is free from the pejorative cast that is associated with pity, e.g., consider the insult, "I pity you," the condescending attitude toward those we pity; the description "you pitiful wretch," the frequency with which pity is rejected—I don't want your pity," and desirability of self-pity. This pejorative cast, lacking in compassion, is in full flower in the emotions Nietzsche analyzes. I would, thus, agree with Jean Stambaugh's assessment that Nietzsche's writings lack a conception of "compassion." See her "Thoughts on Pity and Revenge," *Nietzsche Studien* (Berlin, 1971), I, 27-35. If what I say is true, any comparison between Nietzsche and Schopenhauer's conceptions of *Mitleid* should take into account that although they use the same German noun, they are referring to different emotions. I have not taken this into account in my explanation of Nietzsche's criticism of Schopenhauer's ethics primarily because these particular criticisms are such that they would apply to any emotion Schopenhauer might claim is the basis of morality.

[47] Nietzsche, *Will to Power*, Section 477. Of course, Kant anticipated Nietzsche in teaching the phenomenality of the inner world. This is suggested by his opacity thesis, but, more importantly, by his distinction between the empirical and the transcendental self or the phenomenal and noumenal self. For example, see his *Critique of Pure Reason*, B154-B158.

of interpretation. We are not simply retriving mental facts. We impose form, organize, and categorize our inner experiences just as we do our outer experiences. If, Nietzsche might suggest, this is sufficient to show that there is something, some unknown component to the outer world— a Schopenhauerian will, a Kantian thing in itself—this is also sufficient to show an unknown component in our inner world. This unknown element, Nietzsche conjectures, could be the true springs and motors of our behavior and it may be different from our interpreted, and hence falsified, account of the inner springs of our actions.

Nietzsche reinforces his criticisms of these methods for assessing the moral worth of actions and characters by mentioning less metaphysically charged problems. Not only are introspective techniques problematic because they are essentially interpretive, they are also misleading because self-consciousness is subject to deception, false forms of consciousness, and rationalizations. For example, our love of others, Nietzsche observes may just be an example of a bad love of ourselves. Instead of being concerned for others because of their own worth, we may be concerned for their well-being because we hate ourselves; my interests and well-being, etc. are so unimportant, I am so worthless, that others count more than myself. On the other hand, this concern for others may be a symptom of our own lack of self-respect and self-confidence, a way of turning away from our own problems because they are too hard:

. . . all such arousing of pity and calling for help is secretly seductive, for our "own way" is too hard and demanding and too remote from the love and gratitude of others, as we do not really mind escaping from it—and from our own conscience—to flee into the conscience of the others and into the lovely temple of the "religion of pity." [48]

These may be the real reasons why one pities others, reasons which are very self-interested and personal, the immorality behind morality, Nietzsche observes. One has been taught, conditioned, and threatened, however, not to be immoral. Thus we hide these facts and deceive ourselves. Our pity is viewed simply as our concern for others, our "benevolence," our simple respect for the moral law. These are, Nietzsche suggests, masks and veils behind which lies the truth. Yet it is the veils and masks which Schopenhauer and Kant use to assess the worth of action and characters.

University of Wisconsin—Whitewater.

---

[48] Nietzsche, *Gay Science*, Section 338.

V

JANE ADDAMS ON HUMAN NATURE [1]

By Merle Curti

It is somewhat curious that in tributes to Jane Addams (1860–1935) occasioned by her centennial year, no serious consideration has been given to her place in American intellectual history. One finds merited praise of her personality and of her contributions to the woman's movement, to social welfare, and to international peace. Her understanding and appreciation of the immigrants in our midst and what she did to help them become Americans without losing a feeling for their Old World heritage have been rightly recalled. But the ideas she held, their relation to her time and her life, have not apparently seemed worthy of analysis and evaluation.

Three main considerations go a long way toward explaining this. Jane Addams did not in any of her writings systematically set forth her social ideas in a way to please the scholars nowadays who set great store on what is called intellectual sophistication. Her ideas, in her books and essays, are subordinated to the larger social and human purposes and activities to which her life was dedicated. The pages abound with straightforward, unpretentious but often moving and penetrating reports of interviews with well known public figures and of participation in meetings of social workers and advocates of peace. Her writings are chiefly concerned with her everyday experiences over forty odd years at Hull House.

A second reason for the neglect of Jane Addams' thought may be that in her own day a public image was developed in some quarters which did her scant justice. She was widely appreciated, but certain critics, influenced by the stereotype of the sentimental do-gooder which was common among intellectuals, were close to condescension in their judgments of her. Agnes Repplier, for example, wrote of her "ruthless sentimentality." Theodore Roosevelt once dubbed her "poor bleeding Jane" and "a progressive mouse." Such judgments no doubt have lingered and confirmed many in accepting a stereotype—a Jane Addams whose easy optimism blinded her to the depth of the "tragic view of life" so popular now in many intellectual circles.

The neglect of her ideas may also be related to a present discouragement over the uses women have made of the vote, to which she attached so much importance, and, even more likely, to the contemporary strength of nationalism and of the forces in the world that make the abolition of war seem at best remote.

It is not my purpose to try to elevate Jane Addams into a major

[1] This essay was presented as the first William I. Hull Lecture at Swarthmore College, October 16, 1960, under the joint sponsorship of the William J. Cooper Foundation and the Swarthmore College Peace Collection.

figure in our intellectual life. But on re-reading her ten books [2] it seems clear that if justice has been done her heart and her social vision, it has not been done her mind. Her ideas illuminate in sensitive and often keen ways major movements of thought in her time. Nor can the significance of her life be understood unless thoughtful attention is given to the rôle that ideas played in that life. Further, at its best, the writing in which her ideas are expressed rises to a level of literary distinction.

The thought of Jane Addams might be considered in any of a number of ways. I have chosen to use a central theme as a key to her ideas and feelings—her conception of human nature. The term itself occurs frequently in her writings. It was not common in her time to give the term an explicit, formal definition, and she herself did not do so. But it is clear that she did not limit it to the native equipment of men. For her, human nature encompassed the experiences and potentialities of the growing organism, in infancy, childhood, adolescence, and old age. She appreciated the dynamic factors in motivation and saw in the universal desire of individuals to be recognized and appreciated as unique persons, and the consequence of society's failure to make such recognition, the key to much behavior. She recognized the nature and rôle of sex in the life of the individual, but she also saw its relation to civilization. In her view of human nature, play and recreation are basic needs which brook denial only at heavy cost. Fighting is of course a part of human nature, but so is cooperation. Above all, her image of man emphasized the idea that the differences separating social classes and distinguishing immigrants and Negroes from old stock Americans, are far less important than the capacities, impulses, and motives they share in common.

In *Twenty Years at Hull House* the author noted that in 1889, when she went to live on Halstead Street, she was without any preconceived social theories and economic views. These, she added, were developed out of her experiences in Chicago. True, but the foundations for these theories and views rested on already formulated conceptions of human nature which, as she herself recognized, began to take shape in early childhood. Such recognition was natural enough, for by 1910, when the book was published, social workers as well as parents and educators were familiar with the great importance G.

[2] All of Jane Addams' books were published by the Macmillan Company: *Democracy and Social Ethics* (1902), *Newer Ideals of Peace* (1907), *The Spirit of Youth and the City Streets* (1909), *Twenty Years at Hull House* (1910), *A New Conscience and an Ancient Evil* (1912), *The Long Road of Woman's Memory* (1916), *Peace and Bread in Time of War* (1922), *The Second Twenty Years at Hull House* (1930), *The Excellent Becomes the Permanent* (1932), *and My Friend Julia Lathrop* (1935); *Jane Addams, A Centennial Reader,* edited by Emily Cooper Johnson, 1960. The Jane Addams papers are in the Swarthmore College Peace Collection.

Stanley Hall had long been attaching to childhood experiences. And so it was natural for Miss Addams to begin her autobiography by referring to the theory that "our genuine impulses may be connected with our childish experiences, that one's bent may be traced back to that 'No man's land' where character is formless but nevertheless settling into definite lines of future development."

These reminiscences reveal some of the basic conceptions of human nature later to be more or less explicitly formulated in writing and richly implemented in living. One finds repeated reference, for example, to the presumably innate tendency of children to seek in ceremonial expression a sense of identification with man's primitive life and kinship with the past, perhaps a compensation for the child's slowness to understand the real world about him, and certainly an instrument toward that end. This conviction, made intellectually respectable by early XIXth-century German philosophers and in Jane Addams' young womanhood by G. Stanley Hall (the recapitulation theory), was to figure in the importance she attached to the esthetic impulse and to children's play. The theory that in play children satisfy an innate need to live over the experience of the race seemed to her both reasonable and realistic. Adolescent behavior, which some thought stemmed from original sin, she looked upon as a natural expression of an instinct too old and too powerful to be easily recognized and wisely controlled. She noted also that children love to carry on, either actually or in play, activities proper to older people. This trait she thought of as also grounded in the need to repeat racial experience, and as expressing itself regardless of precept or inculcation. "The old man," as she put it, "clogs our earliest years."

Another early formed foundation stone for her image of man was the conviction that the basis of childhood's timidity, never altogether outworn, stems from "a sense of being unsheltered in a wide world of relentless and elemental forces." It is at least in part because of this fear and loneliness, she thought, that the child, and the adult which he becomes, needs affection and companionship. Jane Addams realized, of course, long before she wrote the autobiography, that in her own case this feeling of being unsheltered was accentuated by the fact that she had been deprived of her mother by death in her third year and by the further fact that a physical deformity both isolated her and gave her a sense of inadequacy and inferiority. But she was sure that all children share in greater or less degree this sense of fear and loneliness and that its major antidote is understanding and love. Also in her case the sense of timidity and loneliness was compensated for by the close and affectionate father-daughter relationship. The father's way of assuring her of his acceptance of her cemented the bond more tightly. It is hard, she reflected, to account fully for a child's adoring affection for a parent, "so emotional, so irrational, so tangled with the affairs of the imagination."

It came to be clear to Jane Addams, as it is so patently clear to us, that her father greatly influenced her ideas about the nature of mankind. A substantial miller imbued with the democracy of the Illinois frontier and of his hero Mazzini, John Addams' views of human nature reflected his abolitionism, his great admiration of Lincoln, and his commitment to Hicksite Quakerism. His complete lack of racial prejudice and his firm conviction that the similarities of men far outweigh the differences, were an indelible influence in the forming of the daughter's view of human nature. So too was his belief in the essential equality of men and women. These beliefs were reinforced by his Quaker heritage and the essentially classless society of this Illinois farm community. When his young daughter was troubled about the doctrine of foreordination, and asked her father to explain it to her, he replied that probably neither she nor he had the kind of minds capable of understanding the doctrine. In other words, as Jane Addams later recalled the conversation, some minds are capable and fond of dealing with abstractions while others are at home with concrete facts and immediate problems: this simple typology explained much that she later observed at Hull House in heated discussions over socialism and anarchism. Her father continued by adding that it made little difference whether one was the sort to understand such doctrines as predestination as long as he did not pretend to understand what he didn't. "You must always be honest with yourself inside, no matter what happens." This idea, so basic in Quaker tradition, stuck with the girl. The discussion ended with the suggestion that there may be areas of unfathomed complexity, incapable at least at the present stage of man's rational development, of being fully comprehended. In Jane Addams' view of human nature there was a large place for the contemplation of life's mysteries.

The instruction and associations of Rockford Seminary did not greatly alter these foundations for a conception of human nature. Jane Addams, like her fellow-students, read textbooks on mental philosophy, but the static and sterile approach in most treatises of this kind at best stimulated discussions outside class on such questions as the freedom of the will. The reading of Emerson strengthened her sense that human nature includes both rational and intuitive capacities. But as she was introduced to new ranges of feminism, she felt dissatisfied with the old belief in the ascendancy of intuition in the feminine mind. Under the influence of the positivism which she discovered, she concluded that women ought to study intensively at least one branch of natural science to make the faculties clear and more acute. Following graduation from Rockford, she tried studying medicine in Philadelphia but found she had little taste or aptitude for the sciences and dropped the course.

During the Rockford years and the brief Philadelphia experiment, Miss Addams' awareness of death and sorrow took on, especially through her study of Plato, a universal dimension: human existence had always been an unceasing flow and ebb of justice and oppression, of life and death. She heard about Darwinism and accepted it. The acceptance and interpretations she gave to evolution became a fresh and vastly important component in her image of man.

Like so many young women college graduates of the time, Jane Addams went to Europe in search of further culture. The four years she spent abroad were shadowed by long and painful illnesses and a depressing sense of failure. Thus her years of further education were not altogether roseate. But she continued to learn. Experiences in the great art galleries and study of man's early artistic expressions in the pyramids and in the catacombs sharpened her vague feeling that the esthetic component is basic in man's nature. But this was not all, for she interested herself further in the positivism which she had discovered in her reading at Rockford.

When she saw that for all their enthusiasm about human brotherhood, the positivists did little or nothing to implement the idea, she sought light elsewhere. This she found in her growing awareness of the human wretchedness in the great urban slums and in the programs of the British social settlement pioneers. Increasingly she felt that many college women in their zest for learning and in their search for individual culture departed too suddenly from the active, emotional life led by their grandmothers and great grandmothers. The rewards of the search for individual knowledge and culture paled as she became more deeply convinced of the far greater importance of learning from life itself. Education and artistic effort, she decided, were futile when considered apart from the ultimate test of the conduct it inspired, when there was no relationship between these and the human need of the poor and the suffering. Thus without benefit of William James and John Dewey, who only later reenforced her views of human nature, she became, as her friend Dr. Alice Hamilton said, something of a pragmatist, determined to test ideas and values about life in the actual laboratory of life. But the pragmatism that later provided support for an enlarged view of human nature did not lead to a rejection of presuppositions more or less unconsciously acquired and interwoven with Christian humanism and Christian mystery.

Closely related to pragmatism and more important in her own intellectual growth had been the doctrine of evolution. No one of the other late XIXth- and early XXth-century movements of thought— the so-called new psychology of the experimental laboratory, or

Freudianism, or Marxism—to all of which she responded, exerted so far-reaching an influence on Jane Addams' view of the nature of man as did the teachings of Darwin and his disciple Kropotkin, who spent some time at Hull House in 1901.

For Jane Addams, the evolutionary view of human nature postulated certain primordial types of behavior and potential types of behavior. On many occasions she referred to these, in the fashion of those days, as instincts. Man shared some of these with other animals. But in the process of evolution, of survival through adaptation, he came to have impulses that set him apart from other animals in somewhat the way that the human hand enabled him to claw his way to a civilization denied his less well equipped fellow creatures.

Her view of the inherited basic equipment of man emphasized the special importance of the extremely early appearance in man's long struggle upwards, of the tribal feeding of the young. This human instinct sprang out of or was at least closely related to man's innate gregariousness and to the ability first of mothers and then of males to see in the hunger of any young symbolical relationship to the hunger of their own offspring. Our very organism, Jane Addams wrote, holds memories and glimpses of "that long life of our ancestors which still goes on among so many of our contemporaries. Nothing," she continued, "so deadens the sympathies and shrivels the power of enjoyment, as the persistent keeping away from the great opportunities for helpfulness, as a continual ignoring of the starvation struggle which makes up the life of at least half the race. To shut oneself away from the race life is to shut one's self away from the most vital part of it; it is to live out but half the humanity to which we have been born and to use but half our faculties." This desire for action to fulfil social obligation was so deep-seated a heritage that to deny its expression, she thought, was more fatal to well-being than anything save disease, indigence, and a sense of guilt.

Here we have the corner stone of all that Jane Addams did in sharing her life with less fortunate neighbors, in encouraging measures designed to prevent the young and the old from being exploited, and in mobilizing in war-time food for helpless hungry mouths wherever they might be. For marvelous though human nature was in its adaptability, it had never "quite fitted its back to the moral strain involved in the knowledge that fellow creatures are starving."

The reading of Kropotkin and others led to the belief that this human instinct or trait appeared perhaps a million years or more before man developed a proclivity to kill masses of his own kind. This method of settling differences, many anthropologists held, had become common among human beings a mere twenty thousand years ago. It was used by only one other species, ants, which like human beings, were property holders. Thus Jane Addams might respectably hold, and she did, that the earlier instinct, with its implications of human solidarity, could under proper conditions exert an even stronger pull over behavior than competing forces, less deeply seated. In other words, man's primordial concern for group feeding of the young and the sense of responsibility for helping those in need which was related to it, might check and control the more recently acquired habit of mass killing of one's own kind. In the growth of international institutions and the evidences that love of man was crossing provincial and national boundaries, she saw hope for an emerging pacifism that in time would make war as obsolete as slavery had become. In sum, her reading convinced her that war, like slavery, was a relatively recent man-made institution. The argument that pacifism could never triumph because of man's inborn and unchangeable pugnacity, was no more valid, she thought, than the pre-Civil War argument of Southerners that slavery could never be abolished because it is ingrained in human nature itself.

In an address at the Boston Peace Congress of 1904, Miss Addams began to spell out the implications of this position, a position more positive in character than the non-resistance ideas of her hero, Tolstoy. In that address she anticipated William James' "Moral Equivalents of War" in suggesting that the subhuman and dark forces which so easily destroy the life of mankind might be diverted into organized attacks on social maladjustments, on poverty, disease, and misfortune, on one hand, and into the closely related "nurture of human life" on the other. It might in particular be diverted from destructive outburst into war by taking heed from the successful example of the immigrants of diverse and even hostile traditions who had learned to live as friends in America's cities. This view was developed in her book *Newer Ideals of Peace,* published in 1907. In the poorer quarters of our cosmopolitan cities she found multitudes of immigrants surrendering habits of hate and of aggression cherished for centuries, and customs that could be traced to habits of primitive man. She not only saw that they surrendered these habits, she also witnessed innumerable and sustained examples of the pity and kindness based on an equally ancient, or even more ancient, instinct: the instinct of pity and kindness toward those in the group whose need was even greater than that of the others. "In seeking companionship in the new world the immigrants are reduced to the fundamental equalities and universal necessities of life itself. They develop power of association which comes from daily contact with those who are unlike each other in all save the universal characteristics of man." To put it in other words, the pressures of a cosmopolitan neighborhood seemed to be the simple and inevitable foundations for an international order in somewhat the same way that the foundations of tribal and national morality had already been laid.

This hope suffered a blow during the first world war when an

emotional crisis showed that many immigrants had not in living together actually shed the heritage of Old World hatreds. But the outbreak of the war brought to the fore another belief also rooted in her
conception of human nature. Jane Addams found a great many
soldiers in hospitals in the several belligerent countries who expressed
the wish that women everywhere would use their influence to end the
struggle. She knew, of course, that women as well as men in all the
fighting countries were supporting the war. Yet she reflected that,
just as an artist in an artillery corps commanded to fire on a beautiful
cathedral would be "deterred by a compunction unknown to the man
who had never given himself to creating beauty and did not know
the intimate cost of it, so women, who have brought men into the
world and nurtured them until they reach the age of fighting, must
experience a peculiar revulsion when they see them destroyed, irrespective of the country in which these may have been born."

Such intimations received confirmation at the meeting of women
from several countries at The Hague in 1915. Here it was said again
and again that appeals against war and for a peaceful organization
of the world had been made too largely a matter of reason and a sense
of justice. If reason is only part of the human endowment, then emotion and the deepest racial impulses must be recognized, modified,
utilized. These deep racial impulses admittedly include the hatred of
the man who differs from the crowd: but this would be softened by
understanding and education. Also involved are those primitive human urgings to foster life and to protect the helpless of which women
were the earliest custodians. Involved too are the gregarious instincts
shared with the animals themselves—instincts which women as non-
combatants might now best keep alive. Such were some of the supports in her concept of human nature on which Jane Addams now
leaned.

When her own country entered the war in 1917 she kept faith with
the instrumentalist conviction that the processes or methods by which
goals are approached or achieved, are more important than acceptance
of so-called practical means that are in fact incompatible with the
ends. She had always felt that temperament and habit—also important ingredients in human nature—kept her in the middle of the road.
Now circumstances drove her to the extreme left of what had been
the peace movement. She faced the opprobrium of society and the
loneliness of standing out against mass judgment, wondering at times
if such deviation as hers might not be only arrogance. But she fell
back on the lesson her Quaker father had taught her: that what was
most important was always to be honest with oneself inside, no
matter what happened, that the ability to hold out against friends
and society in a time of crisis depends "upon the categorical belief
that a man's primary allegiance is to his own vision of the truth and
that he is under an obligation to affirm it."

She also found comfort in reminding herself of the universality of sorrow and death and in pondering—she knew it was at the risk of rationalization—on what seemed to be one of the lessons of the evolutionary view of human nature. If the deviant pacifist invited the deeply rooted biological hatred meted out to one who by nonconforming threatened the security of the group, there was after all another side of the evolutionary coin. All forms of growth begin with a variation from the mass. Might not the individual or group that differed from the mass be initiating moral changes and growth in human behavior and affairs? Might not he who was damned as a crank or pitied as a freak in times of stern crisis actually be leading in the growth of a new moral sense for his society? In view of the complexity and mystery of life's purposes, who could say? And finally, the difficulties of being a pacifist in war time were made a bit more bearable by keeping in mind what seemed another lesson from evolution: that the virtues of patriotism and the martial traits remained only as vestiges after they had actually become a deterrent to future social progress.

In other ways, too, the evolutionary view deeply influenced without moulding Jane Addams' ideas about human nature. This view also influenced, in an unknown measure, her own conduct. During the first years on Halstead Street nothing was more pitifully clear to her than "the fact that pliable human nature is relentlessly pressed upon by its physical environment." The Socialists, more than any other group, seemed to realize this, and seemed also to be making an earnest effort to relieve that heavy pressure. She would have been glad to have the comradeship of that "gallant company" had the Socialists not so firmly insisted that fellowship depended on identity of creed. In making this comment she was for the moment probably overlooking a Socialist emphasis on class conflict: for though she recognized the existence of such a conflict, she was not convinced that it was inevitable.

And so, unable to find comfort in a definite ideology which "explained" social chaos and pointed to logical bettering of physical conditions, Jane Addams went at the matter differently. Without bitterness or self-righteousness she tried to help labor and management learn the lesson of cooperation. She tried to educate public opinion and legislators to an appreciation of the fact that there is a definite relation between physical conditions and human behavior: that long and exhausting hours of labor at deadening tasks are likely to be followed by a quest for lurid and exciting pleasures. Moreover, the power to overcome such temptation reaches its limit almost automatically with that of physical resistance. "The struggle for existence," she wrote in *Democracy and Social Ethics* (1902), "which is so much harsher among people near the edge of pauperism, sometimes leaves ugly marks on character." Society had begun to apply this evolutionary principle to the bringing up of children. It had finally come to expect certain traits and behavior under certain conditions, to adapt methods and matter to the child's growing and changing needs. But society was slow to apply this principle to human affairs in general. In our attitudes toward the poor, the alcoholic, the prostitute, the outcast, she wrote, we think much more of what a man or woman ought to be than of what he is or what he might become under different and better conditions.

Here is an important factor in Jane Addams' approach to social work. She sensed the limitations in what the scientific charity groups and case workers had come to look on as the only true kind of helpfulness but what all too often seemed to those to be aided, ruthless imposition of conventions and standards that were incomprehensible. Pity might seem capricious and harmful to the new type of social case worker, but she should not forget that a theory of social conduct is a poor substitute for tenderness of heart which need not be blind to the complexity of the situation.

The deeply human interest in and appreciation of all sorts of people, including those in trouble, led Jane Addams to an early appreciation of the rôle of sex in deviant behavior and tragedy. It is noteworthy that a girl reared in the Victorian period was able to speak as frankly as she did and to recognize sex as "the most basic and primordial instinct of human beings." It is remarkable that she so early saw in the sex instinct a source of creativity in the arts and that she recognized its close association with play, which she also thought to be an inherent need in humankind. Basic and all important as the sex instinct was, it had always, from the beginnings of the race itself, been in some way controlled in the expression it took. But, in her view, our modern industrial city as it was in the 1890's not only failed to provide sensible, humane, and necessary forms of regulation of the instinct but invited its commercial degradation and exploitation and encouraged its expression in delinquent behavior and in enduring human tragedy.

More specifically, the American city with its anonymity, its uprooted families, its ill-adjusted immigrants, its commercial exploitation of the labor of girls and boys and young men and women in grim shops and factories in an almost never-ending workday, provided no opportunities for the development of comradeship and recreation save in gaudy and sensation-evoking saloons, dance halls and similar money-making establishments. Loneliness was the fate of innumerable girls who struggled against poverty and who had no decent opportunities for making friendships. "It is strange," wrote Miss Addams in 1911, "that we are so slow to learn that no one can safely live without companionship and affection, that the individual who tries the hazardous experiment of going without at least one of them is prone to be swamped by a black mood from within. It is as if we had to build little islands of affection in the vast sea of impersonal forces lest we be overwhelmed by them." Boys, to be sure, found companionship in gangs. But deprived of opportunities for natural expression of adolescent revolt in healthy recreation, the gang was at best an antisocial institution leading naturally to delinquency and a life of defeat, alcoholism, violence, and crime.

One might suppose in view of the innumerable examples of the rôle of sex in leading to ruthless exploitation one the one hand and to grim tragedy on the other, that Jane Addams would have accepted the Calvinist theory, with which she was familiar, of the innate depravity of mankind. On the contrary, with her faith in the pliability of human nature she held that just as our society brings out unfortunate behavior, so it is also capable of evoking wholesome relationships, social idealism, and artistic creativity if society assumes responsibility in a great area of human drive and experience, sex, which it had ignored, or condemned, or permitted to be degraded. She quoted General Bingham, Police Commissioner of New York, to the effect that there is "not enough depravity in human nature" to keep alive the very large business of commercial prostitution. "The immorality of women and the brutishness of men have to be persuaded, coaxed, and constantly stimulated in order to keep the social evil in its present state of business prosperity."

Jane Addams, like other Americans imbued with the teachings of pragmatism, did not draw any separating line between theory and practice. If, as she insisted, the regulation of this great primitive instinct had a long history and if that regulation had evolved with civilization, indeed, with the race itself, it was important to recognize the fact that its regulation now needed to be better adapted to the conditions of urban and industrial life.

Understanding the nature of sex was the first step in developing a better regulation of it. The cooperation of parents and schools might do much to bring about a more healthy understanding of and attitude toward sex. Sane education could be furthered not only through classes in biology and hygiene. It could also be encouraged through the study of literature and history which provide rich examples of the ill-effects of mere suppression or mere indulgence, and which also give abundant illustration of the ennobling expression of sex in altruism. Also important in her view was the expression of the creative aspects of the sex instinct in music and art—which the ancient Greeks had so well understood. "In failing to diffuse and utilize this fundamental instinct of sex through the imagination," she wrote, "we not only

inadvertently foster vice and enervation, but we throw away one of
the most precious implements for ministering to life's highest need."
It is, to be sure, no easy thing to substitute the love of beauty for
mere desire, to place the mind above the senses. But "the whole history of civilization," as she kept reminding her generation, "has been
one long effort to substitute psychic impulsion for the driving force
of blind appetite." Jane Addams took pains again and again to make
clear that this was quite different from the mere parental and social
imposition of repression.

Understanding the nature and potential relationships between
sex, altruism, and esthetic creativity was, however, not enough. What
was also needed was community provision for the expression of the
sex impulse in wholesome companionship, in social idealism put into
practice, and in the provision by society of adequate means for the
expression and development of the play instinct. For this too was so
basic and inherent a constituent of human nature that it could neither
be safely repressed nor, in modern urban life, left to chance. The
thwarting of all these basic instincts, the failure of contemporary
society to provide proper channels for their expression, explained, Jane
Addams insisted, much of the tragedy that stemmed from leaving the
sex instinct isolated from intelligent direction and manifestation. It
is worth noting in passing that she came to these views without benefit of Freud, at least as far as we know. When, in the 1920's, she first
spoke of him in her writings, it was less to find support for her thesis
than to regret the popular interpretation which focused attention on
the driving need for direct and overt sex expression.

But understanding and sublimation of the sex instinct are not in
her view enough. Society, she insisted, must put an end to certain
conditions that tempted boys and girls into degrading expressions of
the sex impulse. It can not do this merely by sanctioning benevolent
welfare capitalism, such as that exemplified in the paternalism at
Pullman. For like a modern King Lear, George Pullman could not
understand that his regimentation of the workers presumably in their
own interest led to "a revolt of human nature" against the denial of
their own participation in what affected every detail of their lives.
State intervention against long hours, poor pay, and the grueling
monotony of tending machines in factory and sweatshop was a more
positive need. The trade unions were working in this direction and
early found in Jane Addams a strong supporter. But the community,
she said, must also provide an environment in which, after an exhausting workday, youth and older workers might find the right sort
of companionship and release from nervous tensions. Only by this
means and through adequate pay would the toilers be freed from the
temptation and necessity of finding pleasure in saloons and dubious
dance halls.

Society can, in short, Miss Addams believed, reestablish under modern conditions the ancient tie between the sex impulse and artistic creativity and wholesome relaxation from the nervous tension of modern industrial labor. And it can also provide the means by which the social idealism of adolescence can find constructive outlet in helping others. Hull House pioneered in all this; but Jane Addams was sufficiently realistic to appreciate the need of a broader institutionally and socially supported program, and to work toward that end. In brief, people need not be allowed to fall into esthetic and social insensibility and into an indulgence of basic instincts that is unsatisfying, wasteful, and often tragic.

How much of the analysis of human nature which Jane Addams so unpretentiously made seems valid in the light of experience and present-day knowledge? One must report that some of her concepts are no longer entertained by competent psychologists. The theory that children in their growth recapitulate racial experiences, for example, now has few adherents. Nor would psychologists describe as instincts some of the motives and behavior she regarded as inborn and unlearned. But in her day psychologists did accept the instinct theory, and in following them she was *au courant*. She was on more solid ground in early emphasizing the importance of childhood experiences and of sex well before even psychologists had generally recognized it. It is true that she was too optimistic in thinking that degrading forms of expression of the sex impulse would disappear if bitter poverty were eliminated and adequate recreation made available. Our society has gone far toward achieving these ends, yet the degrading forms of expression seem to be as much of a problem as ever. But it is hard to measure the effects of changing conditions, and a great deal can of course be said for her conviction that the sex impulse can be modified and channeled into varied and often elevating expressions.

Miss Addams was also a pioneer in America in appreciating and using constructively the now well established fact that the great modes of adjustment in life, whether considered individually or socially, develop through influences of which each participant is often unconscious as he struggles to adapt himself to continuing and changing conditions. And though motivation research, unknown in her day, has made substantial progress, her discussion of motivation was unusually perceptive and is still largely acceptable. Her explanation of the deviant behavior of youth as a blundering effort to find adventure and self-expression in a society which provides few opportunities for either, is still central in the most informed approaches to the problems of delinquency. A case can also be made for her thesis that the talents and experiences of women in bearing children, in nurturing life, and in housekeeping and homemaking have been important factors in what they have done with the vote and through organization in helping to raise standards of community welfare.

It is perhaps in Miss Addams' discussion of the relation of war to human nature that the limitations of her analysis and her program are most apparent. One need not minimize the contributions of women in the continuing struggle against war. But her ideas about the potential rôle of women in this struggle, which she associated with a strongly ingrained compassion and reverence for life, would probably seem to her, were she alive today, to have been overstressed. The fact that immigrants in the United States seem quickly to forget ancient hatreds and learn to live together in peace, has been cited by various writers here and abroad. But Miss Addams' expectation that this demonstration would have an effect on international cooperation does not appear to have been realized. It also seems clear that she overstressed as a factor for peace what she regarded as the primordial appearance in the race of group responsibility for feeding infants and children regardless of parentage. The fact that loyalty to the nation and mass killing appeared historically late has not thus far rendered these patterns of behavior subordinate to the compassionate traits in human nature which she thought to be much older and therefore stronger in pull.

On the other hand, social scientists generally endorse Miss Addams's early arrived at insistence that the things that make men alike are more important than the things that differentiate them. If this is the case, then it may be that in our trials and errors and in our efforts to adjust our behavior to the world community we now recognize as a fact, we have not yet found adequate means for institutionalizing the implications of the fact that men share common characteristics regardless of culture. Also relevant to the discussion is the general agreement of psychologists and other social scientists that man's action or behavior is largely explained in terms of his social relationships.

Perhaps we have not yet sufficiently tested Jane Addams' conviction that there will be no peace until the world community is no longer divided into the repressed, dimly conscious that they have no adequate outlet for normal life, and the repressing, the self-righteous and the cautious who hold fast to their own. Perhaps we have not yet tested sufficiently her overarching conviction that if life is often mean, unprofitable and tragic, if it is at other times feeble and broken, it is because we have not yet learned the lesson, and acted on it, that these evidences of what some call the tragic flaw in human nature, result not from man's essential and unchangeable limitations, but rather follow from our failure to understand ourselves and others.

University of Wisconsin.

PART TWO

RACE AND ETHNICITY

A.   American Questions on Race

VI

DR. BENJAMIN RUSH AND THE NEGRO

By Donald J. D'Elia

"I love even the name of Africa," declared Benjamin Rush in 1788: these words of the co-founder, secretary, and later president (1803–13) of America's first abolitionist society (in Pennsylvania) were more than rhetorical.[1] For Rush realized that his revolutionary program of social, political, and religious reform, a program dramatized by his signing the Declaration of Independence, required the abolition of slavery.[2] Anything less than freedom for all men, black and white, would, he knew, give the lie to the republican idealism of '76. This Rush believed with great certainty. And so from that day in 1766 when, bound for studies at Edinburgh, he, a "free-born son of liberty," was outraged by the sight of a hundred slave ships in Liverpool harbor, to his death in 1813, Rush dedicated himself to Negro freedom and prosperity in a free America.[3]

If there was any one person who inspired Rush's crusade against slavery it was Anthony Benezet. The gentle Quaker reformer and philanthropist was to young Dr. Rush, back in his native Philadelphia in 1769 after study abroad, one of the most disinterested men of all time. Friend Anthony Benezet urged Rush to publish his thoughts on slavery, and the young physician's *An Address to the Inhabitants of the British Settlements in America, upon Slave-Keeping* appeared in Philadelphia, Boston, and New York in 1773. The *Address* was the first of many attacks by Rush on the social evils of his day, and perhaps his best.[4] And to his lifelong campaign against slavery and his great work in promoting the welfare of the Negro, the *Address* was to be an inspiring monument.

Negroes, Dr. Rush argued scientifically, were not by nature intellectually and morally inferior. Any apparent evidence to the contrary was only the perverted expression of slavery, which "is so foreign to the human mind, that the moral faculties, as well as those of the understanding are debased, and rendered torpid by it." He continued in the *Address*:

All the vices which are charged upon the Negroes in the southern colonies and the West-Indies, such as Idleness, Treachery, Theft, and the like, are the

[1]Rush to Jeremy Belknap, August 19, 1788, Lyman H. Butterfield, ed., *Letters of Benjamin Rush* (2 vols., Princeton, 1951), I, 482. Rush (1746–1813) and James Pemberton (1723–1809), the Quaker philanthropist, were the chief organizers of the Pennsylvania Society for Promoting the Abolition of Slavery, and the Relief of Free Negroes Unlawfully Held in Bondage (1774).

[2]The standard biography is Nathan G. Goodman, *Benjamin Rush, Physician and Citizen, 1746–1813* (Philadelphia, 1934). L. H. Butterfield's editorial commentary on Rush's letters and his "Benjamin Rush as a Promoter of Useful Knowledge," Proc. American Philosophical Soc., XCII (March 8, 1948), 26–36, are indispensable to what follows.

[3]Rush, "Journal Commencing Aug. 31, 1766," Indiana University MS, (Oct. 28, 1766), 13.

[4]Rush to Barbeu Dubourg, April 29, 1773, and to Granville Sharp, May 1, 1773, *Rush Letters*, I, 76, 80–81; George S. Brookes, *Friend Anthony Benezet* (Philadelphia, 1937), 93.

genuine offspring of slavery, and serve as an argument to prove that they were not intended by Providence for it.[5]

Science, then, made clear that human bondage was monstrous and that it not only vitiated the body but the faculties as well.[6] Restore the mind and the body to their natural state of freedom, the young medical philosopher asserted, and the vices of slavery would inevitably disappear and a new, more virtuous humanity emerge.

Rush was not content with mere professions of equality, however noble. Facts were what he needed, and in his early pamphlet on slavery and in later writings he marshalled all that he could find to prove the Negro's fitness for civilized society. Even as he wrote in 1773, the Negro poet Phillis Wheatley was charming Boston audiences with her literary gifts. The girl, it was true, was free and talented—no average Negro in America—but Rush believed that she shared with the most primitive African in the slave trade and with all human beings the inborn principles of taste and morality, which slavery corrupted and perverted, yet could not destroy. For God Himself had given men and women of every color a native appreciation of the sublime and the beautiful.[7]

Certainly, Rush argued, the only hope for the Negro (and for the moral reformation of the white society that had enslaved him) was emancipation and education. Separately emancipation and education were powerless to effect real and lasting changes in the Negro's status. What they could accomplish together was strikingly evident in the case of Rush's friend and brother physician, James Durham, about whom Rush wrote in the *American Museum*:

I have conversed with him upon most of the acute and epidemic diseases of the country where he lives, and was pleased to find him perfectly acquainted with the modern simple mode of practice in those diseases. I expected to have suggested some new medicines to him, but he suggested many more to me. He is very modest and engaging in his manners. He speaks French fluently and has some knowledge of the Spanish language.[8]

As a slave boy in Philadelphia, Dr. Durham had been educated in reading, writing, and the Christian religion; then he had served as a kind of apprentice under three physicians, the last finally allowing him to purchase his freedom.[9] Of course Rush, as secretary of the Pennsylvania Abolition Society and

---

[5]*An Address to the Inhabitants of the British Settlements in America, upon Slave-Keeping* (Philadelphia, 1773), 2-3.

[6]Rush to Granville Sharp, July 9, 1774, John A. Woods, ed., "The Correspondence of Benjamin Rush and Granville Sharp 1773-1809," *Journal of American Studies*, I (April 1967), 6-7, hereafter "The Correspondence."

[7]*An Address to the Inhabitants of the British Settlements in America, upon Slave-Keeping*, 2; Rush to Granville Sharp, July 9, 1774, Woods, ed., "The Correspondence," 6-7. Phillis Wheatley's *Poems on Various Subjects, Religious and Moral* appeared in 1773 (*DAB*).

[8]Rush to the Pennsylvania Abolition Society, Nov. 14, 1788, *Rush Letters*, I, 497; this letter was printed in *The American Museum*, V (Jan. 1789), 61-62. Another letter by Rush, submitted at the same time to the Society, concerned the Negro slave prodigy, Thomas Fuller, the illiterate "African Calculator." See Prof. Butterfield's note, *Rush Letters*, I, 497-498.   [9]*Ibid.*, 497.

a leading doctor and medical teacher, relished this opportunity to inform the public of a former slave's competence in the practice of medicine. Later, in the terrible yellow fever epidemic of 1793, when Rush was in dire need of help in treating the sick, and Durham was absent, other black men assisted him in battling death. Male nurses like the faithful Marcus demonstrated to him anew that the Negro was inferior in neither skill nor courage.

Marcus, Rush's friend and household servant, was no Dr. Durham. But his value to Rush and the ailing humanity of Philadelphia in the great plague of 1793 is evident in letter after letter from Rush to his wife, who was safely in New Jersey. Weak himself with the fever, Rush wrote on September 21 of the comforting presence of his devoted Negro assistant:

Marcus has not, like Briarius, a hundred hands, but he can turn his two hands to a hundred different things. He puts up powders, spreads blisters, and gives clysters equal to any apothecary in town.[10]

And a month later, now seriously ill but improving under Marcus' tender care, the grateful Doctor confided to Mrs. Rush that "with a little instruction" Marcus "would exceed many of our bark and wine doctors in the treatment of the present fever."[11] Rush owed his life to Marcus, just as Marcus and Peter, a little mulatto servant boy who assisted Rush in treating fever victims, owed their lives to him.[12] To Rush this was dramatic evidence of the moral equality of all men!

Outside his household but dear to him as friends and humanitarians were Absalom Jones, Richard Allen, and William Gray, leaders of the Negro community in Philadelphia. It was they who nobly joined the battle against yellow fever at Rush's request by providing Negro nurses and workers for the stricken city.[13] After the deadly and seemingly interminable epidemic was over, Rush once again took up his pen to defend the Negro—this time because of the charge that the black nurses had exploited the helpless and dying whites they had attended during the crisis. In a letter to Mathew Carey, who was preparing an account of the fever, Rush tried to set the record straight:

In procuring nurses for the sick, Wm. Grey and Absalom Jones were indefatigable, often sacrificing for that purpose whole nights of sleep without the least compensation. Richard Allen was extremely useful in performing the mournful duties which were connected with burying the dead. Many of the black nurses it is true were ignorant, and some of them were negligent, but many of them did their duty to the sick with a degree of patience and tenderness that did them great credit.[14]

[10]Rush to Mrs. Rush, *ibid.*, II, 673. The best account of the yellow fever epidemic is John H. Powell, *Bring Out Your Dead; The Great Plague of Yellow Fever in Philadelphia in 1793* (Philadelphia, 1949).

[11]Rush to Mrs. Rush, Oct. 14, 1793, *Rush Letters,* II, 716.

[12]*Ibid.,* Sept. 22, 1793, Oct. 17, 1793, 674–675, 717; Powell, 117.

[13]Rush to Mathew Carey, Oct. 29, 1793, *Rush Letters,* II, 731–32; George W. Corner, ed., *The Autobiography of Benjamin Rush: His "Travels through Life" Together with His Commonplace Book for 1789–1813* (Princeton, 1948), 221 and Dr. Corner's note; Powell, 94–101.

[14]Rush to Mathew Carey, Oct. 29, 1793, *Rush Letters,* II, 731–732; also, Rush's classic *An Account of the Bilious Remitting Yellow Fever, As It Appeared in the City of Philadelphia, in the year 1793* (Philadelphia, 1794) for his praise of the Negroes.

What made their conduct even more exemplary, Rush noted dramatically, was the discovery that Negroes did not possess the immunity to yellow fever that Rush himself and the public had attributed to them during the epidemic.[15]

Working together in great humanitarian causes was not new to Rush, Jones, Allen, and Gray. At the very time the fever raged these men and John Nicholson, another white philanthropist, were seeing their dream of an African church in Philadelphia come true. The African Episcopal Church of St. Thomas, dedicated on August 22, 1793, was America's first Negro church; and for Rush, who had done so much to bring it about, the event marked a turning point in the history of the Negro's quest for freedom.[16] He and others had pioneered the antislavery movement which had won a triumph in 1780 with the passage (in Pennsylvania) of the nation's first abolition law.[17] To add to her honor, Rush's state now had a church for the advancement of her freedmen in religion and morals.

The revolutionary significance which Rush attached to the Negroes' having their own church is nowhere better expressed than in his commonplace book:

I conceive it will collect many hundred Blacks together on Sundays who now spend that day in idleness. It may be followed by churches upon a similar plan in other States, and who knows but it may be the means of sending the gospel to Africa, as the American Revolution sent liberty to Europe? Then perhaps the Africans in America may say to those who brought them here as slaves, what Joseph said to his brethren when they condemned themselves for selling him into Egypt.[18]

Indeed, there was no doubt in Rush's mind that what he called the "Spirit of the Gospel" was regenerating the world in his time: that just as the political evil of monarchy had been destroyed by the divinely commissioned American Revolution, in which Rush himself had so actively participated, so the moral and social evil of slavery was being destroyed, too, by a merciful God acting through the agency of Rush and other reformers. The historic ignorance and misery of the Negroes, accordingly, were predestined to give way before the civilizing forces of religion and education, which God in His infinite wisdom had released in the epoch of the American Revolution. Rush believed that the United States was the center from which God was reforming the world through perfected reason and progressive revelation.[19]

[15]Rush to Mathew Carey, Oct. 29, 1793, *Rush Letters,* II, 731–732; Powell, 95.

[16]Rush to John Nicholson, Nov. 28, 1792, to Mrs. Rush, July 16, 1791, August 22, 1793, and to John Nicholson, August 12, 1793, Rush *Letters,* I, 624, 599–600, II, 639–640, 636–637; Corner, 202–203.

[17]Ira V. Brown, *Pennsylvania Reformers: from Penn to Pinchot* (University Park, 1966), 7.

[18]"Now therefore be not grieved, nor angry with yourselves, that ye sold me hither: for God did send me before you to preserve life." Genesis XLV, 5; Corner, 202–203; Rush to Granville Sharp, August 1791, *Rush Letters,* I, 608–609.

[19]Rush to Jeremy Belknap, June 21, 1792, to Rev. Elhanan Winchester, Nov. 12, 1791, and to Thomas Jefferson, August 22, 1800; *ibid.,* I, 620–621, 611–612; II, 820–821; Rush to Granville Sharp, Oct. 29, 1773, "The Correspondence," 3; Corner, 161–162. Rush, "Lectures on Pathology. Influence of Government upon Health," Library Company of Philadelphia, Rush MSS (Yi2/7396/F22), 312–314.

That America was chosen by God as the place for man's ultimate deliverance from slavery was evidenced, Rush believed, in the New World's providing a religious and political sanctuary for Europeans from earliest times. Closer to his own day, Quaker antislavery reformers and educators of the Negro like John Woolman and Anthony Benezet manifested in their work the special divine presence. Rush himself had written his *Address* under the spell of Benezet and, again because of the Quaker's influence, had opened a lifelong correspondence with Granville Sharp, the English abolitionist.[20] To Sharp, in fact, he wrote excitedly of the Continental Congress's pledge of October 1774 *"never* to import any more slaves into America." "This resolution does our Congress the more honor," he observed with transparent pride, "as it was proposed and defended entirely upon *moral* and not political principles."[21] Congress's motives in the Continental Association were, of course, not so simple and noble, but Rush viewed the resolution idealistically as a sign of his country's moral regeneration:

Thus have we stopped the avenue of a vice which we have good reason to fear brought down the vengeance of Heaven upon our country—a vice so infinite in its mischief upon the liberty, morals and happiness of a people that no wisdom, or power could have established an empire which it would not have destroyed. We have now *turned from our wickedness.* Our next step we hope will be to do that *which is lawful and right.* The emancipation of slaves in America will now be attended with but few difficulties except such as arise from instructions given to our Governors, not to favour laws made for that purpose.[22]

There was hope, Rush went on, even the probability that, should Americans persevere in this antislavery feeling, Negro bondage would disappear from the continent in forty years.[23] Then Britain's shame as the creator of the African Company would be complete.[24] The very climate and rich soil of the slave colonies seemed to cooperate with the new moral purpose in that forced labor was unnecessary in the divine economy. "The natural fertility of the earth in all warm countries," Rush argued teleologically, "shows that heaven never intended hard labor to be the portion of man in such countries."[25]

Rush believed, too, that the hand of God could be seen in the Declaration of Independence, which he signed as a delegate from Pennsylvania. And for him there was absolutely no doubt that the Negro possessed (and had been denied) the natural rights which the Declaration celebrated. So certain was Rush of divine wrath at the Anglo-American enslavement of the Negro that he fearfully suggested that a bloody civil war might be necessary "to expiate their guilt."[26]

The triumph of American arms in 1783 was also unmistakable evidence to

[20]Rush to Granville Sharp, May 1, 1773, "The Correspondence," 2; Rush to Thomas Jefferson, Oct. 6, 1800 and to Mrs. Rush, June 1, 1776, *Rush Letters,* II, 825–826, I, 102; Rush, *An Address to the Inhabitants,* 28.

[21]Rush to Granville Sharp, Nov. 1, 1774, "The Correspondence," 13.   [22]*Ibid.*   [23]*Ibid.*

[24]Cf. Rush, *An Address to the Inhabitants,* 21; Rush to Nathanael Greene, Sept. 16, 1782, *Rush Letters,* I, 286.   [25]*Ibid.;* Rush, *An Address to the Inhabitants,* 8.

[26]Corner, 119; Rush, *An Address to the Inhabitants,* 7, 30; Rush to Nathanael Greene, Sept. 16, 1782, *Rush Letters,* I, 286; Rush to Granville Sharp, July 9, 1774, "The Correspondence," 8; Rush, *An Address to the Inhabitants,* 30.

Rush of God's being on the side of freedom—for black and white. "I remember the time (about 15 years ago)," he wrote to Granville Sharp in November, "when the advocates for the poor Africans were treated as fanatics, and considered as the disturbers of the peace of society. At present they are considered as the benefactors of mankind and the man who dares say a word in favor of reducing our black brethren to slavery is listned (*sic*) to with horror, and his company avoided by every body."[27] This was not true, he hastened to admit, in South Carolina. But there and in the other southern states reason and Christianity were prevented from operating successfully by a collective mental disease which Rush, in his investigations as a medical philosopher, called "negromania."[28]

A form of madness, which in Dr. Rush's broad definition meant "a want of perception, or an undue perception of truth, duty, or interest," negromania had before the Revolution affected people in all parts of the country. Now, in 1783, the disorder was prevalent only in the South. Negromaniacs in their collective illness and misery failed to perceive that Negro slavery violated the laws of nature and God and that the interest, health, and happiness of white Southerners lay in their own free honest labor.[29] Any healthy-minded person could see that God had not created the Africans for hard work. It was obvious to any man of sound perceptions that the Divine Governor of the universe had placed Africans in easy tropical surroundings and fitted them only for light employments. In seven years, though, the revolutionary Doctor was confident, the negromania could be cured, at least in South Carolina.[30]

Rush's faith in the Revolution as the harbinger of an age of freedom and equality among black and white seemed to be gloriously confirmed when in September 1787 the proposed Federal Constitution appeared to prohibit the importation of slaves, beginning in 1808. Later as a member of the Pennsylvania state convention to consider ratification of the Constitution, he would have much to do with its acceptance in his home state. But even before ratification Rush proudly wrote to his English abolitionist friend, John Coakley Lettsom, of his native province's role in ending the slave trade:

To the influence of Pennsylvania chiefly is to be ascribed the prevalence of sentiments favorable to African liberty in every part of the United States. You will see a proof of their operation in the new Constitution of the United States. In the year one thousand seven hundred and eight (*sic*) there will be an end of the African trade in America.[31]

[27]Rush to Granville Sharp, April 7, 1783, and his November 28th letter from which the quotation is taken, "The Correspondence," 17, 20; Corner, 161–162.

[28]Rush to Granville Sharp, Nov. 28, 1783, "The Correspondence," 20; Rush, "On the Different Species of Mania," D. D. Runes, ed., *The Selected Writings of Benjamin Rush* (New York, 1947), 212–13. This edition of Rush's writings should be used only when absolutely necessary—as in this instance—and with extreme caution; see L. H. Butterfield, "The Reputation of Benjamin Rush," *Pennsylvania History,* XVII (1950), 19.

[29]Rush, "On the Different Species of Mania," 212–13; Rush to Granville Sharp, Nov. 28, 1783, "The Correspondence," 20; Rush, *An Address to the Inhabitants,* 7–8.

[30]Rush to Granville Sharp, Nov. 28, 1783, "The Correspondence," 20.

[31]Goodman, *Benjamin Rush,* 78; Rush to John Coakley Lettsom, Sept. 28, 1787, and to James Madison, Feb. 27, 1790, *Rush Letters,* I, 442, 541.

So pervasive was the spirit of liberality and humanity among all the framers of the Constitution, Rush triumphantly declared, that nowhere did the words "slaves" or "Negroes" appear in the great document. The use of those ugly words, it was agreed, would serve only to "contaminate the glorious fabric of American liberty and government."[32]

By December 25, 1787 Rush had seen his early optimism for the Constitution's adoption redeemed. Delaware, Pennsylvania, and New Jersey had by now ratified and hopes were high for general adoption by the states. Rush was ecstatic at the thought that the slave trade was doomed in America. "O! Virtue, Virtue, who would not follow thee blindfold? The prospect of this glorious event more than repays me for all the persecution and slander to which my principles and publications exposed me about 16 or 17 years ago."[33] With the abolition of the slave trade assured and the revolutionary spirit of liberty becoming everywhere more powerful and obvious, Rush directed his energies to destroying slavery itself, and to ameliorating the Negro's miserable condition and preparing him for real social and political equality.

Rush, a physician and medical teacher as well as a humanitarian, was convinced that slavery was physically and morally injurious to the Negro. This was so despite proslavery arguments that the Negro was merry, as could be seen in his singing and dancing, and therefore perfectly happy. The Negro slave was merry, true, but his mirth had nothing to do with happiness. The Africans' merry singing and dancing were, in fact, "physical symptoms of melancholy or madness, and therefore are certain proofs of their misery." This was science—not a slave-master's fancy. The life and health of man, Rush's science and revealed religion confirmed, depended upon the natural stimulus of liberty. Slavery deprived man of liberty which, like the other natural stimuli of food, clothing, and fuel, was essential to life and health. Without liberty there was only fear, which was destructive of life. No wonder, then, that slaves suffered from peculiar disorders of mind and body like melancholy, lockjaw, the many dietary diseases, and dangerous child-bearing complications. Christianity and natural reason should be outraged by such unnecessary human misery![34]

A practicable and God-given way of helping to end slavery, Rush believed, was to be found in the manufacture and use of American maple sugar rather than West Indian slave-produced cane sugar. "Whoever considers that the gift of the sugar maple trees is from a benevolent Providence," he wrote

[32]Rush to John Coakley Lettsom, Sept. 28, 1787, *ibid.*, 442.

[33]Rush to Elizabeth Graeme Ferguson, Dec. 25, 1787, *ibid.*, 446–447; Wayland F. Dunaway, *A History of Pennsylvania* (2d ed.; Englewood Cliffs, 1961), 190; Sylvester K. Stevens, *Pennsylvania: Birthplace of a Nation* (New York, 1964), 121.

[34]Rush to Jeremy Belknap, May 6, 1788, and to John Coakley Lettsom, April 21, 1788, *Rush Letters,* I, 460, 457–458. For the quotation on singing and dancing as symptomatic of melancholy, see *ibid.,* 458–459. In his famous *Medical Inquiries and Observations upon the Diseases of the Mind* (Philadelphia, 1812), 41, Dr. Rush again noted a connection between Negro insanity and "the toils of perpetual slavery." In the same work, 39, he observed that "fear often produces madness," but his most elaborate discussion of this idea and the natural stimulus of liberty is to be found in "An Inquiry into the Cause of Animal Life in Three Lectures," Rush, *Medical Inquiries and Observations* (5th ed.; 2 vols., Philadelphia, 1818), I, 39, 13, *et passim.*

Thomas Jefferson, who was much interested in the project,

that we have many millions of acres in our country covered with them, that the tree is improved by repeated tappings, and that the sugar is obtained by the frugal labor of a farmer's family, and at the same time considers the labor of cultivating the sugar cane, the capitals sunk in sugar works, the first cost of slaves and cattle, the expenses of provisions of both of them, and in some instances the additional expense of conveying the sugar to market in all the West-India Islands, will not hesitate in believing that the maple sugar may be manufactured much cheaper and sold at a *less price* than that which is made in the West-Indies.[35]

What this meant in Rush's teleological view was that God had planned free maple sugar to replace slave cane sugar at this revolutionary time in the history of the world. "In contemplating the present opening prospects in human affairs," he concluded his letter,

I am led to expect that a material part of the general happiness which Heaven seems to have prepared for mankind will be derived from the manufactory and general use of maple sugar, for the benefits which I flatter myself are to result from it will not be confined to our own country. They will I hope extend themselves to the interests of humanity in the West-Indies. With this view of the subject of this letter, I cannot help contemplating a sugar maple tree with a species of affection and even veneration, for I have persuaded myself to behold in it the happy means of rendering the commerce and slavery of our African brethren in the sugar islands as unnecessary as it has always been inhuman and unjust.[36]

Here certainly was a workable program of undermining the economic foundations of slavery.

Negroes, though rescued from slavery and unnatural fear, needed special care, Rush held. He observed of the almost 3,000 freedmen in Philadelphia in 1791 that they were "still in a state of depression, arising chiefly from their being deprived of the means of regular education and religious instruction."[37] The fine educational work of Anthony Benezet and the other Quakers notwithstanding, it was imperative that bold, new projects be undertaken for the Negro's relief.

One of these projects, as we have seen, was the founding of Negro churches like that of St. Thomas. Rush was so excited about this cause that he took the matter to the President of the United States himself, who pledged a contribution. And to Granville Sharp, Rush wrote, "The favor I now solicit for them is more substantial than even freedom itself. It will place them in a condition to make their freedom a blessing to them here and prepare them for happiness beyond the grave."[38] Sharp responded generously with his own and other English contributions. As late as 1810 when, by Rush's information, there were in excess of 12,000 Negroes in Philadelphia, their indefatigable partisan

[35]Rush "To Thomas Jefferson: An Account of the Sugar Maple Tree," July 10, 1791, *Rush Letters,* I, 592–593; Goodman, *Benjamin Rush,* 286–287. For Jefferson's interest, see the "Account," 587.

[36]*Ibid.,* 596–97; Corner, 177; Butterfield, "Benjamin Rush as a Promoter of Useful Knowledge," 28–32.

[37]Rush to Granville Sharp, August 1791, *Rush Letters,* I, 608.

[38]Rush to Mrs. Rush, Aug. 12, 1791; to Granville Sharp, Aug. 1791, *ibid.,* 602, 609.

was still trying to collect money for new African churches.[39]

Another of Rush's enterprises to help the "poor blacks" of the nation was his projected Negro farm settlement. Named "Benezet" in honor of the dead Quaker reformer, who had so influenced Rush in his career as a benefactor of the Negro, the model farm colony was planned for Bedford County, Pennsylvania, where Rush in February 1794 had purchased 20,000 acres. Near the end of the year he saw a perfect opportunity to advance his project. Determined to act on his belief that yeoman farming was the best way of life for the Negro, Rush presented 5,200 acres of his Bedford holdings to the Pennsylvania Abolition Society. Along with his offer, Rush characteristically suggested a plan by which the land might be distributed in fee simple to worthy Negro farmers. Should the enterprise fail, a possibility he realistically conceded, the Negro could still benefit, as the lands could then be sold and the proceeds "applied for the emancipation and melioration of the condition of the blacks."[40] Invincibly optimistic, the good Doctor made even possible failure serve his humane purposes. A decade later, though, he was still confident enough in the project of Negro farm colonies to make another donation of land to the Society, this time in Cambria County, Pennsylvania.[41]

We have seen that all of Rush's programs to help the Negro were carefully reasoned and planned. And, again typically for the Age of the Enlightenment in which he lived, Rush employed science—as he understood it—to destroy fear and superstition and to advance the civilization of man. Science demonstrated, for example, that slavery was contrary to nature, that it corrupted the faculties of slaves and masters and, by the natural laws of association, of all men.[42] Rush argued, too, in a scientific paper read before the American Philosophical Society, that even the Negro's black skin color was explicable in natural terms—as symptomatic of a leprous disease. "The inferences" of this for the Negro, he noted to Thomas Jefferson, "will be in favor of treating them with humanity and justice and of keeping up the existing prejudices against matrimonial connections with them."[43] Another and truly radical

[39]Rush to Mrs. Rush, Oct. 17, 1793, and to Samuel Bayard, Oct. 23, 1810, *ibid.*, II, 717, 1071; Rush to Granville Sharp, June 20, 1809, "The Correspondence," 37.

[40]The deep respect that Rush had for Anthony Benezet can be seen throughout his writings but most notably in his "Biographical Anecdotes of Anthony Benezet" and his "Paradise of Negro-Slaves—A Dream," Rush, *Essays, Literary, Moral, and Philosophical* (2d ed.; Philadelphia, 1806), 302–304, 305–310. On Rush's planned Negro farm colony, see his letter to the President of the Pennsylvania Abolition Society, [1794?], *Rush Letters*, II, 754–55, and Prof. Butterfield's note on 755–56; Goodman, *Benjamin Rush*, 303.

[41]Rush to the President of the Pennsylvania Abolition Society, [1794?], *Rush Letters*, Prof. Butterfield's note on II, 755–56.

[42]Rush, *An Address to the Inhabitants*, 2–3, 6, 21–22; Rush, "On the Utility of A Knowledge of the Faculties and Operations of the Human Mind to A Physician," *Sixteen Introductory Lectures to Courses of Lectures upon the Institutes and Practice of Medicine. . . .To Which are Added Two Lectures upon the Pleasures of the Senses and of the Mind; with an Inquiry into Their Proximate Cause* (Philadelphia, 1811), 270; Rush to American Farmers About to Settle in New Parts of the United States, March 1789, I, 504; Corner, 219–20, 176.

[43]Rush to Thomas Jefferson, Feb. 4, 1797, *Rush Letters*, II, 786. His paper, "Observations Intended to Favour a Supposition That the Black Color (as It Is Called) of the Negroes Is Derived from the Leprosy," was read in July 1797 and published in the

implication, more helpful to the Negro, was that a cure would someday be found in the perfection of medicine for his leprous skin disease.

But Rush's science, for all its integrity and ingenuity, was really the handmaid of his theology, as was his humanitarian concern for the Negro itself. Ultimately, the Negro was important and his freedom and prosperity necessary because of the perfect divine creation in which Rush implicitly believed and whose benevolent purposes he sought to discover and explain. God's benevolent purpose in allowing Negro slavery was a question that deeply troubled Rush. But it was a question that he seems to have answered to his satisfaction. "And when shall the mystery of providence be explained which has permitted so much misery to be inflicted upon these unfortunate people?" he wrote his Boston friend, Rev. Jeremy Belknap. "Is slavery *here* to be substituted among them for misery *hereafter?* They partake in their vices of the fall of man. They must therefore share in the benefits of the Atonement. Let us continue to love and serve them, for they are our brethren not only by creation but by redemption."[44]

Slavery, it appeared, was a special means of salvation granted to Negroes by God. It was a condition of relatively short worldly misery greatly preferable to the long, almost infinite, punishments which other men must undergo after death in order to achieve the same reconciliation with God. When Rush's reason and science failed, it was this teleological explanation of the Negro slave's place in the divine government that sustained Rush. Most of his projects for the Negro's freedom and welfare came to nought: the Negro farm colony of "Benezet" never materialized; the American sugar maple tree was never to be as widely cultivated as he hoped. And in the end, as Rush had gloomily foreshadowed, a civil war between English-speaking people was necessary to end slavery.

But Negro slavery *was* abolished officially—first in Great Britain and then in the United States. Negro churches and colleges *have* flourished, and the African-American has increasingly taken his place as a major force in American life. For the Negro, however, the potential meaning of the American Revolution, with respect to freedom and prosperity, is only beginning to be realized: "THE REVOLUTION IS NOT OVER!"[45]

State University, New Paltz, N.Y.

Transactions of the American Philosophical Society, old ser., IV (1799), 289–97. For an interesting and thoughtful discussion of Rush's "supposition," see Daniel J. Boorstin, *The Lost World of Thomas Jefferson* (Boston, 1960), 89 ff. Prof. Boorstin's comparison of Jefferson's and Rush's ideas on the Negro, as well as on other subjects, is always insightful. A more general study is Winthrop D. Jordan, *White Over Black: the Development of American Attitudes Toward the Negro, 1550–1812* (Chapel Hill, 1968), which examines the subject of the Negro in a different context. The revolutionary (and political) character of Rush's medical ideas is treated in Donald J. D'Elia, "Dr. Benjamin Rush and the American Medical Revolution," *Proceedings of the American Philosophical Society*, CX (Aug. 23, 1966), 227–34.

[44]Aug. 19, 1788, *Rush Letters,* I, 482–483; Rush, "Paradise of Negro-Slaves.—A Dream," *Essays, Literary, Moral, and Philosophical,* 306; Donald J. D'Elia, "The Republican Theology of Benjamin Rush," *Pennsylvania History,* XXXIII (April 1966), 187–203, esp. 197.

[45]Rush, "An Address to the People of the United States....On the Defects of the Confederation," *American Museum,* I (Jan. 1787), 8–11. The quotation comes from H. Niles' reprint of the "Address" in his *Principles and Acts of the Revolution in America* (Baltimore, 1822), 236.

VII

ARISTOTLE, PLATO, AND THE MASON–DIXON LINE

By Harvey Wish

In the bitter slavery controversy, defenders of the peculiar institution found next to the Bible itself a deep source of inspiration in Aristotle, whose heavily qualified and contradictory statements on the justice of slavery were taken as a flat endorsement.[1] Dismissed by most historians as mere rationalization, the broader significance in American thought of this employment of Aristotle has been overlooked. For just as Aristotle proved a major prop to antebellum Southern romanticism for the leisure class ideal of Greek democracy, so his master Plato inspired the numerous Utopias and transcendentalist theories of Northern romanticism. Western Europe was then surrendering to the cult of Greece reborn in the worship of Byron while American architecture bowed to the sway of the Greek Revival. This vogue affected the style of thought. "Plato is philosophy, and philosophy, Plato," Emerson told his audiences; in another lecture he added, "As they say that Helen of Argos had that universal beauty that every body felt related to her, so Plato seems to a reader in New England an American genius."[2]

Aristotle's well-nigh supreme intellectual dominion in medieval philosophy and science made him too intimate an ally of Catholicism to be warmly accepted within the Puritan tradition. His system of logic, for example, was flatly denied in the sixteenth century by a Huguenot philosopher, Pierre de la Ramée, who had contended in his master's thesis at Paris in 1536: "Whatever has been said by Aristotle is wrong." Ramée influenced Protestant Europe considerably and affected the Puritans on both sides of the ocean.[3] To the Puritans, jealous of heathen rivals to the Bible, the attack of Ramée and his disciples upon the pagan Aristotle was usually welcome. Besides, the new experimental

[1] See Book I, chs. VI–VII of Aristotle's *A Treatise on Government, or The Politics of Aristotle* (Everyman's Library, London, 1939).

[2] "Plato; or The Philosopher," in Brooks Atkinson (ed.), *The Complete Essays and Other Writings of Ralph Waldo Emerson* (Modern Library, New York, 1940), 471–72. Whether Aristotle and Plato were fundamentally opposed in actuality is largely irrelevant for this paper.

[3] Perry Miller, *The New England Mind* (New York, 1939), 116–206.

science, especially the Newtonianism which Puritan Harvard was quick to accept, challenged the cosmology of Aristotle and the medieval scholastic textbooks based on his science, thus reducing his prestige by the end of the seventeenth century.[4]

As Renaissance and Reformation thought weakened the sway of Aristotle, there came a corresponding enhancement of Plato's stature. Puritan intellectuals questioned Aristotle's psychological principle, ''There is nothing in the mind that was not first in the senses.'' This, they felt, left no room for the mystical Platonic ideal of innate ideas and its theological equivalent in the New England ''conscience'' existing independently of the physical self.[5] This strain of mysticism, in an increasingly Platonic form, can be traced through Jonathan Edwards's writings in the early eighteenth century, Emerson's school in the mid-nineteenth and to some extent in the ''inner light'' doctrines of Quakerism and its variants.[6]

Formulas of a perfect society, conceived in the spirit of an earthly kingdom of righteousness, probably derived as much from Plato's *Republic* as from the Reformation emphasis on a Bible Commonwealth. Thomas More, who coined the term ''Utopia,'' was a true Renaissance humanist attracted to Greek speculation on the ideal state. Jesuits in seventeenth-century Paraguay wrought, however imperfectly, to realize such a community among the Indians. Puritan New England during its early communistic stage was conscious of its Platonic origins, as Bradford tells us; and William Penn's Holy Experiment in Pennsylvania belonged to the tradition of Utopia-making. By the early nineteenth century, Plato-inspired Utopias, whose theoretical structure Aristotle had derided, dotted the landscape—largely above the Mason-Dixon line—with socialist commonwealths, millennial communities, and intellectual retreats.[7]

To certain of the New England Democrats, like John Wise of Massachusetts, the popular theory of the social compact by which

[4] Samuel E. Morison, *The Puritan Pronaos: Studies in the Intellectual Life of New England in the Seventeenth Century* (New York, 1936), ch. X.

[5] Miller, *op. cit.,* 270–277.

[6] I. Woodbridge Riley, *American Thought from Puritanism to Pragmatism* (New York, 1915), 173; H. W. Schneider, *History of American Philosophy* (New York, 1946), Pt. I.

[7] Alice Felt Tyler, *Freedom's Ferment* (University of Minnesota Press, Minneapolis, 1944), *passim.*

government rested only on consent clashed with Aristotle's organic theory of the state which viewed society as a natural growth arising from man's gregarious nature. In 1717, Wise was busy defending the freedom of each congregation from hierarchical pressure, and chose to base his case on eighteenth-century doctrines of natural rights. He took issue with Aristotle's dictum, "Nothing is more suitable to Nature, than that those who excel in understanding and prudence should rule and control those who are less happy in those advantages." Against this Wise turned to the Roman law and the rule of Ulpian in the *Digest* that "by a natural right all men are born free."[8] The Aristotelian view, which began with the natural inequality of men and property, was promptly taken up by conservatives, North and South, such as John Adams, whose distrust of majorities led him to favor a system of checks and balances, thus combining the Aristotelian classification of government by the one, the few, and the many. Replying to John Taylor of Caroline, Virginia, a Jeffersonian Democrat who refused to consider legitimate any property not "fairly gained by talents and industry," he measured the consequences of this belief, "You must recur, Mr. Taylor, to Plato's republic and the French republic, destroy all marriages [and] introduce a perfect community of women—before you can annihilate the distinctions of birth."[9] This type of argument was to be taken up by the militant proslavery propagandists in their attacks on Northern Utopianism.

Jefferson, the outstanding eighteenth-century liberal, had popularized the democratic social compact philosophy in his Declaration of Independence, which left no place for Aristotle's organic theory of the state's origin. In addition, he was critical of Aristotle's *Politics* as antiquated because it omitted "the new principle of representative democracy."[10] Like the Puritans he added the staple of "conscience" to Aristotle's realistic doctrine that

[8] John Wise, *The Law of Nature in Government* (Old South Leaflets, General Series, vol. 7, no. 165, Boston, 1905), *passim*.

[9] Letter of John Adams to John Taylor, quoted in Richard McKeon, "The Development of the Concept of Property in Political Philosophy: A study of the Background of the Constitution," *International Journal of Ethics*, XLVIII (1937–38), 297; 366.

[10] Letter to Isaac H. Tiffany, August 26, 1816, in Andrew A. Lipscomb (ed.), *The Writings of Thomas Jefferson* (Washington, 1905), XV, 65–66.

knowledge comes solely from the senses. While he still retained an admiration for certain features of Aristotle's philosophy, he spoke harshly of Plato's "dealing out mysticism incomprehensible to the human mind, [one who has] been deified by certain sects usurping the name of Christians; because in his foggy conceptions they found a basis of impenetrable darkness whereon to rear fabrications as delirious, of their own invention."[11]   His reaction to Plato, like that of Adams, suggests the attacks of the later proslavery group.

The South, particularly during Jefferson's day, shared in some of the dreaded "isms" she later decried, but circumstances were to direct her intellectual course in other directions.   With the accession of King Cotton, the fastening of the patriarchal plantation system, the explosive racial situation, and the persistent rural character of the South, there developed a conservative environment hostile to social experimentation and philosophic individualism.   To some extent the traditions of Protestant dissent, critical of Aristotle, were modified by the Episcopalian influence among the Virginia ruling class and by the Catholicism of the French and Spanish Louisianans.   In this setting Aristotle's prestige was to soar ever higher.

Proslavery writers attacking Jeffersonianism and natural rights drew freely upon Aristotle, ignoring the fact that he defended only the "natural slave," a backward individual in any society; actually Plato and perhaps most Greek philosophers shared this belief, intimating that natural slaves had no human rights.[12]   Pioneer in the Southern conservative reaction (though of course not the first proslavery writer) was Professor Thomas R. Dew of the College of William and Mary—Jefferson's Alma Mater—who defended slavery in Aristotelian terms as a perpetual institution and the basis of an ideal Greek democracy; his arguments did much to still the older abolitionist sentiment yet active in the Virginia legislature of 1831–32.[13]   Dew's example was

[11] Letter to William Short, October 31, 1819, in Adrienne Koch and William Peden (eds.), *The Life and Selected Writings of Thomas Jefferson* (Modern Library, New York, 1944), 693.

[12] Robert Schlaifer, "Greek Theories of Slavery from Homer to Aristotle," *Harvard Studies in Classical Philology*, XLVII (1936), 192–199.

[13] Thomas R. Dew, *Review of the Debate in the Virginia Legislature of 1831 and 1832* (Richmond, 1832) ; id., *An Essay on Slavery*, in *Proslavery Argument as*

avowedly influential among the younger proslavery propagandists such as James D. B. De Bow, George Frederick Holmes, George Fitzhugh, and a host of journalists.[14]

Into this propaganda there crept in more or less explicitly the notion of a direct antithesis in social philosophy between Aristotle and Plato, which was applied to the sectional conflict. Thus, a "Southron" wrote in the *Southern Literary Messenger* of 1838:

To Aristotle, one of the most profound of the philosophers of antiquity, we confidently appeal, and with the more confidence, because in this iron age of utilitarianism, his material philosophy, fortified with all the powers of the "greatest, wisest, meanest of mankind" has been preferred to the spiritual sublimity of the divine Plato. Aristotle has expressly declared that "in the natural state of man, from the origin of things, a portion of the human family must command and the remainder obey"; and that the distinction which exists between master and servant is a distinction at once natural and indispensable; and that when we find existing among men freemen and slaves, it is not man, but nature herself who has ordained the distinction.

"Southron" went on to attack the natural rights theories, the social compact, and the alleged right of revolution as a harmful product of the individualistic French revolutionary philosophy and "its school of unbelievers." Insubordination, he observed in Aristotelian accents, meant the ruin of the social fabric.[15]

Another contributor to the *Messenger,* a decade later, drew a similar antithesis between the two Greek philosophers. "The former [Plato] delighted more to revel in the pure and lofty regions of imagination, and sometimes lost himself in the mazes of his own refined and subtle speculations. The latter [Aristotle] with far more judgment and far more success devoted his gigantic powers to the elucidation and unfolding of subjects of much more use to his fellow men than metaphysical abstractions."[16] In 1852, "J. H. B.," reviewing an edition of Emerson's essays, spoke disparagingly of the latter's transcendentalist "dreams of Germany"

Maintained by the Most Distinguished Writers of the Southern States (Charleston, 1852), 287–462.

[14] Harvey Wish, *George Fitzhugh, Propagandist of the Old South* (Southern Biography Series, Baton Rouge, 1943), 45–47.

[15] "A. Southron," "Thoughts on Slavery," *Southern Literary Messenger,* IV (1838), 737–747.

[16] ———, "Ancient Greece: Her History and Literature," *ibid.,* XIV (1848), 129–139.

as un-American and a mere pretense to "Plato's brain." He concluded his attack on idealism and Northern Utopianism by stressing the Aristotelian idea of man's social duties and dependence on society.[17]

John C. Calhoun of South Carolina, indifferent to documentation, obviously borrowed much from Aristotle's *Politics,* directly or indirectly. This included the classification of governments, the problem of conflicting economic interests, and the anti-majoritarian basis of the check-and-balance system, and finally his rejection of the social contract and natural rights in favor of an organic state. Men, far from being born free and equal in a state of nature, he argued, "are born subject, not only to parental authority but to the laws and institutions of the country where born and under whose protection they draw their first breath." Calhoun's attempt to defend the anachronistic institution of slavery led him to borrow from conservative doctrines he found in Aristotle and the reactionary Polish "liberum veto" used to thwart the majority.[18]

A fellow-South Carolinian, somewhat more moderate than Calhoun, was William J. Grayson, author of *The Hireling and the Slave* (1856), a reply in verse to *Uncle Tom's Cabin.* Attacking the evils of modern industrialism as far worse than the paternalistic slavery system, he rested his case fundamentally on Aristotle, to whom he attributed Calhoun's chief theories:

The maxim of Mr. Calhoun is, that a democratic government cannot exist unless the laboring class be slaves; that if the man who has nothing is allowed to rule, there can be no safety for property—property would soon be voted robbery. A democracy, therefore, must consist of freemen and slaves. This is the substance of the dogma. It is not a new thing, but is two thousand years old. So far from being "first enumerated" by Mr. Calhoun, it is as ancient as Aristotle. In his "Politics"—which should be a textbook in all Southern colleges—in words as clear and emphatic as language can furnish, he lays down the maxim, that *a complete household or community is one composed of freemen and slaves.* He was writing to democracies. He maintains also, that the slaves should be barbarians, not Greeks, as Mr. Calhoun now holds it to be an advantage that the slaves of the South are negroes, a barbarian race sufficiently strong and docile for

[17] J.H.B. (John H. Bernard?), "Ralph Waldo Emerson—History," *ibid.,* XVIII (1852), 247–255.

[18] John C. Calhoun, "A Disquisition on Government and a Discourse on the Constitution and Government of the United States," in Richard K. Cralle (ed.), *The Works of John C. Calhoun* (New York, 1883), 44–45; 58; 71; 82.

labor. The whole proposition, both as to slavery itself and the race of the slave, is distinctly stated by the Greek philosopher.[19]

Undoubtedly the most brilliant and creative of the proslavery school was George Frederick Holmes, son of an English planter and official of Demarara, British Guiana, who had come to Charleston as a youth after attending the University of Durham, England, later joining the literary circle of Legaré, Simms, and Lieber, and editing several Southern journals; during 1857–1897 he was to be a professor of literature and history at the University of Virginia. Upon the death of President Thomas R. Dew of the College of William and Mary, where Holmes had taught briefly, he published a significant proslavery essay in the *Southern Literary Messenger,* "Observations on the Politics of Aristotle Relative to Slavery." He chose to use a sociological analysis to buttress slavery through "a comprehensive study of the phenomena of societies and the history of nations." As a text for his pioneer essay in social science, he chose Aristotle's statement from the *Politics:* "Nature has clearly designed some men for freedom and others for slavery;—and with respect to the latter, slavery is both just and beneficial."

Slavery, as Holmes defined it, was "continuous, involuntary, and unlimited dependence." This was part of the historical order of society, for all society has ever been divided into the dependent and those on whom they depend." He theorized, "Circumstances and degrees of civilization, the comparative density and the proportions of the population, the amount and distribution of capital, may vary the forms in which this dependence is exhibited, the names by which it is known, and the mode by which it is enforced." Rejecting *a priori* reasoning as the sole basis for the analysis of social organizations, he placed his reliance on history and experience to discover the motives and operations of human beings in society: "whatever is natural is just, except in those cases where the dictates of natural instinct are clearly rebuked by the higher law of divine revelation." Hence he found slavery and serfdom the norm of human history, except for the present period in the Northern states of this country. He explained, "The free vent for superfluous energy and labour afforded by the States and Ter-

[19] William J. Grayson, "Mackay's Travels in America—The Dual Form of Labor," *De Bow's Review,* XXVIII (1860), 48–66.

ritories of the West and the singularly rapid increase of labour-employing capital at the North, has retarded and still modifies the development of the relation of master and servant.'' However he noted a ''fatal velocity'' towards pauperism in cities like Boston and New York, which would eventually resemble conditions in England, France, and Germany.   Wherever slavery disappears, free competition inspires class conflicts between labor and capital.

He agreed with Aristotle that the slavery of kindred races was pernicious and maintained that Negroes, unlike Caucasians, had always been slaves throughout history.   Showing a certain racialist bias in his thinking, he held that in all ages progress has been exclusively in the hands of the Indo-Germanic races.   In his final exposition, he relied on Aristotle's organic theories of the state to refute Rousseau's idea of the Social Contract and sought to explain away Ulpian's phrase that all men are born free as intended to exclude slaves who ''are scarcely regarded as men by the Civil Law.''[20]

As a pioneer in the then novel field of sociology, Holmes sought his scientific foundation in Aristotle.   The highest compliment he could bestow upon his contemporary Auguste Comte, ''father of sociology,'' whose works he was the first American to review extensively, was that the Frenchman's inductive philosophy was ''the only considerable enlargement of Logic which has been effected since the writings of Aristotle.''   By 1866, Holmes had tempered his praise by adding that there was little in the Comtian system of positivism not already anticipated ''in a juster spirit'' by Aristotle.   Again, as the first American to write a college textbook on sociology, *The Science of Society* (1883), which was a series of lectures given to his classes at the University of Virginia, he refused to follow the current Anglo-American trend of individualistic sociology fostered by Herbert Spencer and William Graham Sumner but based his science on the Aristotelian analysis of the social nature of man.[21]

[20] George Frederick Holmes, "Observations on a Passage in the Politics of Aristotle Relative to Slavery," *Southern Literary Messenger,* XVI (1850), 193–205.

[21] Harvey Wish, "George Frederick Holmes and the Genesis of American Sociology," *The American Journal of Sociology,* XLVI (1941), 698–707; *id.,* "George Frederick Holmes and Southern Periodical Literature of the Mid-Nineteenth Century," *The Journal of Southern History* (1941), 343–356; Charles A. Ellwood,

As one of the leading book reviewers of the Old South, Holmes gave his influential support to other proslavery writers who borrowed his version of Aristotle. Among these were Professor Albert T. Bledsoe, a mathematician of the University of Virginia and author of the much-discussed *Essay on Liberty and Slavery* (1856). Bledsoe's position was strikingly similar to that of Holmes; beginning with the Aristotelian idea of man as born into a society of which he is therefore an organic part and attacking the whole natural rights philosophy which made man prior to society, he came to similar conclusions regarding the justice of slavery.[22]

The most significant proslavery propagandist of the South, judging from the frequency with which he was quoted in articles, newspapers, pamphlets, congressional debates, and travellers' books, was George Fitzhugh, a lawyer and journalist of Port Royal, Virginia, who held editorial posts temporarily with the fire-eating Richmond *Examiner* and the Richmond *Enquirer* and wrote scores of articles for *De Bow's Review*. In 1854 he published a proslavery book in scientific dress entitled *Sociology for the South, or the Failure of Free Society,* and continued this theme in an interesting sequel, *Cannibals All! or Slaves Without Masters* (1856). Fitzhugh's views on slavery resembled Holmes's so closely as to suggest collaboration; their literary friendship actually began after the publication of Fitzhugh's earlier essays of 1849, which contained most of the ideas later developed in his books. Despite his use of Aristotle's analyses, he had never read any of the philosopher's writings. In a letter to Holmes of April, 1855, he admitted, "I received from Mr. Appleton's, a week ago, Aristotle's *Politics* and *Economics*. I find I have not only adopted his theories, his arguments, and his illustrations, but his very words. Society is a work of nature and grows. Men are social like bees; an isolated man is like a bird of prey. Man and society are coeval." In another letter written the same month to

---

"Aristotle as a Sociologist," *Annals of the American Academy of Political and Social Science,* XIX (1902), 227–238.

[22] George F. Holmes, "Bledsoe on Liberty and Slavery," *De Bow's Review,* XXI (1856), 132–147; "R." "Liberty and Slavery—Professor Bledsoe," *Southern Literary Messenger,* XXII (1856), 382–388; George Fitzhugh, "Bledsoe on Liberty and Slavery," *Daily Richmond Enquirer,* July 24, 1856.

Holmes, he observed worriedly, "All these things which I thought original with me, I find in Aristotle. I am in a fix. If I did read him I am a plagiarist. But if I write again, I'll make a clean breast and acknowledge my pseudo-learning is all gathered from the Reviews."

Like Holmes, Fitzhugh argued that all history revealed that the normal form of society had been based on slavery or the "subordination" principle. Jeffersonianism, the notion of human equality, laissez-faire, were all in violation of normal social behavior and grounded on a jungle ethics of "dog-eat-dog." Fitzhugh knew the concept of the survival of the fittest through the writings of Malthus on population theory and denounced the idea (as Holmes did) that the competition of organisms could produce anything better or finer as a result of the process. Between the normal society described by Aristotle and the unstable society associated with the competitive principle there could only be war. This was expressed in a Richmond *Enquirer* editorial which apparently inspired Lincoln's "House Divided" speech:

Social forms so widely differing as those of domestic slavery and [attempted] universal liberty cannot long co-exist in the Great Republic of Christendom. . . . The one form or the other must be very wrong. . . . The war between the two systems rages everywhere; and will continue to rage till the one conquers and the other is exterminated.

In his mind the failure of competitive societies was seen in Europe's unemployment, her slums, the socialistic revolutions of 1848, and the prevailing unrest on that continent. So far these consequences had not fully overtaken the Northern States, largely because of free lands, but even there the innumerable Utopian and socialistic experiments were products of a desperation born of a bankrupt social system. Instability was a principle incarnate of free society and led to religious, political, and economic radicalism. The Satanic inspiration for free society he found in Plato's *Republic* with its promiscuous marriage ideas which contrasted sharply with Aristotle's teaching that the duty of the state was to preserve the family. Eventually Fitzhugh was to become a racialist of a type startlingly similar to the modern fascist. He applauded Gobineau's then novel ideas of Aryan superiority, praised war and intense (Southern) nationalism as ennobling, lauded the planter class as "a master race," and after the Civil War justified monopoly capitalism as far preferable to competitive enterprise.[23]

Aristotle's popularity in the classics-loving South was not limited to the proslavery writers. Even in the Southern controversy over the repeal of the usury laws in various states, the authority of Aristotle, almost as in medieval times, weighed heavily in some circles. Had Aristotle not held that money was sterile and therefore could not beget money?[24] While traditionalists like Fitzhugh respected this classical ban on usury, other commercial-minded Southerners showed impatience with attempts to employ Aristotle in the arguments. Southern students of oratory, like their Northern fellows, paid the highest respect to Aristotle's rules of rhetoric —an important factor in a region where oratory ranked among the finest of arts.[25] As for Aristotle's logical principles, these were not minimized as elsewhere as a triumph of the sterile syllogism, but praised as an anticipation of Bacon's inductive principles of science.[26] In psychology, the Stagirite's pioneer influence was enthusiastically acknowledged. "It first belonged to Aristotle," wrote one Louisianan, "to penetrate into the depths of human reason, to submit it to the same scalpel which has produced the history of animals, to determine and to describe all its elements under the denomination, since so celebrated, of categories."[27]

The classicists of the South were not unchallenged. Even James D. B. De Bow of Louisiana, federal Superintendent of the Census, whose famous *Review* contained superlative praises of Aristotle by Holmes, Fitzhugh, Grayson, and other well-known contributors, was himself a champion of modern commercial education and jealous of the Southern domain ruled by Aristotle.

[23] This is largely abridged from the writer's *George Fitzhugh, Propagandist of the Old South, supra.*

[24] See two unsigned articles in *De Bow's Review,* VII (1849), "Usury Laws and the Value of Money," 123–128, and "The Value of Money and Usury," 501–507; W. J. Ashley, "Aristotle's Doctrine of Barter," *Quarterly Journal of Economics,* IX, (1894–95), 333–341.

[25] "S.L.C.," "Rhetoric as a Part of the College Course," *Southern Literary Messenger,* XV (1849), 705–710.

[26] W. S. Grayson, "Bacon's Philosophy and Macaulay's Criticism of It," *ibid.,* XXIX (1859), 177–183.

[27] C. S. Farrar, "The Science of History," *De Bow's Review,* V (1848), 127–134.

Invited to hold the first chair of political economy at the University of Louisiana, he chose as his opening lecture, "The Commercial Age." Criticizing Southern schools for neglecting practical subjects, he observed, "Theory and fact are the poles of ancient and modern philosophy. Bacon has risen up against Aristotle, and vindicated *fact* in the face of all nations and men." He pointed to a world trend among colleges and universities "against the antique" in favor of engineering, economics, agriculture, chemistry, and commerce. The South must no longer be content with "actual or alleged inferiority," and commerce must be placed on the proud pedestal "it is yet destined to occupy." Deriding the traditional Southern leadership, he observed, "The sons of the planters have preferred to stock the learned professions beyond the possibility of demand, or to indulge in idleness, vice, and dissipation."[28] This note is occasionally struck by Southern college trustees who called for more practical subjects, including modern languages, at the expense of the classics. In this vein a Virginian minister wrote his article, "Speculative Philosophy: Cui Bono?" Attacking ancient "abstraction run mad, logic on stilts" as responsible for modern trends in sensual philosophies, wholesale divorces, and radicalism, he asserted that no real improvement for mankind had come from the principal schools of antiquity.[29]

Many philosophers of our day will scarcely recognize their Plato or Aristotle in most of the American variants which came to serve the purposes of propaganda or eccentric causes, North and South. Certain of the proslavery writers, as we have seen, found the symbols of the Southern fight in the ancients and plumbed the depths of the timeless problem of freedom versus authority, of liberty versus organization. Fittingly enough, the new Republican Party, claiming a prior right to Jefferson's party label above the time-serving Democrats, chose to inscribe the Declaration of Independence with its social compact philosophy into their political platform.

Fondness for the classics was of course shared by North and South, but with certain significant differences of emphasis, as the Aristotle-Plato antithesis in the South shows. Aristotle was

[28] J. D. B. De Bow, "The Commercial Age," *ibid.*, VII (1849), 225–239.

[29] W. C. Crane, "Speculative Philosophy: Cui Bono?," *Southern Literary Messenger*, X (1844), 357–359.

drafted into the service of the South in its self-conscious efforts to deny the sectional inferiority which economic facts imposed upon it.   Isolated in the Western World, which condemned slavery as an anachronism, the South found compensation in Aristotle to flaunt a moral superiority over Northern radicals imbued with the "isms" of Plato, the anti-traditionalism of the Enlightenment, and a militant liberalism full of implications hostile to slavery both in the New World and the Old.

Western Reserve University.

VIII

THE IDEOLOGY OF WHITE SUPREMACY

By James W. Vander Zanden

It has been now almost a century since Appomattox. Yet in many respects even today the South remains a land set apart from the nation. It has developed a way of life in its essentials common with all America, yet its uniqueness is inescapable. This has been not for want of sharp internal variations and contrasts. Perhaps no American region possesses greater internal diversity than the South in historical background, geography, cultural composition, economic structure, and political and social outlooks. Still, pervading the whole, there has been an inner cohesiveness which has given the Southland its distinctive way of life. And central to this way of life in one way or another has always been the Negro.

On May 17, 1954, a large cornerstone of this Southern way of life was placed in jeopardy. On that date Chief Justice Earl Warren delivered the unanimous opinion of our nation's highest court " that in the field of public education the doctrine of ' separate but equal ' has no place." [1] In so doing the Supreme Court raised upon the Southern horizon the prospect of a social revolution with considerable scope. But as the first year following the decision rolled by, and then a second, third and fourth year, it became increasingly unclear as to what the nature or extent of this social revolution would be, or whether, in fact, it might not be largely abortive.

The prospect of major changes in the region's racial patterns was perceived by the great mass of Southern whites as constituting a distinct threat. To this threat they responded by resistance, unleashing a flurry of activity and a surging social movement. More than 90 segregationist organizations mushroomed across the face of the South, such as the Mississippi Association of Citizens Councils claiming 65 chapters and 80,000 members. From Richmond to Austin officials busied themselves with legal alchemy, frantically searching for a magical potion to escape the high court's ruling, enacting in the process more than 196 new segregationist bulwarks. And communities such as Milford, Clinton, Little Rock, and Sturgis captured world headlines as angry mobs milled before desegregating schools intent upon thwarting integration.

Knitting Southern whites together in their adamant hostility toward integration is a group of ideas revolving about the Negro. These ideas give the movement its ideological cohesion—the glue which unites the movement's members in a fellowship of belief. Underpinning the segregationist position are three major ideological premises:

1. Segregation is part of the natural order and as such is eternally fixed.

[1] For the text of the decision see the *New York Times*, May 18, 1954.

2. The Negro is inferior to the white or, at the very least, is " different " from the white.

3. The break-down of segregation in any of its aspects will inevitably lead to racial amalgamation, resulting in a host of disastrous consequences.

From time to time various treatises have appeared subjecting one or more of these beliefs to searching scientific scrutiny. Here we can pause merely to note that regarding such a key tenet as inherent Negro inferiority, contemporary anthropologists and geneticists are agreed that such an assertion has not been scientifically demonstrated while its racist overtones are blatantly false.[2] What is of immediate concern to us is that these Southern beliefs, correct or incorrect as they may be, have a potent, living reality about them. They are alive by virtue of the fact that they are held by men, and by men who act on the basis of them. As an outstanding American sociologist, W. I. Thomas, has noted, " If men define . . . situations as real, they are real in their consequences." [3]

Deeply embedded in Southern thinking is the firm conviction that segregation is inextricably rooted in nature and as such is eternally fixed. In seeking to convey their sentiment regarding segregation, Southerners have frequent recourse to such phrases as " instinctive," " a natural order," and " a universal law of nature." Thus Louisiana State Senator W. M. Rainach, chairman of his state's special legislative segregation committee, declares: " Segregation is a natural order —created by God, in His wisdom, who made black men black and white men white." [4]

And in his concurring opinion upholding the denial of admission of Virgil Hawkins, a Negro, to the all-white University of Florida, Florida Supreme Court Justice Glenn C. Terrell reasoned in a somewhat similar manner.[5] The Citizens Councils have likewise given prominence to this position. A widely circulated pamphlet of the Mississippi Association asserts:

Animals by instinct mate only with their own kind. . . . The fact that man is also a gregarious animal and that human beings everywhere and under all conditions of life tend to segregate themselves into families, tribes, national or racial groups, only goes to prove that all human relations are regulated by this universal law of nature.[6]

[2] In this connection see: M. F. Ashley Montagu, *Man's Most Dangerous Myth: The Fallacy of Race* (New York, 1945) and *Statement on Race* (New York, 1951); also, Ruth Benedict, *Race: Science and Politics*, rev. ed. (New York, 1945).

[3] W. I. Thomas, " The Relation of Research to the Social Process," in *Essays on Research in the Social Sciences* (Washington, D. C., 1931), 189.

[4] *Southern School News*, I (Nov. 1954), 3.　　　　[5] *Ibid.* (Nov. 1955), 4.

[6] " A Christian View on Segregation," pamphlet of the Mississippi Association of Citizens Councils (Greenwood, Miss., n.d.), 5.

This premise is the lineal descendant of the ante-bellum position that slavery was based upon the " laws of nature," an argument appearing early in the Southern ideological arsenal.   In 1700 the first positive statement of the anti-slavery school appeared in Boston, written by Samuel Sewell, then Judge of the Superior Court.   His pamphlet, *The Selling of Joseph, A Memorial*, received wide distribution and influenced the progress of the anti-slavery movement throughout the colonies.[7]   The following year John Saffin replied to Sewell in a pamphlet entitled, *A Brief and Candid Answer to a Late Printed Sheet, Entitled the Selling of Joseph*.[8]   One by one Saffin sought to answer Sewell's arguments in what was probably the first written defense of slavery in America.   Saffin denied the general principle of natural equality as constituting the order of the universe.   He suggested that Sewell had inverted " . . . the order that God hath set in the World, who hath ordained different degrees and orders of men, some to be High and Honourable, some to be Low and Despicable; some to be Monarchs, . . . Masters, . . . others to be subjects, and to be Commanded; Servants of sundry sorts and degrees, bound to obey, yea some to be born Slaves, and so to remain during their lives. . . . " [9]

The " natural order " position was a carry-over from the pre-Enlightenment Period.   Social and economic inequalities were justified as part of the " natural order " and God's ordained plan for the world.[10]   Human servitude, economic classes, social estates and even the differing status of men and women were explained on this ground.   The position had been strongly influenced by Aristotle and other Greek thinkers who had justified slavery in logic as conforming to nature.[11]

The argument was a mainstay in the defense of slavery and became an important bulwark in the philosophic defense that formed to meet the natural rights attack of the Revolutionary period.[12]   The anti-slavery school had early advanced the position that slavery was contrary to nature's law.   They frequently appealed to nature as a higher law that overrode all man-made sanctions for slavery.[13]   In their thinking they were influenced by John Locke who held there

[7] Reprinted from an original in George H. Moore, *Notes on the History of Slavery in Massachusetts* (New York, 1866), 83–87.   Also see William Sumner Jenkins, *Pro-Slavery Thought in the Old South* (Chapel Hill, 1935), 4–6.

[8] Reprinted from an original in Moore, *op. cit.*, 251–256.   Also see Jenkins, *op. cit.*, 4–6, 39.

[9] Moore, *op. cit.*, 251–2.

[10] See, for example, John of Salisbury, *The Statesman's Book* (*Polycraticus*), trans. by John Dickinson (New York, 1927), Book IV, Chaps. I and II and F. Max Mueller, ed., *The Sacred Books of the East: The Laws of Manu* (Oxford, 1886), Vol. 25, Chaps. I, II, III and IV.

[11] See Aristotle, *Politics*, trans. by W. Ellis (New York, 1928), Chap. II, XIII, and *passim*.   [12] Jenkins, *op. cit.*, 44–46.   [13] *Ibid.*, 121.

could be no slavery under the law of nature; rather, slavery resulted from the withdrawal of the protection of that law. The pro-slavery advocates sought to answer this argument by pointing to the state of inequality that existed in nature.[14] Southerners, such as John C. Calhoun argued that the natural rights position, holding that all men are born free and equal in a state of nature, was contrary to universal observation. Calhoun asserted that instead of being born free and equal in a natural state, man was "born subject, not only to parental authority, but to the laws and institutions of the country where born, and under whose protection they draw their first breath."[15]

Southerners such as George Frederick Holmes, an ante-bellum teacher in several Southern colleges, sought historical support for the natural law position. He argued that as slavery existed "in a very considerable degree under all forms of civilized society, we may consider it a necessary consequence of social organization (or may even go further and with Aristotle regard it as a necessary constituent thereof), and as this is admitted to be natural, so we may consider its consequences to be consonant with the laws of nature."[16] Others sought evidence of an empirical sort from anatomy and ethnology seeking to demonstrate that inequality, not equality, was the natural order of the universe.[17] As the slaveholder viewed nature, variety and inequality characterized every work of the Great Creator; in a word, nature was governed by unerring laws "which command the oak to be stronger than the willow; and the cypress to be taller than the shrub."[18]

Closely allied with the natural order position, was the elaborate Biblical argument formulated in defense of slavery.[19] It was no wonder that in 1863 the Presbyterian Church, South, met in General Synod and passed a resolution declaring slavery to be a divine institution ordained by God. Today segregationists have taken over the ante-bellum scriptural defense of slavery in its virtual entirety, finding in it an ideological bulwark for the segregated order.[20]

The "natural order" argument continued as a major support of the caste-order in the post-bellum period finding frequent expression in the defense of the Southern racial structure. Thus in 1907, Bishop William Montgomery Brown, prominent official in the Protestant Episcopal Church, could write that race prejudice was "a deep-rooted, God-implanted instinct,"[21] and that the "Anglo-American citizen is prevented by a law of nature from allowing the Afro-American to be

---

[14] *Ibid.*, 138. [15] *Ibid.*, 126. [16] *Ibid.*, 135.
[17] *Ibid.*, 137–40. [18] *Ibid.*, 138. [19] *Ibid.*, 200ff.
[20] See "A Christian View on Segregation," *op. cit.*, 8–13.
[21] William M. Brown, *The Crucial Race Question* (Little Rock, 1907), 118.

associated with him in the government of these United States. . . . " [22]
Accordingly Bishop Brown reasoned: " From every point of view, the
conclusion is unavoidable that it is not only right for Anglo-Ameri-
cans to recognize the Color-Line in the social, political and religious
realms, but more than that it would be a great sin not to do so." [23]

A corollary of the " natural order " argument holds that " members of each race prefer to associate with other members of their race
and . . . they will do so *naturally* unless they are prodded and inflamed
and controlled by outside pressures." [24]   Thus U. S. Senator Sam J.
Ervin of North Carolina reasons that racial segregation is not the offspring of bigotry or prejudice, but the product of " a basic law of
nature—the law that like seeks like . . . man finds his greatest happiness when he is among people of similar cultural, historical and social
backgrounds." [25]   Likewise, for the Southern white segregation is not
a moral question.   Former South Carolina Governor James F. Byrnes
declares: " It is useless for me to argue whether the racial instinct
[for segregation] is right or wrong—it exists." [26]

This argument became prevalent following the Civil War as a
justification for the establishment of separate facilities for Negroes
and whites, including separate churches.   The Methodist Episcopal
Church, South, had made an effort following the war to retain their
Negro congregations.   When this failed, Atticus Greene Haygood,
then president of Emory College in Georgia, and later a Methodist
bishop, sought to explain the situation in these terms:

. . . nature asserts herself.   In nearly all of the States the Conferences are
now unmixed; in all of them where the negroes are sufficiently numerous to
form separate organizations.   As oil and water diligently shaken together in
a vessel mix for a time, but without chemical union, so these two races
mixed in the Conferences for a time.   When the mixture settled, lo! the oil
and the water touched, but were distinct.

. . . instinct is supreme; the colored brethren were restless till they had their
own Conferences.   It was the same instinct, for instinct it is, that led to the
formation of a number of African Church organizations in the North long
ago. . . .

[22] *Ibid.*, 125.   Also see Henry W. Grady, " What of the Negro," in *The Possibilities of the Negro in Symposium* (Atlanta, 1904), 63, and Thomas Nelson Page, *The
Negro: The Southerner's Problem* (New York, 1904), 310.

[23] Brown, *op. cit.*, 135.

[24] From the report of the North Carolina Advisory Committee on Education
(Pearsall Committee).   *Southern School News*, II (May 1956), 7.   Italics added.

[25] Sam J. Ervin, " The Case of Segregation," *Look* (Feb. 24, 1956), 134.

[26] James F. Byrnes, " Race Relations Are Worsening," *U. S. News & World
Report* (Feb. 22, 1957), 113.

This instinctive disposition to form Church affiliations on the color basis may be wise or unwise. But it is in them—deep in them. The tendency is strengthening all the time. This instinct will never rest satisfied till it realizes itself in complete separation.[27]

As Guion Griffis Johnson has pointed out, this was a convenient theory as it relieved churchmen of the burden of applying the ethics of the Golden Rule to the Negro. Except for extremists, they did not deny the concept of the Fatherhood of God and the brotherhood of man, but the theory of race instinct made it possible to hold that the full implications of brotherhood could not apply to the Negro. " If brotherhood *could* not be applied, it was an easy step to the conclusion that brotherhood *should* not be applied. . . . Southern churches, both white and Negro, thus tended to become the most militantly race conscious institutions in the post-war era." [28]

The notion of innate racial inferiority and superiority became a prominent public issue in relatively recent times—probably not earlier than the late seventeenth and early eighteenth centuries.[29] Physical differences were known to exist between groups of mankind before this time but the notion of the biological inferiority of particular groups was absent. Thus in the early period of American slavery Negro servitude was justified not on biological grounds but rather on grounds that the Negro was a heathen and a barbarian.[30] When Bishop Berkeley visited the Colonies around 1730 he found the notion prevalent that " being baptized is inconsistent with a state of slavery." [31] This belief among the slaveholders probably constituted the main obstacle to the conversion of the Negroes, as the slaveholders feared that baptism would alter the status of the slave. Jenkins suggests that this idea probably grew out of the old patristic theory which held that slavery was based upon man's original sin rather than upon nature. Thus as long as the slave was a heathen, slavery was lawful, but the sacraments washed away original sin and the basis of slavery

[27] Atticus G. Haygood, *Our Brothers in Black* (Nashville, 1881), 232–235. Also see Atticus G. Haygood, *Pleas for Progress* (Nashville, 1889), 39.

[28] Guion Griffis Johnson, " The Ideology of White Supremacy, 1876–1910," in *Essays in Southern History*, ed. Fletcher Melvin Green (Chapel Hill, 1949), 145.

[29] See Montagu, *Man's Most Dangerous Myth, op. cit.*, 16; Benedict, *op. cit.*, 3–4; Ralph Linton, *The Study of Man* (New York, 1936), 46; and Oliver Cromwell Cox, *Caste, Class, and Race* (New York, 1948), 322ff.

[30] See Helen Tunnicliff Catterall, *Judicial Cases Concerning American Slavery and the Negro* (Washington, 1926), I, 53–71; James Curtis Ballagh, *A History of Slavery in Virginia* (Baltimore, 1902), Chap. II; Edward Raymond Turner, *The Negro in Pennsylvania, Slavery, Servitude, Freedom, 1639–1861* (Washington, 1911), 17–21; and John H. Russell, *The Free Negro in Virginia* (Baltimore, 1913).

[31] Jenkins, *op. cit.*, 18.

fell.[32] The slaveholders' apprehension apparently was so great, that in 1727 the Bishop of London, who was in charge of missionary work in the Colonies, sent a pastoral letter to slave-masters declaring: [33] " . . . Christianity, and the embracing of the Gospel, does not make the least Alteration in Civil Property, or in any of the Duties which belong to Civil Relations; but in all these Respects, it continues Persons just in the same State as it found them." Likewise a number of Colonies enacted statutes to set at rest the apprehension of the slave-owners so that the work of religious instruction might proceed.

As time progressed and the Negro was converted to Christianity, the heathen or infidel buttress no longer constituted a satisfactory defense of slavery. Gradually, then, the biological argument came into prominence. As Montagu has indicated:

Their [the Negroes'] different physical appearance provided a convenient peg upon which to hang the argument that this represented the external sign of more profound ineradicable mental and moral inferiorities.[34]

The situation was not too different in South Africa. MacCrone states that the earliest practice in South Africa was to free slaves that had been baptized. Such a practice, however, constituted a costly economic burden and challenged the status system. " When, in 1792, the question was explicitly raised by the Church Council of Stellenbosch, whether owners who permitted or encouraged their slaves to be baptized would be obliged to emancipate them, the matter was referred to the Church Council of Capetown for its opinion. That body replied that neither the law of the land nor the law of the church prohibited the retention of baptized persons in slavery, while local custom strongly supported the practice. . . ." [35] Thus the ideological bulwark, originally symbolized by religion, became symbolized by race.

Notions of innate Negro inferiority apparently arose rather early in the Colonies. Overtones of this thinking are found in Saffin's answer to Sewell, and Bishop Berkeley in his visit to the Colonies noted that " an irrational contempt of the blacks, as creatures of another species, who had no right to be instructed or admitted to the sacraments, has proved a main obstacle to the conversion of these poor people." [36] As Jenkins has observed: " The inferiority of the Negro was almost universally accepted in the South by all groups of pro-slavery theorists as a great primary truth." [37]

Some writers such as George S. Sawyer, a prominent member of

---

[32] Ibid., 18–19.   [33] Quoted by Jenkins, ibid., 19.   [34] Montagu, op. cit., 19.
[35] I. D. MacCrone, Race Attitudes in South Africa (New York, 1937), 135.
[36] Quoted by Jenkins, op. cit., 17.   [37] Ibid., 252.

the Louisiana bar, sought to establish Negro racial inferiority by means of the historical argument:

The social, moral, and political, as well as the physical history of the negro race bears strong testimony against them; it furnishes the most undeniable proof of their mental inferiority. In no age or condition has the real negro shown a capacity to throw off the chains of barbarism and brutality that have long bound down the nations of that race; or to rise above the common cloud of darkness that still broods over them.[38]

Others such as Samuel George Morton and Dr. S. A. Cartwright sought physiological support for the belief." [39]

In the early 1840's under the impetus of the work of Dr. Josiah Clark Nott, a physician of Mobile, Alabama, the theory of a separate origin of the white and Negro races began to gain currency in the South. According to this view, the two races were endowed with a different original nature. This nature was viewed as permanent, incapable of physical or intellectual alteration. Not only was the barrier between the races insurmountable, but nature was seen as setting limits beyond which the Negro was totally incapable of improvement. Thus, "no philanthropy, no legislation, no missionary labors can change this law: it is written in man's nature by the hand of his Creator." [40] The principles of pluralism ran counter to the teachings of the Christian churches. Accordingly, pluralism was denounced by church authorities as advocating a theory of natural causation while denying God a place in the universe. Nevertheless, pluralism gained adherents in intellectual and academic circles.

In the decades following the Civil War three major ideological positions can be distinguished on the issue of Negro inferiority. The first group held that the Negro was innately inferior to the white, and that while as a race Negroes might achieve a certain degree of progress, still they could do so only under the pressure and guidance of the whites, although never reaching the white man's intellectual, cultural, moral or physical level. It was the doctrine of permanent Negro inferiority. This position viewed the Negro as essentially a completed product of evolution, incapable of being assimilated by the whites.[41] Enoch Spencer Simmons, a member of the North Carolina bar, articulated this position in these words: "While we give the negro credit for much and believe him capable of more progressive advancement, in the way of learning and civilization, yet we know he is an inferior

[38] Quoted by Jenkins, *op. cit.*, 244–245.   [39] *Ibid.*, 247ff.

[40] Josiah Clark Nott and George R. Gliddon, *Types of Mankind* (Philadelphia, 1854), 79.

[41] For a foreigner's characterization of the position see W. P. Livingstone, *The Race Conflict* (London, 1911), 14–15.

race, who, under the most favorable conditions, will not and cannot ever achieve what his white friend can, because it is not the purpose of God, the great wise Creator, that he should. . . . " [42]

This group believed that there existed a biological ceiling above which the mind of the Negro could not be improved. The mind of the white, it was alleged, did not attain its full growth until some five to ten years after the full growth of his body, while the mind of the Negro matured several years sooner than his body. Accordingly, there existed an ever-widening gap between Negro and white mental capacity during adolescence and the twenties. E. H. Randle of Virginia typified this point of view: " I would place the matured capacity of the black at about eighteen, and of the white at about thirty. This makes a wide difference in the benefit the two may receive by training." [43]

Some writers took great pains to demonstrate that the Negro did not have " sufficient and the right kind of brain to enable him as a race to reach that high standard of education, refinement and civilization enjoyed by the white man." [44] It was alleged that the skull of the Negro was thicker than that of any other race and the gray matter and the number and depth of the convolutions less than that of the white race.[45] Some even suggested that the brain of the Negro in its physical characteristics approached that of the chimpanzee. Several scientists such as Robert B. Bean published findings attempting to show that the skulls of Negroes were smaller than the skulls of white men, and that the brains were less convoluted and otherwise deficient.[46] In this instance, Bean's work was exposed by Franklin P. Mall who repeated Bean's measurements on many of the same specimens and found that Bean had completely distorted his measurements and conclusions.[47]

The belief in innate Negro inferiority was widely held throughout the South and frequently set forth by Southern spokesmen and ideologists. Thomas Nelson Page, Southern novelist who romanticized the ante-bellum plantation system, firmly believed in " the absolute and unchangeable superiority of the white race—a superiority . . .

[42] Enoch Spencer Simmons, *A Solution of the Race Problem in the South* (Raleigh, N. C., 1898), 30.

[43] E. H. Randle, *Characteristics of the Southern Negro* (New York, 1910), 60. Also see Simmons, *op. cit.*, 74.

[44] William P. Calhoun, *The Caucasian and The Negro* (Columbia, S. C., 1902), 19.

[45] In this connection see *ibid.*, 20–23.

[46] Robert B. Bean, " Some Racial Peculiarities of the Negro Brain," *American Journal of Anatomy* (Sept. 1906), 353–432.

[47] Franklin P. Mall, " On Several Anatomical Characteristics of the Human Brain, Said to Vary according to Race and Sex with Especial Reference to the Weight of the Frontal Lobe, *American Journal of Anatomy* (Feb. 1909), 1–32.

not due to any mere adventitious circumstances, such as superior educational and other advantages during some centuries, but an inherent and essential superiority, based on superior intellect, virtue, and constancy." [48] He found nothing of value emanating from the mind of the Negro " In art, in mechanical development, in literature, in mental and moral science, in all the range of mental action...." [49] Prominent Southerners such as John Temple Graves and Henry W. Grady likewise adhered to this position.[50] Some carried the position to the point of an unreasoning fear of the Negro which amounted to a phobia. Serious proposals were advanced for removing the Negro from the South and transporting him to Africa or a 49th state. Rabid anti-Negro books and tracts made their appearance such as Charles Carroll's *The Negro A Beast*.[51]

The second group, while convinced of Negro inferiority, was less certain as to the " permanence " of this inferiority. In appreciating this position, it is important to realize that even as late as the early decades of the twentieth century it was widely believed in scientific circles that culture was a genetically inherited rather than an environmentally transmitted property, a belief now discredited, but still prevalent in popular thinking. Accordingly, the Negro was viewed as retarded, as thousands of years behind the white race in development.[52] However, this second group was not prepared to rule out the possibility of the Negro " catching up " with the " superior race." Philip Alexander Bruce, with ancestry in the old planter aristocracy of Virginia, clearly set forth this point of view in 1889 in his *The Plantation Negro as a Freeman:*

Whoever seeks to judge the moral character of the negro without having any knowledge of him from personal contact, is very apt to be misled by the notion that he is merely a white man in disposition whom the Creator has endowed with a black skin. Plainly as his complexion distinguishes him from the whites, to the eye, it will be discovered, after association with him for a great length of time, to be one of the smallest points of difference between him and the Anglo-Saxon. Remove all trace of that color with which Nature has painted his rugged countenance, wash away every stain that darkens it, and the moral traits that seem to be peculiar to his race would cause him still to occupy an original and unique position. How far these traits will be modified in the future by the transmitted influences of a more refined and elevated condition remains to be seen. It may be true, as some ethnologists believe, that the highest personal type of civilization is far more a result of inherited instincts and knowledge than of innate superiority of

[48] Page, *op. cit.*, 292–293.   [49] *Ibid.*, 249–250.
[50] J. T. Graves, " The Problem of the Races," in *The Possibilities of the Negro in Symposium*, *op. cit.*, 5–34, and Grady, *op. cit.*, 62–3.
[51] Charles Carroll, *The Negro A Beast* (St. Louis, 1900).
[52] Haygood, *Pleas*, *op. cit.*, 6, and Graves, *op. cit.*, 9.

race. . . . [53]

Bruce viewed the Negro as essentially " illiterate, credulous, feeble in judgment, weak in discrimination, a child in his habits of dependence and self-indulgence, accessible to every temptation and with little ability to resist, without a hope or aspiration above his physical pleasures. . . ." [54] He was alarmed that " The influences that are shaping the character of the younger generation [of Negroes] appear to be such as must bring the blacks in time to a state of nature. . . ." [55] It was essentially a paternal point of view, one which held that the Negro race could be elevated only under the guidance and supervision of an advanced civilized race.

A third group rejected the point of view that the Negro was an inferior or sought to skirt the issue as a major consideration. Instead they held that the Negro race was " different " from the white race. The " difference " was essentially one of social heritage, a heritage in which the white had obtained advantages, the Negro disadvantages.[56] As a consequence the races could be distinguished on the basis of traits peculiar to them, e.g., the nature of the moral code and practices generally prevalent among them. This position more or less characterizes the thinking of Edgar Gardner Murphy, an Episcopal clergyman of Montgomery, Alabama, and Bishop Atticus G. Haygood. Haygood writes:

Wherever the negroes are in large numbers, there, we may be sure, are their characteristics. If they live in the midst of another race, there, also, are the characteristics of that race . . . there are differences as well as resemblances —a simple but important fact not always considered. The differences as well as the resemblances go deeper than the skin. Whether the negroes are superior or inferior, whether better or worse than white people, it will nevertheless be admitted by candid persons that a company of negroes . . . are not, in any State, or city, or town, or country hamlet in the United States, realized in the inmost consciousness of men to be just the same as white people.[57]

Of the three positions the first was by far the dominant. In the latter half of the nineteenth and early twentieth centuries the doctrines of innate Negro inferiority gained considerable impetus.[58]

[53] Philip A. Bruce, *The Plantation Negro as a Freeman* (New York, 1889), 139.
[54] *Ibid.*, 61.   [55] *Ibid.*, 246.
[56] This position was probably most clearly set forth by Samuel Creed Cross, *The Negro and the Sunny South* (Martinsburg, W. Va., 1899). In this work, Cross militantly attacks white supremacy and urges that Negroes be accorded the same rights and liberties accorded the whites.
[57] Haygood, *Our Brothers in Black, op. cit.*, 19.
[58] This was true of anti-Semitism as well. See George Eaton Simpson and J. Milton Yinger, *Racial and Cultural Minorities* (New York, 1953), 106ff.

Three of the more important factors contributing to this development might be singled out. First, the appearance of Charles Darwin's *Origin of Species* in 1859 had an extraordinary influence upon social thought as well as upon the world of science. It laid the foundations for modern biology and demonstrated the effects of selection upon human beings. While Darwin's theory was hotly defended, attacked and modified, race theorists built up their conception of race on its framework. They sought to connect race with the evolution hypothesis and to arrange the races in a hierarchy, from which the thesis followed that the races could not be of equal endowment. In a period increasingly oriented toward scientific thinking, such a position appealed to many as lending " scientific " support for the existing racial structure.

A second factor adding currency to the doctrine of inherent Negro inferiority was the prevalent belief in this period in the preponderance of biological influences on human characteristics and behavior. In psychology and related fields various instinct theories of behavior were widely held. The importance assigned instincts was reflected in McDougall's *Social Psychology,* the most popular text in its field.[59] The importance of learning and culture in the determination of human characteristics and capabilities had been suggested in the early theoretical work of such men as Franz Boas,[60] Charles H. Cooley [61] and George Herbert Mead,[62] but this latter orientation found the going heavy.

Even as late as the 1920's the situation was quite confused. The social sciences were preoccupied with the nature-nurture controversy. But research on race was clearly undermining the theory of innate racial superiority and inferiority, while the various instinct theories were falling into general disrepute. Illustrative was the re-examination of the Army's intelligence testing program during World War I. Originally the finding that Negroes scored lower than whites had been given a racist interpretation by C. C. Brigham.[63] Later analysis, such as O. Klineberg's studies, showed that Negroes in some northern states scored higher than whites in some southern states. Still sociological thinking was confused. Surveying the available evidence

[59] W. McDougall, *An Introduction to Social Psychology* (Boston, 1911).

[60] Franz Boas, *The Mind of Primitive Man* (New York, 1911), and " The Mind of Primitive Man," *The Journal of American Folk-Lore,* Vol. 14 (Jan.–March 1911), 1–11.

[61] Charles H. Cooley, *Human Nature and the Social Order* (New York, 1902), and *Social Organization* (New York, 1912).

[62] George Herbert Mead, *Mind, Self and Society* (Chicago, 1934). This volume was prepared by Charles W. Morris from students' lecture notes after Mead's death. As a result it constitutes a much earlier contribution than its date of publication.

[63] C. C. Brigham, *A Study of American Intelligence* (Princeton, 1923).

on the issue in 1927, P. A. Sorokin in his *Contemporary Sociological Theories* could write:

. . . [the] perfect agreement of all these tests: the historico-cultural, the mental; the absence of geniuses, especially of the highest rank; and the ' superiority ' of the mulattoes, seems to indicate strongly . . . that the cause of such a difference in the negro is due not only, and possibly not so much to environment, as to heredity.[64]

It was little wonder then that such beliefs had wide credence among the general population.

A third factor giving impetus to the doctrine of Negro inferiority was Anglo-Saxonism, a product of modern nationalism and expansionism. For a time it had a particularly powerful grip upon American historians, represented by such men as Herbert Baxter Adams and John Fiske who exalted the rôle of the Anglo-Saxons in history.[65] The Anglo-Saxonist cult was allied with the notion of inevitable Anglo-Saxon " destiny," a notion reflected in the " Manifest Destiny " position. The doctrine found wide acceptance in the South, widely popularized by such Southern spokesmen as Henry W. Grady, who found little difficulty linking Anglo-Saxonism with white supremacy:

The Anglo-Saxon blood has dominated always and everywhere. It fed Alfred when he wrote the charter of English liberty; it gathered about Hampden as he stood beneath the oak; it thundered in Cromwell's veins as he fought his king; it humbled Napoleon at Waterloo; it has touched the desert and jungle with undying glory; it carried the drum-beat of England around the world and spread on every continent the gospel of liberty and of God; it established this republic, carved it from the wilderness, conquered it from the Indians, wrested it from England, and at last, stilling its own tumult, consecrated it forever as the home of the Anglo-Saxon, and the theater of his transcending achievement. *Never one foot of it can be surrendered while that blood lives in American veins, and feeds American hearts, to the domination of an alien and inferior race.*[66]

Today among the great mass of Southern whites the belief in Negro racial inferiority is virtually universal. However, in strictly biological terms the thinking is vague and unclear. An array of traits are attributed " by nature " to the Negro, traits which are believed to be inherent in the " race," and which define the Negro as an " inferior." These alleged traits include unreliability, laziness, thriftlessness, immaturity, immorality, criminal inclination, ignorance, incapacity for sustained mental activity and special susceptibility to certain diseases.

[64] Sorokin, *Contemporary Sociological Theories* (New York, 1928), 297–8.

[65] For an excellent treatment of Anglo-Saxonism see Richard Hofstadter, *Social Darwinism in American Thought*, rev. ed. (Boston, 1955), Ch. 9.

[66] Grady, *op. cit.*, 64–5. Italics added.

The belief finds sophisticated formulation among some Southern intellectuals. Representative of such expressions are the following:

History is not so much the record of the events of nations as a whole as it is the chronicle of the contributed civilizations of the superior races. . . . The negro race, though one of the oldest, has never built a worthy civilization.— [President D. M. Nelson of Mississippi College, Clinton, Miss.] [67]

There is much evidence to show that the Caucasoid people, the white race, have creative talents and abilities that have not been demonstrated to any considerable extent by the Negro race. . . . The white and Negro races differ in talents and abilities that are hereditary.—[Dr. W. C. George of the University of North Carolina Medical School.] [68]

The strength of the belief in Negro biological inferiority tends to vary inversely with educational level. In fact, among white Southerners with some college education there is a tendency to supplant the belief in inherent Negro inferiority with a belief that the Negro is merely " different " from whites, leaving the issue of " innateness " either open or denying it entirely. Kenneth Cass, Greenville, South Carolina mayor, expresses this point of view in a remark to a *Life* writer: " I don't want to argue it [that Negroes are inherently inferior] with anybody, but I don't go along with that. It doesn't sound quite Christian to me. They're human beings just like everybody else." [69]

Still white Southerners are in general agreement that Negroes *are* " different " from whites. Mississippi Senator John C. Stennis sets forth this sentiment to the *U. S. News & World Report:* " The traditions of the races are greatly different. The environment and background of the races are greatly different. Actually there are great social and emotional differences that quickly come to the surface when aroused. Their mental processes are different. . . ." [70] The average white Southerner, when specifying the manner in which Negroes differ from whites, frequently singles out an array of " differences "; these have been summarized by Thomas R. Waring, editor of the Charleston, S. C., *News & Courier,* in a highly publicized article in *Harper's Magazine.*[71] In it Waring attributed to Negroes higher incidences of venereal disease, a lower cultural level, more " casual " marital habits and considerably higher rates of illegitimacy, a greater

[67] D. M. Nelson, *Conflicting Views on Segregation,* pamphlet of the Mississippi *Association of Citizens Councils* (Greenwood, Miss., n.d.), 10.

[68] From a speech at Dartmouth College in Hanover, N. H., fall of 1956.

[69] Robert Wallace, " The Voices of the White South," *Life* (Sept. 17, 1956), 110.

[70] " The Race Issue: South's Plans, How Negroes Will Meet Them," *U. S. News & World Report* (Nov. 18, 1955), 90.

[71] Thomas R. Waring, " The Southern Case Against Desegregation," *Harper's Magazine* (Jan. 1956), 36–45.

crime rate, and a lower average intellectual development.

Among whites of lower and even some middle socio-economic class stations one elicits highly emotional responses lacking Waring's level of literary sophistication. It should be understood, however, that the white Southerner holding beliefs such as these is not dishonest or engaged in deliberate deceit. His ideas conform to his personal experience and observation, selective as they may be. The Negro's living standards, though rising, are still low; rates of extramarital households and illegitimacy, of tuberculosis and venereal disease, and of crimes against persons and property are considerably higher among Negroes than whites; and results of standardized, national I.Q., achievement, reading and related tests from Virginia to Texas show consistently lower scores for Negro than white children when taken as a racial group. The average Southern white is not aware of the multitude of social and cultural facts and forces which have fostered these situations. Rather he associates them with the visible physical characteristics of the Negro and concludes the Negro is inherently inferior or at the very least " different."

Given these beliefs concerning the Negro, the prospect of school integration evokes widespread fear in the mind of the Southern white. At the same time the beliefs function as an ideological bulwark of the existing caste system. For if the Negro occupies a position in the biological order lower than the white and nearer to the animals, or if his basic personality and behavior pattern is " different " from that of the whites (a pattern which whites commonly define as socially unacceptable or reprehensible), then a segregated order is in no need of moral defense. Accordingly, from the white point of view, the Negro does not enjoy " rights " but merely " privileges." These " privileges " are seen by the white as testifying to his generous, unprejudiced nature and as satisfying the dictates of Christian charity.

Gunnar Myrdal in his monumental study, *An American Dilemma*,[72] postulates the existence of a struggle within the heart of America between its democratic creed of equality and justice and its segregated, castelike system. What Myrdal failed to comprehend is that for most Southern whites there is no such moral dilemma. The doctrine of Negro inferiority or " differences " serves to place the Negro beyond the pale of the American democratic creed. This is illustrated by an experience I had while walking near a Negro section in Augusta, Georgia. As I was passing a number of white children who were hurling stones and insults at a nearby group of Negro children, I inquired of the former: " Why are you throwing stones at those children? " They replied: " Mister, they ain't children, they're niggers! "

[72] Gunnar Myrdal, *An American Dilemma* (New York, 1944).

Closely associated with the doctrine of Negro racial inferiority is the belief that interbreeding or crossing between races results in inferior offspring. According to popular superstition, the offspring of interracial unions inherit all the bad and few of the good qualities of the parental stocks. In turn these bad qualities are allegedly passed on to future generations during which time the good qualities are further sifted out through continued interracial unions. The net result is the mental and physical deterioration of the group.[73]

Articulate current expression of this belief is represented in the following statements:

We publish to the world that we protest the attempts being made to desegregate the races, because we believe such would inevitably lead into a hybrid monstrosity that would defy the word and will of God.—[Resolution of the Missionary Baptist Association of Texas composed of some 300 East Texas churches.] [74]

... history shows that nations composed of a mongrel race lose their strength and become weak, lazy and indifferent. They become easy preys to outside nations.—[Georgia Senator Herman Talmadge.] [75]

... the intermingling of breeding stock results invariably in the production of " scrubs " or mongrel types, and the downgrading of the whole herd. The same principle applies with equal force to the process of human development.—[A Citizens Council pamphlet.] [76]

Southern thought on racial amalgamation can be traced to the ante-bellum period. A number of prominent Southern ante-bellum scholars, most noted of which was Dr. Josiah Clark Nott,[77] advanced the theory that the races were not intended to mix. Nott argued that the offspring of whites and Negroes would speedily merge into one or the other of the original types, or become extinct from defective organization. According to Nott, " the superior races ought to be kept free from all adulterations, otherwise the world will retrograde, instead of advancing, in civilization." [78]

After the Civil War the belief was invested with new, highly accentuated emotional qualities as it became linked with the cult of white womanhood—the " woman on the pedestal " pattern.[79] The

---

[73] See Brown, *op. cit.*, 106–109; Randle, *op. cit.*, 117–118; and *The Possibilities of the Negro in Symposium, op. cit.*, 123. This position is similar to that set forth by Arthur de Gobineau, *The Inequality of Human Races*, trans. by Adrian Collins (New York, 1915), 209.

[74] *Southern School News*, I (Dec. 1954), 15.

[75] H. E. Talmadge, *You and Segregation* (Birmingham, 1955), 44–45.

[76] " A Christian View on Segregation," *op. cit.*, 6.

[77] Nott and Gliddon, *op. cit.*   [78] *Ibid.*, 405.

[79] " The white women of the South are pure. They are a high-minded, proud, spotless race. If they were not this, the Anglo-Saxon people in America would

Negro male was depicted as ruled by an inordinate sexual craving for white women, making all Negro men potential rapists. Through the years it has fostered a deep-seated anxiety among whites for the safety of their women.[80] This fear has been played upon by white supremacist leaders in the current controversy who have exhorted whites that the ultimate goal of the N.A.A.C.P. " is to open the bedroom doors of our white women to the Negro man." [81]

By the turn of the twentieth century the miscegenation doctrine had been elevated to a cardinal position in the Southern ideological structure. In 1904 Edgar Gardner Murphy could write: " The doctrine of race integrity, the rejection of the policy of racial fusion, is, perhaps the fundamental dogma of Southern life." [82] And in 1910 Sutton E. Griggs wrote: ". . . the problem of keeping Negro blood out of the veins of the white race is the paramount problem with the Southern white man, and to it all other questions, whether economic, political or social are made to yield." [83]

For the Southern white the prospect of racial intermarriage or amalgamation is viewed with considerable alarm. It appears to him as a real, imminent prospect—the epitome of evil and danger. For him it is a taboo—*the* taboo of taboos. Throughout the world societies have erected about sex their most heavily-charged emotional and coercive sanctions. This the South has done with interracial marriage. And as is true of taboos in general, the South has invested this taboo with mystical properties. Viewed as inextricably bound with obedience to it, is the fate of humanity and society. To violate the taboo is to desecrate the sacred (Southern white womanhood)

---

rapidly degenerate into a low-grade, mongrel breed, and that would be the end of American civilization, and the beginning of barbarism." Brown, *op. cit.*, 106. Regarding white women who had sexual relations with Negro men, Bruce writes: " The few white women who have given birth to mulattoes have always been regarded as monsters; and without exception, they have belonged to the most impoverished and degraded caste of whites, by whom they are scrupulously avoided as creatures who have sunk to the level of the beasts of the field." Bruce, *op. cit.*, 55. On the same matter Simmons writes: " Over the few marriages between white women and Negro men, which occasionally occur in the North, we draw the mantle of charity, and attribute such folly in white women to mental derangement and temporary insanity. No self-respecting white woman, in the full possession of her senses, North or South, would ever be so lost to shame and love of race pride as to unite herself in marriage with a negro, to become the mother of a hybrid mulatto race. God forbids such a union." Simmons, *op. cit.*, 30.

[80] See Bruce, *op. cit.*, 83–85.

[81] A statement by Alabama State Senator Walter C. Givhan, a frequent speaker at Council meetings. *Southern School News*, I (Jan. 1955), 3.

[82] Edgar Gardner Murphy, *Problems of the Present South* (New York, 1904), 34.

[83] Sutton E. Griggs, *Wisdom's Call* (Nashville, Tenn., 1911), 113.

and to unleash inevitable tribulation. As the Southerner views interracial marriage, it is something which cannot be grasped by secular or rational understanding. In this sense the belief is actually magical in character.

The taboo on intermarriage is focused upon the white woman. It covers not alone formal marriage but illicit sexual intercourse with Negro men. But the taboo does not operate with the same intensity to bar illicit intercourse between white men and Negro women. In the latter situation the white blood is " saved " from " pollution " by Negro blood, since paternity does not establish parentage with the certainty of maternity, and the offspring, regardless of the lightness of complexion, is automatically assigned to the Negro group. In short, a white woman has from an interracial union a " Negro " child but a Negro woman from an interracial union never has a " white " child.

It is this doctrine on interracial marriage that in the last analysis constitutes the South's main defense of the segregated system. Firmly embedded in Southern white thinking is the belief that the breakdown of segregation in any of its aspects would lead to the cultivation of such attitudes and social intimacies as would inevitably result in intermarriage. As the white Southerner perceives the segregation issue, *the* question remains: " Would you want your sister or daughter to marry a Negro? "

For many in America the Southern beliefs outlined here are offensive, evoking strong emotional reaction. But this merely underlines the fact that the contest between the forces of integration and segregation is to a considerable measure a conflict of ideologies. The current school-desegregation controversy has served not only to magnify the differences in ideology within America, especially between sections, but to buttress, intensify and solidify them through the heightened consciousness engendered by the resulting struggle.

In the years since World War II the movement within American life to realize for Negroes the full benefits deriving from the American democratic creed has gained increasing momentum. But as has been true throughout history, movements of social reform have encountered opposition and resistance. Movement has begot counter-movement; ideas have begot counter-ideas. Thus William Sumner Jenkins in his *Pro-Slavery Thought in the Old South* observes of the ante-bellum slavery controversies, " Slavery had defenders whenever defenders were needed; the exact nature of the defense was determined to a great extent by the degree to which and by the way in which the welfare of slavery was endangered." [84] Today the story is being repeated with the lineal descendant of slavery: segregated institutions.

Duke University.

[84] Jenkins, *op. cit.*, 49.

IX

MARX AND JEWISH EMANCIPATION

By Shlomo Avineri

That Karl Marx was an inveterate antisemite is today considered a commonplace which is hardly ever questioned. Marxists feel rather uneasy about it and try to evade the issue by pushing his essay *Zur Judenfrage* into the background, wishfully hoping that it will be ultimately forgotten. The essay is seldom translated or even separately published in the original German, nor is it quoted by orthodox Marxists above the absolute minimum. They, as well as non-Marxists, are usually perplexed by the enormity of Marx's anti-Jewish outbursts; [1] others see in it one more evidence of an antisemitic undercurrent in European socialism.[2] That Marx's essay was later accompanied by such uncomplimentary remarks about Lassalle as *'Baron Itzig,' 'Jüdel Braun,'* or *'Ephraim Gescheit,'* [3] seems to give weight to this contention. The fact that Bebel and Bernstein, as first editors of the Marx-Engels correspondence, carefully deleted every anti-Jewish remark of the Master from their edition, only attests to the burden Marx left as a legacy to his disciples in this as in many other respects.

Marx's essay is an answer to Bruno Bauer's two treatises on the Jews.[4] It has mainly two aspects: first, it is Marx's earliest attempt to form his own social philosophy in confrontation with the Young Hegelian tradition in general and with Bauer's 'critical school' in particular. Secondly, it is a fierce invective against what Marx conceives to be the spirit and essence of Judaism as a historical phenomenon. Bauer, according to Marx, in denying the Jews political and civic rights, is mistaken in failing to distinguish between the *political* and the *human* emancipation. *Political* emancipation, which means according to Marx political *formal* equality, can be achieved within bourgeois society, whereas *human* emancipation, which signifies transcending alienation, necessarily presupposes the destruction of bourgeois society as the sphere of men's egotistic interests contrasted with universal human attributes. The problem posed by Jewish emancipation occurs, according to Marx, wholly within bourgeois society and should hence be treated according to the general formal principles of equality underlying it. Bauer misses this, and hence his attitude is mistaken.

But the brunt of Marx's argument about the Jews is in the second part of his essay, where he identifies Judaism with the practice of selling and buying, sees bourgeois society as the manifestation of the Jewish spirit, and ends by saying that "the social emancipation of the Jew is the emancipation

---

[1] S. Hook, *From Hegel to Marx* (New York, 1936), 100–3; A. Cornu, *Karl Marx et Friedrich Engels* (Paris, 1958), II, 254–71; R. C. Tucker, *Philosophy and Myth in Karl Marx* (Cambridge, 1961), 110–13. K. Kautsky, in his *Rasse und Judentum* (Supplement No. 20 to *Die Neue Zeit*, 1914) does not mention Marx's essay at all.

[2] E.g., E. Silberner, "Was Marx an anti-Semite?," *Historia Judaica*, XI (1949), 3–52; the same author, *Sozialisten zur Judenfrage* (Berlin, 1962), 119–27.

[3] *Marx-Engels Gesamtausgabe* (Berlin, 1929), 3e. Abt., III, 213; II, 324, 334, 369.

[4] B. Bauer, *Die Judenfrage* (Braunschweig, 1843); B. Bauer, "Die Fähigkeit der heutigen Juden und Christen frei zu sein," *Einundzwanzig Bogen aus der Schweiz*, ed. G. Herweg (Zürich and Winterthur, 1843), 56–71. Cf. N. Rotenstreich, *The Recurring Pattern* (London, 1963), for a detailed study of Bauer's as well as Marx's views.

of society from Judaism."[5] This image of Judaism is generally conceived to be Marx's Last Judgment on the Jews, and recently an American went to the length of crediting Marx with a racialist antisemitism, postulating a quasi-Nazi view of advocating a *physical* annihilation of the Jews.[6]

Marx's rather unflattering image of Judaism somehow overshadows the question about his actual attitude to the practical question which caused the essay to be written, i.e. the position of the Jews in Prussia. It is certainly right to suppose that this question was a secondary one from Marx's own point of view: the philosophical argument with Bauer took precedence. Still, it has been very much overlooked that Marx comes back in a later context to this question of Jewish emancipation, and in this case engages in a very detailed argument about the problem itself. This is done by Marx a year or so later in *The Holy Family*. In the general argument against Bauer, three sub-sections are devoted to Bauer's attitude to the Jewish question.[7] Marx here takes issue with a series of articles by Bauer which were written by way of response to some Jewish reactions to his initial essays of 1843.[8] Again, Marx's argument is on two levels, a philosophical and a historical one. On the first level Marx reiterates his contention that Bauer mixes up political with human emancipation, and on this count Marx does not really add anything significant to what had already been said by him in his first article in the *Deutsch-Französische Jahrbücher*.

It is, however, on the second plane that Marx plunges deeply into the various issues connected with the polemical literature which sprung up around the question of Jewish emancipation at that time. Here he takes sides in the argument between Bauer and a host of Jewish polemicists (Philippson, Samuel Hirsch, Salomon, Gabriel Riesser, *et al.*). The significant fact is that *Marx completely endorses the views held by the Jewish writers*, though wrily adding that in spite of the fact that they are far inferior to Bauer as polemicists, the latter does not get the better of them in argument.

At the outset Marx supports one of Gustav Philippson's arguments against Bauer. According to Philippson, Bauer's point of departure is irrelevant; instead of posing the question of Jewish emancipation in the context of *existing* society within which the question has arisen, "Bauer imagines a peculiar kind of state—a philosophical ideal of a state, a state as it has never existed and could never exist, a state in which the Sovereign gives public lectures on logic and metaphysics, and in which all the citizens, from the Chief Minister down to the lamp cleaner of the Royal Theater take notes, like Chinese mandarins, of every word uttered by the crowned Pro-

---

[5] K. Marx, *Early Writings*, trans. T. B. Bottomore (London, 1963), 40 (Marx-Engels, *Werke* [Berlin, 1961], I, 377).

[6] D. D. Runes, *Karl Marx, A World Without Jews* (New York, 1959), ix.

[7] K. Marx and F. Engels, *The Holy Family*, trans. R. Dixon (Moscow, 1956), 117–21, 127–32, 143–59 (*Werke*, II, 91–95, 99–104, 112–25); that those sections were written by Marx, cf. *Werke*, II, 724.

[8] B. Bauer, "Neueste Schriften über die Judenfrage," in *Allgemeine Literatur-Zeitung*, Heft I (December 1843) and Heft IV (March 1844).

fessor, so as to make sure that every executive act will be in accordance with what was written down in their school notebook." [9] Marx remarks that this is valid criticism, as Bauer "confuses the state with humanity, the rights of man with man, and political emancipation with human emancipation." [10]

Bauer's theological premises, which combine his Christian valuation of Judaism with his attitude to Jewish contemporary emancipation, are the focal point of Marx's attack on the second, historical level. Bauer and his school, Marx asserts, pose the question in a wrong way: "It thus distorted the Jewish question in such a way that it did not need to investigate *political emancipation* . . . but could be satisfied with a criticism of Jewish religion and a description of the Christian-German state." [11]

Marx points out that XVIIIth-century Enlightenment, by creating the modern bourgeois world, succeeded in neutralizing religious dissent from the political sphere, making religion irrelevant in the realm of the state. Bauer and his colleagues, on the other hand, would like to go back in history and do away with this political neutralization of the religious element in the modern world. Bauer sees the Jewish question as a religious one; no one would deny that, Marx remarks, but it is not *only* a religious question. The roots of the religious problem are deeply imbedded in the actual living conditions of the Jews, and these—like Jewish religion itself—are being constantly recreated and preserved by bourgeois society. Marx reiterates here his Feuerbachian, anthropological attitude to religion, and though he does not budge an inch from his earlier approach which identified Judaism with the bourgeois world, his basic attitude and its practical consequences do not fundamentally differ from those generally held by people who supported Jewish emancipation; even a liberal like Macaulay could not help making clear his aversion to both Jewish religion and economic activity in his essay advocating their enfranchisement.[12]

The religious problem of Judaism cannot, according to Marx, be solved within existing society (as it is just one phenomenal manifestation of human alienation in general); therefore, the political and civil rights of the Jews cannot be decided upon in a religious context: "If a Jew demands freedom and nevertheless will not renounce his religion, he . . . sets no condition contrary to political freedom," Marx points out.[13] This is in direct opposition to Bauer who made it a condition for emancipation that the Jews should renounce their religion. Marx says that Bauer's attitude is characteristic and typical of the Christian-Prussian attitude, and he goes to some length to show that Bauer hypostasizes his idea of a Christian state [14] on the Prussian absolutist *Landeskirche*. Marx jokingly remarks that for Bauer "his faith in Jehovah is changed into faith in the Prussian State." [15] Marx then goes on to support another Jewish writer, Gabriel Riesser (who eventually became a member of the 1848 Frankfort Constituent Assembly), against Bauer: "Herr Riesser correctly expresses the meaning of the Jews'

[9] G. Philippson, *Die Judenfrage von Bruno Bauer* (Dessau, 1843), 5.
[10] *The Holy Family*, 118 (*Werke*, II, 92).   [11] *Ibid.*, 121 (*Werke*, II, 95).
[12] T. B. Macaulay, "Civil Disabilities of the Jews" (1831), *Critical and Historical Essays* (London, 1951), II, 228f.
[13] *The Holy Family*, 150 (*Werke*, II, 118).   [14] *Ibid.*, 151 (*Werke*, II, 118).   [15] *Ibid.*

desire for recognition of their free humanity when he demands, among other things, the freedom of movement, sojourn, travel, earning one's living, etc. These manifestations of *'free humanity'* are explicitly recognized as such in the French Declaration of the Rights of Man. The Jew has all the more right to the recognition of his 'free humanity' as the 'free civil society' is thoroughly commercial and Jewish and the Jew is a necessary link in it." [16] Marx's criticism of bourgeois society and of the rôle the Jews play in it, according to his view, does not prevent him from demanding full civil and political rights for the Jews; not because Jewish emancipation signifies the journey's end, but because those rights are in accordance with the premises of bourgeois society itself.[17] That those principles are but a milestone on the road to ultimate salvation is beside the point when considered in this context; nay more, they become a necessary stage towards this ultimate emancipation. Marx supports Riesser also on another occasion by maintaining that the only legitimate attitude to the Jewish claims is to gauge them by the criteria of the objective juridical norms of bourgeois society; an approach like that of Bauer, based as it is on subjective feeling and consciousness (*'Gemüt und Gewissen'*) throws the door wide open to a host of considerations which are by definition inadequate and irrelevant in deciding questions of rights.[18]

Bauer's theological approach also causes him to view Judaism as outside the pale of historical process and the Jews as existing outside the realm of history, having no historical justification for their continuing existence. Bauer denies Rabbi Samuel Hirsch's contention that the Jews played any part in history.[19] Of course, the Jews contributed 'something' to history, Bauer asserts, but then "an eyesore is something too—does it mean it contributes to develop my eyesight?" Marx seems to have put some of the ancestral rabbinical vehemence into his rejoinder in defending the rabbi against the critical theologian: "Something which has been an eyesore to me since my birth, as the Jews have been to the Christian world, which

[16] *Ibid.*, 153 (*Werke*, II, 120).

[17] This clear distinction between his attitude toward Judaism and the political question of Jewish emancipation is manifested by Marx in a letter to Arnold Ruge. Here Marx relates how as editor of the *Rheinische Zeitung* he was approached by the leader of the Jewish community in Cologne in connection with a Jewish petition on emancipation to be presented to the Rhenish Diet. Marx informs Ruge that though the 'Israelite religion' is 'destestable' (*widerlich*) to him, he will support the petition so as to bring more rationality into the existing 'Christian state' (Letter to Ruge, 13 March 1843, *MEGA*, I, ½, 308).

[18] *The Holy Family*, 130 (*Werke*, II, 102). It is noteworthy that this was also the angle from which Hegel viewed the criteria by which Jewish emancipation should be judged. Marx is in full agreement with Hegel in that both detest Judaism, though for different reasons, yet both go out of their way to point out that Jewish emancipation is a necessary corollary of the universal norms of modern society. Cf. G. W. F. Hegel, *Grundlinien der Philosophie des Rechts*, ed. J. Hoffmeister (Hamburg, 1955), § 209, 270, as well as my "A Note on Hegel's Views on Jewish Emancipation," *Jewish Social Studies*, XXV (April 1963), 145–51.

[19] S. Hirsch, *Das Judentum, der christliche Staat und die moderne Kritik: Briefe zur Beleuchtung der Judenfrage von Bruno Bauer* (Leipzig, 1943), 24.

grows and develops with me, is not an ordinary sore, but a wonderful one, one that really belongs to my eye and must even contribute to a highly original development of my eyesight. . . . However, the criticism quoted above revealed to Herr Bruno [Bauer] the significance of Jewry in 'the *making* of modern times.' " [20]

Marx comes back to this aspect of the place of Judaism in the historical process in another context, and though the tone is less incisive it is not less determined. Marx points out again that the Christian theologian element in Bauer's thought makes him suppose that Judaism actually lost its place in Universal History at the coming of Christ. Marx points out that Bauer is thus merely giving vent to his theological prejudices, clothing in new philosophical garment the 'old theological superstition.' [21] To Marx, Judaism exists within and through the historical process, it can be understood only historically and "the emancipation of the Jews to make human beings of them, or the human emancipation of Jewry, is therefore not to be conceived in the manner of Herr Bauer, as the special task of the Jews, but as the general practical task of the whole world today, which is Jewish to the core. . . . Herr Bauer, a *genuine* though *critical theologian* or *theological critic* could not get beyond the *religious contradiction.*" [22]

One of Bauer's arguments against the Jews preserving their religion after being emancipated was that nationalism is dying out anyway, so there is no special need to preserve one specific nationalism while the world is developing towards a supra-national cosmopolis; the Jews have to merge their individuality in this universalism. Marx's answer to this is significant on three counts: (a) in regard to any notions he may have had about the future existence of the Jews as an *ethnic* group; (b) in connection with the development of his thought on the general problem of nationalism; and (c) regarding his attitude to the question of historical predictability. Marx says in fact that there is no proof whatsoever to the contention that the different nationalities are doomed to disappearance; further, any attempt at historical prophecy is dangerously near to bringing theology back into the picture.[23]

In his first essay on the Jews in the *Deutsch-Französische Jahrbücher* Marx defined the modern state as being characterized by the separation of religion from the state.[24] Now in *The Holy Family* Marx goes one step further in trying to find a formal criterion by means of which it will be possible to gauge the degree of modernity any particular state has achieved. Anyone who has followed Marx's argument closely will not be surprised to find that Marx takes *the degree to which Jews enjoy political and civil rights as the criterion for the modernity of any particular state.* The Rights of Man (i.e. "political" emancipation), have first of all to be achieved in order to be transcended. To quote Marx: "The *Jews* (like the Christians) are fully *politically emancipated* in various states. Both Jews and Christians are far from being *humanly* emancipated. Hence there must be a *difference* between *political* and *human emancipation.* The essence of *political* emancipation, i.e. of the developed, modern state, must therefore be

[20] *The Holy Family*, 119 (*Werke*, II, 93).   [21] *Ibid.*, 147 (*Werke*, II, 115–16).
[22] *Ibid.*, 148 (*Werke*, II, 116).   [23] *Ibid.*, 132 (*Werke*, II, 104).
[24] *Werke*, I, 350–56, 360.

studied. On the other hand, states which cannot yet *politically* emancipate the Jews must be rated by comparison with accomplished states and must be considered as under-developed." [25] It seems that Marx makes it quite explicit, that he is concerned here not only with the inner contradictions of an attitude which would like to deny the Jews equal rights in a modern society, but is out to claim those very rights for the Jews himself.

That Marx was conscious of the limitations of this *political* emancipation in the specific case of the Jews is evident from an episode cited by him as an illustration of the general dichotomy between the merely political and the final human emancipation. The case in question concerns the attitude of the French Jews during the July Monarchy to introducing Sunday as the public holiday in state schools. It may provide an interesting comment on Marx's insight in so far as his general view on the limitations of merely political emancipation enabled him to perceive a dilemma which many optimistically minded liberals, Jewish and Christian alike, have not foreseen, certainly did not in 1845.

When it was proposed in the French Chamber, in December 1840, that Sunday be the public holiday in state schools, some radical deputies objected on the ground that this meant admitting clericalism through the back door. The Jewish deputy Adolphe Cremieux declared, however, that in the opinion of French Jewry, the religion of the majority of Frenchmen must be taken into account, and therefore the Jews will not object to declaring Sunday a public holiday in state schools. Marx remarks: "Now according to free theory Jews and Christians are equal, but according to this practice Christians have a privilege over Jews; for otherwise how could the Sunday of the Christians have a place in a law made for all Frenchmen? Should not the Jewish Sabbath have the same right, etc.?" [26]

This, according to Marx, is the intrinsic contradiction in the modern, constitutional state; political liberalism can solve only the purely *political* problem. The question how Jewish individuality can be maintained within a predominantly non-Jewish society will always remain problematical according to Marx, so long as the human emancipation, i.e. Revolution, will not sweep it away. Marx sees quite clearly the limits of political emancipation; but being conscious of these limitations, as well as accepting the historicity and relativity of bourgeois society and its liberal *ethos,* does not prevent him from voicing the same demands that were expressed by the liberals themselves; though for Marx the values underlying those demands are never ultimate. One has to divorce Marx's acrimonious attack on the rôle Jews played, according to him, in history from his attitude to the question of Jewish emancipation; it was on this second plane that he argued forcefully against those who tried to proceed from their feelings about the historical rôle of Judaism to argue against the civil rights of the Jews.

The Hebrew University, Jerusalem.

[25] *The Holy Family,* 149 (*Werke,* II, 117). One can see a practical application of this criterion in Marx's attitude in 1848, when he viewed cases where restrictions were re-imposed on the Jewish population in some German towns as a clear indication of resurgent reactionary trends. Cf. *Neue Rheinische Zeitung,* 17 Nov. 1848, 29 Nov. 1848, (*Werke,* VI, 25, 75).

[26] *The Holy Family,* 155 (*Werke,* II, 122).

X

"IN THE INTERESTS OF CIVILIZATION": MARXIST VIEWS OF RACE AND CULTURE IN THE NINETEENTH CENTURY

By Diane Paul

On August 7, 1866 Karl Marx wrote the first in a series of letters to Friedrich Engels and Ludwig Kugelmann enthusiastically recommending a new book, *The Origin and Transformation of Man and Other Beings*, by the French traveller and amateur scientist Pierre Trémaux.[1] Marx's enthusiasm was not shared by Engels (who thought the book absurd), or by the scientific community or general public. Like Hume's *Treatise on Human Nature*, it appears to have fallen "dead-born from the press"; unlike the *Treatise*, it enjoyed no revival. Entirely ignored in histories of biology, geology, and paleontology, its importance derives solely from the fact that Marx thought it "a very great advance over Darwin" scientifically and "far more significant in its historical and political applications."[2]

The Trémaux correspondence is fairly well-known, at least among scholars concerned with Marx's and Engels' attitudes toward Darwin. As someone interested in that general topic, I was eventually led to read the original letters, having up until then relied on the summaries and shortened versions in the literature. I was immediately struck by a sentence my studies had not prepared me to find: "As he [Trémaux] indicates, (he was in Africa a long time) the common Negro type is only a degeneration of a much higher one."[3] The strik-

---

[1] Pierre Trémaux, *Origine et Transformation de l'homme et des autres êtres*. Part I (Paris, 1865). Apparently a second volume was planned but never completed, or at least never published. The Marx/Engels/Kugelmann correspondence in the *Marx–Engels Werke* (Berlin, 1966), hereafter cited as *Werke*, is dated as follows (all 1866): Marx to Engels, 7 Aug., Engels to Marx, 10 Aug., Engels to Marx, 13 Aug., Engels to Marx, 2 Oct., Marx to Engels, 3 Oct., Engels to Marx, 5 Oct., and Marx to Kugelmann, 9 Oct.

[2] Marx to Engels, 7 Aug., 1866. All references, unless otherwise stated, are to the *Werke*.

[3] ". . . wie er (er war lang in Afrika) nachweist, dass der gemeine Negertyp nur Degereszenz eines viel höhern ist." *Ibid.* I know a few references to this sentence in the literature, out of at least a dozen discussions of Trémaux: in Conway Zirkle, *Evolution, Marxian Biology, and the Social Scene* (Philadelphia, 1959), 91-111 (a highly polemical treatment of Marx's racial views), in Lewis Feuer, *Karl Marx and the Intellectuals* (Garden City, 1969), 20, and in Saul Padover (ed.), *Marx on History and People* (New York, 1977), although for some reason it is included in the section

ing omission of this sentence in much—though as it turned out not all—of the Marx-Darwin literature led naturally to the following question: What other comments on race may have been more or less systematically edited out of the literature? Marx's view of Jews has been debated for many years, and his and Engels' unflattering references to the Slavs are also fairly well-known. But what of their attitudes toward other groups, such as blacks and the Irish, and the links between their views of various cultures? These questions in turn raise another, logically prior, one: Given the very real differences between the nineteenth- and twentieth-century concepts of race, the links between race and biology, and the content of biology itself, how can we characterize the views of Marx and Engels in a way which is both true to the texts yet avoids looking through a twentieth-century glass darkly at men who were—as we shall see—very much of the nineteenth?

Biology, Race, and Culture in the Nineteenth Century

In the twentieth century, to hold that differences among human groups are biologically-based is necessarily to imply that those differences are largely outside of human control. If human populations are in important ways genetically distinct, there is little that we can do about it, given the imperviousness of genes to direct environmental manipulation. Modern genetics, in turn, has led to a sharp distinction between biological and cultural explanations of human differences, the former assuming relative immutability, the latter, relative plasticity. In this context, the epithet "racist" has come to be applied almost exclusively to those views which ascribe non-trivial differences among human populations to biological, hence more or less permanent, differences.

The nineteenth century did not recognize a sharp break between biological and cultural explanations, nor could it, given the lack of

---

on "Marx and Darwin" rather than "Marx on Negroes and Mongols." The latter section includes but one entry, and that Marx's critique, in *The German Ideology*, of Max Stirner's view! Both Marvin Harris, *The Rise of Anthropological Theory* (New York, 1968), 236-40, and Leon Poliakov, *The Aryan Myth*, trans. Edmund Howard (New York, 1974), 244-46, briefly discuss Marx's racial views in light of the Trémaux correspondence but without reference to that particular comment. Some scholars, clearly familiar with the Trémaux correspondence, nevertheless praise Marx's "anti-racism." Perhaps the most striking example is Lawrence Krader, editor of Marx's ethnological notebooks. In "Marxist Anthropology: Principles and Contradictions . . . ," *International Review of Social History*, **20** (1975—Part 2), 236-72. Krader writes: "Marx was one of the first to denounce the racist cant" (of 19th-century anthropology), 236, but does not say where.

any genetic theory which would make such a distinction plausible. Nineteenth-century genetics was predominantly "Lamarckian," that is, based on the assumption that organisms actively adapt to their environments by acquiring characteristics (both physical and behavioral) that over a period of time become inherited. The view that acquired characters are under certain conditions heritable, though it had its nineteenth-century critics (most notably August Weismann in Germany and Alfred Russel Wallace, Edward Poulton, and E. Ray Lankester in England), was widely accepted even after publication of Darwin's *Origin of Species* in 1859. Although we today recognize the incompatibility of Darwinism and Lamarckism, the nineteenth century did not. Darwin himself was forced to explain the origin of variation at least in part through Lamarckian factors, having rejected the alternatives of saltation (macro-mutation) and hybridization. Moreover, as the result of serious criticisms levelled at his explanation of the mechanism of evolution (i.e., natural selection), Darwin's followers, such as the German Ernst Haeckel, allowed even greater scope to Lamarckian factors in evolution than did Darwin. (Darwin's *critics*, of course, went even further, some to the point of abandoning selection altogether in favor of explanations based on the direct adaptation of organisms to their environment.)[4]

This point is crucial to an understanding of nineteenth-century racial attitudes since Lamarckian assumptions may entail very different conclusions about the nature of racial differences than would modern genetic theory. Given the assumption that acquired characters are heritable, it follows that poor environments, whether natural or cultural, are almost inexorably bound to be reflected biologically. "Backward" peoples, whatever the original reason for their failure to develop, must after centuries of living in deprived environments become biologically degenerate. This was in fact the argument advanced at the beginning of the assault on Mendelian genetics in the Soviet Union by biologists such as Iu. A. Filipchenko. Filipchenko argued that the opponents of Mendelism assumed that only good environments are heritable. A consistent Lamarckian interpretation, he noted, implied that all deprived populations, including the proletariat, would be genetically "lamed."[5] The potentially reactionary character of Lamarckism was also asserted by J. B. S. Haldane, the

---

[4] A good general source on late nineteenth-century evolutionary biology is John Coleman, *Biology in the 19th Century: Problems of Form, Function, and Transformation* (New York, 1971) which also contains an excellent bibliography.

[5] Loren R. Graham, "Eugenics and Human Heredity in Weimar Germany and Soviet Russia in the 1920's: An Examination of Science and Values," unpublished paper, 1977, 37-39.

distinguished Marxian geneticist, who claimed in the British *Daily Worker*:

Lamarckism is now being used to support reaction. A British biologist who holds this view thinks that it is no good offering self-government to peoples whose ancestors have long been oppressed, or education to the descendants of many generations of illiterates. He has, however, to explain why even the children of orators must still be taught to speak, though men have been speaking for hundreds of generations.[6]

The pessimistic, negative side of Lamarckism, with its implication that poor environments are genetically crippling, is illustrated by Engels' discussion of the difficulty of teaching mathematics to bushmen and Australian Negroes. In the *Dialectics of Nature* he writes:

. . . modern natural science has extended the principle of the origin of all thought content from experience in a way that breaks down its old metaphysical limitation and formulation. By recognizing the inheritance of acquired characteristics, it extends the subject of experience from the individual to the genus; the single individual that must have experienced is no longer necessary, its individual experience can be replaced to a certain extent by the results of the experiences of a number of its ancestors. If, for instance, among us the mathematical axioms seem self-evident to every eight-year-old child, and in no need of proof from experience, this is solely the result of "accumulated inheritance." It would be difficult to teach them by a proof to a bushman or Australian negro.[7]

On the other hand, some stressed the *reversibility* of biological degeneration. In this view, genetic differences are seen to be real but transient. Given Lamarckian assumptions, it is possible to emphasize either modifiability *or* the accumulated effects of environment. In *The German Ideology* Marx stresses the former, more positive side of Lamarckism:

[Max Stirner] . . . has not the slightest idea that the ability of children to develop depends on the development of their parents and that all this crippling under existing social relations has arisen historically, and in the same way can be abolished again in the course of historical development. Even naturally evolved differences within the species, such as racial differences, etc., which Sancho [Stirner] does not mention at all, can and must be abolished in the course of historical development.[8]

---

[6] J. B. S. Haldane, *Science and Everyday Life* (London, 1939), 115. Ironically, another article in the same collection is titled: "A Great Soviet Biologist" (i.e., T. D. Lysenko).

[7] Friedrich Engels, *Dialectics of Nature*, trans. & ed. Clemens Dutt (New York, 1940), 314.

[8] Karl Marx, *The German Ideology* in *Karl Marx/Frederick Engels, Collected Works*, Vol. 5 (New York, 1976), 425. In "The Works of Marx and Engels in Ethnol-

In this passage, Marx expresses the optimistic aspect of Lamarckism in an extreme form: all racial differences can, over time, be overcome. This conclusion is not, however, necessarily entailed by a Lamarckian genetics; whether crippled races can be restored depends upon, most importantly, the reasons for their degeneration. Not much can be done about climate, for example. When Marx himself refers to actual races, as opposed to his general, theoretical pronouncements on Race, we shall see that he is sometimes less sanguine about the possibility of improvement. Moreover, for all Lamarckians, whether the time-scale of improvement is brief or lengthy depends upon the extent of degeneration as well as its causes. Marx never suggests how rapidly the improvement he envisages might occur; most probably, he had no clear idea.

Lamarckian assumptions also blur the modern distinction between "nations" and "races." References to the French, Italian, Greek, Jewish, Russian, or Slavic "races" in nineteenth-century literature simply describe peoples with a common language, religion, and history, not peoples who are biologically distinct. But given widespread nineteenth-century assumptions, a human population which maintained a unity of language and culture would *become* a race; nations are, in George Stocking's words, "races in the process of formation."[9] The author of "Heredity and Progress," an article appearing in the English socialist journal *Progress* in 1885, expressed the conventional wisdom of his time when he wrote: "Anyone who considers the Jews will see at once that their character, as much as their noses, are an inheritance. A Scotchman 'caught young' as Johnson said, may lose some of the superficial characteristics, but

---

ogy Compared," *International Review of Social History,* **17** (1973—Part 2), 223-75, Lawrence Krader writes: "The footnote to this passage of *The German Ideology* mentions personal energy of individuals of the various nations, energy through race mixture. This is likewise a step back from a social theory, introducing biological elements which Marx later rejected . . . ," 275. Unlike Krader, I believe *The German Ideology* to represent Marx's most anti-racist position. That Marx never abandoned the view that racial differences affect historical development is indicated by the following quote from volume three of *Capital:* "The form of this relation between rulers and ruled naturally corresponds always with a definite stage in the development of the methods of labor and of its productive social power. This does not prevent the same economic basis from showing infinite variations and gradations in its appearances, even though its principal conditions are everywhere the same. This is due to innumerable outside circumstances, natural environment, race peculiarities, outside historical influences, and so forth, all of which must be ascertained by careful analysis." Karl Marx, *Capital,* Vol. III, Part VI, Chap. XLVII, II (Chicago, 1909), 919.

[9] George W. Stocking, Jr., "Lamarckianism in American Social Science, 1890-1915," in *Race, Culture, and Evolution: Essays in the History of Anthropology* (New York, 1968), 245.

will retain all the national peculiarities of his race; and so will the Irishman."[10]

This is not to assert that the term "race" was never used in a purely cultural sense, but given the nature of nineteenth-century genetics, references to various national and cultural groups as "races" must generally be understood as implying some degree of biological distinctness. That national characteristics are to some extent biologically-based is assumed even by explicitly "anti-racialist" writers. For example, George Plekhanov, criticizing Antonio Labriola's views of the effect of race on historical development, nevertheless concedes:

The temperament of every nation preserves certain peculiarities, induced by the influence of the natural environment, which are to a certain extent modified, but never completely destroyed, by adaptation to the social environment. These peculiarities of national temperament constitute what is known as *race*.[11]

The exact relationship between biology and culture was doubtless unclear to most nineteenth-century writers; it had to be, given a genetic doctrine according to which acquired characters were heritable but which suggested no mechanism by which this process could occur. Hence the question of how readily racial differences, as manifested in nations or other groups, might develop or disappear was simply unanswerable. As a result, though accepting a common genetical framework, various writers were free to stress either the plasticity of traits or the accumulated effects of environment—the positive or negative side of Lamarckism—as it suited them.

What Marx and Engels Said About Blacks

In analyzing Marx's and Engels' comments on blacks there are at least two elements to consider: the content of their views and the style in which they are expressed. As to the content of their views, they wrote little directly on the subject though there is some relevant indirect evidence. As noted in the introduction, Marx commented with approval on Trémaux's contention that Negroes had degenerated from a higher race. Trémaux's general views on race are interesting and shed light on Marx's views of both blacks and Slavs. It is perhaps worth quoting in some detail from Marx's first letter to Engels urging him to read Trémaux's book:

---

[10] J. M. Wheeler, "Heredity and Progress," *Progress*, 5, Nov. 1885, 499.
[11] George Plekhanov, *The Materialist Conception of History* (New York, 1940), 25.

In its historical and political applications, Trémaux is much more important and fruitful than Darwin. Here alone is found a natural basis for certain questions, as of nationality, etc. For example, he corrects the Pole, Duchinski, whose concern over the geological differences between Russia and the West Slavs he otherwise confirms, but in this matter it was not as Duchinski thought, that the Russians were not Slavs being much more Tartars, etc., but that the prevailing geological formation itself tartarized and mongolized the Slavs. As he indicates, (he was in Africa a long time) the common Negro type is only a degeneration of a much higher one. "Against the great laws of nature, the schemes of men are nothing but disasters; witness the efforts of the Tsars to make the Polish people into Muscovites. The same nature, the same faculties, revive on the same soil. The work of destruction never ceases, the work of reconstruction is eternal. The Slav and the Lithuanian races have their true boundary with the Muscovite in the great geological line which extends north of the basins of the Nieman and the Dnieper. To the south of this great line the capacities and types of men proper to this region are and will always remain different from those of Russia." [12]

As this excerpt from Marx indicates, Trémaux's theory relates the nature of the soil to human racial types (a not uncommon kind of argument in the nineteenth century although Trémaux's version is particularly crude).[13] The nature of the soil, according to Trémaux, changes over time. Older—primary or secondary—rocks are less "perfect" than are rocks of more recent periods. It follows that persons who live on more recent terrain are themselves more perfect (except where recent soil is the product of the erosion of old rocks). Perfection in humans is defined largely in aesthetic terms; e.g., Negroes are ugly, not because of their color (which to Trémaux is an unimportant feature of race) but because of their shape, while white Caucasians, especially Greeks, are beautiful.

What makes new terrain more perfect, except that it is in some sense more "complex" or "varied," is not clear from the text. Moreover, Trémaux suggests no mechanism by which the perfection of the soil could be translated into improved human types. His entire argument is, in fact, based upon correlations: people with similar characteristics tend to live on the same kinds of soil. For example, Newfoundlanders (who live on old rocks) are "a sort of Negro."

[12] Marx to Engels, 7 Aug., 1866.

[13] I am greatly indebted to Camille Limoges of the University of Montreal for his patient explanation of the *Origin and Transformation* . . . to someone baffled both by Trémaux's French and by his science. Oddly enough, none of the many scholars who have discussed Marx's view of Trémaux in the context of Trémaux's general attitude toward Darwinism have read the *Origin and Transformation*. . . . Leon Poliakov did read a summary of Trémaux's racial views given in his account of his African travels, *Voyage en Ethiope, au Soudan oriental et dans la Nigrite* (Paris, 1863), Vol. II.

American Negroes, however, are much closer to American whites than to Australian aborigines. There are, therefore, as many different human races as there are soils of different type. Even within France, claims Trémaux, the people of Brittany, who live on old soil, are religious, superstitious, traditional in their allegiances, and willing to place their government in the hands of a king, while the people of Paris, who live on recently developed terrain, are intelligent, industrious, independent, and favor representative government.

The effect of the soil on racial differences is not, however, always that clear-cut. For one thing, there may be interbreeding at the stage when differences have just begun to develop ("the soil diversifies; fecundity unifies"). For another, certain factors, such as the nature of diet, may intervene and mask the action of the soil. Slavery, for Trémaux, is another degenerative force which may work at cross-purposes with the action of the soil. In general, however, there is a parallel between the perfection of human beings and that of the soil. Trémaux even uses his theory to explain why the Confederate South, which was not at all industrialized, was able to hold out against the North for so long. Given the higher quality of Southern soil, he predicts that even if the North wins the Civil War, it will inevitably be governed by the South.

Degenerate races, therefore, are those that migrated to geologically inferior terrain. The Egyptians who moved South, to the Sudan for example, have characteristics less perfect than those in the North. The degeneration of the Mayan civilization is explained as the result of migration to a soil less perfect than the people. Trémaux is clearly a monogenist; he explains human racial differences not in terms of multiple origins but in terms of degeneration from a common type. For example, he insists that the Negro is not a perfected ape but a degenerated human being. Moreover, we are not entirely helpless in the face of geological-cum-racial differences. Besides the possibility of migration, man can have some influence over the quality of the soil through reforestation of lands and the use of fertilizers.

It is interesting to note that Trémaux's extreme environmentalist approach is extended to life on other planets, on which the perfection of life would also be a function of the soil, varying with the degree of development of parasites. Parasites in herbivores, according to Trémaux, do not advance beyond a certain low level of development. When eaten by carnivores whose intestinal tract is more advanced, they too progress. Apparently, the intestinal tract is the equivalent of "soil" for these organisms.

It is certainly not my intention to imply, on the basis of his enthusiasm for Trémaux's book, that Marx accepted all these aspects of the theory. Marx recognizes that the book has many deficiencies (though he is not explicit as to what they are), but his enthusiasm for

Trémaux's general theory, which even by nineteenth-century standards is particularly simple-minded, can only be explained either by the extent of his disenchantment with Darwin or by his desire to find a basis in natural science for his cultural prejudices or, most probably, both.

At Marx's urging, Engels purchased a copy of the book and, appalled at what he found, replied:

. . . I have arrived at the conviction, that there is nothing to his theory if for no other reason than because he neither understands geology nor is capable of the most ordinary literary historical criticism. One could laugh oneself sick about his stories of the nigger Santa Maria and of the transmutations of the whites into Negroes. Especially, that the traditions of the Senegal niggers deserve absolute credulity, *just because the rascals cannot write*! Besides it is nice to blame the soil formation for the difference between a Basque, a Frenchman, a Breton, and an Alsatian; and of course, it is also its fault that these people speak four different languages. Perhaps this man will prove in the second volume, how he explains the fact, that we Rhinelanders have not long ago turned into idiots and niggers on our own Devonian Transition rocks. . . . Or perhaps he will maintain that we are real niggers.

This book is not worth anything, a pure fabrication, which defies all facts and would have to give a proof for every proof which it adduces.[14]

Marx does not appear to have been much swayed by Engels' criticism, for on the next day he wrote back, defending Trémaux, in a letter which ends: "Trémaux's basic idea on the influence of the soil is, in my opinion, an idea which needs only to be announced, to secure for itself once and for all the right of citizenship in science and, at that, entirely independent of Trémaux's presentation."[15] Engels replied two days later in a letter much softer in tone than his first one, admitting that the Trémaux book might have some value after all (he had only read a third of the book at the time of his original reply to Marx). In particular, he notes:

This man has the distinction of having stressed the influence of the soil upon racial and, logically, species formation more than has happened so far. And secondly, of having developed more correct opinions on the effect of the crossing than his predecessors (though in my opinion very one-sided ones). . . . There is something tremendously plausible about the hypothesis that the soil becomes in general more favorable for the development of higher species in proportion to its belonging to newer formations.[16]

In spite of these concessions, the thrust of Engels' letter is primarily critical: he repeats arguments made previously and suggests new

---

[14] Engels to Marx, 2 Oct., 1866. Quoted in Zirkle, 93. All italicized phrases are emphasized in the original.

[15] Marx to Engels, 3 Oct. 1866.   [16] Engels to Marx, 5 Oct. 1866.

ones as well. At this point, the correspondence between Marx and Engels concerning Trémaux apparently breaks off, but Marx does write shortly afterward to Ludwig Kugelmann recommending the book "in spite of its diffuse style, geological errors and deficiency in literary–historical criticism" as an advance over Darwin.[17]

Although Engels more or less dismisses Trémaux's book, nothing in his comments indicates any disagreement with either Trémaux's or Marx's characterization of blacks (or Slavs) or the view that cultural differences reflect biological ones. Engels' complaint is that Trémaux is a poor geologist. Engels himself clearly believes that at least some human races degenerated from higher ones. As he writes in "The Part Played by Labour in the Transition from Ape to Man":

At first, therefore, the operations, for which our ancestors gradually learned to adapt their hands during the many thousands of years of transition from ape to man, could only have been very simple. The lowest savages, even those in whom a regression to a more animal-like condition, with a simultaneous physical degeneration, can be assumed, are nevertheless far superior to these transitional beings.[18]

If, for Engels, degeneration cannot be explained on the basis of geology, then how can it be explained? To the extent that Engels considers this problem at all, he appears to think that the introduction of milk and meat to the diet produced larger brains in some human races. Apparently he accepted literally Feuerbach's famous dictum *Der Mensch ist was er isst* ("Man is what he eats."). In the *Origin of the Family, Private Property, and the State,* Engels writes:

The plentiful supply of milk and meat and especially the beneficial effect of these foods on the growth of the children account perhaps for the superior development of the Aryan and Semitic races. It is a fact that the Pueblo Indians of New Mexico, who are reduced to an almost entirely vegetarian

---

[17] "Ich empfehle Ihnen auch Trémaux: *'De l'origine de les* [sic] *etres* etc.' Obgleich verlottert geschrieben, voller geologischer Schnitzer, viel Mangel an literarisch-historischer Kritik, enthält es—with all that and all that—einen Fortschritt über Darwin." Marx to Kugelmann, 9 Oct., 1866.

[18] Frederick Engels, "The Part Played by Labour in the Transition from Ape to Man," in *Dialectics of Nature*, 281. Compare Engels' view with that of Edward Aveling, Marx's son-in-law and a popularizer of Darwin's works in socialist circles. Aveling argued that the gap between the highest and lowest human races was much greater than that between humans, in general, and apes—in fact, that certain human races cannot interbreed. See, for example, his *The People's Darwin: Or Darwin Made Easy* (London, n.d.), esp. 20-22. An interesting article on later socialist attitudes toward blacks is Robert C. Reinders, "Racialism on the Left: E. D. Morel and the 'Black Horror on the Rhine,'" *International Review of Social History*, 13 (1968) Part I, 1-28.

diet, have a smaller brain than the Indians at the lower stage of barbarism, who eat more meat and fish.[19]

Engels was probably influenced in this view by Lewis Henry Morgan about whose book *Ancient Society: Or Researches in the Lines of Human Progress from Savagery through Barbarism to Civilization* Engels wrote: "On the original states of society there is a *definitive* book, a book as definitive as Darwin's for biology: it has, of course, been discovered by Marx; Morgan, Ancient Society, 1877."[20] Marx made extensive excerpts with notes from Morgan and, to a lesser extent, from the works of the anthropologists Henry Maine, John Lubbock, and John Phear.[21] Engels later used Morgan's book as the starting-point for the *Origin of the Family . . .* whose subtitle is "In the light of the Researches of Lewis Henry Morgan." In *Ancient Society,* Morgan expresses the view that those Indian tribes which domesticated animals, and hence were able to incorporate meat and milk into the diet, developed larger brains as a result. He goes on to suggest:

. . . the Aryan and Semitic families owe their preeminent endowments to the great scale upon which, as far back as our knowledge extends, they have identified themselves with the maintenance in numbers of the domestic animals. In fact, they incorporate them, flesh, milk, and muscle into their plan of life. No other family of mankind have done this to an equal extent, and the Aryan has done it to a greater extent than the Semitic.[22]

It is worth noting in this context that Morgan held, in relation to blacks, extreme racist views. In fact, although he is usually described as a monogenist, Morgan believed the black race to be so backward as to refute the notion that all human races have a common origin. He was, still, a fervent abolitionist, at least partly on the grounds that the black race would die out if emancipated. As he said to William Seward: "It is too thin a race intellectually to be fit to propagate and I am perfectly satisfied from reflection that the feeling towards this race is one of hostility throughout the north. We have no respect for them whatever."[23]

[19] Frederick Engels, *The Origin of the Family, Private Property, and the State* (New York, 1972), 91. This view is discussed in greater detail in "The Part Played by Labour. . . ." 287-88.

[20] Engels to Karl Kautsky, 16 Feb., 1884.

[21] These have been published as *The Ethnological Notebooks of Karl Marx,* transcribed and ed. Lawrence Krader (Assen, 1972).

[22] Lewis H. Morgan, *Ancient Society* [1877] (Chicago, 1909), 25. Marx appears to have been impressed with Morgan's general views about the relationship of types of subsistence to levels of culture but not by the specific link between animal protein and brain size.

[23] Quoted in Harris, 139.

Morgan's views on race were most clearly expressed in *Systems of Consanguinity and Affinity*, a book familiar to both Marx and Engels.[24] In this work, blacks are characterized as follows:

Unimportant in numbers, feeble in intellect, and inferior in rank to every other portion of the human family, they yet centre in themselves, in their unknown past and mysterious present, one of the greatest problems in the science of the families of mankind. They seem to challenge and to traverse all the evidences of the unity of origin of the human family by their excessive deviation from such a standard of the species as would probably be adopted on the assumption of unity of origin . . . In the light of our present knowledge the negro is the chief stumbling block in the way of establishing the unity of origin of the human family, upon the basis of scientific proofs.[25]

That Marx and Engels failed to disassociate themselves from Morgan's racial views in itself proves nothing. It acquires meaning only in the context of their overall views. In this regard it is worth noting that both Marx and Engels accepted Ernst Haeckel's theory that "ontogeny recapitulates phylogeny" (that individual development repeats the evolutionary history of the species). It was certainly possible in the late nineteenth century to be a recapitulationist without being a racist. However, Haeckel's views had come to be so closely associated with racism that it might be expected that Engels at least (since he was far more concerned with Haeckel than was Marx) would separate himself from that aspect of his theory, especially since he was critical of Haeckel's general political, and to some extent philosophical, opinions.[26]

Both Marx and Engels sometimes used the English term "nigger" to refer to blacks and to others for whom they had contempt (e.g., the frequent references in their correspondence to "the Jewish nigger Lassalle"). It is amusing to note that the Soviet English-language edition of their letters includes the following explanation: "With reference to the use of the word "nigger" which occurs in this book: Marx used the word while living in England, in the last century. The word does not have the same connotation as it has now in the U.S. and should be read as "Negro" whenever it occurs in the text."[27]

---

[24] Engels refers to Morgan's *Consanguinity and Affinity* in *The Origin of the Family*. . . . Marx also refers to that book in his notes on Morgan's *Ancient Society*.

[25] Lewis H. Morgan, *Systems of Consanguinity and Affinity of the Human Family* (Washington, D.C., 1870), 462.

[26] On Haeckel's racial views and their influence see Daniel Gasman, *The Scientific Origins of National Socialism: Ernst Haeckel and the German Monist League* (New York, 1971) and Stephen Jay Gould, *Ontogeny and Phylogeny* (Cambridge, Mass., 1977), Ch. 5.

[27] *Karl Marx and Frederick Engels: Selected Correspondence, 1846-1895*. Trans. Dona Torr (New York, 1942), vi.

This explanation does not accord with that of the Oxford English Dictionary or with a great deal of other evidence. For example, when John Stuart Mill replied to Carlyle's infamous 1849 essay in *Fraser's Magazine*, "Occasional discourse on the nigger question," he pointedly titled his answer "The Negro question." If the word "nigger" was not so jarring in mid-nineteenth century England as it is in England or America today, it nevertheless was a term of abuse.

Marx's and Engels' public writings on the American Civil War are certainly sympathetic to the cause of "Negroes."[28] It is predominantly in their private correspondence that one finds references to "niggers" and, in relation to Jews, "Yids," "Itzig" [Ikey], "the Jew so-and-so," mimicking of Jewish speech patterns, disparaging references to Jewish physical characteristics, and so forth. To some extent, Marx and Engels both have public and private personae. This will become even more evident when we consider their opinions of Jews.

What Marx and Engels Said About Jews

Marx's and Engels' writings on the Jews have been discussed at length by others (although this has certainly not resulted in anything like general agreement about the nature of their views). In spite of the large literature which already exists, it is perhaps worth making a few points relevant to the debate from the perspective of this paper. First, whether or not Marx and Engels were anti-semitic, they were clearly not racist in the modern sense of holding Jews to be biologically distinct (at least from Aryans as they typically refer to "Aryans and Semites" as one in comparison with other races). However, the question of their attitudes towards Jews is hardly exhausted by that statement. In fact, a close examination of their writings, including correspondence, indicates that no simple characterization of their views is possible. There have been a number of recent attempts to portray Marx, and to a lesser extent Engels, as proto-fascists. George Watson has found in Marx's writings the intellectual origins of the Red Army Faction, one of whose leaders, Ulrike Meinhof, publicly blamed the failure of the German left on its blindness to the fact that

[28] However, abolition for Marx presumably depended upon a certain level of civilization. In a letter to Engels (14 June 1853) Marx writes: "He [Henry Charles Carey in *The Slave Trade, Domestic and Foreign*] shows how the main stock of Negroes in Jamaica, etc., always consisted of newly imported barbarians, since the English treatment of Negroes was such that their numbers not only failed to remain steady but actually declined to two-thirds of the annual slave import; whereas the present generation of Negroes in America is a native product, more or less Yankee-ized, English-speaking, etc. and therefore *capable of emancipation*." Quoted in *Karl Marx on America and the Civil War*. Ed. by Saul K. Padover (New York, 1972), 39.

"anti-semitism is really a hatred of capitalism."[29] Hugh Lloyd-Jones comments that "[Marx's] remarks about Lassalle sometimes recall the tone of Goebbels."[30] W. H. Chaloner and W. O. Henderson claim that Marx "detested his own race."[31] Max Geltman writes that Jews "never knew that Marx had called for their utter disappearance from the face of the earth."[32] And Robert Payne remarks that Marx's "solution of the Jewish question was not very different from Adolph Hitler's."[33]

[29] Quoted in George Watson, "Race and the Socialists," *Encounter*, **47** (Nov. 1976), 23. It is perhaps worth quoting at some length the newspaper report of Meinhof's speech before a German court in 1972. She is reported to have said: "Auschwitz heisst, dass sechs Millionen Juden ermordet und auf die Müllkippen Europas gekarrt wurden als das, als was man sie ausgab - als Geldjuden! Finanzkapital und Banken, 'der harte Kern des Systems' des Imperialismus und Kapitalismus, hätten den Hass der Menschen auf das Geld und die Ausbeutung on sich ab und auf die Juden gelenkt. Diese Zusammenhänge nicht deutlich gemacht zu haben, sei das Versagen der Linken, der Kommunisten gewesen. Die Deutschen waren antisemitisch, also sind sie heute Anhänger der RAF. Sie wissen es nur nicht, weil man vergessen hat, sie vom Faschismus, vom Judenmord, freizusprechen und ihnen zu sagen, dass Antisemitismus eigentlich Hass auf den Kapitalismus ist." *Frankfurter Allgemeine Zeitung* (Dec. 15, 1972), 6. I would like to thank the author of the article, Dr. Peter Jochen Winters, and the *Frankfurter Allgemeine Zeitung* for their permission to quote from their report of Ulrike Meinhof's speech. Watson translates "als was man sie ausgab" as "for what they were" whereas "for what they were presented as" would be more correct. Disturbing as Meinhof's speech is (especially given the at least passive support of the Red Army Faction by many German university students), it is also, taken as a whole, confused and even in places incoherent. Watson's translation and analysis make Meinhof's point appear to be much clearer than in fact it is, and his charge that she "spoke up publicly in the Good Old Cause of revolutionary extermination" is not obviously supported by the text. Watson, 22.
[30] Hugh Lloyd-Jones, "The Books that Marx Read," *London Times Literary Supplement* (Feb. 4, 1977), 188.
[31] W. H. Chaloner and W. O. Henderson, "Marx/Engels and Racism," *Encounter*, **45** (July 1975), 20. They also remark that Engels ". . . had no prejudices against coloured peoples. He rejected the view commonly expressed by explorers and missionaries in his day that native peoples were 'heathen savages' who were obviously inferior to white races," 21. The only evidence adduced to support this view is Engels' account, based on his reading of Morgan, of the "wonderful child-like simplicity" of Iroquois life, *ibid*. Had Morgan's and Engels' attitude toward the Iroquois Indians been as totally admiring as Chaloner and Henderson suggest (it was in reality far more complex) it could hardly support such a broad generalization. Moreover, there exists directly conflicting evidence in the *Dialectics of Nature*, "The Role Played By *Labour* . . . ," and personal correspondence, among other sources.
[32] Max Geltman, "Socialist Anti-Semitism: Marx, Engels, and Others," *Encounter*, **45** (March 1976), 94.
[33] Robert Payne, *The Unknown Karl Marx: Documents* (1972), 14-15. Quoted in Watson, 19.

Sometimes the view of Marx as virulently anti-semitic is based on a particular reading of his two well-known review essays, published in 1844 under the general title *Die Judenfrage* (On the Jewish Question), one of which emphasizes Marx's prediction that Judaism will disappear ("the Jew will become *impossible,*" in Marx's phrase) in a socialist society. But the view of Marx as anti-semitic rests much more frequently on his disparaging comments about Jews as a race and as individuals than on a particular interpretation of the *argument* of *Die Judenfrage*. These unflattering remarks appear primarily in the second essay of *Die Judenfrage*; in *Herr Vogt,* the manuscript of 1860 still untranslated (into English) with its extraordinarily tasteless attack on Joseph Moses Levy, publisher of the London *Daily Telegraph* (the length of whose nose provides the focal point for three pages of abuse); in several articles which appeared in *Die Neue Rheinische Zeitung,* the newspaper edited by Marx and Engels in 1848–49; and in their private correspondence.[34]

The remarks in their private correspondence, especially Marx's comments on the character and appearance of Ferdinand Lassalle, are frequently cited in support of the thesis that Marx was a self-hating Jew. Eduard Bernstein edited these remarks out of the original edition of the Marx-Engels correspondence (1913), and for many years the most famous letter was said to be forged. Its inclusion in the official East German edition of the collected works of Marx and Engels effectively ended that debate. The letter, which is actually more insulting to blacks than to Jews, reads as follows:

The Jewish nigger Lassalle, who fortunately left at the end of the week, had, again fortunately, lost 3000 Thaler in a bad speculation. The fellow would rather throw the money in the gutter than lend it to a "friend" even if the interest and capital were guaranteed. At that, he gives out the impression

---

[34] Marx's and Engels' articles in *Die Neue Rheinische Zeitung* include a number of very disparaging comments about Jews, esp. in Poland. See their articles of June 8, July 8, July 9, August 9, August 12, August 22, September 1, November 29 (all 1848) and January 8, February 21, March 18, April 29 (1849). The most virulently anti-semitic articles to appear in that newspaper were, however, published by others. Of particular note is the series of five articles by Ernst Drönke (one of the publishers of the *N.R.Z.*) which appeared in July 1848. Mr. Lev Golman of the Institute of Marxism-Leninism of the CC CPSU writes: "There is no doubt that the point of view represented in this article, as in other articles by Drönke on the Polish Question, expressed the general position of the editors of the N.R.Z. including its chief editor Marx." Letter to the author, Feb. 20, 1979. I am very grateful to Mr. Golman, who edited the *N.R.Z.* articles for the new English-language edition of the Marx/Engels *Collected Works,* for his help in sorting out the authorship of the articles on the Polish question. Only Marx's and Engels' articles in the *N.R.Z.* are easily accessible in German, Russian, and now in an English edition of their works. There is, however, a German facsimile edition of the *N.R.Z.*

that he must live as a Jewish baron or as a baronial Jew (probably through the countess). . . . Now it is completely clear to me that, as his head shape and hair growth prove, he is descended from the Negroes who joined Moses on the journey out of Egypt (if not, his mother or grandmother on his father's side crossed with a nigger). Now this combination of Judaism and Teutonism with a negroid basis must produce a strange product. The obtrusiveness of the fellow is indeed negroid. . . . One of the great discoveries of our nigger—which he shared with me as a 'most trusted friend'—is that the Pelagians stemmed from the Semites. . . .[35]

In spite of this and similar letters, and comments in some published works, some Marx scholars insist that Marx was not, and given his general philosophical outlook could not have been, anti-semitic. They base this claim upon a particular reading of *Die Judenfrage*, especially the first essay, and to a lesser extent, *The Holy Family*. None of Marx's defenders (that I know of, at least) denies that Marx equated Judaism with the spirit of commercialism and self-interest; the message of *Die Judenfrage* is plain enough:

Let us consider the actual, wordly Jew, not the *Sabbath Jew*, as Bauer does, but the *everyday Jew*.
Let us not look for the secret of the Jew in his religion but let us look for the secret of his religion in the real Jew.
What is the secular basis of Judaism? *Practical* need, *self-interest*.
What is the worldly religion of the Jew? *Huckstering*. What is his worldly God? *Money*.
Very well then! Emancipation from *huckstering* and *money*, consequently from practical, real Judaism, would be the self-emancipation of our time.[36]

Nevertheless, the counter-argument claims that *Die Judenfrage* is not anti-semitic in spirit for the following reasons. First, Jews had become, as a result of their exclusion from guilds, professions, and agriculture a commercial people, buoyed by a commercial religion, who historically played a central role in the development of capitalism, so Marx's "economic-Jew" stereotype may be exaggerated but contains a large element of truth. Moreover, given that Marx was writing at a time before sociological and historical studies exposed the exaggeration of the stereotype—one held by many Jews themselves—Marx at the least ought not to be singled out for special blame.[37]

---

[35] Marx to Engels, 30 July 1862.

[36] Karl Marx, "On the Jewish Question," in *Karl Marx/Frederick Engels, Collected Works*, Vol. 3 (New York, 1975), 170.

[37] For example, see Hal Draper, *Karl Marx's Theory of Revolution: State and Bureaucracy* (New York, 1977), 591-608. Although Draper presents a strong defense of Marx, his argument that everyone on the left, including Jews, accepted the same stereotype as did Marx is greatly exaggerated. It ignores, for example, the highly negative reaction on the part of many Jews to the Portrait of Fagin in *Oliver Twist*, a reaction to which Dickens himself was sensitive.

Second, and more important, the counter-argument continues, the spirit of *Die Judenfrage* is anything but anti-semitic. However offensive its tone to twentieth-century ears with their experience of Hitlerism and other anti-semitic movements, the central thesis of the essays is that political emancipation of the Jews ought not to wait upon general social emancipation. It is, such scholars insist, an argument (directly largely against the Left Hegelian, Bruno Bauer) in favor of granting full political equality to the Jews in the here and now, not in some liberated future. To be sure, political equality represents only a limited step on the road to full social emancipation, for it leaves untouched those property relationships from which the most basic inequalities necessarily follow. Nonetheless, the emancipation of the state from religion (i.e., the separation of the state from all theological concerns) represents a genuine, even if limited, advance in human freedom. Political emancipation ought not to be confused with social emancipation, but they *are* interrelated. Indeed, the extent to which the state has divorced itself from religious concerns (of which Jewish emancipation is perhaps the best index) indicates the degree of a state's modernity. Therefore, those states which had not yet granted Jews political equality must be considered backward.[38] Engels is particularly clear in his condemnation of anti-semitism as reactionary: it "is nothing but the reaction of the medieval, decadent strata of society against modern society, which essentially consists of wage-earners and capitalists; under a mask of apparent socialism, it therefore only serves reactionary ends; it is a variety of feudal socialism and with that we can have nothing to do."[39]

What is most striking about the sharply conflicting arguments over Marxist anti-semitism is that they are based on generally different sorts of evidence. The view that Marx and Engels were anti-semitic is based largely on their *style*, on the contempt they express for Judaism as a religion and for most Jews as individuals, especially (though not exclusively) in their correspondence. The opposed view is based on the *argument* of *Die Judenfrage* and, to a lesser extent, on *The Holy Family* and Marx's philosophical writings in general.

Both kinds of evidence are relevant, and together they indicate that no simple characterization of Marx's and Engels' views is defensible. They did hold a general philosophical position which led them

[38] Shlomo Avineri, *The Social and Political Thought of Karl Marx* (Cambridge, 1968), 43-46.

[39] Engels to an unknown correspondent, 19 April 1890, published in the Vienna *Arbeiterzeitung,* 9 May 1890. The letter is included in *Selected Correspondence, 1846-1895,* trans. D. Torr, 469-72. Engels also criticizes anti-semitism in *Herr Eugen Dühring's Revolution in Science.* trans. by Emile Burns, ed. C. P. Dutt (London, 1934) though his remarks have perhaps the character of a stick with which to beat Dühring who was a rabid anti-semite.

to support full political rights for Jews. It is therefore absurd to imply, as some writers do, that Marx looked forward to "a world without Jews"[40] as though he espoused their physical extermination. On the other hand, it is equally clear that Marx was highly sensitive about his Jewish origins and that he and Engels both disliked most Jews personally and accepted every current anti-Jewish stereotype, including those which from their own personal experience and knowledge of history they should have had reason to doubt.[41] Julius Carlebach has recently shown how little merit there is in the claim of some scholars, such as David McClellan, that Marx's use of the term "Judentum" in *Die Judenfrage* is essentially devoid of religious and racial content.[42] Marx himself asserted that "not only in the Pentateuch or Talmud but also in present society we find the nature of the contemporary Jew, not as an abstract nature but as a supremely empirical nature," and he certainly makes empirical claims about Jewish religion and Jewish history, claims which Carlebach shows to be "even more contemptuous and certainly less well-informed than those of his predecessors" (such as Feuerbach and Bauer).[43] Moreover, both Marx and Engels disapprove of what they take to be every characteristic of contemporary Jews. From Marx's comments in the second essay of *Die Judenfrage*, other published material by Marx and Engels, and especially their private correspondence, we know that they believed Jews to be selfish, interested only in money-making, capable of determining the fate of Europe through their control of international finance, clannish—even greasy.[44]

Taking into account all of the available evidence, I think that the

[40] Dagobert D. Runes, *A World Without Jews* (New York, 1959), all but a few pages of which is a translation of *Die Judenfrage*.

[41] Yvonne Kapp's biography of Eleanor Marx contains an interesting anecdote in this regard. At the death of Marx's wife, an obituary notice appeared in *La Justice*, a journal for which Marx's son-in-law, Charles Longuet, was an editor. It noted that Marx's Jewish origin created prejudice against the marriage, a remark which angered Marx who wrote to his daughter the same day: "I suppose I am not mistaken in crediting Mr. Ch. Longuet's inventive genius with this literary embellishment . . . Longuet would greatly oblige me in never mentioning my name in *his* writings." Yvonne Kapp, *Eleanor Marx*, Vol. One (New York, 1972), 221. Marx never referred to his Jewish origins and showed extreme sensitivity about the comments of others.

[42] Julius Carlebach, *Karl Marx and the Radical Critique of Judaism* (London, 1978), esp. 148-84. Carlebach's is certainly the most thorough and closely-reasoned analysis of the argument of *Die Judenfrage* and is especially valuable in providing a historical context in which to locate that essay.   [43] *Ibid.*, 173.

[44] A few examples: ". . . the loan-mongering Jews derive much of their strength from these family relations, as these, in addition to their lucre affinities, give a compactness and unity to their operations which ensure their success"; Marx in the *New York Tribune* (4 January 1856), quoted in Chaloner and Henderson, 20. On Engels' club, the "Schiller Anstalt"—"What has happened is what always happens when Jews are about. At first, they thank God that they had a Schiller Anstalt, but

attitude of Marx and Engels toward Jews can be reasonably characterized as follows. As a result of their particular historical situation, Jews have developed a wide range of unpleasant characteristics all directly or indirectly associated with money-making. These historically-conditioned traits will inevitably disappear in a society where money-making is not possible; when Judaism loses its practical basis, the Jew as we know him will cease to exist and the Jewish "problem" will simply dissolve. However, it follows that in the present, as opposed to the socialist future, Jews as a class are the kind of people with whom one would not much want to associate. That it is not their fault and that it will not always be thus does not alter the fact that for Marx and Engels almost all Jews were characterized by highly undesirable traits. Though they rationalized their attitude toward particular Jews, they accepted as true this characterization which if accepted by others, could not help but create a socialist attitude of contempt toward the "actual, worldly" Jew. That is the real basis of socialist anti-semitism, the link connecting Marx with the disgraceful position of almost all socialists in the Dreyfus affair and the anti-semitic views of at least a portion of the modern European left.[45]

---

hardly had they got inside than they wanted to build a bigger club house—a true temple of Moses—to which the Schiller Anstalt could be moved"; Engels to Carl Siebel, 4 June 1862, *ibid.* On Lassalle—"a real Jew from the Slav frontier . . . a greasy Jew disguised under brilliantine and flashy jewels"; Engels to Marx, 7 March 1856, *ibid.,* 21. "I begin to understand French anti-semitism when I see how many Jews of Polish origin with German names intrude themselves everywhere to the point of arousing public opinion in the ville lumière . . ."; Engels to Paul Lafargue, 22 July 1892, *ibid.* "So long as they are making money it is a matter of complete indifference to the English middle classes if their workers eat or starve. They regard hard cash as a universal measuring rod. Anything that yields no financial gain is dismissed as 'stupid', 'impractical', or 'idealistic.' That is why these petty Jewish chafferers are such devoted students of economics—the science of making money. Every one of them is an economist"; Engels, *The Condition of the Working Class in England in 1844* (London, 1892), 312. "We discovered that . . . the German national simpletons and money-grubbers of the Frankfurt parliamentary swamp always counted as Germans the Polish Jews as well, although this meanest of all races, neither by its jargon nor by its descent but at most only through its lust for profit, could have any relation of kinship with Frankfurt"; Engels in the *N.R.Z.* (29 April 1849), in *Marx/Engels, Collected Works,* 360. On Joseph Moses Levy, publisher of the London *Daily Telegraph*—"But of what use is it for Levy to attack Mr. Disraeli . . . , so long as Mother Nature has inscribed, with the wildest black letters, his family tree in the middle of his face? The nose of the mysterious stranger of Slawkenbergious (see *Tristram Shandy*), who fetched himself the finest nose from the promontory of noses, was merely a week's talk in Strasbourg, whereas Levy's nose constitutes a year's talk in the City of London . . ."; Marx in *Herr Vogt,* quoted in Saul K. Padover, "The Baptism of Karl Marx's Family," *Midstream,* **24** (June/July, 1978), 44.

[45] For the most part, socialists were either indifferent or active anti-Dreyfusards.

A Note on the Irish

There is a striking parallel between Marx's and Engels' opinion of the Jews and of the Irish. The Irish also, as a result of historical circumstances, possess many undesirable traits, traits almost the reverse of those which characterize the Jews. The Irish are stupid, addicted to drink, coarse, dirty, passionate by nature, brutal when drunk though otherwise light-hearted and happy, in short, at their best they have the virtues of small children, but at their worst they are animal-like. (However, even in their most degraded condition the Irish rise above the level of savages, another indication of the nineteenth-century Marxist view of non-Western societies.) Lest this seem an exaggeration, a few excerpts from Engels' *The Condition of the Working Class in England* will serve to illustrate the point:

One worker needs more than another, because the former is accustomed to a higher standard of living, than the latter. The Englishman, who is not yet wholly uncivilised, needs more than the Irishman, who goes about in rags, eats potatoes, and lives in pigsties. This does not prevent the Irishman's competing with the Englishman and gradually dragging down his wages and standard of living to his own level. Certain jobs can only be performed by workers who have reached a certain degree of civilization and practically all industrial employment falls into this category.[46]

Two things make life supportable to the Irishman—whiskey and his lively, happy-go-lucky disposition. He drinks himself into a state of brutish intoxication. Everything combines to drive the Irishman to drink—his light-hearted temperament, akin to that of the Mediterranean peoples, his coarseness, which drags him down virtually to the level of a savage, his contempt for all normal human pleasures, which he is incapable of appreciating because of his degraded condition, combined with his dirty habits and his abject poverty.[47]

The actual manner in which poverty strikes the Irish may be explained by the history, traditions and national characteristics of the people. The Irish have a strong affinity with the Latin races such as the French and the Italian. The resemblence to the Italians is particularly strong. . . .

In Ireland passions and sentiment rule supreme and reason takes a back seat. The sensuous and excitable nature of the Irish prevents them from undertaking tasks which require sober judgment and tenacity of purpose.

Eleanor Marx was a striking exception; see Aileen Kelly, "Eleanor Marx, Heroine," *New York Review of Books,* 24 (Jan. 26, 1978), 29-30. The French socialist leaders Jules Guesde and Jean Jaurès issued a manifesto supporting "nonparticipation in the Dreyfus affair, on the ground that while the reaction wishes to exploit the conviction of one Jew to disqualify all Jews, Jewish capitalists would use the rehabilitation of a single Jew to wash out 'all the sins of Israel.'" Quoted in Geltman, 92.

[46] Engels, *The Condition of . . . ,* 89-90.   [47] *Ibid.,* 106.

Obviously such a people are not able to engage in industry as it is carried on today.[48]

It is less clear with the Irish (than it is, say, with the Jews) that their distinctive national characteristics, particularly the "sensuous and excitable nature" which they share with the Latin races, will entirely disappear in the course of historical development. There is an ambiguous quality to Engels' comments on the Irish which, as noted early in this paper, is typical of nineteenth-century discussions of nationality. Nonetheless, whatever their peculiarities as a "race," the problems of the Irish are primarily the result not of their nature but of an oppressive social structure.

That social structure is internal; Engels does not believe that the degraded condition of the Irish can be attributed to English rule, a fact which will become abundantly clear after that rule has ended. Nonetheless, both Marx and Engels are fairly consistent supporters of Irish independence (and apparently not just for tactical reasons). As with the Jews, therefore, the Irish are viewed as having a wide variety of unpleasant characteristics, characteristics which will not be altered by Irish independence. Nonetheless, as with the Jews, political emancipation is not made to wait upon general social emancipation.

What Marx and Engels Said About the Slavs

We have already seen in their discussion of Pierre Trémaux something of the attitudes of Marx and Engels toward the Slavs. Their letters indicate a willingness on Marx's part to adopt, at least temporarily, a biological explanation for the course of Slavic history. While Engels dismisses the book initially as bad science (later admitting that soil may have some influence on race), nothing in his replies indicates disagreement with Marx's characterization of the Slavs. Their letters and published articles, particularly in the *Neue Rheinische Zeitung*, reflect a life-long preoccupation with the "Slavic question" and a personal distaste for Slavs on the part of both men. In fact, their opinion of the Slavs is so low that beside it their portraits of the blacks, Jews, and Irish appear almost flattering. And in Engels' case, the ultimate solution to the Slavic question is to be found not in general social emancipation but in the extermination of the Slavs as a people. This solution follows from Engels' view of historical development in general and Slavic history in particular, not, at least obviously, from any belief in "natural" Slavic inferiority.

---

[48] *Ibid.*, 308-09.

The objections of Marx and Engels to Pan-Slavism have been thoroughly discussed elsewhere.[49] What is of interest for this paper is that first, Marx tried to buttress his anti-Slavic views with geo-biological arguments and that second, although Engels did not, his characterization of the Slavs and solution to the Slavic question were considerably harsher than Marx's, a good indication of the difficulty (and perhaps futility) of distinguishing "racial" from purely "cultural" views of inferiority in the nineteenth century. At the least, the difficulty provides a warning against the too easy twentieth-century assumption that cultural theories of human differences are necessarily more benign in their implications than are those based on nature. Not only German hegemony over the Slavs but also American expansionism was defended by Engels "in the interests of civilization." The striving for self-determination on the part of peoples "without a history," peoples who have not followed that course of historical development leading to capitalism, is viewed with contempt. Engels' remarks on American expansionism (in an article denouncing Slavic nationalism) illustrate this attitude. As part of an argument with Bakunin he writes:

> How does it happen then, that between both these republics [the U.S. and Mexico] which according to the moralistic theory should be "brotherly" and "federated," a war broke out over Texas, that the "sovereign will" of the American people, supported by the bravery of American volunteers, for "geographic, commercial and strategic necessities" moves a boundary line drawn by nature a few hundred miles further south? And will Bakunin reproach the American people for waging a war which to be sure deals a severe blow to his theories based on "Justice and Humanity," but which none the less was waged solely in the interests of civilization? Or is it perhaps a misfortune that the splendid land of California has been wrested from the lazy Mexicans who did not know what to do with it? Is it a misfortune that through the rapid exploitation of the gold mines there the energetic Yankees have increased the medium of circulation, . . . have built great cities, have opened up steamship lines, are laying railroads . . . ? Because of this the "independence" of a few Spanish Californians and Texans may suffer, occasionally "Justice" and other moralistic principles may be injured, but what do they count compared to such world historic events?[50]

The Czechs and South Slavs, like the "lazy Mexicans" and assorted other peoples, lack the historical requisites for independence; their nationalisms are necessarily counter-revolutionary:

> Except for the Poles, the Russians, and at best the Slavs in Turkey, no Slavic people has a future, for the simple reason that all the other Slavs lack

---

[49] A good summary of their views is provided by Joseph A. Petrus, "Marx and Engels on the National Question," *Journal of Politics*, **33** (Aug. 1971), 797-824.

[50] Engels, "Der demokratische Panslawismus," *Die Neue Rheinische Zeitung* (Feb. 1849). Trans. as "Democratic Panslavism" in Paul W. Blackstock and Bert F. Hoselitz (eds.), *The Russian Menace to Europe* (Glencoe, Ill., 1952), 70-71.

the most basic, historic, geographic, political and industrial prerequisites for independence and vitality.

Peoples which have never had a history of their own, which from the moment they reached the first, crudest stages of civilization already came under foreign domination or which were only forced into the first stages of civilization through a foreign yoke, have no vitality, they will never be able to attain any sort of independence.[51]

Or as expressed in a different essay:

There is no country in Europe which does not contain in some corner one or several ruins of people, left-overs of earlier inhabitants, pushed back by and made subject to the nation which later became the carrier of historical development. These remains of nations which have been mercilessly trampled down by the passage of history, as Hegel expressed it, this ethnic trash always becomes and remains until its complete extermination or denationalization, the most fanatic carrier of counterrevolution, since its entire existence is nothing more than a protest against a great historical revolution.

Such in Scotland were the Gaels, the supporters of the Stuarts from 1640 to 1745. Such in France were the Bretons, the supporters of the Bourbons from 1792 to 1800. Such in Spain were the Basques, supporters of Don Carlos. Such in Austria are the Panslavist South Slavs, who are nothing more than the waste products of a highly confused development which has gone on for a thousand years.[52]

Moreover, Engels' solution to the Slavic question comes at least close to what some scholars have (I argued earlier, mistakenly) seen as Marx's solution to the Jewish question. A few brief excerpts from Engels' articles in the *Neue Rheinische Zeitung* illustrate his fanaticism:

Then it is war. 'A ceaseless fight to the death' with Slavdom, which betrays the Revolution, a battle of annihilation and ruthless terrorism—not in the interests of Germany but of the Revolution![53]

The next world war will cause not only reactionary classes and dynasties but also entire reactionary peoples to disappear from the earth. And that too would be progress.[54]

Among all the nations and petty ethnic groups of Austria there are only three which have been the carriers of progress, which have played an active role in history and which still retain their vitality—the Germans, the Poles and the Magyars. For this reason they are now revolutionary.

The chief mission of all the other races and peoples—large and small—is to perish in the revolutionary holocaust.[55]

Conclusion. Marx and Engels are said by some to have been extreme racists, by others anti-racists. They were neither. The only

---

[51] *Ibid.*, 72.

[52] Engels, "Der Magyarische Kampf"; trans. as "Hungary and Panslavism" in Blackstock and Hoselitz, 63-64.   [53] Engels, "Democratic Panslavism," 84.

[54] Engels, "Hungary and Panslavism," 67.   [55] *Ibid.*, 59.

thing striking about the racial views of Marx and Engels is their ordinariness. Their attitudes were the typical attitudes of nineteenth-century Europeans who, regardless of their ideology, thought in terms of a hierarchy of cultures with their own at the top and who occasionally used biology to provide a scientific basis for their categorization of societies into higher and lower forms. The use of biology by Marx and Engels, like that of many of their contemporaries was sporadic, *ad hoc,* and sometimes inconsistent (as in Marx's geo-biological explanation of Slavic history, which, however, evidently did not apply to the Poles for whom both he and Engels had the highest regard). Moreover, for them biological differences were, in some cases at least, capable of amelioration. As Engels' view of the Slavs indicates, in the nineteenth century the judgment that a people lacks "a history of its own" may be harsher than the opinion that, as a result of soil, diet, or other natural factors, a people is biologically degenerate.

There is a widespread, and I believe unfortunate, tendency to transform Marx and Engels into progressives on every issue of twentieth-century concern. It was Marx who wrote:

With the same right with which France has taken Flanders, Lorraine and Alsace, and, sooner or later, will take Belgium, with that same right Germany takes Silesia: with the right of civilization against barbarism, of progress against stability . . . this right is worth more than all treaties, for it is the right of historical development.[56]

Yet the anti-colonialist image of Marx and Engels is hardly affected by this and other contrary evidence. They were not consistent anti-colonialists, and they were not progressive about race either; they were simply no better or worse than most of their contemporaries.

More than fifty years ago, Georg Lukács wrote in *History and Class Consciousness* that all philosophies, including Marxism, reflect certain assumptions of the age in which they were born.[57] The important question today is to what extent Marxist categories are informed by the nineteenth-century cultural prejudices of Marx and Engels.

University of Massachusetts at Boston.

---

[56] Karl Marx in *Die Neue Rheinische Zeitung* (Aug. 12, 1848); cited in Bertram D. Wolfe, *Marxism: One Hundred Years in the Life of a Doctrine* (New York, 1965), 26.

[57] Georg Lukács, "The Changing Function of Historical Materialism," *History and Class Consciousness: Studies in Marxist Dialectics,* trans. Rodney Livingstone (Cambridge, Mass., 1971).

XI

SIGMUND FREUD, HIS JEWISHNESS, AND SCIENTIFIC METHOD:
The Seen and the Unseen as Evidence

By Sigmund Diamond

In Chapter V of his *Group Psychology and the Analysis of the Ego,* Sigmund Freud discusses the differences between leaderless groups and groups with leaders, and he illustrates those differences by referring to examples of "highly organized, lasting, and artificial groups"—the church, more particularly the Catholic Church, and the army. What characterizes these groups is the libidinal tie which attaches the followers to the leader and makes possible their attachment to each other; the disintegration of the tie between the leader and his followers results in panic. When the Assyrian soldiers learn that Holofernes has actually lost his head, they metaphorically lose their heads: "The loss of the leader in some sense or other, the birth of misgivings about him, brings on the outbreak of panic, though the danger remains the same; the mutual ties between the members of the group disappear, as a rule, at the same time as the tie with their leader."[1]

Freud's discussion of the disintegration of a church is far briefer than his discussion of the disintegration of an army; indeed, it is confined to the last two short paragraphs of the chapter. The next-to-last paragraph reads:

The dissolution of a religious group is not so easy to observe. A short time ago there came into my hands an English novel of Catholic origin, recommended by the Bishop of London, with the title *When It Was Dark.* It gave a clever and, as it seems to me, a convincing picture of such a possibility and its consequences. The novel, which is supposed to relate to the present day, tells how a conspiracy of enemies of the person of Christ and of the Christian faith succeed in arranging for a sepulchre to be discovered in Jerusalem. In this sepulchre is an inscription, in which Joseph of Arimathaea confesses that for reasons of piety he secretly removed the body of Christ from its grave on the third day after its entombment and buried it in this spot. The resurrection of Christ and his divine nature are by this means disproved, and the result of this archeological discovery is a convulsion in European civilization and an extraordinary increase in all crimes and acts of violence, which only ceases when the forgers' plot has been revealed.[2]

Freud's English translator, James Strachey, identifies *When It Was Dark* as a "book by 'Guy Thorne' (pseudonym of C. Ranger Gull) which enjoyed extremely large sales at the time of its publication in 1903."[3]

[1] Sigmund Freud, *Group Psychology and the Analysis of the Ego,* trans. James Strachey (New York, 1960), 38.   [2] *Ibid.*   [3] *Ibid.*

In the entire chapter Freud cites no empirical evidence to support his statements about the character of the church and about the causes and consequences of the dissolution of a religious group. We are presented not with evidence but with an illustration from a then eighteen-year old novel, not from the record of historical or contemporary events. My curiosity was aroused, however, not by the somewhat dubious methodology—Freud's Q.E.D. is placed not after a logical inference or some confirmatory data, but after a reference to a work of fiction—but by what seemed to me to be an interesting similarity between the novel cited by Freud and some others I had read in the same genre. Literary curiosity, not scientific analysis, was my goal.

Some years ago I had read Honor Tracy's *The Straight and Narrow Path* (New York, 1956), an always clever, sometimes profound book on the unanticipated consequences of a rationalist scholar's attempt, for the best of reasons, to cleanse the Irish villagers (among whom he was living) of their superstitions by showing the similarity between their religious practices and paganism. The result was a religious revival; the joke was on the rationalist. More recently I had read a current best-seller, Charles Templeton's *Act of God* (New York, 1979), a novel in which the possibility of continued belief in the divinity of Christ is threatened, not by the planting of faked evidence, but by the discovery of genuine evidence that the real grave of Jesus had just been found and that his skeleton was intact. True, there were some differences between the two novels. Tracy's protagonist is an anthropologist recovering from a recent breakdown; the discoverer of the real tomb of Jesus in Templeton's novel is an archeologist who had "wangled a grant from the Ford Foundation." What added enchantment was the circumstance that in both novels the crucial discovery was made by a professor (in one case he may not even have had tenure). Both novels seemed to meet the specifications for which Freud had selected the third—the observation of "the dissolution of a religious group"—and I thought that by reading the third I would begin research on what seemed to be an interesting genre of literature: novels in which Christianity is faced with the danger of dissolution as the result of a discovery, sometimes faked, sometimes genuine, that seems to threaten the authenticity of the Resurrection or the validity of other miracles. Such an inquiry promised to provide an interesting avenue into changing definitions of religion and, especially, into what has been felt to be its particular vulnerabilities. I have now read *When It Was Dark,* and I must confess some degree of failure in my attempt to use it to help map the changing contours of religious vulnerability. For the fact is that the novel hardly deals at all with what Freud maintains is its central issue and does make of paramount importance something about which Freud is totally, and uncharacteristically, silent. Why, then, did Freud see in the novel what is hardly there and why did he not see what is so crucial? Did he suppress what he saw? Did he really see what was there? Did he even read the novel?

I. Before presenting what the novel does deal with, let me summarize briefly what Freud saw in it and the use he made of what he saw:

1) It is "an English novel of Catholic origin, recommended by the Bishop of London . . ." which deals with "a conspiracy of enemies of the person of Christ and of the Christian faith" to expose Christianity as a hoax through the planting of false evidence which denies the historicity of the Resurrection.

2) The result of this "archeological discovery is a convulsion in European civilization and an extraordinary increase in all crimes and acts of violence, which only ceases when the forgers' plot has been revealed."

3) The dissolution of the religious group is accompanied not by fear, as would be appropriate in the case of an army overcome by panic, but by "ruthless and hostile impulses toward other people," impulses previously held in check by the restraining influence of "the equal love of Christ" which characterized membership in the group.

4) Even religions of love, like Christianity, "must be hard and unloving" to non-communicants; "cruelty and intolerance toward those who do not belong to it are natural to every religion." Summing up his conclusions on the relation between religion and intolerance, conclusions apparently confirmed or at least illustrated in the testimony of the novel, Freud writes: "However difficult we may find it personally, we ought not to reproach believers too severely on this account; people who are unbelieving or indifferent are much better off psychologically in this matter [of "cruelty and indifference"— Strachey]. If today that intolerance no longer shows itself so violent and cruel as in former centuries, we can scarcely conclude that there has been a softening in human manners. The cause is rather to be found in the undeniable weakening of religious feelings and the libidinal ties which depend upon them.[4]

In short, Freud sees in the novel confirmation of his conclusions concerning the relation between group belief and group behavior. What did he not see in the novel?

When It Was Dark is so rich and intricate in its simplicities that merely to summarize the plot is a matter of some complexity. Characters move onstage and off, manipulated by the author sometimes to advance the narrative, sometimes to afford him an opportunity to comment on current intellectual fashions and social trends. The most striking theme of the book—the influence of social and cultural status on the behavior of groups—is sounded virtually from the start.

[4] *Ibid.*, 38, 39.

The Reverend Ambrose Byars, vicar of Walktown, near Manchester, has two classes of people to contend with in his community: wealthy Jews, now Unitarians, and Lancashire natives, a "hard uncultured people."[5] He is musing over an apparently charitable offer to endow two scholarships for boys, scholarships which religious schools are eligible to receive on condition that no religious questions be asked on the examinations the boys must take. That condition has been rejected by the Catholic schools in the neighborhood, but Byars accepts—and so he becomes the beneficiary of the philanthropy of Constantine Schwabe, a rich, powerful, charitable businessman and politician (he is a Liberal), among whose attributes is that he is a former practicing Jew whose current secularism represents the evil of the anti-Christ. Schwabe is spinning a plot that is literally devilish in its implacable secular rationalism, a plot which depends for its success on the participation of Robert Llewellyn of the British Museum, the world's foremost authority on the archeology of the Near East. Fortunately for Schwabe, Llewellyn is vulnerable to blackmail. Unhappily married, he leads a double life; he desires things he cannot afford on his British Museum salary—saffron Saloniki cigarettes, garnet-colored cassis—and he is maintained in this luxurious style of life by borrowing from, of course, Constantine Schwabe. The source of his corruption is his infatuation for Gertrude Hunt, a voluptuous Jewish music-hall actress. The plot is for Llewellyn, in return for forgiveness of his debt to Schwabe, to plant a tomb in Palestine with the Greek inscription: "I, Joseph of Arimathaea, took the body of Jesus, the Nazarene, from the tomb where it was first laid and hid it in this place." The reason for the plot is stated by Schwabe in words similar to Freud's, at the end of Chapter V, on the relation between tolerance and the weakening of religious feeling:

A great intellectual peace will descend over the civilized world. Should not one exult at that, even though men must give up their dearest fetishes, their secret shrines; even though sentiment must be sacrificed to Truth? The religion of Nature, which is based upon the determination not to believe anything which is unsupported by indubitable evidence, will become the faith of the future, the fullfilment of progress. It is as Huxley said, "Religion ought to mean simply reverence and love for the Ethical Ideal, and the desire to realize that Ideal in life." Miracles do not happen. There has been no supernatural revelation. (188-89)

The sentiments that Freud expresses as his own on the relation between civility and the weakening of religious belief are, in the novel, expressed by the Jewish anti-Christ.

---

[5] Guy Thorne [pseud. of Cyril Ranger Gull], *When It Was Dark* (New York and London, 1906). Page numbers in the text refer to this work.

Gradually the novelist lengthens the cast of characters who will be caught up in the plot, some as victims, willing or unwilling, some as implacable enemies of the Satanic Schwabe. Among the latter are Helena, Byars's daughter, a "simple Christian" (would it not have been appropriate for Freud to have indulged himself here in the activity he engaged in so often in other contexts, namely, to point out that she bore the same name as the mother of the Emperor Constantine who, carrying the cross at the battle of the Milvian Bridge, heralded the triumph of Christianity with the words: "In hoc signo vinces"?), and Basil Gortre, a curate in love with Helena. Ultimately, a key figure in the toppling of the Jewish anti-Christ is the far from simple Sir Michael Manichoe, patron of St. Mary's of London, Gortre's church, a Conservative member of Parliament, son of a rich Roman banker, and, as it happens, a converted Jew. So intensely High Church has Sir Michael become that he even has a private chaplain, Mr. Wilson. Had Freud read the remarkable confrontation scene between Chaplain Wilson and Mr. Schwabe somewhat more carefully, he might have formulated the concept of cognitive dissonance long before Professor Leon Festinger or, at least, provided a somewhat richer account of the variables affecting the connection between the discovery of new "fact" and the toppling of old "belief." Mr. Wilson is speaking:

... go and tell a devoted man of the Church that he has been fed with sacraments which are not sacraments, and all that he has done has been at best the honest mistake of a deceived man, and he will laugh in your face, as I do!.... He also says, "Whether He is a sorcerer or not I know not; one thing I know, that whereas I was blind, now I see!" It is easy to part with one in whom one has never really believed. We can easily surrender what we have never held. But you haven't a notion of the real Christian's convictions, Mr. Schwabe. (191)

When the violence that follows the news of the discovery breaks out, it appears first in Palestine among the Moslems and "lower-class Jews" who initiate anti-Christian riots, not, as Freud implies it ought in his discussion of the dissolution of the church, among the Christians who ought to be the most affected by the discovery. The Vatican simply forbids the reading of articles about the discovery, and so disciplined are the Catholic masses that they do not panic like a leaderless army nor engage in crime like the members of a church who have lost faith in their leader.

Still, Christians are affected by the discovery, but the novelist's discussion of who is affected and how those effects are manifested suggests influences that mediate the relationship between belief and behavior about which Freud is silent. Through what medium does the public learn about the discovery of the tomb? Through the press, of course. The *Daily Wire* was the first newspaper to break the news, and its judgment of the significance of the event must have influenced the perception of its readers:

Old and venerated institutions will be swept away; minds fed upon the Christian theory from youth, instinct with all its hereditary tradition, will be for a while as men groping in the dark. But the light will come after this great tempest, and it will be a broader, firmer, more steadfast light than before, because founded on, and springing from, Eternal Truth. The mission of beneficent illusion is over. Error will yet reign for a generation or two. . . . Let us rather turn from the saddening spectacle of a fallen creed and rejoice that the ''Infinite and eternal Energy'' man has called God—Jahweh, Theos—that mysterious law of Progress and evolution, is about to reveal man to himself more than ever completely in its destruction of an imaginary revelation. (213)

That editorial had been approved by the three principal owners of the paper in a conference with Mr. Ommaney, the editor. Why?

Once more commercial and political influences were at work, as they had been two thousand years before. The little group of Jewish millionaires who sat in Ommaney's room had their prototypes in the time of Christ's Passion. Men of the modern world once more were enacting the awful drama of the Crucifixion. Constantine Schwabe was among the group; his words had more weight than any others. The largest holding in the paper was his. The tentacles of this man were far-reaching and strong. (214)

As in Palestine, so in Walktown: news of the discovery first affects the behavior not of the devout, but of infidels, dissenters, and doubters. It is not, despite Freud, that morale disintegrates among those who believed, but that it disintegrates among those who never believed or did not believe strongly enough:

The strong forces of Unitarianism and Judaism, always active enemies of the Church, were enjoying a moment of unexampled triumph. Led by nearly all the wealthy families of Walktown, all the Dissenters and many lukewarm Church people were crowding to these same synagogues. (214)

There were, of course, citadels of resistance. The Catholic Church refused to make any concessions to the discovery, even to recognize it. As a result, it was subject to popular scorn and hatred; riots broke out in Liverpool between Irish dockers and those ''who called themselves Protestants last year and 'Rationalists' to-day'' (221). Many in the Low Church deserted to Unitarianism; Methodists, however, showed fewer desertions—among them, revivalism grew.

The novelist shows a refreshing realism in placing his discussion of the consequences of the plot in a complex social matrix. Who is affected by the discovery is mediated by, among other things, intensity of religious belief, previous denominational affiliation, class position, geographical location—all matters about which Freud is silent. "What did it matter to these sturdy Nonconformists" in a fishing village in the west of England that "*savants* denied Christ? All over England the serene triumph of the Gospel, deep, deep down in the hearts of quiet people, gave the eternal lie to Schwabe and his followers. . . . Everyone came to service just the same as usual, life went on in unbroken placidity. The fishermen . . . absolutely *refused* to believe or discuss the thing. So utterly different from town people! They simply felt and knew intuitively that the statements made in the papers *must* be untrue. So . . . they ignored it." (241, 258)

Even the influence of one aspect of ideology on the ability to tolerate another is considered; for example, the effect of advocacy of women's rights on perception of the significance of the archeological discovery. Charlotte Armstrong, a novelist and rationalist—"Jesus is a great teacher"—approves of the desacralization of Christianity. Her sister Catherine Paull is head of the "World's Woman's League":

The Indian lady missionaries and doctors . . . were affiliated to it. The English and American vigilance societies for the safeguarding of girls, the women of the furtive students' duels in Russia, the Melbourne society for the supply of domestic workers in the lonely up-country stations of Australia, while having their own corporate and separate existences, were affiliated to, and in communication with, the central offices of the League in Regent Street. (273)

Miss Paull disagrees with her sister; the exposure of religious belief as an illusion will not usher in an era of toleration:

You, Charlotte, are at the moment concerned with the future and with abstractions. I am busied with the present and with *facts* . . . in my official capacity, and more, in the interests of my life work, I am bound to deplore what has happened. I deplore it grievously. . . . *We* know, here, what is going on beneath the surface. *We* are confronted by statistics and theories pale before them. (276-77)

What were the statistical facts that demolished abstract theories? Comparison of the statistics for the current month with those for the month before the discovery of Jesus's "tomb" in Palestine showed that criminal assaults against women had increased 200 percent in Wales, "scarcely less" in England, while in Ireland, "with the exception of Ulster . . . only eight percent." (278)

"But," asks a shocked Mrs. Armstrong, "is it *certain* that this is a case of cause and effect?" Miss Paull is "absolutely certain." She has received more than a thousand responses to a questionnaire, free of sectarian bias, she has sent to people interested in the work of the League all over the world. The evidence is overwhelming. Crimes against women are rampant in Europe and the United States. In New York and Chicago, consideration is being given to legalizing brothels in every city ward. The laws against polygamy in Utah are about to be repealed. Women are being flogged in the copper mines of Rhodesia, and the capitalist owners of the mines are pressing for the re-establishment of slavery ("This was the only way . . . by which the labour problem in South Africa could be solved. . . . It would be the best thing for the Kaffir, perhaps, this wise and kindly discipline. So the proposal was wrapped up"), (295). The Moslems were preaching Holy War against the Christians in the Balkans. In India, the native troops were mutinous and the pre-Christian caste system revived. Christian fanaticism, never far below the surface in sullen, mysterious Russia, had erupted, and the masses were being urged to war against England for its infidelity. The darkness was yet to deepen. In the words of a London newspaper: "The terrible seriousness of the situation need hardly be further insisted on here. Its reality cannot be more vividly indicated than by the statement of a single fact: Consols are down to sixty-five." (299)[6]

The crisis itself is not the same phenomenon to everyone. Men and women are implicated in it in different ways, and so different is the course of life from the course of logic that even those who formed the conspiracy with a clear-eyed sense of the purpose it was to achieve are puzzled, disappointed, even endangered by its unanticipated outcome. At the first news of the discovery, Schwabe was a hero to all but the religious—had he not been in the forefront of the secular rationalists? But the attitudes of everyone were changing. With consols at 65, with bread prices rising and war imminent, his investments were in danger of being wiped out. And, perversely, the people were not acting in anticipated ways. The mob was turning against anti-Christians as well as against Christians:

With an absolute lack of logic, the churches were crowded again. The most irreligious cried out for the good old times. Those who had most coarsely exulted over the broken Cross now bewailed it as the most awful of calamities. Christianity was daily being terribly avenged through the pockets and stomachs of the crowd. (307-08)

The rationalistic feminist Mrs. Armstrong is dismayed. She had always known that " 'The decisive events in the world occur in the intellect.' Yes, but how soon do they leave their parent and outstrip its poor control?" Now she knows. "There was no need for women

---

[6] Consols: consolidated annuities formed from certain British perpetual and lottery annuities bearing interest; they were in the late nineteenth century an important part of the British national debt and a symbol of national stability.

now. That was the bitterest thought of all. The movement was over—done with. A private in the Guards was a greater hero than the leader of an intellectual movement. What a monstrous *bouleversement* of everything!" Mrs. Armstrong has a strong sense of moral duty, and she is frightened by the cool detachment of Ommaney, the editor, who has only a technician's interest in events, not a moral involvement: "The highly trained journalist, to whom all life was but news, news, news, was a strange modern product which warred with her sense of what was fitting" (314-315).

Sir Michael Manichoe, former Jew, now High Church Anglican, is motivated by the highest religious principles, but his conviction is buttressed by interest. At a time when the price of consols is plummeting catastrophically, he is buying them. The only way for him to make a profit would be to prove that the discovery is a hoax, for then so great would be the relief that the price of consols would skyrocket. It is not altogether clear whether the mixture of principle and interest that motivates him is proof that cupidity is hard to expunge even among former Jews, or that, among Christians, virtue provides more than its own reward. (Freud apparently read too hastily to notice the obvious play on words, Manichoe-Manichean: Manichoe—once a Jew, now an Anglican; Manichean—Man the product of Satan but containing a spark of the light of God.)

The Byzantine corruptionists who have fabricated the monstrous plot are betrayed by the devout simplicity of the innocent. The word "Byzantine" to characterize the plotters is mine; the novelist's phrase for the conspirators is "a Sanhedrin of the great" (235). Llewellyn tells Schwabe that he has talked about the plot to his mistress, Gertrude, the Jewish music-hall actress, who has now disappeared but has been seen with Curate Gortre. Schwabe cringes in fear and anger: "The beauty of his face went out like an extinguished candle. His features grew markedly Semitic; he cringed and fawned, as his ancestors had cringed and fawned before fools in power hundreds of years back" (319). But Schwabe sees a way out; Gortre and Gertrude Hunt can be murdered. Time, however, had run out; Christianity, born of a Jew, almost destroyed by a Jew, would be saved by a former Jew. Gertrude Hunt, stricken with remorse, dying, reveals the plot to Gortre, Manichoe, and their friends, and the conspiracy quickly unravels. Ionides, the Greek workman who was bought by Llewellyn to bury the tomb confesses; Llewellyn returns to his wife, who deserts him, then in mercy returns with a Cross just as he dies; Gertrude Hunt, spiritually reborn, dies peacefully in the bosom of the church. The most sordid and contemptible fate is Schwabe's. Five years after these events, three young sisters are taken on a visit to an insane asylum. There they see Schwabe:

> On a bed lay the idiot. He had grown very fat and looked healthy. The

features were all coarsened, but the hair retained the color of dark red. He
was sleeping. . . . *It* got up with a foolish grin and began some ungainly
capers. . . .

"I liked the little man with his tongue hanging out the best," said one.

"Oh, Mabel, you've *no* sense of humor! That Schwabe creature was the
funniest one of *all!*" (389-390).

All is peaceful now in Walktown. While the idiot Schwabe grins
and capers, Mr. Byars and Helena are listening to the Sunday sermon
of her husband, Dean Gortre—"Christ is risen."

II. Clearly, there are some extraordinary differences between
Freud's reading of the novel and what the novel says. The most trivial
is that it is not, as Freud says, a novel of "Catholic origin" at all; it
is written from a High Church Anglican point of view. Was Freud
misled by the endorsement of the novel by "the Bishop of London?"
If so, then he apparently did not know, despite his great affection for
England, that there are bishops in the Anglican hierarchy as well
as in the Roman Catholic. Indeed, there is no "Bishop of London" in
the Roman Catholic hierarchy; that title is unique to the Anglican
hierarchy. The comparable Roman Catholic position is "Bishop of
Westminster."

More important, the novel does not support Freud's conclusions
(in Chapter V) as to the causes and consequences of the dissolution
of a religious group, and it clearly contradicts Freud's explicit statements about the relation between religious belief, on the one hand,
and violence or tolerance, on the other. Freud may be correct in what
he says about that relation, but he can draw no comfort from what the
novel says about it. Why did he think the novel supported his views?
Finally, and most puzzling of all, Freud is absolutely silent on the
novel's single most striking characteristic—its blatant anti-Semitism.
"No villains need be; passions spin the plot," George Meredith
wrote;[7] but the passions that spin the plot of Guy Thorne arise precisely from villainy—the villainy of Jews. What defeats that villainy
is the new-found faith of one-time Jews, Jesus of Nazareth and Gertrude Hunt, the modern Magdalene. What might account for Freud's
silence about the novel's anti-Semitism? Perhaps it was overlooked.
But why assume that it was overlooked? Perhaps Freud saw it but
chose not to comment upon it. Or perhaps he did not see it at all. What
in Freud's life might provide clues to the answer to a question which
is at once biographical and methodological, having implications for
the understanding of his character and of his work?

Some authorities have presented views of Freud that, at least on
two counts, make his silence the more puzzling. The conspiracy in the

[7] *Modern Love* (London and New York, 1892), Stanza XLIII, p. 59.

novel depends on the planting of faked archeological evidence. That the archeology of antiquity, especially sculpture, was, in Peter Gay's words, "an addiction" of Freud's is well known. One of his first forays into the psychoanalytic interpretation of literature was his essay of 1907 on the meaning of Wilhelm Jensen's novella, *Gradiva*, in which the patient-protagonist is an archeologist who sees in Rome a Pompeiian bas-relief that reminds him of a girl for whom he has borne a long-suppressed love. Freud himself bought in Rome a similar bas-relief, which he added to his collection of antiquities and placed on his wall next to a copy of Ingres's "Oedipus Interrogating the Sphinx." As Peter Gay remarks: "Collecting antiquities both freed him from his work and brought him to it. . . . It is striking, and has not gone unnoticed, that Freud liked to draw on archeology for his metaphors." In the Pantheon of those with whom, at one time or another, he compared himself was Heinrich Schliemann; the psychoanalyst is an archeologist: "Digging down from layer to layer, he seeks the buried city."[8] Freud, struck by the similarity between his own and Jensen's interests in archeology and human behavior, and perhaps nettled by Jensen's ideas about neurosis, delusions, and psychosis that Freud regarded as his own, was drawn to make inquiries of Jensen himself about the sources and meaning of his ideas.[9] Is it not at least somewhat curious that Freud's interest in a novel, published at almost the same time as *Gradiva*, ignores half of the equation of archeology and human behavior about which he was so passionate?

The same authorities comment on still another characteristic of Freud's that makes his silence in the face of the novel's anti-Semitism seem odd. "Facing up to things as they are characterizes Freud's life," Peter Gay says:

It was not easy to be a Jew in Imperial Austria, especially a Jew with aspirations. . . . Yet Freud persisted, both in doing psychoanalytical work and in calling himself a Jew. . . . A laboratory for every known species of anti-Semitism, Vienna virtually compelled Freud to see himself as one among a band of potential victims, as one among Vienna's Jews. It was a role . . . that he took upon himself with his accustomed courage. But the core of that courage was neither sectarian nor local. It was intellectual. Freud was, first and last, the scientist, bravely following the evidence wherever it led.[10]

---

[8] Peter Gay, *Freud, Jews and Other Germans* (New York, 1978), 43, 46. See also Suzanne Bernfeld, "Freud and Archeology," *American Imago,* **8** (1951), 107-28. Freud's "Delusions and Dreams in Jensen's *Gradiva*" is printed in James Strachey, ed., *The Standard Edition of the Complete Psychological Works of Sigmund Freud,* 24 vols. (London, 1953-74), IX.

[9] Ernest Jones, *The Life and Work of Sigmund Freud,* 3 vols. (New York, 1953-57), II, 343.   [10] Gay, *op. cit.,* 77.

Ernest Jones agrees with that verdict:

An overpowering need to come at the truth at all costs was probably the deepest and strongest motive force in Freud's personality, one to which everything else—ease, success, happiness—must be sacrificed. And, in the profound words of his beloved Goethe, "The first and last thing required of genius is love of truth."[11]

But if Freud was "compelled" to see himself as a Jew; if he assumed that role with his "accustomed courage"; if that courage was "intellectual" at its core; if everything was sacrificed for the "over-powering need to come at the truth"; and if the courage to sustain that need was at hand, then why was Freud so insensitive as not to see the anti-Semitism in the novel he cited to support his views, or, if he did see it, why was he silent?

III. Freud *was* a courageous man, but his feelings toward Judaism and his own Jewishness were not compounded of courage alone. They were, to say the least, complex. Though the authorities may not be sure about what kind of Jew Freud was or what being Jewish meant to him, they are sure—and cite abundant evidence—that he never denied being Jewish, that he was extremely sensitive to the fact of Jewishness, and that he often showed great courage in facing the indignities he suffered because he was Jewish and the rewards that tempted him to give up his Jewishness. He may have regarded himself, as he said in a letter to Oskar Pfister, as a "quite Godless Jew," but he charged into a group of anti-Semites, brandishing his cane, when they confronted Freud and his family returning to their hotel while on vacation in the Bavarian Alps.[12] He wrote to Barbara Low on the death of her brother-in-law, David Eder:

We were both Jews and knew of each other that we carried this miraculous thing in common, which—inaccessible to any analysis so far—makes the Jews.[13]

In reply to the Italian writer Enrico Morselli who had sent him his book on psychoanalysis and his essay on Zionism, Freud expressed some reservations about the first, none whatever about the second:

. . . your brief pamphlet on the Zionist question I was able to read without any mixed feelings, with unreserved approval, and I was pleased to see with

---

[11] Jones, *op. cit.*, I, 321. See also Friedrich Heer, "Freud, the Viennese Jew," in Jonathan Miller, ed., *Freud, the Man, his World, his Influence* (Boston and Toronto, 1972): "It is important to remember that" Freud's "acceptance of his Jewishness was made in a climate of rabid anti-Semitism" (3). But this begs the question, since the precise meaning of Freud's "acceptance of his Jewishness" is the point at issue.

[12] Jones, *op. cit.*, II, 15, 199.

[13] Quoted in Marte Robert, *From Oedipus to Moses: Freud's Jewish Identity* (Garden City, N.Y., 1976), 35.

what sympathy, humaneness, and understanding you were able to choose your point-of-view concerning this matter which has been so distorted by human passions. . . . I am not sure that your opinion, which looks upon psychoanalysis as a direct product of the Jewish mind, is correct, but if it is I wouldn't be ashamed. Although I have been alienated from the religion of my forebears for a long time, I have never lost the feeling of solidarity with my people. . . .[14]

To Ernest Jones, Freud was "pretty sensitive" to the "faintest" signs of anti-Semitism.[15] In a letter to Sandor Ferenczi on April 24, 1900, commenting on an attack against him at the Medical Society of Hamburg, he wrote: "Between the lines you can read further that we Viennese are not only swine but also Jews. But that does not appear in print."[16] Sixteen years later, commenting on an attack on psychoanalysis by Professor Franz von Luschan of Berlin, Freud wrote, "An old Jew is tougher than a Royal Prussian Teuton."[17] In the midst of the war, depressed because nothing was going well, he wrote to Karl Abraham: "The only cheerful news is the capture of Jerusalem by the English and the experiment they propose about a home for the Jews."[18] "You may be sure that if my name were Oberhuber," he wrote to Abraham, "my new ideas would despite all other factors have met with far less resistance."[19] He identified with, among countless others, the Jewish Moses (though he came to have doubts about Moses' Jewishness) and the Semitic Hannibal; the Jewish Bible was an endless source of imagery and ideas; his formal writings and letters are studded with references to Jewish jokes, Jewish stories, and Jewish history. His own view of the matter is perhaps best summed up in the address he gave on May 6, 1926, his seventieth birthday celebration, at the Vienna chapter of B'nai Brith. He had joined the Order in 1895, when, "despised and universally shunned" as a result of his earliest publications, he was "seized with a longing to find a circle of picked men of high character who would receive me in a friendly spirit. . . ." For many years he had been regularly attending the meetings on alternate Tuesdays, and he had even given lectures on "The Interpretation of Dreams" there, just as, in 1896, he gave his first public lecture on the subject at the Judisch-Akademische Lesehalle at the University of Vienna:

That we were Jews could only be agreeable to me; for I was myself a Jew, and it had always seemed to me not only unworthy but positively senseless to deny the fact. What bound me to Jewry was (I am ashamed to admit)

---

[14] *Ibid.*, 41.
[15] Jones, *op. cit.*, II, 163.   [16] *Ibid.*, II, 116.
[17] *Ibid.*, II, 119; see also *ibid.*, II, 398-99.   [18] *Ibid.*, II, 191.   [19] *Ibid.*, II, 49-50.

neither faith nor national pride. . . . But plenty of other things remained over to make that attraction of Jewry and Jews irresistible—many obscure emotional forces, which were the more powerful the less they could be expressed in words, as well as a clear consciousness of inner identity, the safe privacy of a common mental construction. And beyond this there was a perception that it was to my Jewish nature alone that I owed two characteristics that had become indispensable to me in the difficult course of my life. Because I was a Jew I found myself free from many prejudices which restricted others in the course of their intellect; and as a Jew I was prepared to join the opposition and to do without agreement with the "compact majority."[20]

But Freud's attitude toward Jews and his own Jewishness had more ingredients than the courage with which he acknowledged the emotional sources of his identity with Jews and the intellectual and characterological indebtedness he owed to Judaism. The evidence of Freud's ambivalence to Judaism and his own Jewishness is so much commented upon and is so extensive as to need no citation here for the purpose of an offer of proof, but merely to illustrate how pervasive it was, affecting, as it did, his waking life, his dream life, his personal life, his professional life, what he remembered and what he forgot. To take but a few examples, and to begin with perhaps the less important:

Freud in his writings makes no mention of Theodor Herzl and virtually no references to Zionism, yet, in his explication of his own dream, "My son, the Myops," Freud notes that shortly before having the dream he had seen a play, *Das Neue Ghetto*, which dealt with the "Jewish problem, concern about the future of one's children, to whom one cannot give a country of their own. . . ."[21] Freud does not mention that the author of the play was his fellow-Viennese, Theodor Herzl; the play is mentioned in a footnote in *The Interpretation of Dreams*, but it is not listed in the bibliography of works cited in the text—nor is the author mentioned, "an omission which hardly ever occurs," one writer says, in Freud's "numerous literary references."[22] The omission of Herzl's name seems more unusual in the light of a letter he wrote on September 28, 1902, to Herzl. On the recommendation of a member of the editorial board of the *Neue Freie Presse*, Freud sent a copy of *The Interpretation of Dreams* to Herzl to be reviewed: "But at all events"—that is, even if it should

[20] Freud's "Address to the Society of B'nai Brith" is in Strachey, *op. cit.*, XX, 273-74. See also Sigmund Freud, *The Origins of Psychoanalysis: Letters to Wilhelm Fliess, Drafts and Notes, 1887-1902* (New York, 1954), 211, 238, 267, 312; Ernst Simon, "Sigmund Freud, the Jew," *Publications of the Leo Baeck Institute, Year Book II* (1957), 276; Jones, *op. cit.*, II, 270.

[21] Quoted in Peter Loewenberg, "A Hidden Zionist Theme in Freud's 'My Son, The Myops . . .' Dream," *Journal of the History of Ideas*, XXXI (1970), 130.

[22] Simon, *op. cit.*, 274; Strachey, *op. cit.*, V, 442.

not be reviewed—"may I ask you to keep the book as a token of the high esteem which I—like so many others—have had [for] many years [for] the poet and fighter for the human rights of our People."[23]

Freud read many English novels; among them was George Eliot's *Daniel Deronda,* regarded as one of the earliest pro-Zionist novels. (The American consulate in Jerusalem is located at the intersection of Rehov Agron and Rehov George Eliot). Ernest Jones tells us that the novel "angered" Freud "by its knowledge of Jewish intimate ways that," as he said in a letter to Martha Bernays, " 'one spoke of only among ourselves.' "[24] But why was he apparently not angered by—indeed, why was he oblivious to—the anti-Semitism of Thorne's novel?

Ernest Jones has described the complicated quality of Freud's relationship to Judaism during his engagement to Martha Bernays. His future mother-in-law " 'little knows what a heathen I am going to make of you,' " he wrote to Martha. " 'She is fascinating but alien, and will always remain so to me.' " On another occasion he wrote to her: " 'They would have preferred you to marry an old Rabbi or Schochet.' " When Freud's friend Joseph Paneth married Sophie Schwab, Freud "gazed at the scene with a fascinated horror and then wrote a letter of sixteen pages describing all the odious detail in a spirit of malign mockery." During his long engagement with Martha Bernays, he considered conversion to one of the Protestant confessions because he was revolted by the thought of standing under the canopy. He spoke to Joseph Breuer about it. " 'Too complicated,' " Breuer advised. And despite the fact that Martha made it as easy as possible for him to go through the marriage ceremony, by having the wedding on a weekday so that few friends could attend, Freud, Jones says, "probably bit his lip when he stepped under the Chuppa [canopy]. . . ."[25]

The letters that Freud wrote to Karl Abraham in connection with the developing controversy with Jung are not exactly unequivocal in the expression of his attitude toward Jewishness. Was Freud being complimentary toward Judaism, or was he a bit resentful, when he wrote Abraham:

Be tolerant, and don't forget that really it is easier for you to follow my thoughts than for Jung, since to begin with, you are completely independent,

---

[23] Quoted in Leo Goldhammer, "Herzl und Freud," *Theodor Herzl Jahrbuch,* Tulo Nussenblatt, ed. (Vienna, 1937), 266-68, translated in Raphael Patai, ed., *Herzl Year Book* (New York, 1958), I, 194-96. See also Simon, *op cit.,* 274, note 13.

[24] Jones, *op. cit.,* I, 174.

[25] Jones, *op. cit.,* I, 116, 134, 140, 167; Simon, *op. cit.,* 277; Jones, *op. cit.,* I, 150; see also Robert, *op. cit.,* n. 13, 79 ff.

and then racial relationship brings you closer to my intellectual constitution, whereas he, by being a Christian and the son of a pastor, can only find his way to me against resistance. His adherence is therefore all the more valuable. I was almost going to say it was only his emergence on the scene that has removed from psychoanalysis the danger of becoming a Jewish national affair.[26]

And again, quite testily: "After all, our Aryan comrades are quite indispensable to us; otherwise psychoanalysis would fall a victim to anti-Semitism."[27]

In his dreams, too, Freud provides us with impressive evidence concerning his ambivalence toward Jewishness. In a discipline as much characterized as psychoanalysis by the desire to ferret out heterodoxy by the close examination of texts, it is striking to see such broad agreement on the interpretation of Freud's Roman dreams and on the central importance of his father to the meaning of his dreams and to his life.

Reference has already been made to "the Myops dream." "By the waters of Babylon we sat down and wept"—Freud describes the dream scene at the Porta Romana in Siena in the words of the Babylonian exile of the Jews. As to the content of the dream, the precise balancing of the son's untranslatable farewell to the woman, "Auf geseres," and his farewell to the man, "Auf ungeseres," has been taken as an expression of Freud's relief that his own son had not inherited either the physical or intellectual one-sidedness that he regarded as a Jewish constitutional trait, a one-sidedness that he had inherited from his father. If Jewish one-sidedness had not been transmitted to his son, perhaps Freud was intimating—or wishing—that the inheritance of specifically Jewish impediments had stopped with him and that he could not be accused of inflicting upon his sons the burdens his father had inflicted upon him. The burdens imposed upon him by his father were quite severe. In his explanation Freud is envious of his relatives who, years before, had escaped the anti-Semitism of the Austro-Hungarian Empire by going to England, and he remembers, quite angrily, a story his father once told him. To demonstrate that the situation of the Jews in the Empire had improved, Freud's father told the ten- or twelve-year-old Sigmund that once, years before, he had had his new fur hat knocked into the street by a Christian who had ordered him off the sidewalk. When Sigmund asked what had happened, the old man said only that he had stepped off the sidewalk to retrieve the hat from the mud. In the dream, Freud stays with his people and leaves Rome, but he was bitterly resentful of his "vague" father who "had doomed his children by leaving them no other possibility than submission to outward oppression or a

---

[26] Jones, op. cit., II, 48.   [27] Ibid., 51.

shameful inner exile." For nearly three quarters of a century Freud did not alter his judgment. As the faithful Ernest Jones tells us: "Submission was not in his nature, and his father never regained the place he had held in his esteem after the painful occasion when he told his twelve-year old boy how a Gentile had knocked off his new fur cap into the mud and shouted at him, 'Jew, get off the pavement.' "[28]

How cowardly was the behavior of the father in contrast with the brave militancy of the Carthaginian father and son, Hamilcar and Hannibal, the son bound to the father by an oath to avenge him against Rome—and so we are led to the briefest consideration of the Roman dreams. Whatever subtle differences may exist among interpreters of those dreams, there is widespread agreement that they are central to Freud's painful self-analysis and to the understanding of the Rome-Jewish polarity. Acceptance, respect, honor, fame, glory—all this was Rome, and all this Freud passionately desired. But not even the heroic Semitic Hannibal succeeded in conquering Rome by frontal assault, and so he never entered the golden city, and Freud was unwilling to pay the price of the other ticket of admission—conversion. He himself contrasted Hannibal's strategy—militant attack—with that of Johann Joachim Winckelmann, the great eighteenth-century Protestant classical scholar, who was converted to Catholicism as the price of being appointed librarian of the Vatican. Professor Carl Schorske's gloss on the Freud texts is that Freud eventually abandoned the Hannibal strategy of vengeance. Winckelmann's Rome was not Hannibal's Rome—it was "the Rome of pleasure, maternity, assimilation, fulfillment," and its capture took the course neither of conquest nor conversion, but science: "Science would have to defeat politics and lay the father's ghost."[29]

Schorske's conclusion is curious. Hannibal's road to Rome is the political; Winckelmann's is the scientific: "Not Hannibal the general, but Winckelmann the scientist." But surely the problem that was posed for both Winckelmann and Freud was not that of pursuing science, but that of deciding how high a price to pay for enjoying the kind of scientific career each one wanted to have. Winckelmann purchased his career with conversion. Freud was never willing to pay that price—he did not, therefore, follow "in the footsteps of Winckelmann"—and he never achieved the serenity over remaining Jewish that Winckelmann obtained in giving up Protestantism. Be that as it may, it is clear that a decisive element in Freud's dreams and in his life, and, following Schorske, in his professional work was his attitude

[28] Loewenberg, op. cit., 129-32; Strachey, op. cit., V, 444; Robert, op. cit., 113, 118-19; Jones, op. cit., I, 22; II, 16-18.
[29] Carl Schorske, "Politics and Patricide in Freud's Interpretation of Dreams," American Historical Review, 78 (1973), 339.

toward his father. He struggled painfully to discover his identity and
he hammered out his identity against the anvil of his father's. The
result, on the whole, is an unheroic, even somewhat contemptuous
picture of his father, and in that portrayal the story of his servile father
submissively stepping off the sidewalk plays the key role. That the
ten- or twelve-year-old Sigmund should have been disappointed is not
surprising; that, as Ernest Jones says, he never got over his disap-
pointment is somewhat surprising. Marthe Robert has pointed out that
Freud's knowledge of Jewish matters was more discursive than it was
scholarly or profound. Perhaps if his knowledge had been deeper he
would have seen his father's behavior in a different light. Freud had
available models of resistance to Roman tyranny that were more than
merely Semitic; they were specifically Jewish. There was the model
of Rabbi Akiba, for example, martyrized by the Romans for his support of the Bar Kochba rebellion. But there was also a non-violent
resistance, a spiritual resistance; after the destruction of the Temple,
Rabbi Yochanan ben Zakkai petitioned the Emperor Vespasian for,
and received, permission to establish a new center for the study of
Talmud at Yavneh. Akiba and ben Zakkai, the militant and the
accomodationist, provided two strategies for spiritual and national
survival. If Sigmund at ten or twelve thought that his father was a
coward, did he have to continue to think so when he was 30, 40, or 50?
Perhaps his father was in the mold of Yochanan ben Zakkai; one may
argue the merits of that model, but it is certainly not contemptible to
feel that at some times, in some places, it suggests a not unworthy
strategy. Why, in short, did Freud endow his father with an unchang-
ing identity, and an unworthy one at that? Had Freud's knowledge of
Jewish history been a bit deeper he might perhaps have come to
different views about his father, and therefore about himself. Identity,
the Bible tells us, is not a garment which is placed upon us at birth and
which we wear unaltered; we can through struggle and activity change
it as Freud did with his. Jacob the patriarch created a new identity in
his struggle with the Angel of Heaven, and corresponding to the new
identity he was given a new name; from Jacob the crafty, the trickster,
he became Israel: "Thou hast persevered with God and with men, and
hast prevailed." The name of Freud's father was Jacob. Why did this
not suggest to Freud that his father's identity was not fixed? Freud
changed his own name in 1878 from Sigismund, "Vienna's favorite
term of abuse in anti-Jewish jokes," to Sigmund. Schorske says that
by "reducing his own political past and present to an epiphenomenal
status in relation to the primal conflict between father and son, Freud
gave his fellow liberals an ahistorical theory of man that would make
bearable a political world spun out of orbit and beyond control." For
Freud, however, to have seen his father as not contemptible, his
father's character would have had to appear different to him—as a

consequence his own character would have had to be different. It would also follow necessarily, if Schorske is to be believed, that Freud's conclusions on the "primal conflict between father and son" would have had to be altered. In that case, the distinction between phenomenon and epiphenomenon would not be as clear, and Freud's conclusions about "primal conflict" between father and son, while less universal, would also have been less ahistorical.[30]

Marthe Robert modifies Schorske's account only slightly:

. . . if he had not avenged his father as he had sworn to by following in the footsteps of Hannibal, neither had Rome vanquished him; he had not succumbed to the spells of the mythical city, which for him was the symbol of ambition and disavowal. He had destroyed the city in his own way, by destroying the tissue of illusory images that transformed it into an inviolable site, sacred in the twofold ancient sense of the word, that is, holy, forbidden to the profane and protected by a mortal taboo.

The victory over his personal myth . . . gave him the certainty that he could now win a leading position "on the other side" without fear of disavowing himself. . . .[31]

IV. The question of Jewishness was so central to Freud's life, to his social and professional relations, to his sense of himself and his painful struggle to see himself as he was and to define his scientific program, and proved ultimately so resistant to solution, either Hannibal's or Winckelmann's, that I am sure his failure to see the anti-Semitism of Thorne's novel was not the repression of what was so

---

[30] *Ibid.*, 342, 347; Robert, *op. cit.*, 98, 106-13; Heer, *op. cit.*, note 6. Immanuel Velikovsky's contrast between Freud's interpretation of his own dreams and Velikovsky's interpretation of them hinges upon the story of Freud's father and the Christian and Freud's preference for Hannibal's militance over his father's cringing. But in Velikovsky's analysis, the point is not the struggle between militance and slavishness but Freud's feeling that his desire for unhampered advancement was being thwarted by his Jewishness. By this reading, Freud's problem arises not so much from a quality of his father—the lack of militance in affirming his Jewishness—as from a quality of his—the ambivalence he felt about how far to go in achieving the success he so desperately wanted. Immanuel Velikovsky, "The Dreams Freud Dreamed," *Psychoanalytic Review* (1941), 487-511.

[31] Robert, *op. cit.*, 130. In this matter, Robert follows Schorske closely, in my judgment too closely. "Science would have to defeat politics and lay the father's ghost," Schorsky says, referring to Freud's conquest of Rome—and of his father—by the choice of Winckelmann's road to Rome rather than Hannibal's. Freud's "Revolutionary Dream" of August 1898—seen in the political context of the German-Czech language controversy, the Galician pogroms, and growing Austrian-Magyar tension—is interpreted by Schorske in such a way as to support his conclusion that Freud's resolution of the problem of his relation with his father provided a *scientific* alternative to a *political* solution, an alternative which, moreover, allowed him to put aside the vestigial remnants of guilt he felt as a result of his earlier decision to renounce politics. One day, after actually seeing Count Franz Thun at a railway

deeply painful. Throughout his life, the pain came breaking through.[32] Perhaps then, he just forgot, but I do not think so. Freud himself would have been the first to reject the explanation of forgetfulness. In the first place, he had come across the novel, with its strident anti-Semitism, only "a short time ago." When he wrote *The Interpretation of Dreams*, he traced his enthusiasm for Hannibal to a book he had read as a child: "One of the first books that I got hold of when I learned to read was Thiers's *History of the Consulate and Empire*. I can still remember sticking labels on the flat backs of my wooden soldiers with the names of Napoleon's marshals written on them. At that time my declared favorite was already Masséna (or to give the name its Jewish form, Manasseh)."[33] It is unimportant that Freud was

---

station and being enraged by his arrogance, Freud dreamed of Thun's castigating a German student leader. Freud identified himself with Adolf Fischhof, a Jewish medical student leader in 1848; but, unlike Fischhof, had denied the possibility of combining a medical career with politics and had renounced the latter. In his dream, Freud flees the scene of the political confrontation with Thun and goes to the university. He returns to the railroad station to leave town, and sees an old blind man—his father—to whom he offers a urinal. For Schorske, the dream dissolved Freud's political impulses and his guilt at turning his back on them; Freud had taken Winckelmann's road to Rome, the "scientific" road; he "ministered" to his father and got his way: the wisdom of the choice he had made earlier in assessing Fischhof's life—the renunciation of politics for medicine—had been proved. Perhaps—but Schorske's interpretation of the dream—and his identification of Freud with Winckelmann—rests upon a strained definition of "science." To "minister" to a person in pain is not to do science, but to do good. In Freud's dream, the person in pain was his father, to whom he was saying, "Though you denied me, yet do I love you." Just as Freud never saw the possibility of his father's being in the mold of Yochanan ben Zakkai rather than Akiba, so Schorske does not see the possibility of an alternative model for Freud's behavior: not Winckelmann, but the suffering—yet loving—Jesus, with whom Freud often identified. Freud's limited knowledge of Jewish history perhaps did not allow him to see a truth about his father. Schorske's interpretation of Freud's dream does not allow him to see a truth about Freud—that he did not choose the "scientific" road to conquer both Rome and his father. Schorske, 339-42. On Fischhof, see Werner J. Cahnman, "Adolf Fischhof and his Jewish Followers," *Publications of the Leo Baeck Institute*, Yearbook IV (1959), 111-39.

[32] Consider, for example, his agony at a moment of triumph. In 1901, he was finally able to enter Rome. "It was an overwhelming experience for me," he wrote to Fliess on September 19, 1901, "and, as you know, the fulfillment of a long-cherished wish." But it was also "slightly disappointing"—and worse. He loved classical Rome, the first Rome; modern Rome, the third Rome, was likeable." Catholic Rome, based on the "lie of salvation," made him "incapable of putting out of my mind my own misery and all the other misery which I know to exist." Freud, *Origins of Psychoanalysis*, 335-36. Freud could well have been pleased by the plot in Thorne's novel to expose the "lie of salvation," but why could he not go beyond his "own misery" which, he implied, was the result of that "lie" and see that Thorne's novel made villains and victims of all Jews?

[33] Strachey, *op. cit.*, IV, 196-98.

wrong in his intimation that Masséna was Jewish; what is important is that he remembered a Jewish reference in a book he had read as a child more than 40 years before, but could not remember the blatant anti-Semitism of a novel he had read only a "short time ago." Fritz Wittels disconcerted Freud by catching him in a lapse. Was it of memory? He pointed out that Freud's reproduction of the inscription on the medallion struck by the English to memorialize the destruction of the Spanish Armada leaves out the word Jehovah. Freud's explanation of the lapse is a little lame: "The English medallion bears the deity's name in Hebrew lettering on a cloud in the background. It is so placed that it can be taken as being part either of the design or of the inscription."[34] So the name of the Jewish God was excluded because it was part of the design, not the inscription; the explanation is disingenuous, but the episode does not prove deliberate suppression.

Freud is silent, one must recall, not only about the novel's anti-Semitism, but about the fact that it does not support—indeed it contradicts—some of the statements in Chapter V for which it was introduced as proof. Ernest Jones tells a revealing story. Dr. Ludwig Jekels told him that Babinski, whom Freud knew at Charcot's clinic, heard Jekels give an address on psychoanalysis at a neurological congress in Warsaw in 1918, showed great interest, and asked him to come to Paris so that he could learn more. Jekels spoke about the matter to Freud. "Freud asked how old Babinski was, and on being told that he was of the same age as himself burst out laughing, saying, 'As old as I am, and yet you expect him to give up his theory in favor of mine!' "[35]

I am inclined to believe that someone like Freud, direct enough to comment on the difficulties created for Babinski by the contradiction between Babinski's views and his own, would have commented on the differences between Thorne's theories and his own, if he had seen them, just as he would have commented on Thorne's anti-Semitism if he had seen it.[36] Ambivalence did not lead to suppression, nor did

---

[34] Quoted in Robert, *op. cit.*, 204, n. 44.

[35] Jones, *op. cit.*, I, 239, note.

[36] In fiction in which he plays a role, Freud is more outspoken in his reaction to anti-Semitism than when he comments on fiction in which anti-Semitism is rampant. In the recent best-seller by Nicholas Meyer, *The Seven-Per-Cent Solution* (New York, 1974), Freud, in the course of treating Sherlock Holmes for cocaine addiction, takes Dr. Watson to the Maumberg Club for a game of indoor tennis. He is insulted by one of the members: "*Juden* in the Maumberg! I say, this place has gone to the dogs since I last set foot here." Imperturbable, Freud responds to the challenge of a duel by suggesting a game of tennis; of course he wins, though he is years older than his opponent. That opponent, Manfred Gottfried Karl Wolfgang Von Leinsdorf, with a "livid wicked face" and an "unsavory reputation," turns out to be the villain whom it takes the combined talents of Freud and Holmes to subdue (126, 130).

forgetfulness, to silence. I think Freud never read the novel; he may have seen a notice of it somewhere, but more likely he was told about it by someone who knew that Freud was interested in the disintegration of a church and called his attention to it on that account, but said nothing about the anti-Semitism of the novel because that was not central to his interests. And what Freud was not told about the book he did not know.

I think I am right in my conclusion, but I hope I am wrong. Suppression may be an example of human frailty. It is easy to feel sympathy for the suppression of painful emotions when those emotions follow from an ambivalence that is experienced by its victims as the tragic outcome of history. It is not so easy to feel sympathy for pretence, though that, too, is human.

Columbia University.

XII

DISRAELI, FREUD, AND JEWISH CONSPIRACY THEORIES

By L. J. RATHER

"So you see, my dear Coningsby, the world is governed by very different personages from what is imagined by those who are not behind the scenes."—*Coningsby; or, The New Generation.*

1. When Benjamin Disraeli, the future Lord Beaconsfield, placed the above words in the mouth of his fictional character, the all-powerful Jew "Sidonia," he was a member of Parliament and spokesman for the Young England group of Tories. Disraeli's words presumably startled the uninstructed reading public, just as the eccentricities of dress and behavior of this quintessential outsider become insider had once startled London society. The international Jew "Sidonia" of *Coningsby* (1844) and of its companion novel *Tancred; or, The New Crusade* (1847) is himself one of those "very different personages . . . behind the scenes." Sidonia's protégé Coningsby is—like Tancred, whom Sidonia dispatches to the Holy Land—an uninstructed young Englishman of the ruling class. Both Coningsby and Tancred learn from Sidonia something of the true nature of the moving powers in control of historic events in the great world of politics and human society. We may not find Disraeli's revelation through Sidonia to our liking today. But his dictum contains an important element of truth: to one degree or another every "world" is manipulated by insiders, and the outsider is always in danger of mistaking the image for the reality.

Less than sixty years after *Coningsby,* Sigmund Freud (1856-1939) argued that, even in the little world of human beings, hidden powers influence apparently surface-motivated thoughts and acts and that seemingly unmotivated thoughts, acts, and lapses of memory may be rationally explained by probing behind the scenes. In doing so (as has often been pointed out) Freud was elaborating in his own fashion the nineteenth-century German romantic conception of the unconscious—"the monstrous realm of the unconscious, the real inner Africa [of the soul]," as Jean Paul (Richter) wrote in *Selina, oder über die Unsterblichkeit der Seele* (1827).[1] Freud's psychological version of Sidonia's dictum has an

---

[1] Jean Paul (Johann Paul Friedrich Richter), *Werke* (7 vols.; Munich, 1960—), VI, 1182; the original reads "das ungeheure Reich des Unbewussten, dieses wahre innere Afrika." The only reference to Disraeli in Freud's collected works is to be found in *Moses and Monotheism* (1930). Freud argues that since "Moses" is an Egyptian name we are entitled to infer that Moses himself was an Egyptian. He adds: "Thus we are not in the least surprised to find it confirmed that the poet Chamisso was French by birth, that Napoleon Buonaparte, on the other hand, was of Italian extraction and that Benjamin Disraeli was indeed an Italian [*sic*] Jew, as we should expect from his name" (*Standard*

inescapable element of truth. We may prefer to discard Freud's particular revelation, but the truth remains.

Bruno Bauer suggested in 1882 that the figure of Sidonia in *Coningsby* and *Tancred* reflected Disraeli's fantasy of himself as an all-powerful ruler and leader.[2] Disraeli's novels, as will be shown below, also express his passionate desire to vindicate European Jewry, based in part on his claim for the inherent superiority of the "Hebrew race" to which he believed he belonged. Disraeli held that the continued stability of European society necessitated this vindication, for—as he argued in his political writings as well as in his fictions—if the Jews were not allowed to rise to their rightful place at the top, they would inevitably conspire from below to topple the society that had rejected them. As we shall see, Disraeli's continued insistence that the foundations of European society were being undermined by the activities of subversive secret societies largely controlled by Jews aroused widespread comment. Unfortunately for those whom he wished to vindicate, Disraeli's claims fed the imaginations of others who were hostile toward the Jews, or toward what Disraeli called the "Semitic principle" in European civilization. Freud too was motivated in part by a wish to vindicate European Jewry; he fantasized himself as an avenging Hannibal advancing on "Rome," or alternatively as the Moses of a psychoanalytic movement that would lead believers to the promised land. Disraeli was nominally a Christian, and Freud was an atheist or at least an agnostic; both men were concerned with the Jewish "race" (as they called it) rather than the Jewish religion. There is thus a parallel of sorts between the Disraelian macrocosm and the Freudian microcosm: things are not always what they seem. In the present essay some historical aspects of this parallel will be explored.

2. Freud was eventually made famous by his *Interpretation of Dreams,* first published in 1900 and followed a year later by his equally influential *Psychopathology of Everyday Life.* The second chapter of the later work, entitled "Forgetting of Foreign Words," analyzes at length a single case, that of a young Jew of academic background who found himself at a crucial point unaccountably unable to recall a certain Latin word in a frequently cited verse from the *Aeneid.* Freud tells us that while on vacation he and the young man (with whom he was already acquainted) had "drifted" into a discussion of the "social position of the race to which we both belonged." The young man, according to Freud, "bemoaned the fact that his generation was prevented from developing its talents and gratifying its desires." To point up his remarks, the young man then attempted to cite the "familiar verse . . . in which the unhappy

---

Edition of the Complete Psychological Works, translated under the editorship of James Strachey [23 vols.; London, 1953-74], XXIII, 9).

[2] Bruno Bauer, *Disraelis romantischer und Bismarcks sozialistischer Imperialismus* (1882; repr. Darmstadt, 1969), 60, 247.

Dido leaves her vengeance on *Aeneas* to posterity." The verse he had in mind was *Exoriare aliquis nostris ex ossibus ultor* ("Rise, some avenger, from my bones!" *Aeneid,* IV, 625). But try as he would, the young man could not recall the indefinite pronoun *aliquis.* After a short interval of mocking observation, Freud supplied the missing word. The young man then challenged Freud to account for the blocked flow of memory. Freud says that he gladly accepted the challenge.

Using the free association technique (described in the *Interpretation of Dreams*) in accordance with Freud's instructions, the young man first came up with the odd notion of dividing *aliquis* into *a-liquis.* This was followed by a chain of words, "reliques-liquidation-liquidity-fluid." Next he recalled "the old accusation which has been brought against the Jews again" (probably a reference to the Tisza-Eszlar affair of 1882).[3] By way of several intermediary steps, he then recalled the miraculous liquefaction of the blood of St. Januarius, said to take place on a fixed date each year at a church in Naples. Finally, he "thought of a woman from whom [he] could easily get a message that would be very annoying to us both." Freud stepped in at this point, remarking that the message, obviously, would be that the woman in question had missed her period. Surprised and astounded, the young man admitted that Freud was right; the woman was an Italian, and he had recently visited Naples in her company.

With the reader as his Watson, Freud explains:

The speaker [had] deplored the fact that the present generation of his people was deprived of its rights, and like Dido he presaged that a new generation would take upon itself vengeance on the oppressors. He therefore expressed the wish for posterity. In this moment he was interrupted by the contradictory thought: "Do you really wish so much for posterity? Just think what a predicament you would be in if you should now receive the information from the quarter you have in mind! No, you want no posterity—as much as you need it for your vengeance."[4]

Amplifying Freud's explanation somewhat, in 1957 Ernst Simon suggested that in all likelihood the young man's mistress was one of the *goyim,* hence inherently incapable of bearing a Jewish Hannibal: "Would

---

[3] The defendants, charged with blood ritual murder, were acquitted partly as a result of the testimony of Paul de Lagarde, an admitted anti-Semite. Lagarde, professor of Oriental languages at Göttingen, had been called in as an expert at the request of a Hungarian rabbi. Lagarde cited his testimony in his later writings in order to distinguish "anti-Semites" from "Jew-haters" (*Ausgewählte Schriften* [2nd ed.; Munich, 1934], 231-32).

[4] Freud, *Psychopathology of Everyday Life.* Authorized English edition, with introduction by A. A. Brill (London, 1935), 19-26. Both Freud and Brill leave the line untranslated. My version is partly based on Dryden's *Aeneid* (IV, 901): "Rise some avenger of our Libyan blood." Freud's young man was in effect substituting "Jewish" for "Libyan."

the daughter of this people, the Roman-Italian mistress, really give the Jews the man who would avenge their misfortune?"[5]

Freud's path back to the source of the blocked memory really has much in common with the method of an Auguste Dupin or a Sherlock Holmes. There the logical fallacy of reasoning from the consequent to a particular one of an indefinitely large number of antecedents is blatantly evident. But Poe and Conan Doyle, omnipotent in their fictional worlds, arrange matters so that the one path chosen always proves to be the right path. In real life the purloined letter would probably turn up in a lawyer's safe, and Watson would prove to have been daydreaming (in *The Cardboard Box,* where Holmes astounds Watson by breaking into his train of thoughts *à la* Dupin) of, say, some sexual misadventure in India long ago rather than of the futility of war as a means for settling international disputes.

Freud's stories are usually as convincing as those of Poe and Conan Doyle, although some readers may find the story of the young man of academic background an exception. But whatever the reason for the young man's inability to recall the full text of Dido's prayer for an avenging Hannibal to arise from her bones—the Carthaginian general is of course the *aliquis ultor* in question—it is clear that he harbored a fantasy of revenge against "Rome." And it is equally clear that, to Freud, this fantasy was firmly based on the fact of Jewish social repression. We are not surprised, therefore, to learn that Freud himself had harbored the same fantasy since childhood. "Hannibal and Rome symbolized for me," he had written in the *Interpretation of Dreams,* "the antithesis between the tenaciousness of the Jew and the organization of the Catholic Church." Freud added that as a boy he had been much put off by an account of his father's calmly nonaggressive response to the insult of a Christian and that he had contrasted it unfavorably with the story of Hannibal's father, Hamilcar, "who made his boy swear on the domestic altar to take vengeance on the Romans."[6]

An equally well-known verse from the *Aeneid* appears on the title page of the book that made Freud famous: *Flectere si nequeo superos, Acheronta movebo,* "If I cannot bend the powers above, I shall move the regions below," (*Aeneid,* VII, 312).[7] These words are spoken by Dido's

[5] Ernst Simon, "Sigmund Freud, the Jew," *Publications of the Leo Baeck Institute of Jews from Germany,* Year Book II (London, 1957), 301-302, n. 132.

[6] Freud, *Interpretation of Dreams.* Authorized translation of the third edition with an introduction by A. A. Brill (London, repr. 1922), 164-5. Freud was a student of the Punic Wars, yet in the first German edition (1900) of this work he called Hannibal's father "Hasdrubal." Freud's explanation of his memory lapse will be found in Brill's translation of the *Psychopathology of Everyday Life,* 250, 253.

[7] Only three citations from Vergil occur in Freud's writings, the third being *forsan et haec olim meminisse juvabit* ("Perhaps we shall rejoice some day in these memories," *Aeneid,* I, 203) in his essay "Screen Memories" (1899). All three are to be found in the

Olympian counterpart, Juno, when she sees that Carthage, the city that she had hoped would rule over the world, will inevitably—as Jove's far-reaching plans unfold—be destroyed by Rome. Ernst Simon remarked that Freud may well have been aware of Ferdinand Lassalle's earlier use of this verse, once (in 1859) as the epigraph for a political pamphlet and again (in 1863) as the closing words of a speech.[8] Aside from his use of the words as the epigraph of the *Interpretation of Dreams,* Freud also introduced them into the text of the work. There he tells us that Juno's words graphically describe the transmission of repressed material from the depths of the unconscious to the surface of the conscious mind. Freud of course left the Latin untranslated. The editors of the *Standard Edition,* aware of the needs of the new generation, render them as "If I cannot bend the Higher Powers, I shall move the Infernal Regions."[9]

Freud's *sortes Vergilianae*—those predictions of the future once made by choosing at random a passage in Vergil—are not altogether happy ones. Dido's curse on Rome is the prelude to her own immediate death and the future destruction of Carthage. Further, the verse that Freud hit on to serve as a metaphor for the return of the repressed can at best serve to picture the repressive process itself. Lassalle's use of *Flectere si nequeo superos, Acheronta movebo* is more to the point: economic, social, and political repression call forth a terroristic response from below. But here, too, doubts arise. Lassalle presumably believed that the revolution would triumph in the end. But Juno knows that her cause is doomed from the start. She may thwart Aeneas, but Rome will come into being; a Hannibal will appear in answer to Dido's prayer, but Carthage must be destroyed. Juno's words do, however, nicely fit in with the metaphorical topography of the mind explored by Jean Paul, Schopenhauer, and others long before the advent of Freud.[10]

3. According to a recent writer on the subject of secret societies, J. M. Roberts, Disraeli's insistence that far-flung international conspiracies constituted the real motive force of nineteenth-century history marks him as a "typical rather than eccentric figure" of his time.[11] (The same may be said of Disraeli's elitist, highly "racist" views, although there were of course those who objected to Disraeli's choice of race.) Disraeli's spectre began to haunt Europe four years before the *Communist Manifesto*

---

fifty-odd citations from Vergil listed in Georg Buchmann's *Geflügelte Worte* (9th ed.; Berlin, 1898).

[8] Ernst Simon, "Sigmund Freud, the Jew," 305.

[9] Freud, *Standard Edition of the Complete Psychological Works,* V, 608.

[10] An English physician, Henry Maudsley, wrote in 1867 that the "results of the mind's unconscious workings flow, as it were, from unknown depths into consciousness." For similar references to mental topography in Jean Paul, Schopenhauer, Schelling, and Kant, see L. J. Rather, *The Dream of Self-Destruction: Wagner's "Ring" and the Modern World* (Baton Rouge, 1979), 110-15.

[11] J. M. Roberts, *The Mythology of the Secret Societies* (London, 1972), 1-11.

(1848) of Marx and Engels laid it down that class struggle, now hidden, now open, was the true motive force of all social history. In *Coningsby,* Disraeli's Sidonia tells his young English protégé of his various intrigues with the Russian minister of finance and with sundry Prussian, French, and Spanish ministers and presidents (all of whom, Sidonia claims, are Jews). Sidonia concludes this lesson with the dictum stated above: "So you see, my dear Coningsby, that the world is governed by very different personages to [*sic*] what is imagined by those who are not behind the scenes."[12]

Sidonia's pronouncement to Coningsby first appeared as an epigraph on the title page of Gougenot des Mousseaux's *Le Juif, le judaïsme et la judaïsation des peuples chrétiens* in 1869. This book, at least according to its author, attacked not the European Jews themselves but rather the baneful influence of "Pharisaic orthodoxy" and the "savage and unsociable tradition of the Talmud" on the Christian peoples of Europe, the French in particular.[13] (Like his German contemporary Paul de Lagarde, des Mousseaux tried to distinguish anti-Semites from Jew-haters.[14]) Fifty years later, in her still widely-read work *Secret Societies and Subversive Movements,* Nesta Webster's epigraph is a pronouncement made by Disraeli in a speech before the House of Commons on July 14, 1856: "It is useless to deny, because it is impossible to conceal, that a great part of Europe—the whole of Italy and France and a great portion of Germany, to say nothing of other countries—is covered with a network of these secret societies."[15]

Sidonia's (as well as Disraeli's) twin obsession is the purity and superiority of the race to which he believes he belongs. Leaving aside a few desert Arabs, says Sidonia, the "Hebrew race" is the only one of the "Caucasian races" that has kept its blood pure; it boasts "the most ancient, if not the only, unmixed blood that dwells in cities." The Hebrews are "the aristocracy of Nature," we read further. Sidonia instructs his protégé as follows:

No penal laws, no physical tortures, can effect that a superior race should be

---

[12] Disraeli, *Coningsby; or, The New Generation* (Leipzig, 1844), 234.

[13] Gougenot des Mousseaux, *Le Juif, le judaïsme et la judaïsation des peuples chrétiens* (2nd ed., Paris, 1886), 128. The first edition of 1869 is said to have been bought up in its entirety and destroyed (*ibid.,* v).

[14] See note 3 above. *The Jewish Encyclopedia* (12 vols.; New York, 1901-1906) states that the term "anti-Semitism" *(anti-Semitismus)* was coined in 1879 by Wilhelm Marr (*ibid.,* I, 641-2). Not all "anti-Semites" accepted the distinction made by Lagarde, however. Under German National Socialism it was thrown overboard: "This term [anti-Semitism] is incorrect insofar as the defense is directed against the *Jews,* and not against the Semitic peoples who do not belong to Judaism" (Theodor Fritsch, *Handbuch der Judenfrage* [32nd ed.; Leipzig, 1933], 504).

[15] Nesta H. Webster. *Secret Societies and Subversive Movements* (2nd ed.; London, 1924), iv.

absorbed in an inferior, or be destroyed by it. The mixed persecuting races disappear; the pure persecuted race remains. At this moment, in spite of centuries, of tens of centuries, of degradation, the Jewish mind exercises a vast influence on the affairs of Europe. . . . You never observe a great intellectual movement in Europe in which the Jews do not greatly participate. The first Jesuits were Jews: that mysterious Russian Diplomacy which so alarms Western Europe is organized and principally carried on by Jews; that mighty revolution which is at this moment preparing in Germany, and which will in fact be a second and greater Reformation . . . is entirely developing under the auspices of Jews, who almost monopolise the professorial chairs of Germany.[16]

Disraeli's Sidonia—whose name, by accident or design, inevitably recalls Vergil's "Sidonia Dido"—warns Coningsby that Jewish patience has its limits. If prevented from developing his talents and gratifying his desires, the Jew will not "tamely continue under a system that seeks to degrade him." He will turn against the establishment, armed with the purse and the vote:

The Tories lose an important election at a critical moment; it is the Jews who come forward to vote against them. The Church is alarmed at the scheme of a latitudinarian university and learns with relief that funds are not forthcoming for its establishment; a Jew immediately advances and endows it. Yet the Jews, Coningsby, are essentially Tories. Toryism is indeed but copied from the mighty prototype which has fashioned Europe. And every generation they must become more powerful and more dangerous to the society which is hostile to them.[17]

Flectere si nequeo superos, Acheronta movebo, Disraeli might have added.

Sidonia's views were too close to Disraeli's heart to be expressed in a work of fiction alone. Seven years after the publication of *Coningsby* he spelt them out in his biography of Lord George Bentinck (champion of the political emancipation of English Jews and Catholics). In a chapter entitled "The Jewish Question" Disraeli makes the following six points: (1) "The Jews [are] a superior race [and] shall never be destroyed or absorbed by an inferior." (2) "The Jews . . . are a living and the most striking evidence of the falsity of that pernicious doctrine of modern times, the natural equality of man . . . , a principle which, if it were

---

[16] *Coningsby; or, The New Generation,* 204, 232. According to Sidonia, the Jews almost monopolize European music: "Almost every great composer, skilled musician, almost every voice that ravishes you . . . spring[s] from our tribes. . . . There is not a company of singers, not an orchestra in a single capital, that are not crowded with our children under the feigned names which they adopt to conciliate the dark aversion which your posterity will some day disclaim with shame and disgust" (*ibid.,* 235).

[17] *Ibid.,* 231-32. The words *Sidonia Dido,* i.e., "Dido of Sidon," occur in three passages in the *Aeneid* (I, 446; I, 613; XI, 74), "Sidonian" being used here by synecdoche for "Phoenician." Hence, although Dido came from Tyre, she is often referred to as Sidonia. Disraeli might have recalled the seventh Duke of Medina Sidonia, who led the Spanish Armada to its downfall in 1588. For the poetic use of Sidonia as Phoenician, see Harper's *Latin Dictionary* (New York, 1889), s.v. Sidon; also Ovid, *Metamorphoses,* XIV, 80.

possible to act on it, would deteriorate the great races and destroy all the genius of the world." (3) "The native tendency of the Jewish race, who are justly proud of their blood, is against the doctrine of the equality of man." (4) "Persecution, . . . although unjust, may have reduced the modern Jews to a state almost justifying malignant vengeance. They may have become so odious and so hostile to mankind, as to merit for their present conduct, no matter how occasioned, the obloquy and ill-treatment of the communities in which they dwell." (5) "Destruction of the Semitic principle, extirpation of the Jewish religion, whether in the Mosaic or Christian form, the natural equality of man and the abrogation of property, are proclaimed by the secret societies, and men of the Jewish race are found at the head of every one of them. The people of God co-operate with atheists; the most skillful accumulators of property ally themselves with communists; the peculiar and chosen race touch the hands of all the scum and low castes of Europe!" (6) "Thus . . . the persecution of the Jewish race has deprived European society of an important conservative element and added to the destructive party an influential ally."[18]

The thesis that a civilization or culture can maintain its integrity only so long as the dominant race which created that culture maintains its blood purity is laid down in both *Tancred* and *Lord George Bentinck.* Anticipating Gobineau's racist theories in the *Essai sur l'inégalité des races humaines* (1853-55), Sidonia answers his own question as to the cause of the various declines and falls that litter the course of world history: "Why do not the Ethiopians build another Thebes," he asks in *Tancred,* "or excavate the colossal temples of the cataracts?" And he replies: "The decay of a race is an inevitable necessity, unless it lives in the desert and never mixes its blood."[19] In *Lord George Bentinck,* Disraeli tells us that if ever the founders of the "great Anglo-Saxon republic" in North America should "secede from their sound principles of reserve and mingle with their negro and coloured populations . . . , they would become so deteriorated that their states would probably be reconquered and regained by the aborigines, whom they expelled." After informing his English disciples that France, Spain and Germany are declining, Sidonia explains why England still flourishes, warning that it too may one day be relegated to the dust-bin of history:

A Saxon race, protected by its insular position, has stamped its diligent and methodic character on the century. And when a superior race, with a superior

---

[18] Disraeli, *Lord George Bentinck: A Political Biography* (4th ed.; London, 1852), 452-507, *passim.* Disraeli asserts that the "Iberian Jews," his ancestors, were of Punic blood (*ibid.,* 502). *Cf.* Dryden's translation of Dido's call for an avenger, in note 4 above.

[19] *Tancred; or The New Crusade* (2 vols.; Leipzig, 1847), I, 171.

idea to Work and Order advances . . . we shall perhaps follow the example of the desolate countries. All is race; there is no other truth.[20]

This slogan, "All is race; there is no other truth," was made notorious in Germany by Houston Stewart Chamberlain (1855-1927), who freely acknowledged Disraeli as his teacher. Although Chamberlain rejected any belief in "pure" races, he told the Germans in 1899 to learn from Disraeli that "race is all, that there is no other truth, that every race that carelessly suffers its blood to be ruined will go under." But closer on the heels of Disraeli came the former Marxist and pioneer Zionist Moses Hess (1812-75). Parodying the *Communist Manifesto,* Hess wrote in 1862: "All history has hitherto been motivated by race struggle and class struggle. . . . The race struggle is primary and the class struggle is secondary." Much as Freud would do forty years later, Hess designated the contending factions in nineteenth-century Europe as "Rome" and "Jerusalem." Like Disraeli, Hess insisted that a Jew is a Jew "by virtue of his racial origin, even though his ancestors may have become apostates." The Jews, Hess stated, are "a people, *one* people" *(ein Volk, Ein Volk).*[21]

Disraeli's unrestrained praise of the virtues of the "Hebrew race"

---

[20] *Tancred,* I, 169; *Lord George Bentinck,* 496. Echoes of this passage from *Tancred* can be made out in Wilhelm Ostwald's boast of 1914 that "[we], or rather the Germanic race, have discovered the factor of Organization. Other peoples [specifically, the foes of Germany in the Great War] still live under the regime of individualism. . . . The stage of Organization is a more advanced stage of Civilization" (Romain Rolland, *Above the Battle,* trans. C. K. Ogden [Chicago, 1916], 111). Still another echo, this time from *Lord George Bentinck,* is audible in the claim that the "racially pure and still unmixed Teuton of the American continent has risen to become its master; he will remain master as long as he does not fall victim to blood-pollution" *(Blutschande),* in Adolf Hitler, *Mein Kampf* (Munich, 1939), 313-34. Cf. the biologically "racist" theory of human history in general set forth in 1863 by Hippolyte Taine: "In every case the mechanism of human history is the same. We always find as the mainspring *(ressort primitif)* some very general disposition of the mind and soul, either innate, and naturally attached to the race *(race),* or acquired, and produced by some circumstances acting on the race." Taine describes "race" as the sum of the "innate and hereditary dispositions" that distinguish one people from another, as sharply as do inherited differences of temperament and bodily structure. He finds that the literature of the Aryan races *(les races aryennes)* tends toward the symbolic, metaphysical, and universal, and is thus capable of "rallying about itself the tenderness and enthusiasm of all humanity" *(du genre humain).* In contrast, the literature of the Semitic races *(les races sémitiques)* tends toward the nonmetaphysical and the particular, so that their poetry is often no more than "a series of vehement and grandiose exclamations" that invites man to the exercise of "unchecked passion and limited, fanatic action." Taine adds: "It is in this interval between the particular representation and the universal conception that the germs of the greatest human differences are found" *(Histoire de la littérature anglaise,* [5 vols., 10th ed.; Paris, 1899], I, xx-xiii, my translation).

[21] Moses Hess, *Rom und Jerusalem: die letzte Nationalitätsfrage* (Tel Aviv, 1935), 26-27, 119. For this and other citations from Chamberlain's writings, see L. J. Rather, *The Dream of Self-Destruction,* passim.

annoyed some of his contemporaries and amused others. The young
George Eliot (1819-80) belonged to the first group. Then twenty-nine
years old and known only for her translation of David Strauss's skeptical
Life of Jesus (1846), she wrote in 1848: "The fellowship of race, to which
Disraeli exultingly refers the munificence of Sidonia, is so evidently an
inferior impulse which must ultimately be superseded that I wonder that
even he, the Jew as he is, dares to boast of it. My Gentile nature kicks
most resolutely against any assumption of superiority in the Jews. . . .
Everything *specifically* Jewish is low grade." Six years earlier she had
written to her father that, while the teachings of Jesus were "worthy of
admiration," in her opinion the "system of doctrines . . . drawn as to its
materials from Jewish notions [is] most dishonorable to God and most
pernicious in its influence on individual and social happiness."[22]

Nevertheless, whatever her later views on the subject of race, George
Eliot's *Daniel Deronda* (1876) is, if anything, biased in favor of rather
than against things Jewish. Aside from the eccentric but admirable musician Klesmer and the equally admirable Miss Arrowpoint, the Gentiles
who people this novel are villainous (the depraved English aristocrat
Henleigh Grandcourt and his parasite Mr. Lush), morally "low grade"
(Grandcourt's first mistress, and the aptly named Miss Harleth who sells
herself to Grandcourt at the expense of his first mistress), or mere ciphers.
The Jews, on the contrary, are, or are at least meant to be, noble and
charismatic (Deronda himself, Mordecai, Kalonymous) or humanly appealing (Mirah, Mordecai's rather overdone adopted family of pious
industrious English Jews).[23] Deronda's Jewish mother, who vanished from
his life after arranging for him to be raised ignorant of his heritage in
an aristocratic milieu, is the exception perhaps, but then she was motivated as much by hatred of her own faith as she was by the desire to
pursue her career as an opera singer unencumbered by a child.[24]

Thackeray, George Eliot's slightly older contemporary, responded to
Disraeli's claims with good-natured ridicule. Thus the "Codlingsby" of
his burlesque of *Coningsby:*

Over the entire world spreads a vast brotherhood, suffering, silent, scattered,
sympathizing, *waiting*—an immense Free-Masonry. Once this world-spread
band was an Arabian clan—a little nation alone and outlying amongst the
mighty monarchies of ancient time. . . . Yes, the Jewish city is lost to Jewish

---

[22] *The George Eliot Letters,* ed. Gordon S. Haight (6 vols.; New Haven, 1954), I, 128,
246-7.

[23] "Klesmer" himself may be of Jewish descent: George Eliot probably borrowed this
unique name from the "klezmer" music of East European Jews.

[24] Daniel Deronda shares Sidonia's sense of mission. Deronda's mother, the renegade
Jewess, may owe something to Disraeli's grandmother Sarah de Gabay, said to have been
a beautiful and ambitious woman "who hated the race she belonged to," quoted by
Frederick Greenwood, one of Disraeli's biographers (see art. "Beaconsfield," *Encyclopaedia Britannica,* [11th ed., 1910-11], 2, 563-71).

men; but have they not taken the world in exchange? Mused thus Godfrey de Bouillon, Marquis of Codlingsby.

Disguised as an old-clothes man, Codlingsby's Sidonia (christened "Mendoza" by Thackeray, probably with malice aforethought) then appears on the scene. After a short conversation, Mendoza—who proves to be immensely rich and a superb athlete to boot, capable of polishing off an English tough with his fists and of consoling his widow with a thick roll of banknotes—takes Codlingsby to his luxuriously outfitted home. Lighting his Turkish pipe with a thousand-pound note from a bundle of the same on a piano, Mendoza informs Codlingsby that Jenny Lind, Rossini, and Carl Maria von Weber are (or were) Jews. So also are the Pope of Rome and the exiled king of France, Louis-Philippe. With some shame Mendoza admits that his own blood is not entirely pure. For he is a lineal descendant of Ivanhoe the Saxon: it seems that Ivanhoe, after the death of Rowena, married the beautiful Rebecca and became "a rabbi of some note in the synagogue of Cordova."[25]

Disraeli's continued harping on the theme "all is race" and his warning that unless the Jews of Europe were given their rightful place at the top they would destroy society from below drew a sharp response from *Punch* in the eighteen-fifties: "Well! The Jews, it seems, are conscious of their ill-treatment. *They* join secret societies. *They* . . . topple over thrones with delight. . . . *'All is race.'* What a picture of cool malignity is this! Shadrach luxuriates in locking up the Frank in a sponging-house; he charges him for the 'Semitic Element' and sticks it on the chops and sherry."[26] On March 24, 1874, Cosima Wagner remarked coolly in her diary: "I read some quotations today from a novel [*Coningsby*] by Disraeli—how he claims for Israel all the great men in art, science, even religion (the first Jesuits, he says, were Jews). A very curious phenomenon." Four years later she and Richard Wagner are reading *Tancred*: "We have to laugh over Disraeli's glorification of the Jews. 'I have an idea what he is getting at,' says R., 'racial purity and great men; that ruling genius I dreamed about—only the Jews could produce him.' Yes-

---

[25] William Makepeace Thackeray (1814-63), "Codlingsby," *Works* (22 vols.; Boston, 1899), VI, 15-28. Disraeli's admiring biographer says that in 1835 Disraeli was publicly called "a liar" by one of his early political sponsors, Daniel O'Connell, and he himself admits that on occasion Disraeli could be "daringly mendacious." The Disraelis claimed descent from an ennobled family of Spanish Jews who had fled from Torquemada ("Beaconsfield," *Encyclopaedia Britannica*, 11th ed.). "Mendoza," we may suppose, plays on the Spanish word *mendosa* (mendacious). Perhaps Thackeray was merely alluding to the betrothal, in 1565, of the 7th Duke of Medina Sidonia to Ana de Silva y Mendoza (see art. "Medina Sidonia," *Encyclopaedia Britannica*, 11th ed., XVIII, 66). On Bernard Shaw's choice of the name "Mendoza" for his race-proud English Jew (in *Man and Superman*), see L. J. Rather, *The Dream of Self-Destruction*, 164.

[26] Charles L. Graves, *Mr. Punch's History of Modern England* (4 vols.; London, 1921-22), I (covering the period 1841-57), 109.

terday R. called himself a 'tattooed savage.'" (In *Tancred*, Disraeli, following a hint given out by his father, has Sidonia comment that after all the bishops of England are only a few centuries removed from "tattooed savages.") We have seen the enthusiasm with which Houston Stewart Chamberlain took up Disraeli's phrase, "All is race; there is no other truth" (wrongly tracing it to *Coningsby*), in 1899. In 1915 the then prime minister of England, Mr. Asquith, recalled Disraeli's words in commenting on the proposal of Sir Herbert Samuel to turn Palestine into a Jewish state: "It reads almost like a new edition of *Tancred* brought up to date . . . , a curious illustration of Dizzy's favourite maxim that 'race is everything,' etc."[27] And in 1936 Disraeli's phrase was given an ironic twist by Klaus Mann in his anti-Nazi novel *Mephisto:* one of the characters remarks bitterly that, for the Nazi ideologues, " 'Race' [is] the only objective truth."[28]

The above lines from *Punch* are taken from Charles L. Graves's *Mr. Punch's History of Modern England* (1921-22). In citing them Graves refers to a "strange passage in Disraeli's 'Life of Lord George Bentinck' foreshadowing the role of world revolutionaries assigned to the Jews in the recent much discussed Jewish Protocol."[29] This juxtaposition of the forged "Protocols of the Wise Men of Zion" and Disraeli's writings makes a valid point. It was to Disraeli that many later Jewish-conspiracy theorists and race ideologues often turned for support. The "Protocols" themselves have been variously traced to a fantastic novel by Hermann Goedsche, written in German sometime in the early eighteen-sixties and later published in Russian translation, to Maurice Joly's attack on the Machiavellianism of Napoleon III, the *Dialogue aux enfers entre Machiavel et Montesquieu, ou la politique de Machiavel aux xix. siècle* (1864), or to a combination of both.[30] Nesta Webster, for her part, cited parallels to the "Protocols" from documents of two subversive secret societies, the *Haute Vente Romaine* and Bakunin's *Alliance Sociale Démocratique,*

---

[27] *Cosima Wagner's Diaries*. Edited and annotated by Martin Gregor-Dellin and Dietrich Mack; trans. with an introduction, postscript and additional notes by Geoffrey Skelton (2 vols.; New York, 1976-77), I, 744, 808, 1121; II, 211-12. Asquith's remark is cited in Nesta Webster, *The Surrender of an Empire* (3rd ed.; London, 1931), 352.

[28] Klaus Mann, *Mephisto,* trans. Robyn Smyth (New York, 1977), 204. It was common knowledge at the time that Chamberlain was Hitler's favorite bedside reading. Klaus Mann's irony is almost surely deliberate. His mother, Katja Pringsheim, was Jewish by descent (her father was the well-known Wagnerian Alfred Pringsheim), and his father, Thomas Mann, had, in 1906, ironically equated the German and the Jewish concern with "race" and "racial revenge" in his long-suppressed short story *Wälsungenblut.* Cf. L. J. Rather, "The Masked Man[n]: Felix Krull is Siegfried," *The Opera Quarterly,* 2 (1984), 67-75.

[29] *Mr. Punch's History of Modern England,* I, 109.

[30] Herman Bernstein, *The History of a Lie* (New York, 1921), 3, 17; *The Truth About "The Protocols of Zion": A Complete Exposure* (New York, 1935), xiii, 260, 371. The latter book is fully documented.

and traced their ultimate source to the late eighteenth century *Illuminati* of Bavaria.[31]

4. Before returning to Freud and his "movement," we take note of two politically tendentious fictions published in America in the last decade of the nineteenth century. They are Ignatius Donnelly's *Caesar's Column: A Story of the Twentieth Century* and William Hope Harvey's *A Tale of Two Nations*.[32] Donnelly (1831-1901) was a former lieutenant governor of Minnesota and a congressman (1863-69) from the same state, a foe of Eastern banking interests, a powerful advocate of agrarian reform, and a chief founder (1892) of the Populist party. Harvey (1851-1936) too was a Populist. He was also an advocate of bimetallism, i.e., of the free coinage of silver, who is said to have given the impetus to William Jennings Bryan's "cross of gold" speech during the presidential campaign of 1896.

Donnelly's anti-Utopian *Caesar's Column* was first published in 1891. In view of its gloomy prognosis we might be inclined to retitle it "1988," which is the year of its fictional action. Whether Donnelly had in mind Disraeli's *Coningsby* and *Tancred* when he wrote is an open question. However this may be, *Caesar's Column* can be read as an extrapolation of Disraeli's fictions. In New York City, as indeed almost everywhere else in the world, the Jewish bankers and their allies have won total control. How this came about is explained to an untutored visitor from Switzerland (oddly enough the only place left untouched by the money-men):

The task which Hannibal attempted, so disastrously, to subject the Latin and mixed-Gothic races of Europe to the domination of Semitic blood, as represented in the merchant-city of Carthage, has been successfully accomplished in these latter days by the cousins of the Phoenicians, the Israelites. The nomadic children of Abraham have fought and schemed their way, through infinite depths of persecution, from their tents on the plains of Palestine, to a power higher than the thrones of Europe. The world is today Semitized. The children of Japhet lie prostrate at the feet of the children of Shem; and the sons of Ham bow humbly before their august dominion.[33]

"Rome" has at last succumbed to the Carthage-surrogate "Jerusalem." At the head of the financial oligarchy stands a Rothschild-like figure, Prince Cabano by name, whose luxurious palace is reminiscent

---

[31] Nesta Webster, *World Revolution: The Plot Against Civilization* (London, 1921), 296-307; *idem, Secret Societies and Subversive Movements*, 408-44.

[32] See Richard Hofstadter, *The Paranoid Style in American Politics and Other Essays* (New York, 1966), 293-97 for additional comment on these two novels. For detailed study of Freud's faulty reading of still another "Jewish conspiracy" fiction, Guy Thorne's *When It Was Dark* (New York/London, 1906), see Sigmund Diamond, "Sigmund Freud, His Jewishness, and Scientific Method: The Seen and the Unseen as Evidence," *JHI,* 43 (1982), 613-34.

[33] Ignatius Donnelly, *Caesar's Column: A Story of the Twentieth Century,* ed. Walter B. Rideout (Cambridge, Mass., 1960), 98.

of the London residence to which we have seen Thackeray's Mendoza conduct the burlesque counterpart of Coningsby. Another Disraelian touch is evident in that the Jews and their allies comprising the financial oligarchy are themselves threatened from below by an underground organization, "the Brotherhood of Destruction," masterminded by "a Russian Jew . . . , a man of great ability, power and cunning." The military leader of this organization is a "man of great stature" known as Caesar Lomellini (possibly Bakunin). For the time being the rebels have been kept in check by an army of mercenaries, whose airships sail "like great foul birds" over the heads of the insurgents, dropping bombs and poison gas. Donnelly's fiction ends with an air war that leaves Western civilization in a shambles: Caesar's column proves to be an immense heap of skulls. The Russian Jew flies to Palestine with ten million dollars in stolen treasure; there he will "revive the ancient splendor of the Jewish race, in the midst of the ruins of the world." The visitor from Switzerland flies to Uganda with a young woman whom he rescued from Prince Cabano's seraglio; there he founds a populist republic in which usury is forbidden by law. So much for 1988.[34]

William Hope Harvey's novel, which is probably not devoid of some factual basis, has as its theme a plot to abolish bimetallism in the United States of America and thereby to reduce that country to servitude under England (which had been on the gold standard since 1816). The action begins in 1869, and the plotters are two immensely wealthy English bankers. They are "Baron Rothe" and "Sir William Cline." The latter is not Jewish, and he has at least the rudiments of a conscience. Not so Baron Rothe, who is "of Semitic origin." The Baron hopes to make "his country [England] supreme over all the earth," after which "*he* would dictate to nations, while prince and pauper uncovered in humble submission before the power of his gold." Their chosen tool is the American Senator John Arnold (presumably named after America's most infamous traitor), whom the Baron's beautiful daughter Edith intuitively recognizes as a man who, if handled properly, is up for sale. The Senator is duly, if subtly, bribed. But he fails to accomplish his traitorous mission quickly enough. The Baron then sends his nephew Victor Rogasner to Washington, D.C., to spur the Senator on. Arnold proves unexpectedly recalcitrant. "With a baleful light of hatred . . . in his black eyes," Rogasner vows to "destroy the last vestige of national prosperity among them [the Americans], and humble that accursed pride with which they refer to their revolutionary ancestors to the very dust." But he falls in love with John Arnold's beautiful ward Vivian Grace, and he is sorrowfully reproached by his own brother: "An American and a Christian. . . . Are there not women of our own race beautiful enough?" To which Victor (an assimilationist) replies: "As for the blood, it is soon lost in that

---

[34] *Ibid., passim.*

current which has changed but little with the ages." Complications multiply, Victor's machinations are exposed before Vivian, and he loses her and suffers a stroke. "Cleansed" somewhat by his stroke, Victor is nursed thereafter by his former mistress and secret agent, Jeanne Souileffsky, a "splendid Russo-Jewess woman" who "might have been Rebecca solicitous over Ivanhoe."[35]

Connelly's Prince Cabano and Harvey's Baron Rothe are very much in the tradition of Disraeli's Sidonia, and the atmosphere of *A Tale of Two Nations* is very much that of Disraeli's world "behind the scenes." One might in addition be tempted to speculate that Baron Rothe's desire to make "his country supreme over all the earth," as well as Rogasner's vow to humble the pride of the Americans who had revolted against English rule a century earlier may have owed something to rumors reaching Harvey's ears. For the first (1877) of Cecil Rhodes's seven wills calls for the founding of a secret society with the aim of (in Rhodes's words) the "extension of British rule throughout the world . . . [and] the ultimate recovery of the United States of America as an integral part of the British Empire." And in 1891 Rhodes, the journalist William T. Stead, and Reginald Baliol Brett (confidant of Victoria, and later of Edward VII and George V) met in London to organize the projected secret society. Lord Nathan Rothschild was named the trustee of Rhodes's fortune in that same year.[36]

5. But what have Freud and Freudian psychoanalysis to do with secret societies and subversive movements? There was indeed a Freudian secret society. As Ernest Jones tells the story in his biography of Freud, the early defections of Carl Jung, Alfred Adler, and Wilhelm Stekel from the ranks of Freud's loyal adherents had a profoundly disturbing effect on the faithful. Jones therefore proposed to Freud in 1912 that a small group of the "Old Guard"—Napoleon, incidentally, was another of Freud's military heroes—be charged with the task of watching over the three fundamental dogmas of Freudian analysis, namely repression, the unconscious, and infantile sexuality. Jones says that the idea of forming a brotherhood of initiates came to him from his boyhood memories of "many secret societies from literature." Freud, who took to the idea with enthusiasm, emphasized that the committee of guardians "would have to be *strictly secret* in its existence and actions." In addition to Jones (the one non-Jew) and Freud himself, the chosen were Hanns Sachs, Karl Abraham, Sandor Ferenczi, and Otto Rank. Freud, who wore a gold ring set with an intaglio of the head of Zeus (or Jupiter, as Jones says), gave each of the five men an antique Greek intaglio of the head to be

---

[35] William Hope Harvey, *A Tale of Two Nations* (Chicago, 1894), 1, 21, 32, 69, 265, 297 and *passim*.

[36] Carroll Quigley, *The Anglo-American Establishment from Rhodes to Cliveden* (New York, 1981), 3, 33, 35.

mounted on a gold ring. The ceremony of the ring took place in 1913. Seven years later Freud took Max Eitingon into the fellowship of the ring. (Sandor Ferenczi and Otto Rank broke with Freud in 1923: Jones puts it that the two men "developed psychotic manifestations that revealed themselves in, among other ways, a turning away from Freud and his doctrines."[37]) Hanns Sachs gives a similar account of the founding of the secret society, in a chapter entitled "Seven Rings," of his reminiscences, *Freud, Master and Friend*.[38]

Simon, in his revealing paper of 1957 on Sigmund Freud as a Jew, speaks of a "covenant" kept by the brotherhood of the seven rings. "In more than one sense," Simon says, "we have here a parallel to Ahad Ha'Am's, the Zionist thinker's, secret society, named 'The Sons of Moshe.'" He adds that Freud termed Judaism a "compulsive neurosis" in 1907, that Freud identified himself with Moses and had once hoped that Carl Jung would be his Joshua to enter the promised land barred to Freud, and finally that Freud's father came from a Hassidic milieu and Freud himself was a "Mithnaged," an inverted Hassid.[39] A year later appeared David Bakan's *Sigmund Freud and the Jewish Mystical Tradition*, in which a case was made for Freud's debt to the Kabbala. According to Bakan, the hidden message of Freud's celebrated essay on the Moses of Michelangelo was that an "excess of the Mosaic-type Law made for neurosis." Freud, says Bakan, opposed "the Mosaic tradition, most fully expressed in Jewish orthodoxy."[40] In asserting that excessive concern with Jewish religious law "made for neurosis," Bakan was echoing Freud himself.

The well-known American neurologist Percival Bailey observed in his 1960 attack on the validity of psychoanalysis that Ernest Jones's reference to the "secret societies of literature" in connection with the

[37] Ernest Jones, *The Life and Work of Sigmund Freud* (3 vols.; New York, 1955), II, 152-54; III, 45. Although Freud does not mention Richard Wagner's *The Ring of the Nibelung* anywhere in his writings, he no doubt knew of the dwarf Alberich's power-conferring gold ring and the hatred of this erstwhile "Lord of the Ring" (*des Ringes Herrn*) in Wagner's music drama for the god Wotan, who had robbed him of it. Wagner's *Meistersinger* was greatly admired by Freud, and, oddly enough, Hanns Sachs and Richard Wagner (the psychiatrist, not the composer) were among the seven auditors of Freud's 1906 series of lectures on psychoanalysis.

[38] Hanns Sachs, *Freud, Master and Friend* (Cambridge, Mass., 1944). Freud's seven rings will remind some readers of J. R. R. Tolkien's motto in *The Lord of the Rings:* "Seven [rings] for the Dwarf-lords in their halls of stone/ . . . One ring to rule them all." Tolkien certainly borrowed from Wagner, and it is at least conceivable that he had Freud in mind as well.

[39] Simon, "Sigmund Freud, the Jew" (see note 5 above), 295, 298-99. Jones, too, mentions Freud's self-identification with Moses and his hope that Jung would be "the Joshua destined to explore the promised land of psychiatry" (*The Life and Work of Sigmund Freud*, II, 33).

[40] David Bakan, *Sigmund Freud and the Jewish Mystical Tradition* (New York, 1958), 72, 77-78, 129, 136.

seven guardians of Freudian orthodoxy was very much to the point. Citing Simon's paper on Freud in support of his own contention that Freudian psychoanalysts constitute a pseudo-religious sect, always striving for perfect orthodoxy among believers, Bailey argued that the neophyte psychoanalyst, guided by an experienced initiate, had to undergo an effective brain-washing in the course of a "mystical ceremony which resembles in so many ways that employed by the Kwakiutl Indians." (Alternatively, we might say that the teaching analyst guides the neophyte through the terrifying depths of the unconscious to lead him at last to the upper world of enlightenment: the literary parallels are Aeneas guided by the shade of his father and by the Sibyl through the classical underworld, to be discharged at last through the ivory gate of false dreams, and Dante guided by the shade of Vergil through the Christian Inferno and Purgatory.) In Bailey's second attack on Freud in 1965, he expressed his agreement with Bakan's thesis that Freud had been heavily influenced by Jewish mystical thought, in particular by medieval Kabbalism. After pointing to the intermingling of Jewish Kabbalism and Christian Catharism in the south of France during the twelfth century, Bailey revealed the surprising fact that he himself had been raised on Catharist doctrine— with which he still felt himself in sympathy—in the Ozark hills of Little Egypt.[41]

According to the French writer O. Mannoni in 1968, Freud had two models in mind when he framed his secret society. One was scientific, the other political. Freud's revered teacher of physiology, Ernst Brücke, together with Emil du Bois-Reymond and Hermann Helmholtz, came together in 1852 (four years before Freud's birth) "to form a kind of scientific freemasonry . . . , whose goal was to destroy completely whatever remained of the old vitalist ideology." The other model is less well known. "Under the influence of a schoolmate at the Sperl Gymnasium, Heinrich Braun," says Mannoni, "[Freud] had long considered joining a clandestine political group of the opposition as an activist."[42] Freud himself, in an autobiographical study written in 1924, mentions Braun merely as an older friend who grew up to be a well-known politician; in

[41] Percival Bailey, "Rigged Radio Interview with Illustrations of Various 'Ego-Ideals,'" *Perspectives in Biology and Medicine,* 4 (1960), 199-265; *Sigmund Freud the Unserene: A Tragedy in Three Acts* (Springfield, Ill., 1965), 88, 105. Bailey later wrote an account of his own spiritual quest, *Up from Little Egypt* (Chicago, 1969). The best single compilation of critical assessments, pro and con, of Freudian theory remains *Psychoanalysis, Scientific Method and Philosophy,* ed. Sidney Hook (New York, 1959). For a recent all-out attack on the Freudian position, based in large part on new revelations from the Freud Archives, see Frederick Crews, "The Freudian Way of Knowledge," *The New Criterion,* 2, no. 10 (June 1984), 7-24. I thank Professor Hook for calling my attention to this article.

[42] O. Mannoni, *Freud,* trans. Renard Balice (New York, 1971), 168. This passage is from "Afterword: The Future of a Disillusion," 160-93, which is not to be found in the French original of 1968 or the German translation of 1971.

1927, however, in a letter to Braun's widow, Freud says that Braun "awakened a multitude of revolutionary trends in me."[43] All this is much in keeping with Freud's early fantasies of himself as an avenging Hannibal.

David Bakan suggested that Freud's use of Juno's vow to loose the powers of hell (in the form of the Fury Alecto) on Aeneas as an epigraph for the *Interpretation of Dreams* implied something of a "Satanic pact."[44] Mannoni, apparently independently, argued that Freud "compared himself to the repressed; he also was prepared to raise Acheron against all resistance." Mannoni supported this claim with the statement that Freud first intended to use as an epigraph the lines from *Paradise Lost,* "Let us consult/What reinforcement we may gain from hope,/If not what resolution from despair."[45] These lines are drawn from the same passage in which Satan and his fellow fallen angels take counsel, "how we may henceforth most offend/Our Enemy" (*Paradise Lost,* I, 187-91).

The implied charge of Satanism was nothing new. With no holds barred, it had been made in the nineteen-twenties by Egon Friedell, a converted Viennese Jew. Psychoanalysis, Friedell asserts, masquerades as mental science but is in reality a "new earth-embracing revolt against the evangel," a "sect . . . with rites, ceremonies and cathartic conjurations, oracles and divination, secret doctrine and its popular version, proselytes and renegades, priests who are subjected to tests, and daughter-sects that condemn each other in turn." Freud is an "Orpheus from the underworld," a "seer and singer . . . who proselytizes for the powers of darkness." Psychoanalysis itself, says Friedell, rising to the highest pitch of his oratory,

is, to speak again with Nietzsche, "a parasite's attack, a vampirism of pale, underground blood-suckers"; it is a grandiose attempt to spread infection, a stealthy act of revenge on part of the losers: the whole world is to be neuroticized, sexualized, diabolized. Psychoanalysis proclaims the breakthrough of Satan's kingdom. Perhaps it speaks the truth; perhaps the interregnum of the devil is indeed approaching. His worshippers, as connoisseurs of the Black Mass know, pay homage to his phallus and his backside as the supreme Holy places.[46]

For Friedell, evidently, the familiar pun on the word psychoanalysis is the anatomical expression of Freud's inversion of values: psychoanalysis is anal psychosis. For Simon, Freud "was not able—even if he had so desired—to be unburdened by the Tablets of the Law . . . although he

---

[43] Cited from Paul Roazen, *Freud and His Followers* (New York, 1971; repr. New Amsterdam Library, 1976), 34.

[44] Bakan, *Sigmund Freud and the Jewish Tradition,* 209-37.

[45] Mannoni, *Freud,* 68.

[46] Egon Friedell, *Kulturgeschichte der Neuzeit* (3 vols.; Munich, 1927-33), III, 479, 582-83.

turned them completely upside down and explained them from below to above."[47]

From the metaphor of Freudian psychoanalysis as Satanism, as the world turned downside up, a metaphor for which Freud himself gave the cue, we turn in conclusion to the metaphor of psychoanalysis as a disease—as, in fact, the very disease that it pretends to cure. Freud may be the unwitting source of this metaphor as well. Mannoni writes:

[Freud] was convinced that it was in the very nature of psychoanalytic doctrine to appear shocking and subversive. On board ship to America [to speak in 1909 at Clark University, Worcester, Mass.] he did not feel that he was bringing that country a new panacea. With his typically dry wit he told his traveling companions [among them Carl Jung and one future member of the fellowship of the ring, Sandor Ferenczi], "We are bringing them the plague."[48]

Four years later Karl Kraus, another writer of genius in Freud's Vienna but an implacable foe of psychoanalysis, published his most celebrated aphorism: "Psychoanalysis is that mental disease for which it holds itself to be the therapy" (*Psychoanalyse ist jene Geisteskrankheit für deren Therapie sie sich hält*).[49] Whether Kraus had heard of Freud's remark or, as seems more likely, had come of himself to this variation on the old saw of the cure being worse than, or worsening, the disease is an open question. The views of Karl Kraus on psychiatry in general and on Freudian psychoanalysis in particular have been discussed at length recently by Thomas Szasz, and nothing more need be added here.[50] Kraus's aphorism has often been repeated and parodied. The British parliamentarian Ian Gilmour argued in 1960 that the Israeli state had "almost a vested interest in racial discrimination," adding: "Zionism aggravated the disease it professed to cure." And in 1970 Shulamith Firestone, after noting that psychoanalysis had long been recognized as "the disease it purports to cure," stated: "Freud was merely a diagnostician for what Feminism purports to cure." Seemingly unaware that Moses Hess had taken the first step by substituting "race" for "class" as the motive power of history, Firestone brought Engels up to date with the following parody of his words: "Historical materialism is that view of the course of history which seeks the ultimate cause and the great moving power of all historic events in the dialectic of sex."[51] (In German, it should be recalled, *Geschlecht* can mean either "race" or "sex.")

[47] Simon, *Sigmund Freud the Jew*, 304.

[48] Mannoni, *Freud*, 168. No authority for the story is given.

[49] Karl Kraus, *Beim Wort genommen, Werke* (14 vols.; Munich, 1952-67) III, 351.

[50] Thomas Szasz, *Karl Kraus and the Soul-Doctors: A Pioneer Critic and His Criticism of Psychiatry and Psychoanalysis* (Baton Rouge, La., 1976).

[51] Ian Gilmour, cited in Alfred M. Lilienthal, *The Zionist Connection: What Price Peace?* (New York, 1978), 411; Shulamith Firestone, *The Dialectic of Sex: The Case for Feminist Revolution* (New York, 1970), 12, 44.

Fictional embodiment of the notion that Freud was a vector of disease or a bearer of moral poison is not difficult to find. The hapless pilgrim of C. S. Lewis's *The Pilgrim's Regress* (1933), in a chapter entitled "Poisoning the Wells," is imprisoned in a dark dungeon by one "Sigismund Enlightenment."[52] And the mysterious Simon of Charles Williams's equally didactic novel *All-Hallow's Eve* (1945) is undoubtedly modelled after the image of Freud as a bearer of contagion. Part gnostic superman, part Wandering Jew, the necromancer Simon seeks to "spread his miasma over the world." Inverting the unutterable name of the Hebrew God, Simon works his black magic by intoning *à rebours* "the perfect Tetragrammaton."[53] But the most unrestrained attack on Freud in this light is to be found in a seldom-mentioned book by Emil Ludwig, *Doctor Freud: An Analysis and a Warning* (1947). The German original, published in Switzerland in 1946, bears the more expressive title *Der entzauberte Freud* ("Freud demystified"). Like Kraus and Friedell, Ludwig (a pseudonym for Cohn) was by upbringing a Jew. Ludwig calls Freud a "lesser devil," bearer of moral "contagion" or "infection" (to which America is said to be particularly susceptible); he speaks even of the "pus with which [Freud] proposes to inoculate children."[54] And Boris Sokoloff asserts that American youth has been "contaminated by the Freudian ethic . . . , [which] declares that all is permissible."[55]

The belief that there exists a far-flung international "Jewish conspiracy" aimed at subverting the rule of the *goyim* is of course much older than Disraeli, but that he contributed much to its spread and credibility cannot be denied; he was, after all, twice Prime Minister of the empire on which the sun was said never to set. And the semi-conspiratorial character of the psychoanalytic movement at its inception, together with the sense of injury to his "race" that Freud made little attempt to conceal, perhaps inevitably drew Freudian psychoanalysis into the overall orbit of the conspiracy charge. We may note in closing that the early Zionist Lev Semenovich Pinsker (1821-1891) turned the charge back at those who made it. In doing so he may be said to have anticipated by several decades Freud's account of the mechanism of projection in paranoia—in which "I hate him" is projected as "he hates me."[56] According to Pinsker it was rather the whole "hostile and conspiratorial world" that had once and for all set its face against the Jews. "Judeo-phobia," Pinsker

---

[52] C. S. Lewis, *The Pilgrim's Regress: An Allegorical Apology for Christianity, Reason and Romanticism* (New York, 1944; first ed., 1933).

[53] Charles Williams, *All-Hallow's Eve.* With an introduction by T. S. Eliot (New York, 1969; first ed. 1945), 63, 159, 215, 217.

[54] Emil Ludwig, *Der entzauberte Freud* (Zurich, 1946), 90; *Doctor Freud: An Analysis and a Warning* (New York, 1947), 128-29, 148. The German original differs in many respects from the English translation.

[55] Boris Sokoloff, *The Permissive Society* (New Rochelle, 1971), 22.

[56] Jones, *The Life and Work of Sigmund Freud*, II, 270.

wrote, "is a psychic aberration . . . , it is hereditary, and as a disease transmitted for two thousand years it is incurable. . . . [It is] an hereditary form of demonopathy, peculiar to the human race."[57]

Stanford University, School of Medicine.

[57] Lev Semenovich Pinsker, *Road to Freedom*, trans. D. S. Blondheim (New York, 1944; repr. 1975), 78-80. The English translation was first published in 1916 by the Federation of American Zionists. Pinsker's conspiracy charge was reversed again in 1943 by H. G. Wells, and directed against what Wells called a "die-hard minority," an "orthodox remnant," of world Jewry: "The whole question turns on the Chosen People idea . . . . It is difficult not to regard that idea as a conspiracy against the rest of the world . . . . A careful reading of the Bible does nothing to correct it; there indeed you have the conspiracy plain and clear. . . . It is an aggressive and vindictive conspiracy" (*The Outlook for Homo Sapiens* [London, 1943], 76-77). The Zionist movement, Wells added, is the "crowning expression of . . . the obdurate insistence of orthodox and semi-orthodox Jewry on their particularity." And in Germany the Nazis were seeking to "mould the mentality of the entire Reich to this fundamentally Biblical idea of a militant Chosen People—Germanised" (*ibid.*, 82, 106). Wells, it should be said, looked on the variously Pan-Germanic, Judaic, or Illuminist world-conspiracy theories, put forward by Nesta Webster and others, as manifestations of "persecution mania" (*ibid.*, 282-83).

PART THREE

SEX DIFFERENCES
OR
GENDER DISTINCTIONS

XIII

MARGARET FULLER AND THE ABOLITION MOVEMENT [1]

By Francis E. Kearns

Margaret Fuller's reputation as a feminist lies firmly established on two major contributions to the woman's rights movement—the conducting of her Conversation classes for women from 1839 to 1844 and her authorship of the tract *Woman in the Nineteenth Century*. The Conversation classes brought together some of the most intelligent women of Boston for the avowed purpose of rectifying the inadequacies resulting from the inferior education alloted to women at the time, whereas *Woman in the Nineteenth Century*, on the other hand, called for broader educational and employment opportunities for women and propounded a theory of marriage based on only the most idealistic principles. Considering her great contributions to the woman's rights movement, it is surprising that Margaret Fuller never took an active part in another equalitarian struggle which during her lifetime gripped the imagination of American reformers, the Abolition movement.

Many of the leaders in the Abolition cause were outstanding proponents of woman's rights. And it has become a commonplace observation in works dealing with the development of the woman's rights movement in America, works ranging from the early *History of Woman Suffrage* by Elizabeth Cady Stanton and Susan B. Anthony [2] to the recent *Century of Struggle* by Eleanor Flexner,[3] that the anti-slavery struggle was actually the progenitor of the woman suffrage movement. Through their efforts in behalf of the Negro slave, women first learned to organize, to hold public meetings, and to conduct petition campaigns. In the social position of the slave they saw an analogy with their own lot and soon began to evolve a philosophy of their basic rights. Indeed, it was as a direct result of the anti-slavery movement that the first woman's rights convention in America was held. In 1840 the American delegation which attended the World Anti-Slavery Convention in London included in its ranks several women, but the convention refused to seat female delegates. Two of the American delegates thus rejected, Elizabeth Cady Stanton and Lucretia Mott, both graduates of Margaret's Conversation classes, left London determined to establish an organized movement for the emancipation of women; and in 1848, at Seneca Falls, New York, they convened the first Woman's Rights Convention in America. Margaret Fuller was aware of the connection between the two movements, for in *Woman in the Nineteenth Century* she declared: "Of all its [freedom's] banners, none has been more steadily upheld, and under none have more valor and willingness for real sacrifices been shown, than that of the champion of the enslaved African. And this band it is, which, partly from a natural following out of principles, partly because many women have been

[1] This study has been made possible by a grant from the Penrose Fund of the American Philosophical Society.
[2] (Rochester, London, and Paris, 1889), I, 52.   [3] (Cambridge, Mass., 1959), 4.

prominent in that cause, makes, just now, the warmest appeal in behalf of woman." [4]

The fact that she perceived this connection makes her unwillingness to join the ranks of the Abolitionists all the more puzzling. Moreover, there are other factors in Margaret Fuller's background which would seem to have impelled her toward a sympathy with the Abolition movement. Many of her friends, including James Freeman Clarke and W. H. Channing, were closely identified with this cause. Theodore Parker, whom she knew through the Transcendental Club and her editorship of the *Dial*, preached against slavery and actively assisted in the escape of fugitive slaves. Furthermore, several of the women who attended the Conversations, in particular Mrs. Ellis Gray Loring and Lydia Maria Child, the latter having assumed the editorship of the New York *Anti-Slavery Standard* in 1841, were active participants in the Abolition movement. In Margaret's own family there was a strong tradition of anti-slavery feeling. As a Representative from Massachusetts, her father opposed the Missouri Compromise in 1820; and, indeed, his first speech in Congress was made in an effort to defeat a bill designed to curb the activities of the underground railroad. [5]

Here an important distinction must be made between disdain for the Abolitionists, many of whom combined religious fanaticism with their equalitarian sentiments, and disdain for the anti-slavery movement itself. For, although Margaret Fuller steadfastly refused to join the ranks of the Abolitionists, she manifested throughout her life a thorough sympathy for the anti-slavery principle. It was only the jaundiced eyes of her more zealous contemporaries, people completely embroiled in the struggles of the Abolition group, which could view her attitude as aloof. The warmth with which she regarded the anti-slavery cause in *Woman in the Nineteenth Century* increased steadily and appears in all her works. In this respect it is interesting to note the growing intensity which she brought to her four articles on the slavery question for Greeley's *New York Tribune* during 1845, her first full year of work with the newspaper. On January 7th she greeted the appearance of *The Liberty Bell*, an annual published in Massachusetts for the benefit of the Anti-Slavery Fair, in cordial but restrained terms. [6] She complimented the Abolitionists on their clarity of argument and loyalty to principle and noted that the essays written by former slaves were incontrovertible evidence of the innate capacities of the Negro. But nowhere in the article does she indicate personal support for the Abolition movement. On March 29th she reported on a lecture given by Frederick Von Raumer before the Scientific Union in Berlin on the slavery question in the United States. [7] Von Raumer confined himself to the pro-slavery arguments and

[4] (New York, 1845), 17–18.

[5] See Leona Rostenberg, "Diary of Thomas Fuller in Congress," *New England Quarterly*, XII (Sept., 1939), 523–524; see also *Debates and Proceedings in the Congress of the United States*, Fifteenth Congress, First Session (Washington, 1854), 825.

[6] "*The Liberty Bell* for 1845."

[7] "Frederick Von Raumer upon the Slavery Question."

Margaret observed that: "The lecture was certainly in an anti-abolition spirit, so as to cause much distaste to the women present, and to all those who believe no improvement impossible on which the human soul is bent with earnest desire." Still Margaret's tone was impersonal, despite her evident distaste for Von Raumer's remarks. By June, however, her anti-slavery sentiment made itself felt in a more forceful manner. In a review of the autobiography of Frederick Douglass, an escaped slave, she declared: "The inconsistencies of Slaveholding professors of religion cry to Heaven. . . . Clergymen to-day command Slaves to obey a Gospel which they will not allow them to read, and call themselves Christians amid the curses of their fellow men." [8] So strong did her feeling against racial intolerance become, that by December she wrote an article attacking an instance of anti-Negro prejudice in the North. She rejected the action of the Lyceum at New Bedford, Massachusetts, in denying membership to Negroes and restricting them to segregated seating facilities. She labeled this policy "unchristian" and complimented Ralph Waldo Emerson and Charles Sumner on their decisions to cancel lecture engagements at the Lyceum.[9]

A few years later, after her experiences in the Roman revolution against Austria, she even expressed regret for her earlier hostility against the Abolitionists. In 1847, after she had settled in Rome, Margaret Fuller either secretly married or became the mistress of Marchese Giovanni Ossoli, a member of the Civic Guard and an ardent Republican. When in 1849 the Republic of Rome was declared and French forces assaulted the city in order to restore the Pope to temporal power, the Marchese took up his post on the walls of the city and Margaret assumed the rôle of director of the Hospital of *Fate Bene Fratelli*, to which the wounded were sent every day. In one of the articles she hastily wrote for the *Tribune* in an effort to arouse American support for the Republican cause, Margaret declared: "How it pleases me here to think of the Abolitionists! I could never endure to be with them at home, they were so tedious, often so narrow, always so rabid and exaggerated in their tone. But after all they had a high motive, something eternal in their desire and life; and if it was not the only thing worth thinking of, it was really something worth living and dying for to free a great nation from such a terrible blot, such a threatening plague. God strengthen them, and make them wise to achieve their purpose." [10] It was not uncommon for New England travellers in mid-nineteenth-century Italy to be drawn to sympathy for the anti-slavery movement as a result of noting the analogy between the situation of the Italians, subjected to Austrian domination and the condition of the American Negro slaves, subjected to another form of vassalage. Holmes and Lowell both reacted in this fashion. So complete was this influence on Margaret Fuller, however, that at least one scholar, Edmund G. Berry, has expressed the view that she might have

[8] *"Narrative of the Life of Frederick Douglass,"* June 10, 1845.

[9] "Lyceum of New-Bedford, Mass.," Dec. 9, 1845.

[10] Quoted in Margaret Fuller, *At Home and Abroad*, ed. by A. B. Fuller (Boston, 1856), 255.

emerged as a leader in the Abolition cause, had not she and her husband perished at sea while returning to America in 1850.[11]

Margaret Fuller's earlier abhorrence of the Abolitionists is not difficult to explain. Among her chief objections to the leaders of the movement was the tone of excess and exaggeration which characterized their pronouncements. Like Thoreau, she was an adherent of self-reliance and self-culture, and, like Emerson, who in "The Chardon Street Convention" had classed Abolitionists along with "Madmen, madwomen, men with beards, Dunkers, Muggletonians, Come-outers, Groaners, Agrarians, Seventh-day Baptists . . . ,"[12] she found it difficult to sacrifice her hard core of New England common sense for the zeal demanded by Abolition or any other extreme reform movement. Time and again she complimented the Abolitionists on the nobility of their aims but at the same time excoriated their methods. Commenting on the preface which William Lloyd Garrison, the noted Abolitionist, had written for the *Narrative of the Life of Frederick Douglass*, she observed: "His motives and his course have been noble and generous. We look upon him with high respect, but he has indulged in violent invective and denunciation till he has spoiled the temper of his mind. Like a man who has been in the habit of screaming himself hoarse to make the deaf hear, he can no longer pitch his voice on a key agreeable to common ears."[13] Similarly, she found in Archy Moore's *The Slave*, one of the earliest, perhaps the first, anti-slavery novels, evidence of "distortion and sophistry,"[14] but she was willing to overlook these faults in view of the book's humanitarian purpose.

Margaret Fuller was by no means alone in her distrust of the Abolitionists. Many New England luminaries, including, as we have seen, Ralph Waldo Emerson, were repelled by the excesses of these anti-slavery zealots and took no active part during the early years of the struggle to free the Negro. Yet they managed to escape the charge of indifference to the anti-slavery movement. What was there then about Margaret Fuller's inaction that appeared so censurable to her contemporaries and to many later scholars? Part of the answer lies in the fact that Margaret was a life-long advocate of social action and was fond of lecturing fellow transcendentalists on the inadequacies of their more cerebral lives. Thus in a letter to W. H. Channing she declared: "Is it not nobler and truer to live than to think? . . . Really to feel the glow of action, without its weariness, what heaven it must be!"[15] And to Emerson she wrote: " . . . your excellence never shames me, nor chills my next effort, because it is of a kind wholly unattainable to

[11] "Margaret Fuller Ossoli, 1810–1850," *Dalhousie Review*, XXX (Jan. 1951), 376.

[12] *Complete Works of Ralph Waldo Emerson*, ed. by Edward Waldo Emerson, Vol. X, *Lectures and Biographical Sketches* (Boston and New York, 1911), 374.

[13] "Narrative of the Life of Frederick Douglass," *New York Daily Tribune* (June 10, 1845).

[14] "The Slave; or Memoirs of Archy Moore," *ibid.*, Feb. 4, 1845.

[15] Quoted in F. A. Braun, *Margaret Fuller and Goethe* (New York, 1910), 137.

me, in a walk where I shall never take a step. You are intellect, I am life." [16]

But Margaret's inconsistency in failing to apply the principle of action to the anti-slavery movement is not the major cause of her later reputation for indifference towards the movement. The chief cause of that reputation is the public attack made on her views of the slavery question by the influential English feminist, Harriet Martineau. In 1834 Miss Martineau made an extensive journey throughout the United States and three years later she published *Society in America*, a compendium of her views on life in this country. Margaret Fuller had met Miss Martineau during her visit to the United States and soon came to idolize the Englishwoman for her independence of mind and freedom from convention. Their relationship was further cemented when Miss Martineau arranged for Margaret to meet Emerson and later tried to help her fulfill a life-time dream of visiting Europe. Nevertheless, despite her discipleship, Margaret Fuller felt that she must inform her idol of her distaste for certain excesses in the latter's recently published *Society in America*. In a letter reassuring the English authoress of her continued friendship, Margaret pointed out that the heavy-handed manner in which the book espoused the anti-slavery movement obscured all other concerns in what was supposed to be a broad examination of American society: "I do not like that your book should be an 'abolition' book. You might have borne your testimony as decidedly as you pleased; but why leaven the whole book with it? It *is* a great subject, but your book had other purposes to fulfill." [17] Such plain speaking did not endear Margaret to the English reformer, eight years her senior. Some forty years later Miss Martineau apparently still smarted with resentment at the disciple's objections, for in her *Autobiography*, the English authoress rebuked Margaret with the charge that the Boston Conversations were a fanciful and shallow means of escaping real threats to American democracy and of shirking duty to the cause of Abolition:

The difference between us was that while she was living and moving in an ideal world, talking in private and discoursing in public about the most fanciful and shallow conceits which the Transcendentalists of Boston took for philosophy, she looked down upon persons who acted instead of talking finely, and devoted their fortunes, their place, their repose, and their very lives to the preservation of the principles of the republic. While Margaret Fuller and her adult pupils 'sat gorgeously dressed,' talking about Mars and Venus, Plato and Goethe, and fancying themselves the elect of the earth in intellect and refinement, the liberties of the republic were running out as fast as they could go, at a breach which another sort of elect persons were devoting themselves to repair; and my complaint against the 'gorgeous' pedants was that they regarded their preservers as hewers of wood and drawers of water, and their work as a less vital one than the pedantic orations which were spoiling a set of well-meaning women in a pitiable way. [18]

[16] Letter, n. d., n. p. Houghton Library, Harvard University, "Fuller Manuscripts," IX, 118b.

[17] Quoted in Margaret Fuller Ossoli, *Memoirs*, ed. by James Freeman Clarke, Ralph Waldo Emerson, and William H. Channing (Boston, 1852), I, 194.

[18] London, 1877, Vol. II, 71.

Harriet Martineau's comment has had a significant effect upon later writers dealing with Margaret Fuller, for many of them have felt compelled to answer the English reformer's charges. In his 1884 biography of Margaret Fuller for the American Men of Letters series, Thomas Wentworth Higginson attempted to remedy the injustice with which he believed Margaret had been treated in "that singularly harsh and unfair book, the 'Autobiography of Harriet Martineau' " [19] by quoting at length from Margaret's letters and Miss Martineau's book in an attempt both to discredit the English woman's objectivity and point up the rôle played in the anti-slavery cause by women who attended Margaret's Conversations. But, as a matter of fact, Higginson only further reinforced the idea of the censurable character of Margaret's attitude toward the anti-slavery movement when he claimed in the same chapter that, "It is a point never yet wholly cleared up, either by her printed memoirs or private letters, why she entered with somewhat tardy sympathy into the anti-slavery movement" (p. 122). In her 1902 *Reminiscences*, Ednah Dow Cheney, who had attended Margaret's Boston Conversation classes, also addressed herself to Harriet Martineau's allegations. Here Mrs. Cheney explained Margaret's failure to enlist in the ranks of the anti-slavery movement on the grounds that the movement itself had not yet passed into its active phase when Margaret departed for Europe in 1846.[20] A more modern commentator, Charles A. Madison, in the *Antioch Review*, has explained the tardiness of Margaret's appreciation for the anti-slavery group as a result of her "aesthetic recoil from the 'rabid and exaggerated' behavior of the Abolitionist leaders," [21] whereas Margaret Munsterberg, in the *Boston Public Library Quarterly*, has suggested that her attitude resulted from an "impatience with platforms." [22]

All of the previously mentioned explanations of Margaret Fuller's lack of enthusiasm for the organized anti-slavery movement—her recoil at the excesses of the Abolitionist leaders, her distaste for platforms and parties, the fact that the movement had not become nearly so widely active by the time of her departure for Europe as it was later to be—are, in varying degrees, valid. But one historically significant explanation is rarely examined. This is the rivalry between the woman's rights advocates and the Abolitionists which began to manifest itself in the 1830's. The part which this rivalry played in Margaret Fuller's attitude toward the anti-slavery movement is made clear by manuscript letters contained in the Boston Public Library's Anti-Slavery Collection. Late in 1840 Maria Weston Chapman, who was Treasurer of the Massachusetts Anti-Slavery Society and was later to edit the *Autobiography* of her long-standing friend, Harriet Martineau, wrote to Margaret Fuller to request that one of the Conversations, which were now receiving wide attention in Boston, be devoted to the topic

[19] Boston, 123.

[20] Boston, 211.

[21] "Margaret Fuller: Transcendental Rebel," *Antioch Review*, II (Sept. 1942), 431.

[22] "Margaret Fuller Centenary," *Boston Public Library Quarterly*, II (July, 1950), 258.

of Abolition. In her reply, written in December 1840, Margaret declined
Mrs. Chapman's suggestion on the grounds that such a talk would interrupt
the schedule already adopted for the Conversation class. In the same letter
Margaret went on to express her respect for the ideals of the Abolition cause
but added her concomitant belief that the followers of the cause demonstrated many of the faults incident to partisan zeal. She concluded:

The late movements in your party have interested me more than those which
had for their object the enfranchisement of the African only. Yet I presume
I should still feel sympathy with your aims only not with your measures.
Yet I should like to be more fully acquainted with both. The late convention I attended hoping to hear some clear account of your wishes as to religious institutions and the social position of woman. But not only I heard
nothing that pleased me, but no clear statement from any one. . . . As far as
I know you seem to me quite wrong as to what is to be done for woman!
She needs new helps I think, but not such as you propose. But I should like
to know your view and your grounds more clearly than I do.[23]

Thus Margaret Fuller felt disappointed that the Anti-Slavery Fair organized by Mrs. Chapman did not clearly insist on the rights of woman as well
as those of the Negro. She regarded herself as having a prior commitment
to the woman's rights cause and did not wish to dissipate her efforts on behalf of woman by spending time on movements "which had for their object
the enfranchisement of the African only."

The question of just how closely they would ally themselves with the
woman's rights movement deeply perplexed Abolitionists in 1840. In that
year, as has been pointed out, the World Anti-Slavery Convention in London refused to seat female delegates; and in this country, in the same year,
when the Anti-Slavery Association passed a resolution permitting women
to become committee members, the action was met with a series of resigna-
tions by less radical members, thus resulting in a crippling split within the
Association. Moreover, there was much opposition to the fact that the
Grimké sisters frequently lectured before mixed audiences on the slavery
question, and in 1836 a Pastoral Letter denouncing such unfeminine and
dangerous conduct had been issued by the Council of Congregationalist Ministers of Massachusetts. Abolition leaders realized that the willingness of
women to participate in their cause was a mixed blessing and many wished
to sever their association with woman's rights agitation. It is not difficult to
understand how in this climate Margaret Fuller could feel that she must
choose between two movements, one to liberate women and the other to
liberate slaves. The note with which Anne Watson, Mrs. Chapman's sister,
answered Margaret Fuller's letter underlines the uneasiness which many
Abolitionists felt at this time when confronted with the woman's rights question. Miss Watson wrote:

Permit me, as a matter of fact to correct one error in your letter. In speaking of the recent Convention you seem to think it a movement of the Anti-
Slavery party—The only object of that party *as such* is the promulgation
of the principle that all men are created with a right to personal liberty

[23] "Weston Papers," MS. A. 3. 14, 82.

and as in this country the Slave is the only being to whom the right is denied, the assertion of his claims is the scope to which Abolitionists *as such* are limited. . . .

. . . The fact that the A. S. Reform is calculated to lead the minds of a community to still further reform is one that we have no disposition to deny—Great changes, religiously & socially must undoubtedly be produced but these results are collateral & not direct & must be modified by circumstances over which the Anti Slavery community have no control.[24]

It would appear then that Margaret Fuller's aloofness towards the anti-slavery movement has been thoroughly exaggerated. Her cautious attitude towards partisans of that movement was caused not by her refusal to come to grips with the problems facing American democracy, as Harriet Martineau would have her readers believe, but resulted from the fact that her equalitarian principles, embracing the desire to liberate not only the Negro but also woman, were far more radical than those embraced by the more conservative reformers constituting the Abolition group.

Georgetown University.

[24] *Ibid.,* MS. A. 3. 14, 83.

XIV

EARLY FEMINIST THEMES IN FRENCH UTOPIAN SOCIALISM: THE ST.-SIMONIANS AND FOURIER*

By Leslie F. Goldstein

I. *Women's Rights vs. Women's Liberation*—It is commonly noted that the feminist movement of the nineteenth and early twentieth centuries was a quest for women's rights, whereas the feminist movement of the late twentieth century is more properly denominated a quest for women's liberation.[1] The central issues of the first wave of feminism were equality in legal and political rights and formal equality of opportunity. These feminists sought the opportunity to vote and hold public office, access to jobs and education, and equality of legal rights in marriage. The last included the rights of married women to own and earn property, to disobey their husbands, to sue for divorce (on grounds comparable to those available to their husbands), to obtain child custody after divorce, and to legal protection against physical abuse by their husbands.

By the mid-twentieth century the goals of the women's rights movement had been, for the most part, written into the law of the United States and much of Western Europe.[2] The 1960s, however, generated a new feminist movement which, while giving attention to some work of the first wave (e.g., seeking ratification of the E.R.A.), was predominantly concerned with women's liberation. A sample list of issues for the contemporary women's movement is "e.g., abolition of marriage, continuation of the nuclear family, payment for housewives, abolition of the housewife role, child care, abortion, access of women to predominantly male occupations, abolition of sex roles. . . ."[3] Even the National Organization for Women (N.O.W.), which has a middleclass and mainstream image, emphasizes these new concerns: their 1968 "Bill of Rights" included insistence on child care centers, tax deductions for working parents for child care, job-

---

* Expansion of a paper originally prepared for delivery at the Annual Meeting of the Midwest Political Science Association, Chicago, Illinois, April 1979.

[1] Gerda Lerner, "Women's Rights and American Feminism," *The American Scholar,* **40** (Spring 1971), 235-49, argues that this is an exaggeration and that the 19th-century American feminist movement included a number of "liberationist" (or "emancipation") elements. However, the *dominant* voice of 19th-century feminism still appeared to call for women's rights as distinguished from women's liberation.

[2] For the remnants of legal inequality still confronting American women at midcentury, see Leo Kanowitz, *Women and the Law* (Albuquerque, 1969). The reader will readily note the vast disparity between the legal inequities discussed by Kanowitz in 1969 and those discussed, for example, by John Stuart Mill in *The Subjection of Women* in 1869.

[3] *The Politics of Women's Liberation* (New York, 1975), 50.

training opportunities, and job-training allowances for poor women (presumably including poor mothers). In short, the core of today's feminism seems to be a concern for liberating women from traditional, sex-based division of labor *within* the family. This concern cuts across various ideological divisions within the movement and is the shared bond among its various segments whether they call themsleves "liberal feminists," "socialist feminists," "lesbian separatists," or "radical feminists." This paper is an exploration of some major intellectual origins of the women's liberationist ideology.

It is not difficult to find roots of the equal rights movement in the classic liberal principles of Hobbes[4] and Locke.[5] Finding the origin of the women's liberation movement is more difficult.[6] A case can be made that Karl Marx, who insisted that the family needed to be "criticized in theory and revolutionized in practice," was a philosophic progenitor of the women's liberation movement.[7] Marx, however, made no secret of his intellectual indebtedness to the utopian socialists of the early nineteenth century.[8] He noted, for example, that Fourier before him had advocated abolition of the family.[9] Fourier, in fact, is credited by modern scholars with having originated the word "féministe."[10] But even before Fourier's ideas attracted

[4] I do not mean that Hobbes was himself a classical liberal, simply that he espoused certain basic premises which laid the groundwork for liberal theory. See Leo Strauss, *Natural Right and History* (Chicago, 1953), and C. B. Macpherson, *The Political Theory of Possessive Individualism* (London and Oxford, 1962). For Hobbes' feminist principles, see *Leviathan,* Chap. 20, Sect. 4.

[5] Melissa Butler, "Early Liberal Roots of Feminism: John Locke and the Attack on Patriarchy," *American Political Science Review,* **72** (March 1978), 135-50; also Terence Ball, "Communication," *Ibid.,* **73** (June 1979), 549-50, and Butler's response, 550-51.

[6] Socrates, of course, suggested revolutionizing the nuclear family, but the earnestness of his suggestion is seriously disputed in the literature. Cf. Allan Bloom, "Interpretive Essay," *The Republic,* trans. Bloom (New York, 1968); and Arlene Saxonhouse, "The Philosopher and the Female in the Political Thought of Plato," *Political Theory,* **4** (1976), 195-221; *idem* with Barbara and George Tovey, "Women's Philosophical Friends and Enemies," *Social Science Quarterly,* **55**, No. 3 (Dec. 1974), 586-605, esp. 589 ff.

[7] See my article, "Mill, Marx, and Women's Liberation," *Journal of the History of Philosophy,* **18** (July 1980), 319-34.

[8] See Sect. III, 3, "Critical-Utopian Socialism and Communism" in the *Communist Manifesto*; also, Marx's lengthy quotation of Fourier in *The Holy Family* (Moscow, 1956), 258-59. Of course, Marx also believed that "scientific socialism" drastically improved utopian socialism.

[9] Sect. III, 3, of the *Communist Manifesto.*

[10] S. Joan Moon, "Feminism and Socialism: The Utopian Synthesis of Flora Tristan" in *Socialist Women,* ed. Marilyn J. Boxer and Jean H. Quatert (New York, 1978), 45, n. 1. The same point is made in Nicholas V. Riasanovsky, *The Teaching of Charles Fourier* (Berkeley, 1969), 208.

widespread attention in France, those of his rivals, the Saint-Simonians, enjoyed quite a vogue.[11] The Saint-Simonians, *unlike* their supposed mentor, Comte Claude Henri de Saint-Simon,[12] openly espoused the cause of complete social and political equality for women.[13]

The purpose of my essay is two-fold. First, by explicating the feminist themes in the thought of the Saint-Simonians and of Fourier, I aim simply to elucidate their respective versions of feminism. Secondly, and more importantly, I draw attention to the very important and overly neglected contribution of these utopian socialists toward originating the ideology of women's liberation.

To be sure, the Saint-Simonians and Fourier were writing and being read during a period of enormous social ferment, a period in which a very wide variety of feminist ideas were "in the air."[14] The attention that they devoted to the oppressive qualities of women's family role and the thoroughness and radicalness of their critique of that role, however, set them apart. These features of their work also identify it as a very appropriate starting point for one wishing to understand the history of women's liberation.

II. *Saint-Simonianism and Women's Liberation*[15]—That the Saint-Simonians endorsed "social equality" for women points to a

[11] Moon, 26-29. St. Simonian prominence lasted from approximately 1828 to 1834. Fourierist groups were in vogue for several years following that period: see Frank E. Manuel, "Children of Saint-Simon" in *The Prophets of Paris* (New York, 1965), 149-95 and notes on 331-34.

[12] Edwin Hedman, "Early French Feminism" (Ph.D. dissertation, N.Y.U., 1954), 102. I use the term "Saint-Simonian" throughout this essay to apply not to the thought of Saint-Simon alone but to the beliefs of the group calling themsleves "Saint-Simonians" who became prominent after his death in 1825.

[13] *Oeuvres de Saint-Simon et d'Enfantin* (hereafter, *Oeuvres*), 47 vols. (Paris, 1865-78), XLV, Chap. 47, "Le Prolétaire et Les Femmes." Essays here are generally undated, and often the author's name is omitted. The chapter following this one, "L'Affranchisement des Femmes" (dated Jan. 1, 1832) is translated by Frank E. Manuel and Fritzie P. Manuel in *French Utopias* (New York, 1971), 293-99.

[14] For a detailed overview of this variety, see Hedman, *op. cit.*

[15] There was, in fact, a variety of Saint-Simonian groupings in France in the 1830s, and this analysis is necessarily partial and tentative because much of the primary source material is available only in 19th-century French journals that I was unable to consult. S. Joan Moon cites *Le Femme Libre* (1832-34), *le Globe* (1830-32), and *l'Organisateur* (1829-1831). My analysis is limited to *The Doctrine of Saint-Simon: An Exposition, First Year 1828-1829*, trans. with intro. Georg G. Iggers (Boston, 1958); and the *Oeuvres*, particularly Volumes XLII, XLIV, and XLV. Also, I consulted the considerable amount of primary (but undocumented) quotation of the Saint-Simonians available in C.C.A. Bouglé, "Le Féminisme Saint-Simonian" in *Chez Les Prophètes Socialistes* (Paris, 1918), 50-110; also, a variety of primary source quotations (carefully documented) appear in S. Joan Moon, "The Saint-Simoniennes and the Moral Revolution," *Proceedings of the Sixth Annual Meeting of the Consortium on Revolutionary Europe* (Athens, Ga., 1976). 162-74.

burgeoning feminist consciousness on their part but leaves many questions unanswered, for the phrase was a catch-all slogan among nineteenth-century progressives. Etienne Cabet, for example, spoke of complete equality for women and men in all opportunities and pursuits but believed that the mother alone should be charged with the first five years of each child's moral and intellectual education.[16] John Stuart Mill endorsed "complete political and social equality" between the sexes while accepting considerable inequality within the marriage institution: "Like a man when he chooses a profession, so, when a woman marries, . . . she makes a choice of the management of a household and the bringing up of a family, as the first call upon her exertions [until her children have attained adulthood and left home.]."[17]

Analysis of the Saint-Simonian version of "social equality for women" reveals that it took women's equality much farther than Cabet and Mill although, in other respects, it seemed to relegate women to permanently unequal status. In still other respects, one simply cannot figure out what the Saint-Simonians intended for women. There is some evidence that they intended to out-do liberals like Mill in equalizing the social tasks of men and women: they advocated women's entry into "social and political functions" and called for marriages of equal partners, proposing a couple-based social system in which each marital couple performed a single "religious or political function." Since each partner would be working on the same social task, the social status of husband and wife would perforce be equal.[18] Saint-Simonians specifically criticized the modern marriage institution not only on its double standard of sexual morality[19] and its

---

[16] Hedman, *op cit.*, 128. Hedman, 133, sees no contradiction between this mandate and total equality between the sexes.

[17] *The Subjection of Women* (London, 1869; rpt. New York, 1970), 89. Mill also believed that the vast majority of women would and should make this choice. See Goldstein, *loc. cit.* (note 3 above), and Tovey and Tovey for further references (note 6 above).

[18] *Oeuvres*, XLIV, Sermon 23, "Le Marriage" (by E. Barrault, n.d.). 77-72.

[19] *Oeuvres*, XLV, Sermon 48, "L'Affranchisement des Femmes," 360-71. The translators (see n. 13 above) list Abel Transom as its author. See also discussion in Frank E. Manuel. Saint-Simonians were deeply distressed at the crass hypocrisy of the double standard and at its links to economic pressures forcing women to prostitute themselves into either "respectable" marriages of convenience or into the open shame of selling themselves on the streets. Consequently, Enfantin propounded a doctrine of permissive divorce (to be regulated by the priest-priestess rulers), the premises of which implied pretty strongly some version of free love. Enfantin himself never made the point explicit, but some of his later followers (still calling themselves Saint-Simonians) argued that he should have drawn the logical conclusion. See Frank E. Manuel, esp. 154-58 and 185-89; C. C. A. Bouglé and S. Joan Moon, "The Saint-Simoniennes . . . ," 164-65.

abominably inequitable property relations[20] but also for its rule that the wife be obedient and do the housework.[21] They even insisted that in the Saint-Simonian future, wives, as equal to their husbands, would no longer change their names.[22]

Fragments of evidence indicate that Saint-Simonian *practice* matched these high theoretical standards of sexual egalitarianism. Once, forty followers of Prosper Enfantin, the leading Saint-Simonian, withdrew to a retreat outside Paris, Ménilmontant, where they adopted a monastic regimen complete with special costumes; a daily schedule of parades, recitations, and other symbolic rituals; and vows of celibacy.[23] At Ménilmontant men shared equally in doing the common household tasks.[24] Moreover, in the meetings and organizational structures of Saint-Simonian groups, women held prominent leadership roles.[25]

Conversely, and despite some similarities to contemporary women's liberation, much Saint-Simonian doctrine would give serious pause to contemporary feminists, raising some fundamental questions about how a Saint-Simonian utopia would bring women the degree of freedom and equality it seemed to promise. Their doctrine envisioned all human history as a progression[26] from the primitive period of interpersonal hostility and antagonism to a golden future of interpersonal peace, harmony, cooperation, and love—the era of "universal association." They believed that the human social unit has expanded historically from family to tribe to city to nation to the international Catholic Church. Next would come the "universal association." As antagonism became civilized, humanity progressed from cannibalism to slavery to wage labor; as humankind continued to progress, wage slavery and inherited property would be abandoned. In "universal association" no one would inherit wealth, each would work according to his/her talents, and each would be rewarded in accordance with his/her works.[27]

However, the "each" rewarded was not to be the human individual but the human couple. The Saint-Simonians believed in three

[20] *Oeuvres*, XLV, Sermon 47, "Le Prolétaire et les Femmes" (n.d.), 354-60.

[21] *Ibid.*, Sermon 23, 80-81. [22] *Ibid.*, Sermon 49, "Aux Railleurs," 381.

[23] Frank E. Manuel, *The Prophets of Paris*, 157 and 185.

[24] Michael St. John Packe, *The Life of John Stuart Mill* (New York, 1954), 94-97. Frank E. Manuel comments (154): "They ennobled the commonest labor by performing it with devotion."

[25] Hedman, 107 and 161.

[26] The progression was not linear but in alternating cycles of "organic" (spiritually unified, well-organized) phases and "critical" phases (eras of doubt, social disorganization, and anomie). The Saint-Simonians believed that the modern "critical" period began in the fifteenth century and needed to be replaced by an organic one to facilitate human happiness.

[27] *The Doctrine*, see n. 14 above.

major human faculties: intellect (reason), the instrument of science; sympathy or morality (love), the source of fine arts; and physical force, the instrument of productive industry. Society had left the moral-loving-artistic faculty underdeveloped, keeping women, who excelled in this faculty, in severe subjugation. As humanity, through Saint-Simonian teachings, began to value human compassion above sterile material industry and cold science, women would be respected for their emotive gifts. Joining men of similar tastes and skills, women would provide the gentle, loving dimension that made each couple the perfect unit of the new society.

To accomplish this, however, it was crucial that women stay as sweet as they are; it was not suitable for women to enter the hostile, competitive, and destructive rat-race of public society. Saint-Simonians announced that they "want women to enter into social and political functions, but not in this world where war (more or less disguised) is what reigns." They meant women to leave domesticity *only* after the new religion had established "the abolition of war, the reign of peace, the amelioration of the fate of the most numerous and poorest class [the proletariat] . . . , the association of all men into a single family." They openly proclaimed:

We declare . . . woman is today legitimately excluded from public life. But we ask, is this exclusion a condemnation of women or is it not rather an express condemnation of your society? . . . To the subjugation of woman and the imperfection of the conjugal union correspond the belief in the principle of evil, bloody sacrifice, war, slavery, privileges of birth, the oppression of industry, the exclusive and hostile development of the faculties of man; to the definitive emancipation of woman and to the perfection of marriage correspond belief in a single God, abolition of the law of blood, the establishment of peace, the eradication of slavery [and] the privileges of birth, the emancipation of industy, and the free development of human activity.[28]

In short, the Saint-Simonians opposed emancipating "la femme" until the world became feminized. Such was the gist of their feminism. They did, however, believe women's emancipation would arrive shortly because the feminization of the world was imminent.

Paradoxically, their belief in the Eternal Feminine produced a more thorough-going dedication to women's autonomy than that ex-

---

[28] This paragraph summarizes the sermon of E. Barrault, "Le Mariage," from *Oeuvres*, XLIV, Sermon 23. The material in quotation is my translation from 74, 95-96, 76, and 78. A small off-shoot group of self-proclaimed "Saint-Simonian" women, who published the monthly journal, *La Femme Libre*, from Aug. 1832 to Jan. 1834, evidently differed from the leadership on this stay-at-home belief and denied that the couple was the true social unit. See S. Joan Moon, "The St. Simoniennes. . . ." They did accept the St. Simonian premises of universal association and the special qualities of the female nature.

hibited by writers like Mill who hedged on the question of woman's nature. Precisely *because* woman was and always would be a very different creature from man, Saint-Simonians believed it was and always had been thoroughly wrong for man to establish laws over women.[29] Although Saint-Simonians did not oppose hierarchical rule for their utopia, at the top they wanted not one but two rulers: male and female. For men were so different from women that:

. . . we cannot pretend to regulate definitively the relationships between the sexes as long as the aspirations of women are not united with ours . . . . But we who summon women to equa ity, we would be lying . . . if we pretended to establish a comprehensive anu c finitive moral system before the position of women had been improved to t e point where they could speak without fear and could accept the moral law freely and willingly. . . . Our entire aim at this moment, then, is to give women a sense of their strength and their dignity, so that they can make all their sufferings and desires known without shame. . . . As we come to *achieve* the emancipation of women, we will give every woman the power to speak, that she may herself hurl a challenge not only at her persecutors but at those who judge her. Oh! When women have the strength to speak . . . then will we come to understand the morality of these men who are without pity for women, who give them tasks beyond their strength. . . .[30]

And the cult searched quixotically for the ideal priestess-ruler who could join "priest" Enfantin in leading humanity into the happy world of universal association.

The feminism of the Saint-Simonians, then, was a sharply double-edged sword. Women need autonomy, but the purpose of this autonomy was to ensure that society establish roles suited to the gentle, sweet, and ultimately weak, nature of women. Androgynous rule would supersede masculine rule because male rulers were guilty of assigning women "tasks beyond their strength":[31] thus, the argument for women's social and political equality rested, paradoxically, on the premise of an intrinsic and permanent weakness. The leadership of the Saint-Simonians never detailed woman's special role within each couple, but they did say enough about their view of woman's eternal (and eternally limited) nature to prompt the question: With friends like the Saint-Simonians, did women's liberation need enemies?

---

[29] *Oeuvres*, XLV, Sermon 47, "Le Prolétaire et les Femmes," 358-59, and Sermon 48, "L'Affranchisement des Femmes," 372-73.

[30] This excerpt from *Oeuvres*, XLV, Sermon 48, is from the passage in Frank E. and Fritzie P. Manuel, *op. cit.*, 297-98.   [31] *Ibid.*, 297-98.

III. *Fourier and Women's Liberation*—Like his contemporary Saint-Simonians,[32] Charles Fourier called forthrightly for women's equality and freedom, condemned their servitude within the existing marriage institution, and railed against the double standard of sexual chastity.[33] He too believed that all important jobs should be open to women on the basis of skill and aptitude rather than closed on account of gender. But unlike the Saint-Simonians, Fourier spoke of women as individuals, not as half the human couple. Fourier's concern was to liberate every human individual, man, woman, and child (whom he called the "third" or "neuter" sex), in two senses. First, through education he wished to free their faculties for maximum development. Education was to begin by age two and was to be handled by skilled experts (rather than haphazardly qualified parents), at community expense, for all, regardless of economic status or gender.[34] Secondly, and more radically, Fourier sought the liberation of human passion from all repression and frustration.[35] He believed that if his utopia (Harmony) were established, every human problem could be eliminated: not only the obvious economic wants like hunger and need for shelter but also boredom, anxiety, and sexual frustration.[36]

[32] Actually, Fourier published his first two major works, *La Théorie des Quatre Mouvements* (1808) and *Traité de l'Association Domestique-Agricole ou Attraction Industrielle* (1822; later published as *l'Unité Universelle*), before the death of Comte Henri de Saint-Simon in 1825, and thus before development of the "Saint-Simonian" doctrine of Enfantin and the other self-professed disciples. But Fourier's ideas did not reach a very wide audience until after the apex of Saint-Simonianism in 1832.

[33] For useful surveys of Fourier's thought, see Nicholas V. Riasanovsky, *The Teaching of Charles Fourier* (Berkeley, 1969); Frank Manuel, "Charles Fourier: The Burgeoning of Instinct," *The Prophets of Paris* (New York, 1962), 195-248; and *The Utopian Vision of Charles Fourier: Selected Texts on Work, Love, and Passionate Attraction*, trans., ed. with intro. by Jonathan Beecher and Richard Bienvenu (Boston, 1971).

[34] For a typical example of Fourier's discussions on education, see *Oeuvres Complètes de Charles Fourier* (Paris, 1966-68), in 12 vols. (hereinafter designated *O.C.*), VI, Chaps. 17-24. Although "formal" education began at about age two, childcare would be communal from birth, and babies' faculties were to be scientifically nurtured beginning as early as the age of six months (VI, 176-79).

[35] Fourier did believe that in our present society, "Civilization" (for him, a term of opprobrium), there *were* genuinely anti-social feelings. These were perverted forms of potentially beneficent feelings resulting from initial repression by Civilization. In Harmony, for example, the potential Nero of Rome would turn that inclination toward the socially productive activity of butchering meat (*O.C.*, X, 132-36, first pagination).

[36] His goals included not simply the provision of adequate shelter for everyone's indoor time but also the construction of mall-like buildings so that streets and sidewalks within each Phalanstery (community/town) would be protected from the elements, and, even more ambitiously, control of the elements themselves. Once humankind established Harmony the cosmos would respond by producing a temperate climate on earth (*O.C.*, IX, D2 [632]).

In fact, this distinction between productive faculties and consumption-oriented desires is somewhat alien to Fourier's thought. For him, in a sense, desires *were* stunted faculties needing development: our capacities for feeling, from the gastronomic to the sexual to the loving to the ambitious and conspiratorial, could—with proper techniques—be more fully developed and thus more freely enjoyed. Dulled for 2000 years in "Civilization" (his term for the current epoch), feelings would truly blossom in Harmony: people would live more than twice as long (on the average, one hundred and forty-four years); they would need to sleep only a few hours per night; and waking hours, filled with pleasures "so numerous, so fiery, so varied," would pass as one long ecstatic moment because the individual would live "in a sort of permanent frenzy."[37] Whether one characterizes Fourier's goal with such elevated phrases as "a continuous . . . kaleidoscopic explosion of rapturous joy"[38] or with the more down-to-earth phrases "permanent orgasm" and "eternal convulsion,"[39] the point is clear: his goals for improving human life extended far beyond ameliorating the lot of the poor and the unemployed and providing economic, professional, and political opportunities to women.

Fantastic though his vision was, the feminist message in that vision was an undeniably dominant theme.[40] Fourier's feminist concerns figured in all of his major published works, from the *Théorie de Quatre Mouvements* in 1808 through the two-volume work (published shortly before his death in 1836-37), *La Fausse Industrie*. His thoughts on the importance of women's plight and on the nature of their oppression often have a contemporary ring, even more so than those of the Saint-Simonians. But, as with the Saint-Simonians, other of his major tenets will give serious pause to contemporary proponents of women's liberation.

Fourier announced repeatedly and in forceful terms that women in Civilization have been severely oppressed and particularly victimized.[41] (Moreover, women were even more severely deprived in the stages prior to Civilization.[42]) Their victimization and its solution are two-fold: women are deprived of economic-industrial and amorous fulfillment. Both deprivations are linked to the marriage institutions.

In fact, marriage for Fourier is at the hub of the two axes characterizing any cultural epoch: (1) the method for the social exchange of

---

[37] Fourier, Letter to Napoleon's Attorney-General, 1799, quoted in Manuel, 228.
[38] Riasanovsky, 60.   [39] Manuel, 228.
[40] Riasanovsky, 209, cites a Ph.D. dissertation on Fourier's feminism, to which I did not have access: E. Dessignole, *Le Féminisme d'après la Doctrine Socialiste de Charles Fourier* (Lyons, 1903). See also the somewhat cursory treatment in Hedman, 110-22.
[41] *O.C.*, I, 149-50.   [42] *O.C.*, III, 168-70, 89-90.

commodities (the economic system), and (2) the method of conjugal union between the sexes.[43] Since marriage is both conjugal and economic,[44] Fourier in earlier works stressed the determinative role of the amorous institutions:

There is in each period a characteristic which forms the PIVOT OF THE MECHANISM and whose absence or presence determines the change of period. This trait is always drawn from love. . . . As a general thesis, the Pivotal characteristic, which is always drawn from the amorous customs, brings about all the others; but the characteristics branching off to it do not give birth to the pivotal one, and lead only very slowly to a change of period. Barbarians could adopt up to twelve of the sixteen traits of Civilization [of which many are economic] and still remain Barbarians if they did not adopt the pivotal trait, *the civil liberty of an exclusive wife.*[45]

It was this reasoning concerning the marriage institution, bolstered by the additional premise that "God recognizes as freedom only those liberties extended equally to both sexes," that underlay Fourier's famous italicized assertions that, "As a general thesis: *Social progress . . . occurs by virtue of the progress of women toward liberty, and social decline by virtue of decreases in the liberty of women.*"[46] Thus, the alleviation of women's plight would perforce involve a beneficial transformation of those pivotal institutions of marriage and the family-based economy.

Within Civilization, women's economic and amorous deprivations were intertwined. The typical lot of women, barred from most productive employment, was to be sold into conjugal servitude as soon as they reached marriageable age. For women outside the aristocracy, Fourier lamented that ". . . prostitution more or less prettied up is their only resort."[47] The ever-present knowledge that she will have to attract a buyer-sponsor in the form of a husband had a terribly damaging effect on the personality of a growing girl, Fourier argued, and caused most women to develop vice-ridden characters, marked by servility and deviousness.[48]

---

[43] *O.C.,* XI, 222-23, second pagination. This selection is from manuscripts published only posthumously, in 1857-58. This dual construct parallels assertions by Marx and Engels that the social institutions surrounding the "means of production" (which, in the final analysis, shape human thought and human society consists *both* of relations aiming at material production for the maintenance of life *and* of relations structuring "the production of fresh life in procreation." *German Ideology,* Parts I and III (New York, 1947; originally in unpublished manuscript form in 1845-46), 13-21. See also Friedrich Engels, *The Origin of the Family, Private Property, and the State* (New York, 1972; first pub. 1884), 71-72.

[44] On the economic impact of the monogamous marriage system, see e.g., *O.C.,* XI, second pagination, 108 and 208.

[45] *O.C.,* I, 89. Fourier's emphasis.

[46] *O.C.,* I, 90, 132-33.

[47] *O.C.,* I, 130-31, 149-50; VI, 191.

[48] *O.C.,* I, 147-50.

In Fourier's eyes, the anarchic arrangements of the present economic system produced even more waste and hardship for women than for men. Men faced poor working conditions, unemployment, employment in jobs unsuited to their faculties, and poverty—which produced hunger, ill-health, and despair. Most women not only endured the ills of poverty but also were pressured by gender prejudice out of almost every gainful employment except prostitution or marital subjugation. Once married, the rules were clear: lifetime bondage and obedience to a husband. Fourier even noted that in "civilized" England a husband could still sell his wife to another man.[46]

Besides personal servitude in marriage, women in particular suffered its labor-wasting impact. The main flaw of a household-based economy was tremendous waste, primarily in duplication of functions. Fourier estimated that three-fourths of all women in cities, half of all women in the country, and three-fourths of all household servants—especially kitchen workers—could have their superfluous labor eliminated by the collective efficiency of Harmony.[50]

Fourier's criticism of marriage, however, stressed its emotional and sexual deprivation, especially for women, much more than its economic deprivation.[51] His typical critiques did not tell of wife-beating and household drudgery but focused on women's sexual repression. The nature of women's "oppression" was that "any word or thought consistent with the dictates of nature is imputed to women as a crime." Persecuted "when [they] obey Nature [women must] behave in ways contrary to their desires." This forces them to be fraudulent "in order to free their natural impulses."[52] Thus, "seemly behavior on the part of the stronger sex is treated as a crime on the part of the weaker sex."[53] After noting the solemn decision of the Council of Macon that women had no souls, Fourier points to a British example of legislation that in his judgment is "no less dishonoring" to women: a law permitting a husband to demand pecuniary

[49] *O.C.*, I, 130-31. Thomas Hardy's *The Mayor of Castorbridge* tells of such an incident in England around the first third of the nineteenth century. Fourier's comment appeared in 1808.

[50] *O.C.*, III, 15-16; IV, 173-79; X, 141-43, first pagination.

[51] He believed that marriage had terrible results for men also and that they could be convinced of this. See, e.g., *O.C.*, I, 111-17; IV, 69-85; and XI, 253-64. He did not plan to abolish marriage until he could obtain the consent of husbands and fathers by some sort of world-wide balloting (*O.C.*, I, 104).

[52] *O.C.*, I, 146-47. In writings that were kept unpublished until 1967, Fourier likened this repression of natural impulses to murder: "Fathers are assassinating their daughters, and . . . the laws and prejudices which ignore the natural right to physical love are comparable to the vengeful gods who, according to Calchas, exacted the blood of Iphigenia" (*O.C.*, VII, 440).

[53] *O.C.*, I, 88.

damages from the acknowledged lover of his wife. In the Fourierist calculus, then, the denial of sexual freedom is equated with the denial of an immortal soul. When Fourier contrasts those nations that have dismally failed the "pivotal" test of "the extension of the privileges of women" with those which have not, he writes exclusively of sexual repression or its absence (amorous liberty).[54]

The extension of women's liberty is the key to social progress. "Free love"—and Fourier did use the phrase—did not mean a cruelly anarchic every-person-for-him/herself version, for that would deprive many, especially the old and the ugly, of something as necessary as food. In Harmony, rather than monogamous marriage with its ever-present companion of widespread but dishonestly concealed infidelity that provides some with a wealth of gratification but leaves others emotionally starved,[55] there would be a system of Amorous Guarantees or the Amorous Corporation. In this system, to a "social minimum" of fulfilling work and decent food, clothing, shelter, and entertainment would be added a "sexual minimum" of fulfilling sex.

In Fourier's Utopia people would live in communal households in village units called Phalanxes. Social motivation would be achieved through a complex incentive system based on Fourier's analysis of the 810 personality types—an incentive system that included differential economic rewards, including the right of bestowing inheritances, as well as psychological rewards (e.g., esteem, companionship) and sensual rewards (gastronomic, sexual, etc.). Jobs would be arranged so that work places were always pleasant and people only did tasks that were fun for them, never working at a single job long enough to get bored (i.e., more than two hours). Incentives would also be structured to ensure that everyone received sexual gratification.[56] All physical needs[57] would be satisfied; no one would work or

---

[54] *O.C.*, I, 130-33. See also 150 on Tahiti.

[55] There is a paradox here. Fourier frequently complained that Civilization's sexual double standard oppressed or repressed women, but he just as frequently complained that women as well as men defied the supposed rules and engaged in very widespread debauchery. See, e.g., *O.C.*, XI, 253-64, first pagination, and 219-26, second pagination; IV, 75; IX, 765-71; V, 259-63. He apparently felt that the pressure to be a hypocrite was a terrible burden to bear, and of course it fell more heavily upon women. His yearning for a society in which all human relations could be sincere and authentic was echoed in the movement of the 1960s' New Left, which immediately preceded the contemporary women's liberation movement.

[56] This sexual insurance structure is detailed only in notebooks that were kept unpublished until 1967 (*O.C.*, VII, *The New Amorous World*). But throughout his publications Fourier indicated his intention in a variety of ways, including the use of terms like "Amorous Guarantees." I have focused attention, on the whole, away from this volume because, obviously, it would not have wielded historical influence on the development of a women's liberation ideology. However, it is useful for understanding Fourier's own beliefs.

[57] This included a variety of sexual penchants presently considered deviant, but there would be a strict taboo on sex with or among children. Only after puberty,

make love out of economic necessity; life would be a constant delight. Outside the Phalanxes, massive economic development (e.g., irrigating the Sahara Desert) would be accomplished by volunteer industrial armies, lured from thousands of Phalanxes by Fourier's usual technique of "passionate attraction." The loveliest women would be attracted to the army, some in the virginal group of 15½ to 20 years old for whom the industrial "soldiers" would be contesting. To further attract recruits, the army would engage in nightly amorous festivities. Women would also serve in the ranks of "bacchantes, bayaderes, fakiresses, fairies, magicians, paladines, heroines, and other feminine jobs."[58] The first three are Fourierist terms for amorous adventuresses who use sexual and affectionate wiles to console and distract dejected suitors who have failed in their quest for a beautiful virgin; the second two groups engage in amorous matchmaking; paladines and heroines have honorific titles for impressive accomplishments.[59] What Fourier meant by "other feminine jobs"[60] must be determined by inference.

On occasion, Fourier seems to intend to do away with the sexual division of labor:

one half of the jobs . . . is to be reserved for women; one must avoid relegating them, as among us, to thankless functions, to the servile roles to which they are assigned by philosophy which pretends that woman is made only to scour pots and mend old clothes.[61]

But then emphasis changes from egalitarian group quotas to somewhat more individualized variation:

Although each branch of industry is especially suited to one of the sexes, such as needlework for women and plough-work for men, nonetheless nature loves mixtures, sometimes by halves, and some jobs by a quarter; she wants at least one eighth of the opposite sex in each function. . . . By means of this mixture in each job the feminine sex will form a useful rivalry with the masculine.[62]

Yet Fourier, at other points, made it clear that he expected certain jobs to be performed only by females: the care of babies aged birth to

---

which Fourier placed at 15½, would youths be allowed into the sexual playground (O.C., V, 250-51). Certain social problems that might be anticipated from a system of free love would not trouble Harmony. Fourier admitted that the system would be fully implemented only after venereal disease had been cured (O.C., VII, 220; and I, 150). Overpopulation would not be a problem because when women were well-fed assured his readers (O.C., VI, 335-38; and VIII, 560-61 [these pages are in the section of 457-612, which follows 613-820]). See also V, 252-53.   [58] O.C., VI, 229.

[59] O.C., I, 172-78; IV, 557-64; V, 258-64; VI, 220-30; VII, 156-64, 209-20.

[60] O.C., VI, 229.   [61] O.C., VI, 141.   [62] Ibid., 190-91.

two,[63] needlework,[64] and laundry. In Harmony, he says when the laundry is being cleaned "*women* will not ruin their hands by plunging them into icy or scalding water" (because there will be faucets to regulate the temperature), and he uses only a female term, i.e., laundresses, to describe the laundry workers.[65]

Fourier's basic principles remained: each would work (according to taste and skill) at productive work under pleasant conditions. What varied was his specific conclusion as to how many members of a particular sex would be fulfilled, happy, and competent at needlework, laundry, and babycare. It was crucial that people not be channeled on the basis of gender into an occupation. Fourier even insisted that children aged birth to three should be dressed alike and raised alike so that only their true vocational talents would bloom, rather than a set of conventionally imposed ones.[66] Although the modern reader may see Fourier as short-sighted in failing to realize that excluding male caretakers for the first two years of life might well have a channeling impact on children,[67] one must grant that on the subject of occupation his heart seemed to be in a women's liberation place.

On women's role as bait for industrial armies, however, the problems with Fourier's outlook amount to far more than short-sightedness. To be sure, the "Vestal (virginal) quadrilles" sent by each of the 10,000-100,000 Phalanxes[68] to these armies (in addition to the ten worker-soldiers to be sent) consisted of equal numbers of each sex, but the male half of the quadrille played a very different role from the female. Both were "the best and the brightest" from their respective Phalanxes, both received much honor and luxury and served to attract suitors from the opposite sex into the armies,[69] but their attracting roles varied considerably. In Fourier's eyes the drawing power of a beautiful virgin was intrinsic:

In young women 16-18 years old, nothing commands higher esteem than a virginity beyond doubt, a genuine, unvarnished decorum, an ardent devotion to useful and charitable duties. . . .[70]

---

[63] *O.C.*, VI, Chap. 18; see also 136, where childcare workers have both masculine and feminine titles for children aged two and older (e.g., *mentorin* and *mentorines*) but childcare workers for the babies are only feminine *bonnes* and *nourrices*. Also, Fourier uses female terms for chambermaids and male for stableboys, but there is no clear evidence that he intended to exclude either sex from these two jobs (*O.C.*, IV, 527-30).

[64] *O.C.*, X, 141-42, first pagination.

[65] *O.C.*, I, 178. Emphasis added.   [66] *O.C.*, VI, 180-81.

[67] *Ibid.*, 172-73. See, for example, Dorothy Dinnerstein, *The Mermaid and the Minotaur* (New York, 1976), esp. Chaps. 4-9.

[68] Each Phalanx also sent "ten men" and presumably three women, since women were to total one third of the army (*O.C.*, IV, 557-64).

[69] *O.C.*, I, 172-76.   [70] *O.C.*, V, 235.

Female vestals would naturally be worshipped, and about thirty women per phalanx would be attracted to the role[71] by its prestige and their own penchants. Males were different: they too would have respected "Vestal" roles in Harmony (unlike morally inconsistent Civilization where male virginity was scorned), but within each Phalanx only half as many males as females would be Vestals. Unlike females, youthful male virgins are not intrinsically respectable but seem to be needed in Harmony for two reasons: (1) to provide abstract moral consistency (God favors sex equality),[72] and (2) to mediate between childhood and sexual maturity so that children at younger and younger ages are not prematurely tempted into sexual activity.[73] Moreover, the intrinsic desirability of sexual purity does not attract young men into the Vestalate. Fourier feels the need to explain what sort of men would enter the Vestalate, and he lists three: (1) those who are so distracted and absorbed by the diversified fun of Harmony that they do not start thinking about sex until a later age than usual; (2) those who have their eye on a female Vestal and use this chance to get close to her; and (3) those who want to make a monarchical match for themselves. Royalty will select mates from the industrial army, and being a Vestal gives a young man an early chance to enter the army (to which admission is very competitive). In short, women Vestals are considered prizes *as such*; male Vestals are earning the chance to *become* considered a prize by joining the army where they can perform prodigious industrial feats or excel in competitive games.[74]

Both men and women would be used as societal sex objects: "Love . . . will thus become one of the most brilliant mainsprings of the social mechanism."[75] But the emphasis is on the use of *women* to attract *men* to labor: a cooperative, multi-phalanx "haying is followed by a meal attended by the loveliest women. . . ."[76] Fourier's examples of vestals selecting mates from their various suitors always discuss women vestals, and his treatments of great industrial tasks typically estimate the number of *men* (*hommes*) needed for the job.[77] He makes the point pretty bluntly: "the gathering of the most famous female vestals is one of the baits [*amorces*] which attracts young folks to these armies."[78]

It is precisely this aspect of Fourier's thought that seems to open him to Karl Marx's criticism of "crude proposals" for "the community of women." Marx complained that these end up making woman

---

[71] *O.C.*, V, 235.   [72] *O.C.*, V, 248.   [73] *Ibid.*, 250-51.
[74] *Ibid.*, 251-55.   [75] *O.C.*, I, 178.   [76] *O.C.*, I, 177.
[77] E.g., I, 177, on the job of haying; *O.C.*, IV, 557, 559, 561, and 562. But cf. statement in *O.C.*, I, 176, that "legionnaires of both sexes will execute works the mere thought of which will frighten our mercenary souls."
[78] *O.C.*, VI, 229.

into "a piece of communal and common property. . . . [W]oman passes from exclusive, private marriage to general prostitution."[79] In Fourier's scheme, women's sexual services are bought by society as a whole to further industrial, or generally, economic, productivity. Fourier seems to argue implicitly that the use of sex for economic benefits to the community is not demeaning if the sexual favors are granted to someone for whom one bears genuine affection or some sort of penchant and if the sexual activity is not performed under economic pressure.[80] It is not at all clear that this answer is adequate, however.

If all individuals are to coexist in freedom and equal dignity, it seems deeply problematic to compare lust for another person with hunger for a piece of bread. This outlook on sexual passion prompted Fourier to write in an unpublished manuscript:

[N]ature . . . has provided helpful knights even for individuals who are no longer of an age to be pleasing; here is the proof . . . . In 1816 a young man was tried in France for having raped six women aged 60 to 80 . . . . They found him guilty and sentenced him but perhaps it would have been wiser to distribute pieces of his clothing as religious relics in order to propagate his good example. It is evidence that this young phoenix acted *out of need, and that need of this genre both in men and women can be pushed to the point of urgent necessity quite as much as that for food.*[81] (Emphasis in original.)

Fourier dubbed this rapist of old women a knight ("*champion*") presumably not because he "did them a favor" (in the too-common misogynist formulation) but because he exemplified two Fourierist principles: (1) that there was adequate variety of passions in the natural world to fulfill everyone's sexual needs (including old ladies') on a purely voluntary basis, and (2) that sexual passion was a *need* just like hunger. Still, the example of rapist as hero is revealing, for Fourier's tone takes him all to often to the brink of depicting woman as the

[79] *The Economic and Philosophic Manuscript of 1844*, trans. Martin Milligan (New York, 1964), 133.

[80] Fourier revealed in the manuscripts published only in 1967 that the exchange of sexual favors would not be quite the one hundred per cent free and authentic exchange that he had earlier made it seem. Sexual favors are given to the old and ugly, for example, for a variety of non-personal reasons, e.g., as penance for infidelities or in order to obtain glory as a "saintly" person (*O.C.*, VII, 434-45 and 43-81, esp. 80 on sex with deformed people). Fourier evidently intended to publish even these manuscripts despite their shocking contents of bizarrely detailed and obsessively planned, community-wide sexual orgies, for he wrote that even these contents "merely lift a corner of the veil" and that he would "not provide an outline of all these [sexual activities]; the civilized are not sufficiently free from prejudicies to be initiated into these mysteries" (VII, 393).

[81] *O.C.*, VII, 440.

sexual servicer of society. And if he were ever to discover that his dream of harmonious, free, passional fulfillment for all were unattainable, it is not at all clear that he would have rejected as a next-best alternative the Marquis de Sade's dictum that all humans have a right to total sexual gratification and that any human desired sexually by another thus has a *duty* to oblige.[82]

One need not, however, take Fourier beyond his own stated position in order to criticize him. A world in which human beings perform the societal role of serving as tactile stimulant to other people is a world where some people are treating other people as less than human, as objects. That Fourier's scheme would give women the reciprocal right to treat men as sex objects does not succeed in making the arrangement a humane one.

In certain respects, Fourier's vision took very important strides toward arguing for women's liberation, as that term is understood today. He advocated for women not only legal and political equality but also educational equality beginning in infancy and true equality of occupational freedom. Women, even mothers, would be freed from the specific duties of home and childcare. He also wished to free women from the unfairness of the sexual double standard. It is true that certain aspects of his notion of the perfect society, from a contemporary women's liberation perspective, were less than perfect and tended to approach a socialized version of Hugh Hefner's "Playboy philosophy." It is also true that certain aspects of his vision were sheer lunacy—e.g., his belief that the planets copulated with one another, that the sea would turn into lemonade, etc.[83] These weaknesses, however, do not negate the contribution that his vision has made to the historical development of the women's liberation movement.

IV. *Conclusion*—Although John Stuart Mill and Karl Marx, as more coherent, rational, and careful thinkers, have perhaps deserved the additional attention that they have received as philosophers of feminism,[84] and although the religious mysticism of the Saint-

---

[82] Excerpt from *Philosophy in the Bedroom*, entitled "A Bedroom Discourse" in *French Utopias* (n. 13 above), 228-32. This pamphlet was originally published by a group of Saint-Simonians in 1848 (ed. note, 217).

[83] See summary of these elements in Riasanovsky, 86-100.

[84] See, e.g., Tovey and Tovey (n. 6 above); Goldstein (n. 7 above); Jane Flax, "Do Feminists Need Marxism," *Quest,* 3, No. 1 (1976), 47-58; and Hal Draper, "Marx and Engels on Women's Liberation," in *Female Liberation,* ed. Roberta Salper (New York, 1972), 83-107. In standard anthologies on the history of feminist thought, the inclusion of Mill and/or Engels is (rightfully) *de rigueur,* but the utopian socialists are (wrongfully) excluded. See, e.g., Alice Rossi, ed., *The Feminist Papers* (New York, 1973); and Miriam Schneir, ed., *Feminism: The Essential Historical Writings* (New York, 1972).

Simonians and the quasi-lunacy of Charles Fourier properly exclude them from the ranks of "philosophers," the widespread neglect of these utopian thinkers, particularly by historians of feminism, has been undeserved. Although the women's liberation ideology of the twentieth century did not spring full-blown from the mind of any single nineteenth-century thinker, it also is not lacking in roots within that earlier turbulent era. Both the Saint-Simonians and Fourier himself contributed important seeds to the doctrine of women's liberation, seeds that lay dormant for many centuries but that came to fruition in the more nurturant conditions of the late twentieth century. Their seminal role in the history of feminism deserves acknowledgment.

University of Delaware.

XV

SEX AND SOCIALISM: THE OPPOSITION OF THE FRENCH LEFT TO BIRTH CONTROL IN THE NINETEENTH CENTURY

By Angus McLaren

In the last decades of the nineteenth century the birth rate fell throughout western Europe. In France the decline, which began almost a hundred years earlier, proceeded at an unparalleled pace, plummeting from 34.8 births per 1000 in 1800 to 22.0 per 1000 in 1900.[1] Family planning on so wide a scale could not escape the attention of any serious student of social change, yet at the beginning of this century Georges Sorel noted that there was no problem that socialists had treated so superficially.[2] A rapid perusal of the works of the leading nineteenth-century writers of the French left provides abundant evidence that their discussion of population pressures was not only rudimentary, it was many times confused and eccentric. In what follows I sketch out the general lines of their treatment of the population question and offer some explanations as to why they failed to come to grips with the issue of birth control. In isolating one problem new light will be cast on several of the broader traditions of the French left: its views on women, on the family, on pleasure—especially sexual pleasure—as a measure of happiness, and on the relationship of sex to politics.

Given the small number of historians who have as yet broached the question of birth control it could be easily assumed that the subject was little discussed in the 1800's. It is true that references to actual contraceptive techniques, even those contained in medical manuals, were usually couched in vague and allusive language. Nevertheless, the general question of the role played by family size in the health and happiness of both the nation and the individual household was a topic that attracted the attention of a host of social observers. In *Mémoires de deux jeunes mariées,* for example, Balzac had Mme de l'Estorade advise Mlle de Chaulieu that to bear more than two children was to condemn beloved beings to a life of misery. A thoughtful husband spared his young wife the responsibility of deciding whether or not to limit the family size; he made the decision himself.[3] But could one ex-

[1]J. Bourgeois-Pichat, "The General Development of the Population of France Since the Eighteenth Century," *Population in History,* ed. D. V. Glass and D. E. C. Eversley (London, 1965), 489; also Hélène Bergues *et al., La prévention des naissances dans la famille* (Paris, 1960).

[2]Georges Sorel, *Matériaux d'une théorie du prolétariat* (Paris, 1919), 196. For the purposes of this paper no stringent definition of socialism is necessary; the term "the left" will be used to mean the socialist left.

[3]Honoré de Balzac, *Mémoires de deux jeunes mariées,* in *Oeuvres complètes* (Paris, 1869), I, 202.

pect social reformers to be overly interested in the private practices of upper-class women? Contraception was long popularly associated with the world of aristocrats and prostitutes.[4] Two responses can be made to this objection. First, even if birth control were in fact practiced only by the upper classes the historian has to explain why reformers who were otherwise campaigning for full social equality should seek to prevent the lower classes from aping their "betters" in this particular area. Second, though most observers agreed that the upper classes were the first to limit the size of their families and that the practice was then taken up in the late eighteenth century by the bourgeoisie, there were in the earliest writings on the subject references to members of the lower classes following suit. In 1760 Jean-Philippe Dutoit-Mambrini declared in *L'Onanisme* that the poor were also tempted by "defensive measures."[5] Moheau warned his readers in 1778: ". . . already the deadly secrets unknown to every animal but man have reached the countryside; even in the villages nature is deceived."[6] In 1782 Père Féline agreed that onanism was common among both the rich and the poor.[7] So concerned were the French clergy with the extent of the "vice" that in 1816, 1822, and 1823 they asked the Penitentiary how they should deal with it. By the 1850's the use of *coitus interruptus* by artisans had, according to Dr. Mayer, "devenue à notre époque d'un usage presque général."[8] In the latter half of the century even conservative investigators were commenting sympathetically on the terror experienced by those working-class women still subjected to repeated pregnancies.

Take a worker's wife; she prefers to be beaten than to risk having another child; but as she is the weaker, she often receives at the one and the same time both the beating and the child. The fear of having a child is more frequently than one supposes a cause of discord in the poor households as well as in the wealthy.[9]

By the end of the century working-class women were demanding information on contraceptive measures. One wrote to the economist, Charles Gide,

Our poor working-class mothers see with terror the ceaseless increase of the number of their children. They cannot raise them. They often lose half of them

[4]M. Guyau, *L'Irréligion de l'avenir* (Paris, 1887), 282. Birth control and contraception will be used to refer to practices to prohibit conception during intercourse; family planning could mean anything from abstinence to infanticide.

[5]J. P. Dutoit-Mambrini, *L'Onanisme ou discours philosophiques et moral sur la luxure artificielle & sur tous les crimes relatifs* (Lausanne, 1760), 60.

[6]Moheau, *Recherches et considérations sur la population de la France* (Paris, 1778), II, 102.

[7]Père Féline, *Catéchisme des gens mariés* (Paris, 1880), 9. In *La Terre* 1871), Émile Zola provides perhaps the best known account of a peasant girl demanding her partner to withdraw before ejaculating.

[8]Dr. A. Mayer, *Des rapports conjugaux* (Paris, 1857), 144.

[9]Guyau, *L'Irréligion,* 282–83.

and those left are weak and sickly. They [the mothers] are physically and morally exhausted. The great majority are ignorant of the means employed, it seems, for a long time by the well-to-do classes. . . . What they unfortunately too often do is attempt to remove the beginnings of a pregnancy. They thus injure their health. . . . In order to teach these women already over-burdened with children should we not instruct ourselves *seriously* and *honestly* [sic] on preventive measures so as to tell them about such means?[10]

The responses made to such pleas by the Catholic clergy and liberal economists have been documented elsewhere.[11] The Church was hostile to birth control and true to the injunction "Go forth and multiply." The extent of family planning could not, of course, be ignored; confessors were advised to assume that it was the husband's responsibility and to avoid embarrassing questions that might drive women from the Church. In the eighteenth century most French political economists accepted a growing population as a sign of the nation's well-being, but in the first half of the nineteenth century Malthus' disciples won an increasing number of converts to the theory that a stable population was preferable. Such stability was to be attained by the working class prudently postponing marriage. After France's defeat at the hands of Prussia in 1871, however, fears were expressed in terms of increasing hysteria that the country's slow population growth was leading to moral and political collapse. The century ended with the clergy and many economists rallying to ward off the threat of depopulation.

What was the attitude of the French left? Its most influential representatives opposed the proposition that population could and should be controlled. Their response was motivated by the following concerns which will be examined in detail: first, that the "population question" was a false issue manufactured by reactionaries to turn attention away from the question of social reform; secondly, that though population could not be controlled, nature or providence would ensure that over-population would not take place; thirdly, that if birth control freed women from their natural duties the relationship of the sexes would be changed and the family undermined; and lastly, that sensual pleasure, which might be increased by the practice of birth control, was not a true measure of happiness and should not be pursued.

To begin with the left's refusal to accept the proposition that there was a "population problem" it is necessary to recall that most

[10]Charles Gide, "Le dépeuplement de la France," *La Revue hebdomadaire,* 19 (May 8, 1909), 143 (the addenda are Gide's).

[11]J. L. Flandrin, *L'Église et le contrôle des naissances* (Paris, 1970); T. Zeldin, "The Conflict of Moralities: Confession, Sin and Pleasure in Nineteenth Century France," *Conflicts in French Society* (London, 1870), 13–51; J. T. Noonan, *Contraception: A History of its Treatment by Catholic Theologians and Canonists* (Cambridge, Mass., 1965); J. J. Spengler, *France Faces Depopulation* (Durham, 1938) and "French Population Theory Since 1800," *Journal of Political Economy,* 44 (1936), 577–631; René Goddard, *Histoire des doctrines de la population* (Paris, 1923); Francesco Nitti, *Population and the Social System* (London, 1894).

eighteenth-century writers believed that population growth was both a cause and an effect of a nation's wealth. Rousseau was stating a commonplace when he declared:

What is the purpose of political association? It is the preservation and prosperity of its members. And what is the surest sign of their preservation and prosperity? It is their number and population.[12]

Indeed the old argument that the ancient world had been more populous than the modern, and that France was actually underpopulated, was still being raised at the end of the century. Poverty, declared Mably, Morelly, and Rousseau, was not caused by the natural increase of the nation's numbers but by the faults of the existing form of society. Social inequalities could be eliminated by redistributing wealth and providing for all. The *patriotes* carried on this argument into the revolution, attributing what they took to be a declining population to fiscal injustices and ecclesiastical celibacy. François-Noel Babeuf (1760–97), the heir of the Spartan egalitarianism of Rousseau and Mably, who made the first practical attempt at establishing a socialist state, set the line of the nineteenth-century socialists' discussion of population. Population pressure did not pose a problem to existing society; if it were to become one in the future it still could only be considered a secondary issue.

I believe that even in the case where it was recognized that the means of subsistence of a Nation would not be sufficient to satisfy the appetites of all its members; I believe that then the simple laws of nature command, instead of depopulation, the partial deprivation of each of its members, to satisfy equally, in the usual proportions the needs of all.[13]

Babeuf was addressing himself to a hypothetical case but his concern reflected the spirit of the times; a year after his death in 1798 Malthus published what was to be the most famous study of the problem, *An Essay on the Principles of Population.*

Malthus was not a disinterested observer; he undertook his investigations with the purpose in mind of destroying the egalitarian theories of Godwin and Condorcet. The result of such utopian schemes, declared Malthus, would be that population would soon overshoot the food supply and be overwhelmed by vice and misery. For his contemporaries his most startling revelation, however, was not that food supplies were increasing in arithmetic and population in geometric progressions, but that the major cause of existing poverty was the "reckless overbreeding of the poor."[14] The upper classes in both France and England, slowly

[12]J. J. Rousseau, *Du contrat social* (Amsterdam, 1762), 119.

[13]*Du système de dépopulation* (Paris, an III), 35. Though this passage is taken from his response to the reputed Jacobin plot to depopulate France, it is representative of Babeuf's thinking. The association of depopulation with the excesses of the Terror was a theme later popularized by Taine.

[14]*An Essay on the Principles of Population* (London, 1803), 531.

having to relinquish traditional arguments for the maintenance of their privileged status were now provided with modern, scientific justifications. Malthus had proven to their satisfaction that reform was futile.

After Malthus, French liberal economists swung round to the view that an ever-increasing population was not desirable. Writers on the left who quite naturally viewed Malthus as an advocate of the propertied classes, clung to the older opinion that the failure of a nation to grow had to be seen as a sign of decay; such growth could be more than made up for by the increases in productivity provided by organized labor. Saint-Simon (1760-1825), considered as a man of the left to the extent that he was opposed to individualistic capitalism, was true to the spirit of the eighteenth century in declaring population growth the best test of a country's prosperity.[15] His early associate Auguste Comte (1798-1857) described population as the mother of social progress and decried Malthus' argument as a sophistic theory, an amalgam of "irrational exaggerations," an immoral aberration which revealed the antipathy of the wealthy for the poor.[16] Philippe-Michel Buonarroti (1761-1837) who popularized Babeuf's thought in the *Conspiration pour l'égalité* (1828) carried on the master's message that in the egalitarian state everything would "favor the multiplication of the species."[17] In *Voyage en Icarie* (1840) the communist Étienne Babeuf (1788-1856) claimed that in his reformed society the population would be doubled.[18] P. J. Proudhon (1809-65), though critical of every other contemporary socialist, did agree that Malthus was responsible for the propagation of a doctrine that would destroy both the family and the economy:

. . . the family dies out and with the family property; the economic movement is left unfinished, and society returns to a state of barbarism. Malthus and the moral economists made marriage inaccessible; the physician-economists make it purposeless: both add to the lack of bread the lack of affections, provoke the disintegration of social ties. . . .[19]

The romantic socialist, Pierre Leroux (1797-1871), was of the same opinion; the "population question" was simply another attack launched by liberals on the lower classes.

After having preached to the poor continence, celibacy, and forbidden marriage before the age of thirty, they have invented what they call *checks* or artificial

[15]Frank E. Manuel, *The New World of Henri Saint-Simon* (Cambridge, Mass., 1965), 227-28.

[16]A. Comte, *Cours de philosophie positive* (Paris, 1842), IV, 644ff. Sismonde de Sismondi could be included here as a left-leaning liberal critical of Malthus: *Nouveaux principes d'économie politique* (Paris, 1819), II, 248ff., and *Études sur l'économie politique* (Paris, 1837), I, 130, II, 266ff.

[17]*Conspiration pour l'égalité* (Paris, 1828), I, 120.

[18]*Voyage en Icarie* (Paris, 1842), 121.

[19]*Système des contradictions économiques ou philosophie de la misère* (Paris, 1846), II, 449.

obstacles to population . . . to teach men to satisfy their instincts without obeying the laws of nature, to violate them was a shame reserved for the atheists that are called economists.[20]

In England, wrote Leroux, the same economists, ignorant of both the moral and economic calamities that declining population produced, were going so far as to defend infanticide.[21]

Now it is important to recall that Malthus' famous plea for "moral restraint" was aimed at convincing the poor to postpone marriage as long as possible; the parson did not condone the use of contraception after marriage and was thus in complete opposition to the birth controllers.[22] This nuance in Malthusian thought was overlooked by many of his disciples and critics. Both sides were far more concerned with his major argument that individual self-improvement and social reform were mutually exclusive, antagonistic goals. In adopting this premise the left had no choice but to oppose population control; to accept the social necessity of either contraception or postponed marriage would, it was felt, be tantamount to acknowledging that unemployment and poverty were natural problems to be overcome by individual self-help.

If the left suspected anyone who worried about the population problem of being an enemy of social reform, did this mean that they foresaw the population increasing interminably? This proposition, they recognized, was untenable. They were thus led to elaborate the second theme of their anti-Malthusian argument, that once a socialist society was created the population would be balanced by "natural means."[23] Just as a man stopped growing once he reached maturity, so too the population would cease to increase once society reached some predetermined level of development. A problem arose, however, when the various socialist theorists attempted to explain the means by which benevolent nature would prevent over-population from occurring.

Proudhon condemned contraception and declared that abortion, defended by a certain Dr. G. . . ., was equal to murder. Charles Loudon's theory that population stability could be attained by extending a mother's period of lactation during which she was less fertile (a theory that won Leroux's interest), was also rejected by Proudhon on the grounds that it sprang from a pessimistic appraisal of man's potential.[24]

[20]*Malthus et les économistes* (Paris, 1849), 104–05.

[21]*Ibid.*, 104. Leroux was apparently referring to Marcus, *An Essay on Populousness* (London, 1838), not realizing that it was a Swiftian attack on, not a defense of, infanticide.

[22]Hence Catholics such as De Maistre, Villeneuve-Bargemont, and Charles de Coux could argue that celibacy was not harmful and that indeed only Catholicism could provide the "moral restraint" for which Malthus called. J. P. Duroselle, *Les débuts du catholicisme sociale en France, 1822–1870* (Paris, 1951), 40ff.

[23]The socialist's faith in nature mirrored the Catholic's in the Creator; e.g., Père Féline, *Catéchisme,* 41–42.

[24]*Système des contradictions,* II, 453, 456; Charles Loudon, *The Equilibrium of Population and Sustenance Demonstrated* (London, 1836).

Even the rhythm method which involved no artificial checks which could offend the susceptibilities of the natural law advocate, was declared to be morally unacceptable.

With this easy means of playing without paying, and of sinning without being surprised, modesty is no longer but a stupid and troublesome prejudice, marriage a bothersome and useless convention.[25]

It was the very idea that birth control made life easier for man that most enraged Proudhon. Labor was the essential characteristic of the human being; struggle and sacrifice of pleasure produced progress. The limitation of population could thus be viewed only as a sign of moral advance if it was a consequence not of the pursuit of pleasure but of a greater devotion to labor. Proudhon claimed, as had Comte, that the great men of history had led chaste lives while the lazy and poor had been prolific. This was the real law of population.

The industrial faculty exercises itself only at the expense of the prolific faculty. Labor is an active cause of the cooling of love: it is the most powerful of all antiaphrodisiacs, that much more powerful especially as it simultaneously affects the mind and the body.[26]

The argument of the socialist theoretician Louis Blanc (1811–82) was similar to Proudhon's in that it contained the idea that the cultivation of manners, the displacement of the lower appetites by the higher, would have a depressing effect on the birth rate.[27] He declared that natality was simply a reflection of the standard of living; when the latter reached a certain level smaller families became the norm. To support his thesis he presented data drawn from Paris which revealed that the wealthier *arrondissements* had fewer births per family than the poorer.[28] The question was to be asked, however, why England, which was more prosperous than France, continued to have a faster growing population?

The discussion of the natural levelling-off of population even led Louis-Auguste Blanqui (1805–81), traditionally portrayed as the cool, calculating revolutionary, into realms of bizarre speculation. He shared Blanc's belief that as the standard of living was raised the birth rate dropped, but he interpreted this phenomenon in a most peculiar fashion. The improvements in public health that would inevitably follow the revolution would result in a preponderance of male births. With fewer women there would be smaller population increases although each

[25]*Système des contradictions*, II, 455.   [26]*Ibid.*, II, 477.
[27]T. Dézamy, *Code de la communauté* (Paris, 1842), 193.
[28]*Organization du travail* (Paris, 1848), 152–53. Blanc came close to saying, as had the conservative Catholic H. A. Frégier, that only the sober artisan would have the self-control necessary to practice *coitus interruptus*. Frégier also made the interesting point that the self-centered artisan who adopted the practice would soon shed the traditional lower class sympathy for unwed mothers and illegitimate children: *Des classes dangereuses de la population dans les grandes villes* (Paris, 1840), I, 326–35.

mother would still bear a large number of children. The *faits connus* on which Blanqui based his theory were drawn from contemporary reports on Tibet.[29] Setting aside the exotic trappings of the argument, it is apparent that Blanqui's response to the birth-control issue was essentially the same as that of most other socialists—a refusal to envisage the direct control of conception as either moral or natural and a faith in providence eventually providing a panacea. The antithesis between the class struggle and individual self-help was reiterated. After the revolution a real solution to the population problem would be provided not just for calculating individuals but for all.[30]

The third theme of the French left's argument against birth control was that it was immoral inasmuch as the practice violated not divine, but natural laws. By freeing women from their natural duties and responsibilities it frustrated the purposes of the family and threatened society at large. Here again nineteenth-century social theorists were following their eighteenth-century forebears. The *philosophes* had sought not to tear down but to build up society on surer foundations. Though they criticized ethics based on religious values they insisted that their natural morality would provide a guarantee of public order. The family, in the eyes of such men, was the source of all social cohesion, a natural entity that had to be buttressed, not undermined. Morelly, for example, believed that by marrying and having children a man provided evidence of his interest in the well-being of the community and therefore, in his *Code de la nature* (1755), marriage was made obligatory.[31] It was due to this concern for the family unit that the *philosophes* who, save for Condorcet, were otherwise little interested in women, felt forced to devote some attention to the role of wife and mother. There was always the danger, warned Rousseau, that the weaker sex, in giving in to its natural penchant for indolence and licentiousness by refraining from having children, could undermine both the family and the state.

Since the state of motherhood is onerous, one soon finds the means of avoiding it altogether; one wishes to do a useless task [i.e., have sex but avoid conception] in order to continually redo it, and to the detriment of the species is turned the attraction given in order to multiply it.[32]

Similarly, Babeuf viewed women with their more passionate natures as a threat to the communist society he envisaged in which happiness would not be found in sensual pleasure but in hard work.[33] Future

[29]*Critique sociale* (Paris, 1885), I, 143–44.

[30]For similar arguments on food and falling birth rates see Charles Fourier, *Le Nouveau monde industriel,* in *Oeuvres* (Paris, 1841–45), VI, 337ff., and from the other side of the channel, Thomas Doubleday. *The True Law of Population* (London, 1842), 275.

[31]*Code de la nature* (Paris, 1910), 99.

[32]*Émile ou de l'éducation,* in *Oeuvres complètes* (Paris, 1971), III, 25.

[33]Cited by Buonarroti, *Système politique* (Paris, 1842), 49–50. Babeuf was given to the use of Samson and Delilah imagery.

harmony, he declared, would depend on limiting their education, maintaining their domestic subordination, and dulling their senses by manual labor. According to Buonarroti, however, women's work was not to interfere with their primary function: "The man, destined by nature to [a life of] movement and action, must feed and defend the country; the woman must give it vigorous citizens."[34] Cabet was working towards the same sort of state in which marriage and fidelity would be civic duties. Celibacy and adultery were to be crimes in Icarie; the moral control of the community would in addition preclude youth from having any "secrets." Cabet, instead of discussing birth control presented a plan for both the doubling of the population and the breeding of a super race. Woman was not to be freed from child-bearing; she was to be subjected to the dictates of a *Commission de perfectionnement*.[35]

A radical change in the appreciation of women has been credited by a number of historians to Saint-Simon and his progeny.[36] Saint-Simon himself showed little real interest in improving the status of women. His follower, Barthélemy-Prosper Enfantin (1796–1864) preached the "rehabilitation of the flesh," but it is difficult to determine what his heralded emancipation of women meant in practical terms.[37] In theory he broke down the old laws of matrimony; in practice he and his followers attempted to prove their higher morality by leading an ascetic life at Menilmontant. Enfantin, his time taken up as it was by the more serious business of searching for the Woman Messiah, had no time for such mundane problems as birth control and does not seem to have considered the population problem. Far from freeing woman, he envisaged subjecting both sexes to the theocratic rule of the *Mère* and *Père*.

Enfantin's religious mysticism represented one aspect of Saint-Simon's patrimony; Auguste Comte's positivism another.[38] The Church had presented woman as primarily a propagator of the species; Comte declared that her essential vocation was that of wife. This was hardly emancipation. Wife and husband were not equal; man was superior in force, woman in affection. Comte condemned the "subversive dreams"

---

[34] *Conspiration pour l'égalité,* I, 282–83.

[35] *Voyage en Icarie,* 140, 122. On the idea of systematic procreation reserved for the best physical and intellectual specimens, cf. Comte, *Système de politique positive* (Paris, 1851), IV, 278.

[36] E.g., George Lichtheim, *The Origins of Socialism* (London, 1969), 244; F. Manuel, *The Prophets of Paris* (Cambridge, Mass., 1962), 157.

[37] S. Charléty, *Enfantin* (Paris, 1930); Michel Chevalier, ed., *Religion saint-simonienne* (Paris, 1832), 176–81; Mme de Casamajor (Émile Barrault), *Pathologie du mariage* (Paris, 1847).

[38] Comte was basically a conservative but deserves attention here because many of his ideas were shared by writers on the left. The fourth part of volume one of *Système de politique positive* was devoted to the *Influence féminine du positivisme;* see also L. M. Ferré, *Féminisme et positivisme* (Paris, 1938).

of the feminists and restricted the wife to her "august domestic vocations." Seclusion was necessary because men and women could only be friends if they could not be competitors. The woman, wrote Comte, was to renounce all power and become the priestess of humanity, representing by her abnegation the subordination of politics to morality.

In Comte's writings one finds the same puritanical streak noted earlier in Babeuf and Cabet. Marriage was for Comte the basic relationship of society and accordingly had to be monogamous and indissoluble. The purpose of the marriage was to purge the couple's love of all base passions. Though Comte loathed Malthus, he downplayed the woman's role as child bearer. Sexual desire was, he admitted, necessary to first bring the couple together, but from that point onward this instinct was to be subjected to a "constant and severe discipline" leading to "conjugal chastity."[39]

A remarkably similar aversion to sexuality is found in the works of Proudhon who brought together all the misogynist arguments of the century. Woman, in his eyes, was inferior to man physically, intellectually, and morally, and existed somewhere between him and the animal world.[40] Once her child-bearing function was completed she lost even this position and became a *sorte de métis*.[41] Men and women were, he declared, two distinct species who could form no true society. The only time they came together was during sexual intercourse—an unfortunate duty required for the continuation of the species. It was during these brief encounters, however, that man ran the danger of falling completely under the sway of woman and the sensual desires she incarnated. He was only saved from this fate by the fact that nature had condemned woman to pay a terrible physical price for her brutish lusts.

Man, with his force, his will, his courage, his intelligence, daily falling into the amorous traps of the woman, would never succeed in taming her and making himself master if he were not aided by the maladies and infirmities which beat down this lioness: pregnancies, births, nursings, then all the diseases which follow and permit the man, in withdrawing from the common bed to catch his breath and become himself again, while the woman, beaten down by suffering, is constrained to bow and humble herself; there is the source of domestic peace.[42]

Michelet had also described the woman as a permanent invalid;[43] what he did not appreciate, declared Proudhon, was that only by her physical

[39]*Système de politique positive,* I, 210ff.; IV, 68–69, 276–78. The climax of this process was, logically enough, virgin birth. Polygamy had been displaced by monogamy; now maternity was to be reconciled with virginity! *Ibid.,* IV, 69, 278.

[40]*De la justice dans la révolution et dans l'église* (Paris, 1858), III, 375ff.

[41]*La pornocratie ou les femmes dans les temps modernes* (Paris, 1875), 181.

[42]*Ibid.,* 262–63. On the fear of female licentiousness cf. Alphonse Exquiros, *Paris ou les sciences, les institutions et les moeurs au XIXe siècle* (Paris, 1847), II, 355.

[43]Jules Michelet, *L'Amour* (Paris, 1889), 52ff.

incapacitation could man be free. Her passions had to be bridled by physical suffering if the family was to play its role of providing the dignity, pious calm, and moral sentiment previously furnished by religion. Birth control, which provided the woman with a way of avoiding the consequences of her concupiscence, was thus necessarily viewed by Proudhon as posing the gravest possible threat to the social order.

Pornocracy [Proudhon's term for female emancipation] and Malthusianism must go together. They appeal to one another, they join, unite, harmonize, as cause and effect. One asks that no more children be produced and the other teaches how to have no more than: Polyandry for women. Polygamy for men. Promiscuity for all.[44]

Proudhon was the one major figure on the French left to win a reputation as an unabashed misogynist. It has been assumed by historians that aside from this renegade all nineteenth-century socialists can be classified as feminists to the extent that they envisaged a better future for women.[45] But it was this tendency of the utopian socialists to discuss the state of motherhood only as it would be after the ultimate social transformation that often blinded them to the very real problems posed by child-bearing to nineteenth-century women. The chilling description of the plight of the working-class mother in the fourierist François Vidal's (1812–72) *De la répartition de la richesse* (1846), provides a useful corrective to contemporary effusions on the joys of motherhood.

The towers [of the foundling homes] have been closed, and the poor mother, the working-class girl, has been left no other option than abortion or infanticide. In our bleak society many mothers have cursed their fecundity, and more than one, in thinking of the future which awaits her new-born child, has broken its head against the cobbles, or strangled it with maternal hands, in order *to deliver it from life,* to spare it misery, suffering, to save it from prostitution. Happy those children of the working class who die in the cradle! Happy the sterile woman! Happy the man with no family![46]

But even Vidal, who bitterly portrayed the burden of motherhood in the somberest of tones, did not suggest that an answer was provided by birth control. He too believed that there was only one way to prevent the horrible act of infanticide and that was by the wholesale changing of society. His unstated assumption, shared by most other socialists, was that if society provided the necessary means of support women could be expected to accept pregnancy after pregnancy without complaint.

[44] *La pornocratie,* 227.
[45] But see Marguerite Thibert, *Le féminisme dans le socialisme français de 1830 à 1850* (Paris, 1926).
[46] *De la répartition de la richesse* (Paris, 1846), 285; Ernest Legouvé, *Histoire morale des femmes* (Paris, 1849), 332.

The fact that many writers on the left denied that the sensual pleasure of either the woman or the man could be taken as a true measure of happiness was a final reason for their rejection of birth control. At bottom these writers shared the traditional moralists' pessimistic conception of man. Like them they believed that social cohesion could only be attained by the individual's sacrifice of pleasure. Man had to choose either the frugality and simplicity of the ascetic or the decadence and degeneration of the sensualist.[47]

The consequences of the sexual over-indulgence which contraceptive practices would permit included both physical and moral debility. As the following passage from Leroux makes clear, it was assumed that to free sexual gratification from the consequences of conception would inevitably lead to debauchery.

Do they imagine that they can create, as they counsel, *checks* on the population, without burdening Humanity with evils of all sorts, without afflicting it with every vice, without imposing on it every type of impurity, without making human life an eternal hell![48]

These "checks" would permit promiscuous liaisons before marriage to go undetected and allow sexual excesses after. The doctors P. J. B. Buchez (1796–1865) and U. Trélat (1795–1879), in the midst of their participation in the Carbonari and Saint-Simonian movements, warned the young man: "But if on the contrary he delivers himself to hasty pleasures, he will ruin his constitution, will remain sickly and weak, lose his memory, his will, will use up his life in a few moments."[49] Sexual excess within marriage was defined by the authors as anything more than twice weekly intercourse. Moreover it was the man's responsibility to protect the physical and moral health of the family; one could not expect wives to have such foresight. "Coition is infinitely less tiring for them than for the man, they can repeat it with impunity. . . ."[50] Women were more sensitive but less sensible creatures, wholly dominated by their sexual desires and therefore a real threat to their husbands' welfare.

The question of preserving one's physical health was only a secondary consideration; the moral consequences of the sensual excesses permitted by birth control were the socialists' real concern. Proudhon was sounding a familiar chord when he declared that it was by shunning pleasure and devoting himself to work that man demonstrated his humanity.

[47]Saint-Simon's statement that the happy man was the working man typified this outlook: *Introduction aux travaux scientifiques du XIXe siècle*, in *Oeuvres* (Paris, 1839), I, 220ff.

[48]*Malthus et les économistes*, 183. Proudhon declared: "*Onanism* has as its corollary *beastiality*. It's curious; conjugal onanism has been proposed by the defenders of human exploitation in order to serve as a brake on the population: as if the beastiality of economics was sanctioned by the beastiality of love." *De la justice*, III, 485.

[49]*Précis élémentaire d'hygiène* (Paris, 1825), 219.   [50]*Ibid.*,220.

This antagonism of the physical and moral in man, in the exercise of his industrial and prolific faculties, is the balance wheel of the social machine. Man, in his development, moves ceaselessly from fatality to liberty, from instinct to reason, from matter to spirit. It is by virtue of this progress that he frees himself little by little from the slavery of the senses, as from the oppression of painful and repulsive labors.[51]

Man had to flee "the tyranny of the organs" and seek in marriage a chaste love that would vanquish the passions. Proudhon was in effect saying that the coming of a reformed society would entail as much a moral as an economic and political revolution. "Either humanity must become by labor a society of saints, or by monopoly and misery civilization is only a vast orgy."[52]

Half a century later Georges Sorel (1847–1922) was voicing the same sentiments. He hailed Proudhon as the defender of morality based on family and sexual relations; he ridiculed the feminist programs of Fourier and Bebel. Yet Sorel recognized that women were not happy with their lot.

But it is necessary never to forget that the woman is the great regulator of birth and that everywhere, as soon as she is no longer raised in the superstitious respect of the force of the male, she demands the right of not being transformed into a reproductive animal.[53]

The problem, as Sorel saw it, was how to relieve women of this burden without releasing the destructive forces of sexuality. Like Comte he insisted that the woman not be dragged down to the man's level by giving her rights to *caprices amoureux*. Like Proudhon he insisted that the answer was to be found in greater chastity for all: "We can affirm that *the world will become more just only to the extent that it becomes more chaste;* I do not believe that there is a more certain truth."[54]

Given the lack of sympathy with which the leading socialists viewed the question of birth control it comes as somewhat of a surprise to find that when the practice finally found public apologists in the last decades of the nineteenth century they were on the left. But these later writers were not in the mainstream of French socialism; they were on its liberal and anarchistic fringes. Moreover they could only look back to a handful of thinkers who in the late eighteenth and early nineteenth centuries provided the basis for the neo-Malthusian movement. Malthus had been jolted into writing *An Essay on the Principles of Population* by Condorcet. Referring to the Frenchman's prediction that in the future man would control his reproduction, Malthus declared:

[51]*Système de contradictions,* II, 480.   [52]*Ibid.,* II, 496.

[53]*Matériaux d'une théorie du prolétariat* (Paris, 1919), 198.

[54]*Ibid.,* 199. Compare Babeuf's statement of a hundred years previous: "Les moeurs étant les garantes des Républiques parce que celles-ci basent sur les vertus, c'est des institutions morales que dépend la perfection ou la perversion de l'esprit républicain." *Le Tribune du peuple,* **28** (Paris, n.d.), 240.

He then proceeds to remove the difficulty of over-population in a manner, which I profess not to understand. Having observed, that the ridiculous prejudices of superstition would by that time have ceased to throw over morals a corrupt and degrading austerity he alludes, either to a promiscuous concubinage, which would prevent breeding or to something else as unnatural. To remove the difficulty in this way, will, surely, in the opinion of most men, be, to destroy that virtue and purity of manners, which the advocates of equality, and of the perfectibility of man, profess to be the end and object of their views.[55]

Antoine-Nicolas de Condorcet (1743–94) had in fact set the line of argument in his *Esquisse d'un tableau historique des progrès de l'esprit humain* (1794) which was to be followed by later birth control advocates. He wrote that soon

... men will then know that, if they have obligations to those beings who are not yet here, it consists not of bringing them into existence, but of making them happy; they have for their purpose the general well-being of the human species or of the society in which they live; of the family to which they are attached, and not the childish idea of burdening the world with useless and unfortunate beings.[56]

Condorcet had been one of the few *philosophes* to subject both the status of women and the family to critical examination. He was not satisfied that either had been predetermined by nature to continue in its present form and he thus had no qualms when it came to questioning the value of population growth as a sign of public prosperity. The same question was asked by Sénancour (1770–1846) in *De l'amour* (1806).

In Europe a quarter of the population cannot escape its abject poverty. It is true that this distress is not directly produced by the lack of space, and that foodstuffs are not wanting; but will the increasing of the population reform the habits which are to a large part a result of the number of men collected together under a single ruler?[57]

Condorcet and Sénancour did not suggest that population control would solve every problem; they simply stated that the individual had a right to contraception. More importantly they were insisting that the woman had the right to control her own body.

The sex which forms and feeds has cares to fulfil; often it wishes to avoid them, often it even must. It is the sex which receives the action which has the right of refusing it. ... Men finding no danger here for themselves, easily forget what harm is done in making pregnant a woman who cannot want it. They cannot ignore how odious such indifference is, and all that there is contemptible in this brutal abandonment. But what they almost all seem to ignore is that even in the unions sanctioned by the law, it is imprudent, blameworthy, senseless, to have as many children as chance in some way produces.[58]

[55] *An Essay on the Principles of Population* (London, 1798), 154.
[56] *Esquisse d'un tableau historique des progrès de l'esprit humain*, ed. O. H. Prior (Paris, 1933), 222–23.
[57] *De l'amour* (Paris, 1834, 3rd edit.), I, 332.
[58] *De l'amour* (Paris, 1808, 2nd edit.), 41, 146.

Condorcet and Sénancour accepted the notion that pleasure was an obvious measure of happiness and that women had as much right to pleasure as men.[59] In contrast to those who called for the repression of the passions they optimistically held that, once freed of the trammels of family and society, the free expression of human needs could only lead to good.

The most famous defender of such liberty in the nineteenth century was Charles Fourier (1772–1837). Indeed, he believed that through the very operation of such freedoms his *état sociétaire* would enjoy a stable population. He was frequently attacked for promulgating contraceptive theories, but in fact he was hopelessly utopian when it came to the problem of assuring a low birth rate.[60] He hoped that women would become less prolific due to greater activity, a *régime gastrosophique, moeurs phanérogames,* and *exercise intégral.*[61] Moreover he declared that the changes he envisaged would not come into force until at least a generation after the founding of harmony.[62] Contemporaries were not taken in by these reservations. They recognized that Fourier was clearly advancing a line of thought that defended the right of birth control. He was a resolute critic of the family which served to oppress both the woman and the child. He was a feminist but his feminism, unlike that of his contemporaries, did not consist of seeking to restrict men to the chaste condition heretofore demanded of women. Instead of calling for mortification of the flesh and holding in check sexual feelings, he gloried in their free expression.[63]

Fourier's critique of the family was to have a marked influence on those French socialists later associated with Marx. The "scientific socialists" avoided the pious moralizing of the utopians while skirting the question of the woman's right to avoid pregnancy.[64] It would appear that

[59]Sénancour specifically defended the unmarried woman's right to contraception: *De l'amour* (1808), 145; (1834), I, 245.

[60]For denunciations of Fourier: Proudhon, *Système des contradictions,* II, 451–55 and Sorel, *Matériaux d'une théorie,* 196.

[61]*Le nouveau monde industriel,* in *Oeuvres* (Paris, 1841–45), VI, 337ff. Moreover Fourier believed that the land could support a larger population if organized in horticultural communities; he drew support for his argument from M. Herrenschwand, *De l'économie politique moderne: discours fondamental sur la population* (London, 1786).

[62]*Duperies des détracteurs; Secte Owen,* in *Oeuvres,* VI, 154–55.

[63]*Le nouveaux monde amoureux,* in *Théorie des quatres mouvements et des destinées générales* (Paris, 1967), 245–314. Fourier's followers tended to downplay his interest in sex; e.g., Victor Hennequin, *Les amours au phalanstère* (Paris, 1849). It is of interest to note, however, that Dr. A. Mayer, one of the first doctors to publicly defend contraception hailed Fourier as *"un grand génie moderne" (Des rapports conjugaux,* 106).

[64]E.g., Constantin Pecqueur, *Théorie nouvelle d'économie sociale et politique* (Paris, 1842), 325; Jules Guesde, *Essai de catéchisme socialiste* (Paris, 1878), 72–79, 93–98; Paul Lafargue, *La question de la femme* (Paris, 1904), 22–24; D. E. C. Eversley, *Social Theories of Fertility and the Malthusian Debate* (Oxford, 1959); R. L. Meek, *Marx and Engels on Malthus* (London, 1953).

in the face of the wide-scale family-planning from the 1860's onwards, socialists felt it was prudent to avoid the issue. Nevertheless, it was still tacitly understood that as far as the traditional left was concerned, to espouse the social necessity of contraception was to acknowledge that the plight of the masses was to be solved, not by class struggle but by individual self-help. Robert Hertz wrote:

> Of course, if it pleases a proletarian family to improve its situation in having no children, they are free [to do so]: it is a personal affair which is their business. But in remaining sterile they have no more contributed to the emancipation of their class than a worker who becomes a wine merchant has abolished wage-earning. . . .[65]

If the working class as a whole adopted such practices the results would be an *amoindrissement national,* a rise in unemployment as the number of consumers fell, and a decline of the socialist population relative to the hoards of prolific *barbares,* i.e., Catholics and foreign laborers. The working-class family which had only one child would not produce a socialist militant; "il fera le plus souvent un petit bourgeois bien sage ou un arriviste médiocre."[66]

A number of anarchists were prepared, however, by the last decades of the century to espouse neo-Malthusianism as a weapon in the class war. Paul Robin (1837–1912), nominated to the General Council of the International in 1871 and later expelled for his support of the Jurassiens, defended the tactic in *La question sexuelle* (1878). He failed to win the support of the better known anarchists such as James Guillaume and Peter Kropotkin, but by the end of the century had a small following which included Nelly Roussel, Sébastien Faure, Eugène Humbert, and Manuel Devaldès.[67]

The line of argument of the neo-Malthusian anarchists was that *liberté de maternité* was a basic right that could not be denied to any woman in any society. To proclaim such a right would not postpone the revolution but advance it. Only a sadist could welcome an increase in the number of miserable children and ill mothers as a harbinger of revolution. What the socialist cause needed were healthier, more intelligent workers which only smaller families could produce. If any doubts were had as to the revolutionary potential of the neo-Malthusian tactic it was only necessary to ask who were in favor of workers having large families—it was the capitalists, patriots, priests, and generals.[68]

[65]*Socialisme et dépopulation; Les Cahiers du Socialiste,* no. 10 (Paris, 1910), 16.

[66]*Ibid.,* 14. For a review of Hertz see *Revue socialiste,* 53 (1911), 475–76; also Désiré Descamps, "Le problème de la dépopulation," *Revue socialiste,* 24 (1896), 257–85; André Armengaud, "Mouvement ouvrier et néo-malthusianisme au début du XXᵉ siècle," *Annales de démographie historique* (1966), 7–21.

[67]Gabriel Giroud, *Paul Robin* (Paris, 1937); R. H. Guerrand, *La libre maternité, 1896–1969* (Paris, 1971); Jean Maitron, *Histoire du mouvement anarchiste en France 1880–1914* (Paris, 1951), 319–24.

[68]E.g., Sébastien Faure, *Le problème de la population* (Paris, 1908), and G. Hardy (Gabriel Giroud), *La loi de Malthus* (Paris, 1909).

Contraception was, as the titles of the neo-Malthusian anarchists' works made clear—*La grève des ventres, La chair à canon, Croître et multiplier, c'est la guerre*—the ultimate form of the general strike.

The neo-Malthusians were to form only a small radical fringe of the French socialist movement, and their activities cannot be fully documented here. The purpose of this paper has been rather to ask why the major writers on the left attacked the idea of birth control as unnatural, immoral, and impolitic. The first point to be made is that they were not alone in their inadequate dealing with the question of contraception. Alfred Naquet (1834–1916), the "father of divorce," was referring to every political following when he asked in 1901 why, despite the fact that birth control was practiced on such a wide scale, no one dared to defend it.[69] The socialists' writings on the subject were, of course, prescriptive, not descriptive. It is difficult to determine when authors were seriously condemning specific practices and when they were striking moralistic poses. Even Paris doctors, whose families in the 1890's averaged, one authority informs us, 1.5 children, were extremely circumspect when it came to discussing birth control in public. Their references to the practice were more often designed to alarm than to enlighten: "L'onanisme conjugal, fléau plus cruel, plus meutrier, plus épouvantable que le typhus, la peste et le choléra réunis. . . ."[70]

Though the decline of the birth rate was noted with anxiety from the 1850's by a host of social observers. there were few who chose to regard it as a consequence of simple family planning. Most attributed the decline to whatever aspect of contemporary society they considered most noxious and therefore most likely to result in sterility. The list included conscription, capitalism, clerical celibacy, urbanization, secularization, taxation, equal inheritance, Free Masonry, overeating, bicycling, alcoholism, absinthe, tobacco, and both the emancipation and subjugation of women.[71] A propos of women, it should be noted that those female writers who were campaigning for social and political equality tended to approach the question of birth control in the familiar moralizing fashion. Political freedoms would not, it was promised, be translated into sexual liberties. "To emancipate the woman," wrote Jenny P. d'Héricourt (d. 1875), "is not to recognize her right of using and abusing love. . . ."[72] Indeed the feminists stressed the idea that the liberated woman could

---

[69] *L'Humanité et la patrie* (Paris, 1901), 243.

[70] Dr. Picon, *Aperçu sur les principales causes de la dépopulation* (Paris, 1888), 9. The information on the size of doctors' families is provided by Dr. Minime (Dr. Lutaud), *Le néo-Malthusianisme* (Paris, 1891), 14.

[71] E.g., L. F. E. Bergeret, *Des fraudes dans l'accomplissement des fonctions génératrices* (Paris, 1868); Raoul Frary, *Le péril national* (Paris, 1881); Arsène Dumont, *Dépopulation et civilization* (Paris, 1890); Auguste Laine, *De la dépopulation en France* (Paris, 1891); Camille Rabaud, *Le péril national ou la dépopulation croissante de la France* (Paris, 1891); Dr. E. Maurel, *De la dépopulation de la France* (Paris, 1896): Edme Piot, *La dépopulation* (Paris, 1902).

[72] *La femme affranchie* (Paris, 1860), I, 5–6; II, 106.

help the man stifle his animalistic appetites. The woman, according to Juliette Lambert (1836–1936), was by nature less motivated by sexual desires and sooner and more completely freed of them. The more active the role she played in family and public life the sooner love would be subordinated to reason and justice, the sooner the beastly side would be overcome.[73]

But to explain the response of the left to the challenge of birth control it is not sufficient to state simply that they shared the prudishness of their contemporaries. Equally important was their sensitivity to the conservative's charge that they were propagating immoral doctrines. The vociferousness with which socialists insisted on their moral superiority suggests that many felt constrained to buttress moral norms in order to compensate for their social critiques. They were so concerned to prove that their economic reforms would not lead, as their opponents claimed, to social disintegration that they defended the patriarchal family, reiterated the subordination of women, and condemned any change in the relationship of the sexes as unnatural. Proclaiming, as had traditional moralists, that social cohesion was achieved by the individual's sacrifice of pleasure it followed that they could view birth control as a highly individualistic act prompted by self-interest and contempt for the community.

In 1896 the economist Paul Leroy-Beaulieu said of the neo-Malthusians: "La propagande de ceux-ci est, d'ailleurs, bien inutile; nombre de familles devancent leurs leçons par instinct."[74] If it is true, as Leroy-Beaulieu and later commentators have suggested, that the neo-Malthusians and anti-Malthusians were equally ineffectual in influencing the acceptance of contraception does this mean that their debate was meaningless?[75] It has been the purpose of this paper to show that the controversy is of particular interest inasmuch as it provides a way of setting aside the time-honored superficial political antagonisms and of isolating the more basic but less frequently acknowledged common concerns of nineteenth-century Frenchmen. The left did not break with traditional Judeo-Christian morality. Only a few writers were to declare that sexual and political repression were related; an even smaller number accepted the notion that the freedom of women to control their own bodies was an essential liberty. The subject of "sexual politics" had been broached; the full debate was to await later generations.

St. Antony's College, Oxford.

[73]*Idées anti-proudhoniennes sur l'amour, la femme et le mariage* (Paris, 1858), 106.

[74]Paul Leroy-Beaulieu, *Traité théorique et pratique d'économie politique* (Paris, 1896), IV, 617.

[75]Hertz, *Socialisme et dépopulation,* 17; Armengaud, "Mouvement ouvrier," 7–21.

XVI

VICTORIAN SCIENCE AND THE "GENIUS" OF WOMAN

By Flavia Alaya

It is common to view feminism historically as a movement rather than as a philosophic or ideological tradition. But there is evidence of such a tradition, articulate enough to provide a doctrine that can stand firm against the vagaries of history and opinion, and consistent enough to establish a logical basis for the intellectual history of the idea of woman's "emancipation" and "liberation." Considered in its relation to social theory or ethics, the tradition is of course part of the larger idea of egalitarian justice. But the feminist idea is integral with the philosophical existential ideal of human freedom synonymous with power over self, and thus sets itself against those theories that would prescribe any limits allegedly imposed by "nature" on human personality or human potential.

First fully articulated by thinkers of the Enlightenment, this philosophical egalitarianism, as I shall refer to it, found almost immediate expression in the form given it by feminism, where attention is obviously focussed on questions of *sexual* limitation. This fact in the history of ideas enables us to draw a direct and continuous line from Mary Wollstonecraft's *Vindication of the Rights of Woman* (1792), through John Stuart Mill's *The Subjection of Women* (1869), into the twentieth century and Beauvoir's *The Second Sex* (1953), without noting any substantial increase or diminution of the force of argument. What is *not* revealed by that continuous philosophical line, however, is precisely what the historical study of feminism as a movement *does* reveal: a discontinuity, occurring sometime after Mill, profound enough to have obliged the modern phase of the movement to recapture or rearticulate its most basic underlying principles.

Attempts have already been made to explain this discontinuity, but none, I believe, has sufficiently explored the possibility that it was visible well before the turn of the century, or that it had its origin less in political or practical realities than in a crisis of ideology.[1] This essay represents an effort to explore such an hypothesis and, more particularly, to suggest that the crucial factor in that severance was the impact

---

[1]Betty Friedan's *The Feminine Mystique* (New York, 1963), though acknowledging the role of science, placed the feminist crisis squarely in the twentieth century. More recent scholarship on this question is reflected in William O'Neill, *Everyone Was Brave: A History of Feminism in America* (Chicago, 2nd ed., 1971), and Estelle Freedman, "The New Woman: Changing Views of Women in the 1920's," *Journal of American History*, **61**, 2 (Sept. 1974), 372–93. All of these, it might be noted, work from a fairly narrow national base that tends to obscure the international character of feminist discussion.

of nineteenth-century science, which gave such vigorous and persuasive reinforcement to the traditional dogmatic view of sexual character that it not only strengthened the opposition to feminism but disengaged the ideals of feminists themselves from their philosophic roots.

The interaction of feminism with science in the nineteenth century involved a very complex process of give and take, and took place at many levels of discourse. But there is no doubt that it colored the entire intellectual history of feminism. One of the more obvious reasons for this interaction is to be found at what might be called their spiritual source: both scientific and feminist thought issued from a similar challenge to conventional wisdom and authority; both possessed, in a sense, missionary status, and it is hardly surprising that they should tend at points to coalesce—sometimes within the same individual—as an alliance of heresies against a common orthodoxy. Moreover, the range of spokesmanship on both fronts was very wide. Particularly in the first half of the nineteenth century, scientific popularizers, humanitarian reformers, and active feminists were seldom daunted by theoretical or philosophical inconsistencies when making pronouncements on the education or development of women.

A typical illustration of this form of interaction is provided by the American abolitionist, feminist, and man-of-letters, Thomas Wentworth Higginson (1823–1911), whose thinking on feminist issues was basically formed in the forties and fifties. A true-born son of the revolution, but no less responsive for that reason to intellectual developments occurring in England, Higginson's social vision could be contained within the simple principle that bad external circumstances inhibit human development, and good ones foster it. Prior work in the abolitionist cause had led him to perceive that this principle was no less applicable to women than to slaves: "Great achievements imply great preparations and favorable conditions. . . . Give an equal chance, and let genius and industry do the rest."[2] But as a progressive thinker, Higginson could not resist adding to his arguments any new "scientific" notion that might lend them support. Taking from the English historian and natural philosopher, Henry Thomas Buckle, the idea that women had a special "genius" for deductive and intuitive modes of thought, and from Buckle and a host of other contemporary thinkers the idea that humanity was on an inevitably upward course of civilization that increasingly brought that "genius" into play,[3] Higginson concluded that the

[2]Thomas Wentworth Higginson, *Woman and the Alphabet. The Writings of Thomas Wentworth Higginson* (Boston, 1900), IV, 9–10. The essay containing these remarks originally appeared in *The Atlantic Monthly* in 1859, and was revised and reprinted in 1872.

[3]Henry Thomas Buckle, "The Influence of Women on the Progress of Knowledge," presented to the British Royal Society in 1858, and published in *Essays* (New York, 1864).

feminist hope could be no less than the will of providence. New opportunities for women would be opened by the feminine ethos of modern social development.[4] The complacency of this conclusion (which was, in fact, largely rhetorical—Higginson continued to work long and hard in the cause) was perhaps less perilous than its implicit social and biological determinism. It obliged him to characterize women, equivocally, as possessing "equal powers, but not identical ones" with men, and to offer them as a return for their education the vague promise of an influence on "philanthropy, culture, arts, affections, aspirations."

That Higginson's views were not merely the result of male bias is suggested by the parallels to be found in the work of Margaret Fuller. Her *Woman in the Nineteenth Century,* a very important feminist manifesto, incorporated nevertheless some of the same subtle historical and biological determinism. Though Fuller emphasized that woman must "work as she will," she implied that such work would still be defined by her "especial genius." Male and female, she said, represented the "two sides of the great radical dualism," the female distinctly suited to further "an especial work of our time."[5] She believed with Higginson that theirs was a new age, "auspicious for women," when "the feminine side, the side of love, of beauty, of holiness, was now to have its full chance." She was no less willing than Buckle to characterize the female sex as a system of qualities, "electrical in movement, intuitive in function, spiritual in tendency," able thus to act as "a harmonizer of the vehement elements" (42, 114–15).

This feminist aspiration, with its naive willingness to contribute to the concept of woman's "genius" and all it implied, was scarcely prepared to deal with the more systematic—and often skeptical—scientific pronouncements to come. Only the rare inheritor of the original philosophic tradition remained alert to how the ambiguous connotations of the concept of woman's genius could obscure the subtle boundaries they drew around the potentialities of women. Harriet Taylor and John Stuart Mill, writing in 1851 on "The Enfranchisement of Women," made a special point of commending the American Feminist Convention of 1848 for having *failed* "to entertain the question of the peculiar aptitudes either of women or men, or the limits within which this or that occupation may be supposed to be more adapted to one or to the other." It was a question, they said, that could "only be satisfactorily answered

---

[4]"Till the fullness of time came, woman was necessarily kept a slave to the spinning wheel and the needle; now higher work is ready. . . . No use in releasing her till man, with his strong arm, had worked out his preliminary share in civilization. . . . The queen had waited for her throne till it could be smoothed and prepared for her occupancy." Higginson, *Writings,* IV, 26.

[5]Margaret Fuller, *Woman in the Nineteenth Century* (New York, 1971; a reprint edition based on the posthumous 1855 text), 115–16, 42.

in perfect freedom."[6] Yet the disdainful and satirical tone of their subsequent remarks on motherhood ("a mere multiplication of numbers"), and the alleged "softness" of female psychosexual character, suggests that even they did not, at the time, take too seriously the threat imposed on feminist thinking by appeals to woman's limited "nature" and peculiar "genius."

During the years (1851–1869) that divided "The Enfranchisement of Women" from the publication of *The Subjection of Women*, however, the need for a much more frontal attack must have become increasingly and painfully apparent. That period saw, along with the appearance of Darwin's *Origin of Species*, an immense thrust given to the evolutionary emphasis of science. With an attention slowly mounting to obsession, scientific thinkers, like Spencer, Darwin, and Galton, were drawn by theories of reproduction and selection to questions that inevitably included the role of sexual character in species development and, by analogy, social development. Buckle's gallant expression of hope in a "coalition of the sexes" in the future "progress of knowledge" was to prove a distinctly minority voice in this chorus. A more prophetic harbinger of the attitude that was to prevail among the major scientists was the copious utterance of Herbert Spencer, who riddled his work with ominous reminders of the heavy handicap nature had imposed upon women, leaving them in a virtually permanent state of arrested development. Thomas Huxley's democratic scruples prevented him from denying women their right to legal and political emancipation, but he felt no scruple, as a scientist, in simultaneously denying them any "natural" equality, existing or potential.[7] Gallantry was being swept away by dogmatic scientific conclusiveness, in assertions that not only described the observable range of women's collective "genius" but defined—and often prescribed—the upward limits of its exercise in the individual, i.e., the capacity of women for any exceptional achievement. Taylor and Mill had no objection to the failure of gallantry, which they had perceived to be largely false in any case. What did strike them was the extremely

---

[6] John Stuart Mill [and Harriet Taylor], "The Enfranchisement of Women," *Dissertations and Discussions* (New York, 1873), III, 105, 119. For Harriet Taylor's part in the composition of this essay and *The Subjection of Women*, see F. A. Hayek, *John Stuart Mill and Harriet Taylor* (Chicago, 1951), and Alice Rossi's introductory essay to *Essays on Sex Equality by John Stuart Mill and Harriet Taylor* (Chicago, 1970).

[7] Huxley's views are in "Emancipation—Black and White," *Science and Education: Essays* (New York, 1914). Pertinent comments by Spencer may be found in "The Comparative Psychology of Man," *Essays: Scientific, Political and Speculative* (New York, 1899), I, 362–63, and *The Study of Sociology* (New York, 1893), 373, first published in the sixties and seventies. Auguste Comte is not so frequently alluded to among English and American writers on this subject, but the impact of his early views on women's inferiority should not be overlooked: cf. his *Philosophie Positive* (Paris, 1839), IV, 405–06.

flimsy scientific basis for such assertions: the powerful opening section of *The Subjection of Women* (1869) was thus devoted almost entirely to the pernicious effects of "arguments from nature," even among those who considered themselves enlightened, upon any discussion of the freedom or potential of women.

But by the time Darwin reentered the field with his *Descent of Man* (1871), it became clear that the floodtide of scientific persuasion about sex roles was well on its way to quenching any new feminist brushfires *The Subjection* might have started. In both degree of conviction and force of authority, Darwin outclassed both Huxley and Spencer. He even felt qualified to assume the role of the social historian in his brief section on the "Differences in Mental Powers of the Two Sexes."[8] "If two lists were made of the most eminent men and women in poetry, painting, sculpture, music—comprising composition and performance—history, science, and philosophy, with half a dozen names under each subject," he asserted confidently, "the two lists would not bear comparison." But historical inferiority was nothing compared to natural:

It is generally admitted that with women the powers of intuition, of rapid perception, and perhaps of imitation, are more strongly marked than in man; but some, at least, of these faculties are characteristic of the lower races, and therefore of a past and lower state of civilization (326–27).

What is surprising to the modern reader (as it must have been surprising to Mill), is that Darwin brought not even minimal scientific documentation to his *ben trovato* conclusions.[9] Though his arguments relied almost entirely upon "analogy with lower animals" and what is "generally admitted," their dogmatic character gave them the appearance of simple, unvarnished truth and the credibility of science in the science-fevered seventies. With not even a passing glance at the environmentalist argument that women's unremarkable past was a function of their cultural subjection, and no attention at all to the logic of Mill's simple caution that "a negative fact at most leaves the question uncertain and open to psychological discussion,"[9a] Darwin declared that

[8]Charles Darwin, *The Descent of Man, and Selection in Relation to Sex* (London, 1871), II, 326–27. The citations here are from Part II, Ch. XIX, "Secondary Sexual Characteristics of Man," which appeared virtually unchanged from the 1st to the 2nd ed. (London, 1874), II, 586–89. Some of the cultural and literary impact of Darwin's views on sexual character has been interestingly explored by Christopher Lohmann in "Darwinism and the Victorian Concept of Sex Roles," a paper given at the American Literature section meeting of the Modern Language Association in December 1973.

[9]Ironically, Darwin actually cited Mill's *Subjection* in his one footnote to this subsection in the 1st ed., twisting it neatly to support his own views (328n).

[9a]Mill, *The Subjection of Women*, 490.

"the chief distinction in the intellectual powers of the two sexes is shown by Man's attaining to a higher eminence, in whatever he takes up, than woman *can attain*" (327, emphasis added). At this point he became even colorful:

It is, indeed, fortunate that *the law of equal transmission of characters to both sexes* prevails with mammals; otherwise it is probable that man would have become as superior in mental endowment to woman, as the peacock is in ornamental plumage to the peahen (328, emphasis added).

The Victorian audience of Darwin had barely had enough time to digest *The Subjection of Women,* and certainly not enough to cope with virtually the only work used as a supporting document in this particular subsection of Darwin's book. This was Francis Galton's *Hereditary Genius,* which had entered the intellectual marketplace simultaneously with *The Subjection* in 1869. A pioneer eugenicist and thoroughgoing Darwinian, Galton was an even more formidable scientific opponent than his master on the question of human mental endowment. *Hereditary Genius* had quietly put environmentalist egalitarians on notice that there were to be no more willy-nilly interpretations of the records of the past. Galton's methods of statistical research were to make a respectable scientific enterprise of the scouring of histories and biographies, and they were to declare woe to any philistine who might deny that animal or hereditary "nature" could define human character or prescribe human potentialities.

Curiously enough, Galton's work received the high distinction of notice in the context of Darwin's discussion of mental sex differences without ever having explicitly raised that issue. Yet Darwin was essentially true to the spirit of his source, namely, Galton. Galton had conducted his research via a system of selection so rigorously heroic, in the Carlylean sense, that the geniuses in his pantheon were almost exclusively men—men whose genealogies included intelligent or "able" women only where they might serve to press home the hereditary nature of his heroes' superior qualities. While he never expressed an outright bias against women, Galton was clearly so attracted to virile achievements that women were denigrated by his *de facto* selection. He devoted an enormous amount of study to military commanders, and concluded his work with a section on oarsmen and wrestlers fully as large as that on poets, whom he found on the whole distastefully undisciplined and "irregular." Even his disciple, Karl Pearson, thought Galton had been unduly harsh toward divines, who were cast as a rather puny and sickly lot.[10] In his very telling general conclusion, Galton expressed regret that he had discontinued his plan "to make memoranda of the physical gifts

[10]Pearson, *The Life, Letters, and Labours of Francis Galton* (London, 1922), II, 99.

of my heroes," since he felt that they would have overthrown any theory that physical weakness was "an essential or even usual accompaniment" of genius. "A collection of living magnates in various branches of intellectual achievement is always a feast to my eyes," he wrote ecstatically, "being, as they are, such massive, vigorous, capable-looking animals."[11]

More important for the feminist debate, Galton expressed his absolute conviction that no circumstances whatsoever were capable of repressing great potential. His very definition of genius described a nature that "if hindered or thwarted, will fret and strive until the hindrance is overcome" (38). It is almost a contradiction in terms," he declared, "to doubt that such men will generally become eminent." If a man is gifted "with vast intellectual ability, eagerness to work, and power of working, I cannot comprehend how such a man should be repressed" (39). So much for Higginson's favorable conditions!

Galton's work, inspired and promoted by Darwin, and enjoying all the credit that such support implied, laid the foundations of an immense effort among natural and social scientists throughout Europe and America in the later century to study the nature of "genius," in its more exclusive and extraordinary sense, and to celebrate "success" by the standards so defined. In wonderfully circular fashion, moreover, the study of individual achievement took those standards from a male-dominated culture, tested women against them within the same cultural conditions, found them wanting, and concluded (predictably) that the "genius" of women—collectively—was to be virtually incapable of genius. Mill's one essential scientific argument, eventually to be adapted by socialists like August Bebel, that *no* conclusions on the question of sexual capabilities could be called scientific without parallel analysis of a control group under different conditions (which did not exist), went unheeded. Galton opened an anthropometric laboratory in London which, among other things, established to the satisfaction of much of the scientific establishment that a deficiency of brain weight in women hopelessly deprived them of the mental resources for effective competition with men. Inspired by Galton, Cesare Lombroso also undertook the scientific study of "the man of genius," remarking in the two or three pages of his study relegated to a discussion of "the influence of sex" that women "are rare exceptions" in the history of genius for constitutional reasons. Following Galton's line almost to the letter, he added that "if there had been in women a really great ability . . . , it would have shown itself in overcoming the difficulties opposed to it."[12]

[11]Francis Galton, *Hereditary Genius* (New York, 1870), 332.
[12]Cesare Lombroso, *The Man of Genius* (London, 1891), 137–38. The spread of Galtonism was remarkable and wide; among his other significant progeny was the American

Meanwhile sexual, hardly less than national, politics played their part in the choice of source materials for such massive undertakings as the *Dictionary of National Biography* (its first volumes issued in 1885). Perhaps owing to the moderating influence of its first editor, Leslie Stephen, the *DNB* proved less invidious toward poets or women than Galton and his followers, but it was nonetheless clear that male genius was synonymous with British civilization, which depended heavily on the establishment of the empire of science, if not of empire itself. Ironically, there seemed to be little place for Higginson's or Fuller's version of a "feminized" civilization, or even for Buckle's vision of a "coalition of the sexes," except in the manufacture of more virile human males.[13]

The Mill-Taylor thesis did not have the strength to stay the launching of this propagandistic effort to identify power with "genius" and both with the Anglo-Saxon male character. Sarah Joseph Hale's earlier *Women's Record* (1855), which could contain in two volumes "sketches of all distinguished women, from the Creation to A.D. 1854," had perhaps only supplied ammunition for a repeated scientific assertion epitomized by Lombroso's statement that examples of successful women become all the "more notable because unexpected and exceptional." Laura McLaren's spirited effort to argue "The Fallacy of the Superiority of Man" proceeded mainly by a strategy of challenging scientific authority with other scientific authority. Her essay, moreover, illustrates the degree to which discussions of genius had vitiated the climate of debate: feminists seemed obliged to justify the social and political *equality* of women (their basic right to the full development of their individual potential regardless of normative limits) by proving the capacity of women to be *exceptional*, as though society's commitment to their education and development would otherwise be wasted. They thus implicitly accepted women's unique castehood even among the oppressed. "Women ask but one century more," wrote McLaren, during which "their powers have had a fair trial," to either prove or disprove their "inherent inferiority."[14] Would society presumably be free then to

psychologist, James McKeen Cattell, who was largely responsible for the establishment of experimental psychology as a science in the U.S., and who founded the American Psychological Association and the directory of *American Men of Science*. Cattell studied with Galton in Cambridge and London, and brought back his methods and some of his prejudices.

[13]And not even for much of that. As Havelock Ellis observed in an article on the *DNB*, its editors had not even been reasonably consistent in supplying data on maternal ancestry. Ellis himself had tried to create a model for such biography in the eighties, by including Olive Schreiner in his own essay on "The Ancestry of Genius," and by tracing even-handedly both maternal and paternal ancestry. Both essays are reprinted in *Views and Reviews* (Boston and New York, 1932).

[14]Laura McLaren, "The Fallacy of the Superiority of Man," *The Woman's World* (New York, 1970; a reprint edition of the Oscar Wilde-edited journal of 1888–90), I, 59.

withdraw the "equal condition" it had granted on an experimental basis? Of course, a Victorian society fearful of anarchy and revolution, that saw its stability threatened by any alteration in the status of woman as upholder of the family, was not one that could tolerate any such fair trial.[15] For a variety of reasons, evolutionary science offered ample reinforcement for subordinating the individual to the general welfare. Social progress and upward evolution were by analogy identified with one another; genius—a remarkable individual variation—was equivalent to a minor species variation that assisted ascent, but was ultimately at the service of the race. A further evolutionary analogy only amplified the social and political significance of Darwinism: that same upward ascent was seen as a process by which simpler forms achieved ever greater complexity and interdependency of organization; society was similarly rising toward increased collectivization and mutuality of interests. To promote reforms, therefore, that were consistent with this process, which, in other words, would only accelerate this "natural" change without heaving it out of its normal channel, was a middle way congenial to a socially-conscious scientist.

Such evolution-based welfare or paternalistic socialism found many adherents among English and American reformers in the later century. Scientifically, they found their scripture in an important biological study, *The Evolution of Sex,* published by Patrick Geddes and J. Arthur Thomson in 1889 as the inaugurating volume of the Contemporary Science Series under the editorship of Havelock Ellis. It took Darwin's pronouncements of the early seventies, submitted them to a full reanalysis, and appeared to reopen every question related to the biological limits of sexual personality.

But the most vital clue to the impact of this work on feminism was the depth of the social consciousness that motivated it. Geddes and Thomson refused to let their study remain, "as biological books for the most part are," they claimed, "without point, and its essential thesis useless."[16] *The Evolution of Sex* was widely read in England and America, and sympathetically received by members of the later Victorian avant-garde.

It became, in fact, something of a manifesto. The authors as flatly

[15] Elizabeth Blackwell's views on the vital importance of preserving the conjugal family are a striking illustration of the conservative posture of some activist women historically associated with feminism; cf. esp. her *Counsel to Parents on the Moral Education of Their Children in Relation to Sex* (London, first ed. 1879).

[16] Patrick Geddes and J. Arthur Thomson, *The Evolution of Sex* (2nd ed., London, 1895). A lucid and detailed analysis of Geddes and Thomson and their attitudes toward sexual character is provided by Jill Conway, "Stereotypes of Femininity in a Theory of Sexual Evolution," *Victorian Studies,* 14 (Sept. 1970), 47–62. Conway rightly emphasizes the significance of this work and outlines its impact on Jane Addams and its influence on the philanthropic activities of women, for which I am indebted to her.

disassociated themselves from liberal, egalitarian feminists as from doctrinaire, traditional anti-feminists. They declared scornfully that both schools spoke "as if the known facts of sex did not exist at all, or almost [as] if these were a mere matter of muscular strength or weight of brain." Reflecting the communal consciousness of their generation, they disdained the liberal's concern for "the franchise" and love of individualistic competition. In short, they rejected Millian liberalism. His "idea of equality," they admitted, had been "serviceable." But now it must give way to the "natural, the biological." It was time to reconstitute "that complex and sympathetic co-operation between the differentiated sexes in and around which all progress past or future must depend" (269).

Their own scientific findings had convinced them that the two sexes were "complementary and mutually dependent," and that this dependency extended to functions "not directly associated with sex." In their own jargon, males were characterized by "katabolism," or destructive metabolism, females by "anabolism," or surplusage. But they elaborated this clinical distinction in much more value-ridden language, concluding a long catalogue of antithetical male and female characteristics with the dogmatic assertion that "man thinks more, woman feels more. He discovers more, but remembers less; she is more receptive, and less forgetful" (271). Even more broadly, women were described as tending "to preserve the constancy and integrity of the species," as having "a larger and habitual share of the altruistic emotions," as excelling "in constancy of affection and sympathy," and as exhibiting "continuous patience"—none of these as mere products of "masculine bullying," but as "an expression of constitutional contrast" (270–71).

The connection of women with the altruistic and sacrificial virtues had a profound appeal for socially-conscious, humanitarian feminists. Combined with the assertion that the moral evolution of humanity *depended* upon these "species-regarding" virtues, as Geddes and Thomson called them, which press the individual to become "diminishingly competitive and increasingly subordinated to the social whole," the argument was almost irresistible. If women did not hold the key to mankind's intellectual and artistic progress, they were most surely to be responsible for its moral future, its increasing socialization, its "subordination of individual competition to reproductive or social ends, and of inter-specific competition to co-operative association" (310–11).

Like Buckle before them, but now on what appeared much more solid scientific ground, Geddes and Thomson lent acceptance to the principle that, in the sphere of action, the virtues biological nature had assigned to women must operate through men to effect harmonious social change and human development. Even in the new collectivist order, it would remain woman's responsibility, presumably, to exercise vigilance over the values inherent in the "family" and "home" of the old order—love, patience, compassion. Their assessment exercised the lure that sympathy and appreciation often exercise: it brought Jane Addams from America to lecture at Geddes's International School, and to carry back, in her turn, influential views on the ethical and philanthropic mission of women. Through her agency, and that of other similarly persuaded men and women, much feminist or potentially feminist energy was channeled into the peace movement, settlement-house work, and other forms of benevolent or "rescue" service considered appropriate to the sexual character of women. In the exhilaration of "co-operative" work, it was easy to ignore the subtle, existential distinction between women—and men—as the social order might find it convenient for them to be, and as they might become without preliminary sexual typecasting. That exhilaration, or, more accurately, that sense of social mission, virtually assured to the evolutionary descent of nineteenth-century feminism the natural selection of a theory of "complementary genius."

The irony in this development was the degree to which it paralleled some of feminism's first political and legislative triumphs. The first real loosenings of the legal compulsions upon women built into the social structure were, in other words, accompanied by a reactionary counter trend in the "higher" culture. The pattern bears comparison with that which simultaneously occurred in the area of race relations, where libertarian views were forced to make headway against new ethnological pronouncements about superior and "lower races"—a common scientific phrase in the later nineteenth century that bore the guise of progressive thinking. That comparison is instructive in dramatizing just how exacting a trial the enlightenment faith in liberty and equality was suffering at the hands of nineteenth-century science. What was desired by "freedom" could not help but come into conflict with what was commanded by biological "necessity."

This conflict was not so apparently present in those feminist thinkers who espoused more radical socialist doctrine. In *Woman and Socialism* (1st ed., 1879), August Bebel was quite decisive in his conclusions on the scientific study of women's potential: "Woman has achieved all that was possible to her" under the "most unfavorable circumstances" of a property-based culture. And he decried the culture-bound dogma of the Galton school that declared "there were no geniuses . . . other than the few who are considered such" by the established classes, perpetuating the myth of their own superiority.[17]

[17] August Bebel, *Woman Under Socialism* (New York, 1904; Eng. transl. of the 33rd ed.), 188. The original title went through various changes in the course of reissue and retranslation. It is interesting to note how pronounced are Bebel's echoes of Mill, who was admired as a late convert to socialism.

Yet while it is in this respect a vigorous exemplar of the feminist tradition, Bebel's work is still marred by a post-Darwinian tendency to take the generic view in sexual matters. Repeatedly he invokes the "Kantian" dictum, as he calls it, that "man and woman only constitute jointly the full human being" (86, 124, 204), and is capable of his own rather sweeping generalizations about psychosexual character without inquiring into their basis. Though he is thoroughly incapable of transforming such normative description into social prescription, there can be no doubt from his observation that the sexes are "very different, though of equal value" (204) that he fully accepted the norms. The balance thus struck was a very uneasy one, and unlikely to check the deepening schizophrenia in feminist thought. The scientific socialist was to find it no easier a task to reconcile feminist individualism with collectivist cooperation than the scientific liberal was to find reconciling egalitarian freedom with biological destiny.

No single figure more acutely illustrates this ideological split than the man whose studies prompted Bebel to accept the revisionist doctrine, "very different, though of equal value." That man was Havelock Ellis, one of the most influential voices in the field of sexual psychology prior to what is called the Freudian era and, for a time, one of the most authoritative spokesmen in the feminist cause. Bred intellectually on the dual concerns of sex and "genius," a devoted student of both Mill and Darwin, an admirer of both Whitman and Baron von Krafft-Ebing, the polar dispositions of his mind were to lead him ultimately into almost pathetic contradictions—contradictions that marked his private life no less than his public utterances. It was Ellis who engineered the publication and to some degree the popularization of the Geddes-Thomson thesis, and thereby assisted vicariously in the degeneration of the philosophic feminist tradition. But his own direct contribution to changing the feminist climate in his time makes a fascinating case study in itself.

Ellis's early work served to cement a strong initial alliance with feminism. He was not then visibly Darwinian or deterministic on the issue of sex and society. On the contrary, his stand prior to the encounter with *The Evolution of Sex* perhaps emerges most sharply in his 1884 review of *Woman and Socialism,* where he argued even more strongly than Bebel himself that "the scientific aspects" of the discussion of sexual equality were misleading. But his basic appeal was not directed to the scientific counter-arguments at all; rather, he paraphrased Bebel's restatement of the familiar egalitarian position "that if women were placed under conditions equally favorable to development they would in a few generations be at no point behind men." With the full force of philosophic conviction, he argued that "there must be no artificial hindrances in the way of human development. We may be assured that the first thing necessary is to assert the equal freedom and independence of women with men."[18]

Though Ellis's *Study of British Genius,* published nearly two decades later, seems from his prefatory marks to have had its genesis in this early period, it is clear that his thinking had, in the interval, undergone a considerable alteration. A work apparently inspired by an impulse to challenge Galton ended, in fact, in equivocations that hovered on endorsement. This once proud ally of the school of "favorable conditions" was now content to give them phlegmatic support. He observed that his own percentage of eminent women had proven higher than that of James Cattell, the American scholar on genius, because Ellis's study was not, like Cattell's, concerned with Europe as a whole but with the English, "a people among whom the conditions"—note the remarkably cautious phrasing—"have possibly been more than usually favourable to the development of ability in women."[19] He did not expressly draw attention to the fact, revealed by his own evidence, that forty-four of the fifty-five women in his list had achieved their reputations since 1700, and thirty of those since 1800. Although he allowed that the claims of procreation and domesticity "are in women too preponderant to be easily conciliated with" intellectual or artistic labor (138), he bypassed all opportunity to probe or even hint at the cultural sources of those claims, or to suggest the legitimacy of resisting them.

The process of Ellis's remarkable shift from impassioned feminist advocacy to nervous, scientific self-restraint, is recorded in his widely acclaimed, much translated, and highly influential *Man and Woman,* which sold out its first edition in 1894. This work was revised and reissued several times during the late nineties, when the *Genius* study was being prepared for publication. The "leading aim" of *Man and Woman* was, Ellis said, to answer precisely the question his *Genius* study was to avoid, and the question Geddes and Thomson had provoked and already answered to their own satisfaction—"how far," as Ellis put it, "sexual differences are artificial, the result of tradition and environment, and how far they are really rooted in the actual constitution of the male and female organisms."[20]

[18] Havelock Ellis, "Women and Socialism," *Views and Reviews,* 9–11.

[19] Ellis, *A Study of British Genius* (London, 1901), viii. Ellis may be referring to a presentation by Cattell at the 3rd Annual Meeting of the American Psychological Association (Princeton, 1894), where he analyzed an international list of 1000 "great men," selected according to the space allotted to them in "different biographical dictionaries and encyclopedias." One can guess how women might fare by that criterion! An abstract of this presentation appears in the *Psychological Review,* **2** (1895), 155–56. Ellis remained entirely silent on the possible bias of other genius scholars, or the validity of their data.

[20] Ellis, *Man and Woman* (4th ed., London, 1904), vii.

Sounding from the results was a distinctly Darwinian echo:

There have been thousands of women painters, but only the men have been re-membered; it would be unkind to make a comprehensive list of famous women painters. . . . In sculpture . . . that there have been two or three women whose names deserve honourable mention is the most that can be said (366).

As for music, which to him represented one of the greatest areas of sexual disparity in recognized achievement, Ellis would not concede that the cause of women's "failure" lay in the culture rather than the female constitution. He considered it rather a field where women "have nearly equal advantages with men," thought there was "no art to which women have been more widely attracted," and none in which "they have shown themselves more helpless" (368–69). He made no apologies for the sources on which he supported such judgments, however painfully ap-parent their bias. He characterized as "very felicitous" George Upton's theory, expressed in *Women in Music* (1st ed., 1880), that

woman does not reproduce [emotions] musically because she herself is emo-tional by temperament and nature, and cannot project herself outwardly, any more than she can give outward expression to other mysterious and hidden traits of her nature. The emotion is part of herself, and is as natural to her as breathing. She lives in emotion and acts from emotion. . . . Man controls his emotions, and can give an outward expression of them (369).

Anton Rubenstein's even more disparaging notion, in *Der Musik und ihre Meister* (1892), that the "increase of the feminine contingent in music" was a sign of "musical decadence," was not only given qualified assent, but dignified with a quotation of its "supporting" argument:

Women lack two prime qualities necessary for creation—subjectivity and initiative. . . . For musical creation they lack absorption, concentration, power of thought, largeness of emotional horizon, freedom in outlining, etc.

Ellis's skepticism here was limited only to the observation that Ruben-stein's statement was insufficiently "scientific" (368).

The same pattern was repeated everywhere: the fields in which woman had succeeded were always less demanding than those in which they had failed. Acting required a capacity for little more than emo-tional sympathy and "imitation." Literature was not really an art at all. "It is merely a method of recording very diverse manifestations of psy-chic attitude and artistic impulse" (369). Fiction "makes far less serious artistic demands" than poetry. "It is only when (as in the work of Flaubert) the novel almost becomes a poem, demanding great architec-tonic power, severe devotion to style, and complete self-restraint, that women have not come into competition with men" (371). As for poetry, the art "is very rare in women," among whom it "has a tendency to be rather thin or rather diffuse and formless"; and finally, women were absolutely unfit for metaphysics or philosophy (370).

It would not be too simplistic to describe *Man and Woman* as an elaborate attempt to reinforce Ellis's prior conviction concerning "complementary" sexual characters. Every bald negative pronouncement on women's capacity for artistic achievement—that they must be "less imaginative than men" (376), that "there can be no doubt ... the artistic impulse is vastly more spontaneous, more pronounced, and more widely spread among men than women" (374), and finally, that "the art impulse is of the nature of a male secondary sexual character, in the same sense as a beard" (377)—was a ruthless way of driving home woman's existence for men, whom they could best serve by creating the appropriate atmosphere, by becoming the creative matrix for man's achievement. His scientific reading had convinced him that it was the male sexual drive, a "restless source of energy," that nourished the impulse to create or to destroy.[21] Only woman, with her "less keen sexual emotions" (377) could assure the channeling of that male energy toward the positive pole of creation. "From an organic standpoint," he concluded, "women represent the more stable and conservative element in evolution. It is a metaphorical as well as a literal truth that the centre of gravity is lower in women and less easily disturbed" (421).

It may be relevant to note here that Ellis's personal experiences with women in this period were an undoubted source of suffering for him.[22] *Man and Woman* may have offered an occasion to rationalize that suffering by transmuting it into nature's retribution for a violation of biological law. Happiness, in any case, could be found only in adherence to that law: "a large part of the joy men and women take in each other," he wrote, "is rooted in [their] sexual difference."

In women, men find beings who have not wandered so far as they have from the typical life and earth's creatures; women are for men the human embodiments of the restful responsiveness of Nature. To every man, as Michelet has put it, the woman whom he loves is as the Earth was to her legendary son; he has but to fall down and kiss her breast and he is strong again (426).

Yet whatever the discontinuity between Ellis's personal experience and

---

[21] Especially important were Baron R. von Krafft-Ebing, *Psychopathia Sexualis* (1st ed., London, 1886), Cesare Lombroso, whose 1886 work *L'Uomo di Genio* was translated and edited for Ellis's own Contemporary Science Series in 1891, and John Fergusson Nisbet, *The Insanity of Genius* (London, 1891), all of whom emphasized the pathological nature of genius.

[22] His relations with Olive Schreiner and Edith Lees in particular, both of them outspoken and feminist; Ellis discovered Lees was a lesbian after their marriage; cf. Ellis, *My Life* (Boston, 1939), as well as the correspondence between Ellis and Schreiner in Olive Schreiner, *Letters: 1876–1920,* ed. S. Cronwright-Schreiner (London, 1924).

his "scientific" conclusions, it is perhaps even less problematical than the discrepancy between those same conclusions and the implications for social policy he drew from them. After building so voluminously-documented a case for women's impotency that it amounted to a prescription for their existence for men, Ellis chose to extort from its last pages an opportunity to make new avowals of support for feminist philosophic ideals. Because he had preferred the rhetoric of "they are not able" to "they must not," he felt free to propose a social freedom that would effectively disregard the very roles he had outlined. "Only nature can pronounce concerning the legitimacy of social modification," he concluded.

We are not at liberty to introduce any artificial sexual barriers into social concerns. The respective fitness of men and women for any kind of work or any kind of privilege can only be ascertained by actual open experiment. . . . An exaggerated anxiety lest natural law be overthrown is misplaced. The world is not so insecurely poised (452).

Yet what security did he guarantee by warning at the same time that nature's pronouncement upon such "open experiment" might be "sterility or death" (442)? In his divided mind, Ellis clearly feared the very thing he proposed. *Man and Woman* was, from the point of view of the intellectual history of feminism, an early warning of the Freudian revolution, a strategic opening that would lead to the eventual victory of biological determinism over moral freedom.

If the social and psychological uses of biology effected the scientific disarming of the philosophic tradition of feminism, the force that was to conclude its transformation was anthropology, with its ability to forge into symbol and archetype the "complementary genius" of Geddes and Thomson, and the "joy in difference" of Havelock Ellis. Indeed, by the time those concepts were articulated, anthropologists had already discovered the imaginative figures to embody them, and to give them the force that only such concrete symbols have to anchor elusive ideas in the consciousness of a culture. They had been storing a rich stockpile of such images since the opening of the Darwinian era, in studies of prehistoric and primitive cultures by Bachofen, Morgan, Starke, McLennan, and Westermarck—images of matriarchies, of fertility rituals, and of the magical power inherent in sex, and sexual polarity.[23]

[23]The scholarly initiative in this important development was taken by T. T. Bachofen with his *Das Mutterrecht* (Stuttgart, 1861) and A. Girard-Teulon, *La Mère chez certains peuples de l'antiquité* (Paris, 1867). The American anthropologist, Lewis Henry Morgan, published his influential *Ancient Society* in 1877, which became the basis of Engel's *The Origins of the Family* in 1884. British research picked up considerable momentum by the eighties as well: J. F. McLennan published *Patriarchal Theory* in 1885, and C. S. Wake produced *The Development of Marriage and Kinship* and C. N. Starcke, *The Primitive Family* in 1889; E. Westermarck published his influential *History of Human Marriage* in 1894.

Of course, to read important feminist statements in this period is to be mindful of the benign influence of theories of matriarchates, gynocracy, and *Mutterrecht* on the force of their argumentation, since they at least provided a forceful wedge against the dogma that male supremacy represented the "order of nature." Bebel and Engels (*The Origins of the Family,* 1884) both relied heavily on works like Bachofen's *Das Mutterrecht* (1861) and Lewis Henry Morgan's *Ancient Society* (1877) for laying the opening premise for radical future change. Mona Caird, in *The Morality of Marriage* (1897), developed her own radical feminist thesis out of the same material.[24] Unfortunately for feminist thought in general, however, the ethnographic and anthropological record could not help but be interwoven with the biological: sexual dominion as a variable was obliged to coexist intellectually with sexual character as a constant in the contemporary climate of scientific cross-fertilization.

Even before Geddes and Thomson published *The Evolution of Sex,* the American anthropologist Lester Frank Ward proposed, in an essay "Our Better Halves" (1888), what he called a "gynaecocentric theory" of human development. Women, he claimed, were the "race type," the conservers of the character of the species, men the "sex type," selected by evolution as a more convenient means of reproduction and to reinforce adaptive variations.[25] Ward's theory was more fully developed, along with its social implications, in his *Pure Sociology* (1904).[26] But from the outset it was seen as an attractive support to missionary feminism and an adaptable supplement to the progressive social vision of those who gave feminism only qualified assent. It assigned power to women, in other words, without prohibiting its delegation along certain sexual lines.

Ward's influence on the work of Charlotte Perkins Gilman was especially profound, and was indeed declared by her with almost sentimental fervor. Interestingly, both of them pointed to a *future* that would alter all our preconceptions about sexual character and sexual relations, yet neither could avoid emphasizing the *past* as prologue. In both *Women and Economics* (1897) and *The Man-Made World,* or, *Our Androcentric Culture* (1911), Gilman's energy was spent largely in reinterpretation of the concept of the maternal race-type, the instinctual evolutionary role of women in species preservation and elevation. The sense of cultural mission and cooperative destiny for women was an inevitable part of her message, eagerly and passionately declared. "The

[24]Mona Caird, *The Morality of Marriage* (London, 1897), esp. 21–78.
[25]Lester Frank Ward, "Our Better Halves," *Forum,* 6 (Nov. 1888), 266–75; cf. also Grant Allen's reply, "Woman's Place in Nature," *Forum,* 7 (May 1889), 258–63 (a classic), and Ward's rejoinder, "Genius and Woman's Intuition," *Forum,* 9 (June 1890), 401–08.
[26]Ward, *Pure Sociology* (New York, 1903), 296–377.

most basic of distinctions between the sexes" was supplied by their being "the centripetal and centrifugal forces of the universe."[27] For
Gilman, the female is by nature the guardian of the race, the matrix of
humane civilization, essentially characterized by the nurturing impulse.
An increasingly militarized androcentric society, hell-bent on destruction, would fail to acknowledge the conservative and preservative force
of woman's sexual energy at its peril.

Olive Schreiner provides a parallel illustration of contemporary
feminist statement. Like Ward and Gilman she believed that the future
would be different from the past: work would not be delegated by sex,
because members of either sex would become more and more androgynous, would mutually adopt their best qualities to become more
totally human and less distinguishable from one another. "We take all
labour for our province," wrote Schreiner in *Woman and Labour* (1911).
"Every individual unit humanity contains, irrespective of race, sex, or
type, should find exactly the field of labour which may most contribute
to its development, happiness, and health, and in which its peculiar
faculties shall be most effectively and beneficially exerted."[28] Yet where
those futures were not merely immediate, envisioning women's direct,
benevolent influence on present political and social life (and, by implication, pointing mainly to suffrage) they were invariably vague and
abstract, exercising nothing like the vigorous, compelling hold on the
imagination of concrete, primitive experience. Having read the
ethnologists and ethnographers, and having observed for herself the
lives of native women in her South African homeland, Schreiner concluded that women were under a natural compulsion to work "in the
service of the whole race."

The women of no race or class will ever rise in revolt or attempt to bring about
a revolutionary readjustment of their relation to their society, however intense
their suffering and however clear their perception of it, while the welfare and
persistence of their society requires their submission (14).

Among the male intellectuals who, by end-century, were still sympathetic to feminism, there was a very noticeable capitulation to the impact of anthropology. This impact was made almost irresistible when it
received its full realization in Frazer's *The Golden Bough,* a catalyst of
literary and artistic renewal. And not only did Frazer's work fall in
beautifully with the contemporary scientific climate, but it gave,
through the archetypal image of vital, primitive femaleness, positive
symbolic expression to the interaction of sexual and creative energies

[27]C. P. Gilman, *The Man-Made World* (3rd ed., New York, 1914), 78–79.
[28]Olive Schreiner, *Woman and Labour* (London, 1911), 216.

that had long preoccupied romanticism.[29] One relevant result of the enormous imaginative exploitation of woman as creative sexual matrix, at the turn of the century, was the effective loss to the feminist tradition of the resources of art and literature as preparers of the culture for radical change—resources mid-century feminism had once enjoyed through such writers as Charlotte Brontë, George Eliot, and George Meredith.[30] The culture was instead prepared for the Freudian, not the feminist, revolution, in which the shameless enjoyment of sex was to be induced by fresh emphasis on sexual attraction between spiritual and physical opposites. The social and personal happiness of the future now seemed to rest on the accentuation, rather than the obliteration, of sex differences, and medical experts began to link feminism not only with social instability but with all the ominous dangers of repressed sexuality. Even the supposed friends of feminism among the English prophets of utopian socialism—William Morris, Edward Carpenter, George Bernard Shaw, and others—were also prophets of this sexual revolu-

[29]William Sharp, who wrote under the female pseudonym "Fiona Macleod," offers a striking example of this appeal. Though he was unwilling to admit his literary bisexuality during his lifetime, Sharp had no theoretical difficulty with the male expropriation of "female" qualities. Neither, apparently, did Geddes, who first published Fiona Macleod's works, and helped to baffle detection of their true authorship until Sharp's death in 1905. The idea that the artist-nature was hermaphroditic had already some currency by the time Sharp began his pseudonymous work. He was familiar with Elie Reclus, *Primitive Folk* (London, 1890), which recorded transvestite rituals and behavior among the priests and prophets of certain tribes. The idea had great persistence and appeal (as seen, for example, in the work of James Joyce). Reclus was quoted extensively, along with the work of Charles Leland on this theme (*The Alternate Sex,* 1904), by Edward Carpenter in *Intermediate Types among Primitive Folk* (1921). The close personal as well as intellectual ties among many of the writers on sex and sex roles suggest an informal network that provides a sociological clue to the pattern of reinforcement of scientific ideas on creativity. For a further discussion of this ambience in relation to Sharp's work, see my *William Sharp—"Fiona Macleod"* (Cambridge, Mass., 1970).

[30]The prominence of Hardy and Conrad at this time is symptomatic. It is worth noting that in a retrospective study of Hardy's work ("Thomas Hardy and the Human Pair," 1930), Havelock Ellis declared that Hardy's emphasis on the "elemental" and "primitive" in women was the source of the "permanent veracity" of his novels, and its lack a source of weakness in Meredith's; cf. *Views and Reviews* (Second Series), 189. The variations on this stereotype of female sexuality (and its companion male stereotype) in twentieth-century art and literature, have already been much noted. See especially (for literature): Kate Millett, *Sexual Politics* (New York, 1969), Katharine Rogers, *The Troublesome Helpmate* (Seattle, 1966), and Mary Ellmann, *Thinking about Women* (New York, 1968); *Woman as Sex Object,* ed. Linda Nochlin (New York, 1972), contains some appropriate scattered insights on women in painting and the visual arts, but probably the most important recent essay on this subject is Carol Duncan, "Virility and Domination in Early Twentieth-Century Vanguard Painting," *Artforum* (Dec. 1973), 30–39.

tion, foretelling the "coming-of-age" of love and the redeeming of sexual energies.[31]

Seen against this continuum, it is apparent that the impact of Freudian psychology was merely one more debt the twentieth century owed to the nineteenth. Even Freud's attacks on contemporary feminism were, in a sense, attacks on a shadow-enemy. The intellectual forces of the earlier feminist tradition had already been weakened, and the new recruits were deeply engaged in promoting a feminism that defined its role around the socializing "genius" of women's complementary sexuality.[32] Perhaps the recent, renewed phase of the movement contains some belated appreciation of the Victorian experience—in its tendency to distinguish between the scientific and the philosophic aspects of the debate,[33] and in the willingness of some feminists to credit the wisdom of G. K. Chesterton's observation, that being human may be the most "unnatural" thing in the world.

Ramapo College, New Jersey.

[31]There are no prudes among the blooming domestic caretakers of William Morris's *News from Nowhere* (1892) or in the cozy utopia of Robert Blatchford's *The Sorcery Shop* (1907). Shaw's representation of the male-female polarity, with the female as carrier of the "Life Force" (*Man and Superman,* 1903), is more familiar; cf. also Edward Carpenter, *Love's Coming-of-Age* (New York, 1911).

[32]O'Neill's conclusion, in *Everyone Was Brave,* that everyone was also contented by the benevolent diversion of woman-power into philanthropy may be oversimplified, but not greatly: "The settlements reassured conservatives that liberated women would interest themselves in traditional womanly concerns. . . . [They were seen] as models for adventurous young female activists, and as evidence that the social concerns of free women would not disrupt the existing order" (94–95).

[33]Compare Simone de Beauvoir, *The Second Sex* (New York, 1953), xxix: "Quite evidently the problem would be without significance if we were to believe that woman's destiny is inevitably determined by physiological, psychological, or economic forces."

PART FOUR

FROM RANK TO CLASS

XVII

JEFFERSONIAN REVISIONS OF LOCKE: EDUCATION, PROPERTY-RIGHTS, AND LIBERTY

By David M. Post

This essay considers the history of a particular interpretation of individual liberty during the period it was reconstructed and introduced in the United States by the Jeffersonian Republicans. The interpretation of freedom here considered—a positive or, following C. B. Macpherson, a "developmental" one—showed two faces in the early U.S. republic.[1] Theories of education and of property-right, when taken together, indicate the reworking of prevalent Lockean beliefs about political liberty. The parallel republican deviations from Lockean theory should be examined not only by those wishing to focus a clearer image of the Jeffersonian movement; consideration of these deviations also enriches current debate over what our own conceptions of liberty need to include. Locke's formulation of the natural right to property and knowledge by fully rational members of society remained influential ideas in the early U.S. Departures from Locke by the Jeffersonians, however, indicate a transformation.

Historiographic Perspectives. Sixty years have softened the too-sharp image which Carl Becker presented of Jeffersonian political theory. Today historians have a far broader, though less focused view. "The lineage is direct," Becker had asserted. "Jefferson copied Locke and Locke quoted Hooker."[2] Historians, in reacting to this view of Jefferson as Locke's direct heir, have widened our understanding of Jeffersonian thought. Just as surely, earlier understandings have been eroded, and little agreement now remains as to exactly what any definition of the Jeffersonian Republicans should include. Who were they? One of the most useful characterizations was provided by Louis Brandeis: "Those who won our independence believed that the final end of the state was to make men free to develop their faculties. . . . They valued liberty as both an end and as a means."[3] In order to consider this evaluation, interpretations of the republican movement need to deal with the associated Jeffersonian transformations of educational theory and property theory. And the literature of the period suggests that a key to understanding these transformations is the emergence of a developmental concept of liberty.

The original point of contention following Becker's study concerned Jefferson's deviation from Locke on the inclusion of property among the trilogy of natural rights. Jefferson substituted "pursuit of happiness" within the famous Lockean "life, liberty, and property." Locke's own phrase was preserved in the

---

[1] For an exposition of a "developmental" concept of freedom, aimed at revising the firm division set by Isaiah Berlin between negative and positive liberty, see C. B. Macpherson, *Democratic Theory* (New York, 1973). Such a concept inheres in the premise that "man is not a bundle of appetites seeking satisfaction but a bundle of conscious energies seeking to be exerted" (5). For a defense of positive liberty see Lawrence Crocker, *Positive Liberty* (Boston, 1980).

[2] Carl Becker, *The Declaration of Independence* (New York, 1922), 79.

[3] *Whitney vs. California*, 274 U.S. 357, 375.

standard common law *Commentaries* of William Blackstone,[4] and in such other eighteenth-century American documents as the 1777 *Declaration on the Violation of Rights.* While the historians Adrienne Koch and Stuart Brown continued to affirm Jefferson's basic adherence to Lockean property theory, others began to question this view. In the 1930s and 1940s Gilbert Chinard, T. V. Smith, Eugene Perry Link, and Herbert Schneider, among others, all departed from Becker's thesis. Gary Wills and Morton White have further reinterpreted Jeffersonian thought.[5]

Recently one reviewer has suggested that republican "revisionism" may have over-extended itself with regard to sweeping away Locke's influence. "This new broom has also swept away much that is the truth," notes Isaac Kramnick, and he finds the reports of Locke's intellectual death to be (*pace* Mark Twain) "greatly exaggerated."[6] Nevertheless, in the past half century historians generally have come to accept the deviation of the republicans from parts of Lockean theory. Interpretations now must deal with the character of those republican deviations in order to form a clearer image of early intellectual life in the U.S.A. We should therefore narrow the discussion of republicanism to a question which is central to the understanding of republican style: was the movement, as Brandeis

---

[4] "The third absolute right, inherent in every Englishman, is that of property." William Blackstone, *Commentaries* (Oxford, 1768), I, 138.

[5] Adrienne Koch, *The Philosophy of Thomas Jefferson* (New York, 1943). She reported (175) that "there is ample proof, therefore, for Jefferson's recognition of property as a basic 'natural' right.' "

Stuart Brown, *The First Republicans* (Syracuse, 1954). Brown asserted (10) that "the language of the *Declaration* intended no departure from the familiar concepts."

Gilbert Chinard, *Thomas Jefferson, the Apostle of Americanism* (Boston, 1929). Chinard discovered (84) that "when Lafayette submitted to Jefferson his 'Declaration des droits de l'homme,' Jefferson put in brackets the words 'droit a la propriete,' thus suggesting their elimination from the list of natural rights."

T. V. Smith, "Thomas Jefferson and the Perfectibility of Mankind," *Ethics* (July, 1943). Smith suggested that Jefferson might have viewed property as a social right.

Eugene Perry Link, *Democratic-Republican Societies, 1790-1800* (New York, 1942). Link wrote that Jefferson and Paine probably diverged from Lockean principles.

Herbert W. Schneider, *A History of American Philosophy* (New York, 1946). Schneider found (246) that "the Scottish enlightenment was probably the most potent single tradition in the American enlightenment."

Gary Wills, *Inventing America* (Garden City, 1978). Wills further corroborates Schneider on the influence of the Scottish enlightenment.

Morton White, *The Philosophy of the American Revolution* (New York, 1978). White terms property an "adventitious" right in the Jeffersonian view, and he traces the origin of this idea primarily to Jean Jaques Burlamaqui (1694-1748), the Swiss jurist who based all political rights on principles of natural law.

[6] Isaac Kramnick, "Republican Revisionism Revisited," *The American Historical Quarterly* (June 1982). As Jefferson did consider Locke one of Europe's three greatest thinkers, and hung his portrait at Monticello, it is impossible to dispute this point. More debatable is Professor Kramnick's assertion that "Chapter 5 of the Second Treatise, 'On Property,' became the received wisdom in advanced radical circles in the late eighteenth-century," at least unless American radicals are excepted by Kramnick. On the contrary, it is the very pervasiveness of Locke's influence which makes so significant the departure from his theories of education and property right.

suggested, indeed a move toward what might today be described as a developmental concept of individual liberty? Answers to this question must begin with the parallel concerns of the republican movement, namely, public education and property as a social right, best understood as divergences from the type of individualism which republicans associated with English thought. In departing from a concept of negative liberty championed by Locke, did not the republicans consciously approach a developmental concept of freedom?[7]

If Kramnick is correct in suspecting Locke's influence to be alive and well in the late eighteenth-century, then it is necessary to review the points of Lockean theory from which Americans diverged. Only against the backdrop of Locke's pervasive influence can Jeffersonian republican features be historically appreciated.

Locke on Property and Education. "It is necessary for me to be as I am," wrote Locke, "God and nature have made me so; but there is nothing I have is essential to me. An accident or disease may very much alter my color or shape; a fever or fall may take away my reason or memory, or both; and an apoplexy leave neither sense, nor understanding, no nor life." In Locke's view the relationship of an individual to his behavior, character, or *properties* is similar to an individual's relationship to his knowledge. In both cases all humans equally must acquire their character or knowledge in the world. "So if it be asked," Locke concluded, "whether it be essential to me or any other particular corporeal being to have reason, I say no, no more than it is essential to this white thing to have words on it."[8]

Despite the egalitarian premise, Locke's theory of property attempted to explain and justify as rightful the divisions of social class. He wanted to show "how men might have come to have property in several parts of that which God gave to Mankind in common, and that without any express compact of all the commoners."[9] Justification for the institution of property was obtained first by granting man control and propriety over his own person. "Though the Earth, and all inferior creatures be common to all men, yet every man has a property in his own *person.* This no body has any Right to but himself. The labor of his body, and the work of his hands, we must say, are properly his." Because Locke regarded individuals the proprietors of their own person, they are able to acquire property freely. "Whatsoever he removes out of the State that Nature hath provided, and left in it, he hath mixed his Labor with and joyned to it something that is his own, and thereby makes it his Property" (*ibid,* 328-29). In the remaining step of explaining the institution of a class society, Locke argued that those who *have* used their labor to appropriate property are also those who most have obeyed God's will—they then must be regarded as the most rational

[7] For a differing interpretation see J. W. Cooke, "Jefferson On Liberty," *Journal of the History of Ideas,* 34 (1973, 563-76). Cooke presents Jefferson as an exponent of negative liberty. However, he does not fully deal with Jeffersonian educational programs or the property theory of republicanism as a movement, nor does he examine Lockean views comparatively.

[8] John Locke, *An Essay Concerning Human Understanding,* Alexander Campbell Fraser, ed., (New York, 1959), II, 58.

[9] John Locke, *Two Treatises of Government,* Peter Laslett, ed., (New York, 1965), 327.

in addition to being the most industrious, for God gave the world "to the use of the Industrious and Rational (and Labour was to be his title to it); not to the Fancy or Covetousness of the Quarrelsome and Contentious" (*ibid,* 333). Thus, Locke was able to justify the ownership of property by the contemporary landowners and gentry, since appropriation had marked that class as the most rational. Macpherson terms the differential rationality in Locke's notion a "bourgeois concept," different from prior, Aristotelian views of masters and slaves. "With Locke the difference in rationality was not inherent in men, not implanted in them by God or Nature; on the contrary, it was socially acquired by virtue of different economic positions." [10]

Having explained the establishment and division of social class, Locke's definition of "property" at once excluded the landless laborer from society while also binding him to it. For the purpose of limiting full membership in the state to the upper class, Locke regarded *land* as representative of *all* property, since civil government was formed by landowners who were its primary participants: "The great and *chief end,* therefore, of men's uniting into Commonwealths, and putting themselves under government, is the *Preservation of their Property.*" States owed their existence to the collective action of the fully rational, property-holding class. One aim of government was the protection of rights to property acquisition; "property" in this sense meant physical capital. However, for purposes of including the landless laborer under the laws of the state, "property" was sometimes broadened to have a meaning nearer to that of "properties" in an environmental sense. Although the right to liberty and property was natural, liberties and human properties were acquired by labor from use of the environment, just as surely as all knowledge was a comprehension of the external world. For the purposes of including the laborer under the law, Locke defined the term "property" broadly to mean "lives, liberties, and estates," including what economists of education today term "human capital." [11] Finally, this ambiguity in Locke's egalitarianism, could result by regarding a proletariat as *in* but not *of* society.

Individuals are born without inherent difference. However, they develop and distinguish themselves in the world just as social classes were developed. Both individuals and classes acquire from the world their properties (in the two senses of the word). But what can be acquired can also be alienated. Thus, because *liberty* and *property* are phrased together in Locke's trilogy of natural rights and have equal status by origin, the terms also have equal economic status. Liberty as well as property may freely be transferred by one class to another in a contract, since Locke gave individuals propriety over their own person. Furthermore, for Locke, appropriation rather than production most fulfilled divine mandate; liberties and labor of the lower classes were acquired in justice.

Lockean educational theory is consistent with his thinking on human development and personality. His *Thoughts Concerning Education* was first written as a letter to Edward Clarke for the benefit of instructing Clarke's son at home. Earlier Locke had written: "Where the hand is used to the plough and the spade, the head is seldom elevated in mysterious reasoning. 'Tis well if men of

---

[10] C. B. Macpherson, *The Political Theory of Possessive Individualism* (New York, 1962), 246.

[11] Laslett, 21.

that rank (to say nothing of the other sex) can comprehend plain propositions."[12] In his *Thoughts* Locke wrote that "virtue is harder to be got than knowledge from the world."[13] Accordingly, moral education was of paramount importance to him. Locke did not think moral intuition was innate, and he stated clearly that "children cannot well understand what injustice is until they understand property" (*ibid.*, 84). Because Locke conceived education as of primarily moral importance, it was understandable that he would advise gentlemen to give their sons a *private* education (i.e., taking place in the private households of the gentry): "A father that breeds his son at home has the opportunity to have him more in his own company, and there give him what encouragement he thinks fit; and can keep him better from the taint of servants and the meaner sort of people than is possible to be done abroad" (*ibid*, 54). In a Lockean perspective, education never was designed to equalize the differential rationality and property-right assumed by his political theory. Locke was clear as to just who should take the time to study: "Those, methinks, who by the industry and parts of their ancestors have been set free from a constant drudgery to their backs and bellies, should bestow some of their spare time on their heads and open their minds by some trials and essays in all sorts of reasoning."[14]

A view of education for the consumption of rational property-owners, education beyond the access of "the meaner sort of people," set the stage for eighteenth-century English debates over grammar and charity schools. Taken to the extreme, Locke's egalitarian epistemological premises eventually led Bernard de Mandeville to criticize educational reform. Mandeville's essay on charity schools, in his 1723 edition of *The Fable of the Bees,* was a frank defense of inequality. "Thinking and reasoning justly, as Mr. Locke has rightly observed, require time and practice. Those that have not used themselves to thinking but just on their present necessities, make poor work of it when they try beyond that."[15] Mandeville was genuinely concerned with the effect on society of educating the poor. Who would perform menial work, if not the poor? Not even the Christian evangelism of the charity-school movement could persuade Mandeville that such education would not have dangerous consequences. "The knowledge of the working poor should be confin'd within the verge of their occupations," he warned, "and never extended beyond what relates to their calling. The more a shepherd, a plowman or any other peasant knows of the world, and things that are foreign to his labour or employment, the less fit he'll be to go through the fatigues and hardships of it with chearfulness and content" (*ibid*, 288).

The Jeffersonian Republicans. When turning to consider the republican divergence from Locke, it is useful to recall the original wording of the *Declaration of Independence:* "inherent and inalienable rights." Because Locke considered

---

[12] John Locke, *The Reasonableness of Christianity,* George Ewing, ed. (Chicago, 1965), 193. Contrast this comment with Jefferson's letter to Peter Carr: "State a moral case to a ploughman and a professor. The former will decide it as well and often better than the latter. . . ." Lee, 146.

[13] Peter Gay, ed., *John Locke on Education* (New York, 1964), 49.

[14] John Locke, *Of the Conduct of the Understanding,* Francis Garforth, ed. (New York, 1966), 53.

[15] Mandeville, *The Fable of the Bees* (Oxford, 1924), II, 190.

virtue and character to be acquired, any notion of moral "development" in the "state of nature" in his theory was out of place. Jeffersonians thought rights inalienable precisely because they had roots inherent in the human being. That property right was not similarly viewed by Jefferson to have such inherent roots is also clear from his substitution of "pursuit of happiness" for Locke's "property."

"Revisionist" historians, to use Kramnick's term, have detected the influence of Scottish moral sense philosophy in Jeffersonian thought. To cite but one example, Henry Home (Lord Kames) reported a universal moral sense, present even in uncivilized man. Moral sense "proceeds from a direct feeling we have upon presenting the object, without the intervention of any sort of reflection. . . ." Home claimed that "the Author of our nature has not left our action to be directed by so weak a principle as reason."[16] Compare Jefferson's statement to Peter Carr: "He who made us would have been a pitiful bungler if he had made the rules of our moral conduct a matter of science." Jefferson then goes on to explain that "the moral sense, or conscience, is as much a part of man as his leg or arm. It is given to all human beings in a stronger or weaker degree, as force of members is given them in greater or weaker degree. It may be strengthened by exercise, as may any particular limb of the body."[17] Jefferson wrote to DuPont de Nemours explicitly: "I believe . . . that morality, compassion, generosity are innate elements in the human constitution."[18]

The Jeffersonian belief in an essentially inherent moral capacity inspired republican views of property and of education quite different from those of John Locke. Since for Jefferson natural rights had roots in human nature, he thought the right to liberty to be in a separate class from the right to property. Locke had treated all rights as though they were properties; indeed, they were represented and symbolized by property and could, like property, be acquired or alienated. Individuals were considered to be without inherent character, but distinctions of both class and individuals were produced by the environment. For Jeffersonians human nature indicated a basic set of rights, but property was incidental and adventitious, a right produced only after formation of a social contract, a social rather than natural right. Thomas Paine gave the most detailed explanation:

Of the first kind there are rights of thinking, speaking, forming and giving opinions, and perhaps all those which can be exercised by the individual without the aid of exterior assistance—or in other words, rights of personal competency. Of the second kind are those of personal protection, of acquiring and possessing property, in which the individual power is less than the natural. . . . These are civil rights or rights of compact, and are distinguishable from natural rights."[19]

Joel Barlow, in 1793, asserted that "it is the person, not the property, that

---

[16] Henry Home, *Essays* (Edinburgh, 1751), 63, 98-99. See also Arthur McGuinness, *Henry Home, Lord Kames* (New York, 1970), 43.

[17] Adrienne Koch and William Peden, eds., *The Life and Selected Writings of Thomas Jefferson* (New York, 1944), 430-31.

[18] Gilbert Chinard, ed., *The Correspondence of Jefferson and Du Pont de Nemours* (Baltimore, 1931), 257.

[19] Cited in Chinard, *Correspondence,* LXXII.

exercises the will, and is capable of enjoying happiness. It is therefore the person for whom government is instituted."[20] It was with this understanding of property right that Jefferson could make his well-known statement to James Madison: "The earth belongs to the living," he charged. "The Portion occupied by any individual ceases to be his when himself ceases to be, and reverts to society. If the society has formed no rules for the appropriation of its lands in severality, it will be taken by the first occupants. . . . But the child, the legatee, or the creditor takes it not by any natural right, but by the law of society of which they are members, and to which they are subject."[21] Comments such as these do support a revision of Becker's thesis, and a conclusion that Jeffersonians deviated from Locke's including property among the natural rights.

Two policies in particular reflect the demotion of property from a natural to a social right. The first was Jefferson's own campaign to abolish primogeniture. His concern was to govern the rules of inheritance by passing a law to divide the Virginia estates of the "pseudo-aristocracy." In his autobiography he reflected that "if the eldest son could eat twice as much, or do double work, it might be a natural evidence of his right to a double portion. But being on par with his brothers and sisters, he should be on par also in the partition of the patrimony" (*ibid,* 45). Yet more revealing than this issue was the linkage Jefferson placed between suffrage and a fifty-acre state gift of land. Like Locke, Jefferson did view landowners as the most responsible guardians of social welfare. They had a physical stake in the preservation of society and were "tied to their country by . . . the most lasting bonds" (*ibid,* 377). However, at the same time that Jefferson limited suffrage to landowners, he also included in the Virginia constitution a provision giving to all white males over twenty-one the necessary property — no great contribution, perhaps, from the viewpoint of those excluded from the plan. And yet, in its direction, does not Jefferson's move verge on the conception, as in Macpherson, of man as a "doer, an exerter, a developer and enjoyer of his human capacities?"[22]

The answer is clearly yes, if one considers the associated views of liberty found in Jeffersonian theories of education. One finds everywhere a linkage between property reform and general enlightenment, for the "pseudo-aristocracy" of wealth was thought challenged by education. Educators were assigned a new responsibility in the republic, and they felt a special mission. Enlightened, literate citizens were seen to benefit society as well as themselves, and their participation was thought at least as important as that of property owners. Therefore education was conceived to be a public task. Jefferson's 1779 *Bill For the More General Diffusion of Knowledge* expressed the provision of education as a positive duty on the state: ". . . Whence it becomes expedient for promoting public happiness that those persons, whom nature hath endowed with genius and virtue, should be rendered by liberal education" capable of government.[23] Years later, in a note to John Adams on Virginia's abolition of primogeniture, Jefferson would recall that "these laws, drawn up by myself, laid the ax to the foot of pseudo-aristocracy. And had another which I prepared been adopted by

---

[20] Joel Barlow, *Letter to the National Convention of France* (New York, 1793), 32.
[21] Koch & Peden, 488.
[22] Macpherson, *Democratic Theory,* 51.
[23] *The Papers of Thomas Jefferson* (Princeton, 1950), Julian P. Boyd, ed., II, 526-33.

the legislature, our work would have been complete. It was a bill for the more general diffusion of knowledge."[24]

Robert Coram, a leader in the Newcastle, Delaware, Patriotic Society, directly attacked the Lockean theory of property in 1791. In a diatribe against Sir William Blackstone, Coram wrote that the English jurist should well have known that "the unequal distribution of property was the parent of almost all disorders of government." Rather than to suggest redistribution of property, Coram saw in this "plain truth a foundation whereon to erect a system, which like the sun in the universe, will transmit light, life, and harmony to all under its influence, I mean—A System Of Equal Education."[25] Coram saw a misuse of schooling in aristocratic societies, which he opposed to an idealized vision of the American Indians. "Among those people all the gifts of providence are in common. We do not see, as in civilized nations, part of the citizens sent to colleges to learn to cheat the rest of their liberties, who are condemned to be hewers of wood and drawers of water."[26] This concern led the Newcastle Patriotic Society to pass a motion recommending establishment of schools "whereby the unfortunate children of indigence and neglect may be educated and enlightened among the children of opulence and vigilance, which is an essential means of preserving that equality so necessary to preservation of a pure republican government."[27]

Samuel Harrison Smith was a co-winner of the American Philosophical Society prize for essays on the type of education proper in a republic. He wrote that "if any circumstance be more connected with the virtue and happiness of the United States than another it is the substitution of works defining correctly political, moral, and religious duty" in accordance with "the radical ideas we have already established and which are in great measure peculiar to us."[28] Although a stalwart federalist on many issues, even Noah Webster could write that "two regulations are essential to the continuance of republican governments: 1) such a distribution of lands and such principles of descent and alienation as shall give every citizen a power of acquiring what his industry merits; 2) such a system of education as gives every citizen an opportunity of acquiring knowledge and fitting himself for places of trust" (ibid, 65).

Republican writers on education exhibited a bias against Lockean individualism. "The republican student," wrote Benjamin Rush (1745-1813), "must be taught to amass wealth, but it must be only to increase his power of contributing to the wants and needs of the state" (ibid, 14). What educational view could be more compatible with Jefferson's comment that "stable ownership is the gift of social law?"[29] Even more than property owners, educated citizens were considered to be the guard against tyranny. Through the individual's pursuit of hap-

[24] Gordon C. Lee, ed., *Crusade Against Ignorance, Thomas Jefferson On Education* (New York, 1961), 164.

[25] Frederick Rudolph, ed., *Essays On Education in the Early Republic* (Cambridge, Mass., 1965), 111.

[26] Rudolph, 130.

[27] Philip S. Foner, ed., *The Democratic Republican Societies, 1790-1800: A Documentary Source Book* (Westport, Conn., 1976), 32.

[28] Rudolph, 216.

[29] Koch & Peden, 630.

piness and development of potential, the general good of republican society was also thought to be increased. "If a nation expects to be ignorant and free, in a state of civilization, it expects what never was and never will be," wrote Jefferson.[30] A nation's freedom was correlated with knowledge, and so was individual liberty. Jefferson told Edward Carrington that to have newspapers without government was preferable to government without newspapers. "But I should mean that every man should receive those papers and be capable of reading them."[31] In his American Philosophical Society essay, which shared honors with Smith's, Samuel Knox also connected knowledge with freedom: "Ignorance, more especially literary ignorance, has often been the parent and stupid nurse of civil slavery." Smith simply stated that "an enlightened nation is always most tenacious of its rights."[32]

The Jeffersonian Republicans consistently drew a connection between the general welfare and the development of its citizens. Perhaps for this reason, despite the pervasiveness of Lockean views, they placed more responsibility for education upon the state. Samuel Knox wrote in his A.P.S. essay that "the celebrated Locke himself not excepted, we find very few who have attempted to offer any plausible objections to a public education." Samuel Harrison Smith agreed. He acknowledged Locke as a partisan of private education because of the "sacrifice, alleged to be produced, of morality and honesty." Smith nonetheless favored public education, outside the control of private households. Associating private education with the aristocracy, Smith observed that "prejudices are as hereditary as titles, and you may almost universally know the sentiments of the son by those of the father" (*ibid*, 307, 208).

If the nation did benefit from the education of its citizens, if the state was to control the process, and if the equal opportunity to develop one's potential was an emerging ideal, then Jeffersonians were also clear that the public must pay for it. Jefferson wrote to the Virginia judge George Wythe that "the tax which will be paid is not more than the thousandth part of what will be paid to kings, priests, and nobles, who will rise up among us if we leave the people in ignorance."[33] Benjamin Rush had similar thoughts: "Shall the estates of orphans, bachelors and persons who have no children be taxed to pay for support of schools from which they can derive no benefit? I answer in the affirmative to the first part of the objection, and I deny the truth of the latter part of it. Every member of the community is interested in the propagation of virtue and knowledge in the state. . . . The bachelor will in time save his tax for this purpose by being able to sleep with fewer bolts and locks."[34]

Republicans were united in a belief that the state had some positive function in raising its citizens from ignorance and servitude to knowledge and freedom. Representative is Joel Barlow's advice to French republicans: "In order to be consistent with yourselves in removing those abuses which have laid the foundation of all offences against society, both in crimes and punishment, you ought to pay a farther attention to the necessity of public instruction. It is your duty

[30] Lee, 18-19.
[31] Koch & Peden, 411-12.
[32] Rudolph, 288, 307.
[33] Koch & Peden, 395.
[34] Rudolph, 6.

to establish a system of government that shall improve the morals of mankind. In raising a people from slavery to freedom, you have called them to act on a new theater, and it is a necessary part of your business to teach them how to perform their parts."[35] New York Governor DeWitt Clinton, President of the Free School Society, had this to say in an 1809 address: "the celebrated Locke . . . devoted the powers of his mighty intellect to the elucidation of education; but in the very threshold of his book we discover this radical error: his treatise is professedly intended for the children of gentlemen. . . . The consequence of this monstrous heresy has been that ignorance, the prolific parent of every crime and vice, has predominated over the great body of people."[36]

The popular appeal of this counter-Lockean movement surfaced in such newspaper editorializing as the following: "it may be said by some that it is reasonable there should be no such [public school] establishment, but that every man should pay for the education of his own children. Let it not be considered, however, that the general fund of knowledge is private property merely: it is public stock on which depends the well-being of the community."[37] Such counter-Lockean sentiments culminated in the rhetoric (if not always actions) surrounding the establishment of early State school systems. In Kentucky, for example, a report of the first Commission on Education (1823) concluded that "the cultivated minds of the people constitute the chief treasure of the state. There is an infinite expansibility in the mind of man; and it is among the first and most important duties of the government to improve the elasticity and cultivate the intellectual energy of the whole community. . . . Knowledge is power, and the only way to preserve an equality of the latter is to promote a general diffusion of the former."[38] Far from the Lockean model which had allowed rational property owners freely to choose an education for their children, Jeffersonians consciously expressed a different ideal. Samuel Harrison Smith, in the A.P.S. essay written just ninety years after John Locke's death, could nonetheless depart radically from Locke's views. Locke had written, "nobody is under an obligation to know everything. Knowledge and science in general is the business only of those who are at ease and leisure."[39] Smith proposed, however, that "it be made punishable by law for a parent to neglect offering his child to the preceptor for instruction."[40]

Care always must be taken to avoid reading nineteenth-century conflicts into prior periods. The Jeffersonian Republicans, after all, were not nascent socialists. Nor can their concerns easily be applied to educational problems of the twentieth-century, or to our ongoing attempt to conceptualize liberty. But the continuing discussion of these issues is deepened by consideration of the Jeffersonians. Locke had emphasized property as a right antecedent to government, and took unequal distribution as proof that property owners were the fully rational members of a society and, thus, its fullest participants. For the Jeffersonians property-right

[35] Barlow, 58.

[36] Carl F. Kaestle, ed., *Joseph Lancaster and the Monitorial School Movement* (New York, 1973), 154.

[37] (Louisville) *Public Adviser*, Nov. 17, 1818.

[38] George Robertson, Broadside, copy in Filson Club, Louisville.

[39] Garforth, 55.

[40] Rudolph, 210.

derived from social life, and reason was equally sufficient in all individuals. They believed that moral education, explicitly as such, was not necessary since there was thought to exist an innate, universal moral capacity. Locke thought virtue to be acquired environmentally and, at his most extreme, had seen education to expand the powers of those having property and leisure. Both in regard to property and to knowledge, Jeffersonians shifted responsibility for the development of human powers away from the exclusive domain of propertied individuals. The divergence of early U.S. thinkers from Lockean educational and property theories marked the start of a divergent view of individual liberty as well. If they valued freedom as an end as well as a means, then they also began to view the opportunity for human development as a proper concern of republican government.

University of Chicago.

XVIII

HEGEL ON PROPERTY AND POVERTY

By Richard Teichgraeber

1. *The Hegelian Origins of Property.*—Hegel's explanation of the nature of property, not unlike his treatment of all the other issues examined in his philosophy, is fully understood only as it is understood within the rational development of his philosophy as a whole. By itself, an argument about the nature of property has no truth. For Hegel, there are no isolated truths; there is only the truth of his whole philosophical system.

In his *Philosophy of Right,* the text I am primarily concerned with here, Hegel's aspiration to systematic truth and coherence does not appear in an historically oriented argument.[1] Hegel's political philosophy is not intended to justify or rationally explain particular historical practices or ideals by speculation upon pre-historical origins. Property, for example, is not to be taken as a philosophical starting-point from which the rest of the argument logically proceeds. There is no one crucial linchpin that secures Hegel's philosophy. His philosophy is politically a structure which is—apparently—everywhere bolted together with irremovable rivets of Reason.

In the Preface to his *Phenomenology of Spirit,* Hegel describes part of the basic strategy that guides the construction of his mature thought: "it is only as science or system that knowledge is actual and can be expounded. Further, any so-called basic proposition or principle, if true, is also false simply insofar as it is merely a basic proposition or principle."[2] Property itself, then, will have no value or meaning apart from its demonstrated role in developing what for Hegel is man's virtually instinctive need to know and realize himself as part of a rationally coherent whole. It has to be emphasized that this development is one in which man as a willful intelligence is bound to engage. Hegel's fundamental presupposition about human nature is that it possesses intelligence, a capacity to reason. For Kant, human beings seem to arrive in the world equipped with reason; Hegel's men, on the other hand, must work at the creation of reason.[3] Human nature is initially neither "free" nor "rational" nor

[1] Hegel claims that his thought is grounded historically only insofar as it claims to have achieved the external goals of human thought through history. Politically, this means that—on most occasions—the Hegelian modern State is to be taken as the perfection of self-conscious reason in the world. However, attitudes in the realms of art, religion, and philosophy remain for each person to struggle with.

[2] *Hegel: Texts and Commentary,* trans. Walter Kaufmann (Garden City, N.J., 1966), 36.

[3] This very likely simplifies Kant unfairly, but the essential point is that his notion of how man behaves in ways that are to be called "rational" is clearly more settled than Hegel's.

"equal"; it appears only with a capacity to develop its potential for thought.

Hegel's understanding of property develops in answer to this question: In observing the process of human intelligence developing in the material world and striving to become explicit in a coherent, rational philosophy, how might one locate and evaluate property? The question so put immediately implies that previous approaches cannot be repeated in giving an answer. Hegel will not seriously consider answers that rest on *a priori* proclamations about human nature. Nor will he accept arguments about the practical necessity or convenience of property. Hegel does speak of the "doctrine of the necessity of private property,"[4] but by this he means that a true understanding of the meaning of property must go beyond simple "external" accounts. Neither empirically unfounded speculations nor justifications of responses to real contingencies in the past will be accepted. "To consider a thing rationally," writes Hegel, "means not to bring reason to bear on the object from the outside and so to tamper with it, but to find the object rational on its own account."[5] It is in carrying out this process that one finds property's "necessity." And thus our work begins not with the fact of property, but with observing intelligence at the work of becoming Reason.

Insofar as human intelligence can be perfectly embodied in the public institutions that structure the life which human beings share in common, Hegel would like us to think that the political organization he describes in *Philosophy of Right*—the State and those various, more localized institutions that both support and compose it—is intelligence's highest achievement. It is intelligence actually become Reason in the world.

I do not intend to examine the particulars of Hegel's structure in full detail here. But this linking together of self-perfecting creative thought and politics is very significant. As an intelligent will man is necessarily political, for Hegel. His development as a self-consciously rational being occurs within and, at the same time, finds itself accompanied by the perfection of that rationally intelligible structure that is the State. "The absolute goal, or if you like, the absolute impulse of the free mind," writes Hegel, "is to make freedom its object, i.e., to make freedom objective as much in the sense that freedom shall be the rational system of the mind, as in the sense that freedom shall be the world of immediate actuality."[6]

This emphasis upon a simultaneous movement toward and realization of rational freedom both internally (in each individual's mind) and externally (in the world that individuals share) is fundamental to understanding all that Hegel claims to have accomplished in his philosophy.

---

[4]*Philosophy of Right*, ed. and trans. T. M. Knox (New York, 1962), 236, par. 46A; hereafter PR.

[5]PR, 35, par. 31.   [6]PR, 32, par. 27.

For our purposes here, it is also crucial in understanding how the argument of *Philosophy of Right* proceeds. Briefly, the upshot of Hegel's claims is that the State is the final "moment" in human intelligence's striving to become Reason in the world. It is, to use Hegel's terminology, the unrealized "concept" of the State at last becoming the realized "Idea" of the State. There are, it would seem, no more particular moments to follow. Yet the end of this striving must mean, at the same time, that the many separate moments are realized again—but now realized all at once. Knowing, as Hegel describes it, that the Idea has various determinations (i.e., Property, Contract, Family, etc.) in its growth as concept, it is important to see that the Idea is not the mere accumulation through time of these determinations. Hegel's point is this:

... a concept's determinancy and its mode of existence are one and the same thing. But it is to be noticed that the moments, whose result is a further determined form of the concept, precede it in the philosophical development of the Idea as determinations of the concept, but they do not go in advance of it in the temporal development as shapes of experience.[7]

Property, therefore, has to be seen as presupposing all of those other determinations of the concept of the State from which property will (in *Philosophy of Right*) be shown to result. Here also, then, one begins to sense how property is located in what Hegel called his philosophical "circle that presupposes its end as its aim and thus has for its beginning ... that which is actual only through its execution and end."[8]

In specific regard to property, these remarks establish the crucial preliminary point: the idea of property has its origins both in the development and in the final accomplishment of Hegel's system. It serves to perfect man's ability to reason and then again appears in place in that perfect structure that reason comes to build. Our study can proceed by observing in more detail Hegel's account of the first stirrings of reason and then move on to see how far property can go in helping to keep thought in motion.

2. *Property's Moment.*—Hegel designates three "moments" in which man *qua* intelligence comes to recognize his power to reason. First, there is his self-proclamation: an individual person's rudimentary recognition of his distinctiveness amidst the rest of the world. Hegel calls this "the pure thought of oneself,"[9] the first moment of freedom when the self attempts to negate all restrictions on the self. This self-assertion is an essential, inescapable task, but its value has substantial limitations—limitations which reason can properly never accept. The "pure thought of oneself" is for Hegel only "negative freedom." In a partially acceptable theoretical form, it might "never be anything in itself but an abstract idea"; but in practice it can easily become a

---

[7]PR, 35, par. 32.   [8]Kaufmann, *op. cit.*, 30.   [9]PR, 21, par. 5.

"fanaticism of destruction."[10] In perfecting his thought, then, man must come to terms with these restrictions and dangers. He moves in a "transition from undifferentiated indeterminancy to differentiation, determination, and positing of a determinancy as content and object."[11] This means that man's abstract, potentially reckless self-proclamation is overcome (here is the first negation of the negation) in the recognition of the "finitude or particularization of the ego."[12]

The success of this second moment is less a victory for reason than a spur to a higher sort of conjugation: man's capacity to rule the universe is yoked to the necessity of giving this rule concrete, detailed definition. Thus we arrive at the third and final "moment" in these first workings of intelligence becoming reason: the appearance of the concept of a will that is *consciously* free to become rational. Here is the capacity for "the *self*-determination of the ego," writes Hegel, "which means that at one and the same time the ego posits itself as its own negative, i.e., as restricted and determinate, and yet remains by itself, i.e., in its self-identity and universality."[13] Herein also lie the elemental facts which intelligence must grasp in its endeavor to be Rational Truth. Because for Hegel "what is concrete and true (and everything true is concrete) is the universality which has the particular as its opposite, but the particular by which its reflection into itself has been equalized with the universal."[14]

With this awareness, we move up from only the first step of the steep spiral staircase of Hegelian philosophy. At this point, we are only speaking of the "will which is implicitly free," which is to say "implicitly rational."[15] We find man aware of his capacity to reason, but the capacity remains of uncertain potentiality. Constrained within a particular will, man's power to move from his own intelligence to universal Reason is first "poured out" into the "mold of immediacy," still lacking "the form of rationality."[16]

To account for the movement from an implicit to a universal rationality is the work of the whole of *Philosophy of Right*. This movement also has its three stages: in the context of this book, a higher level and more intricately developed complement to the movement from intelligence to implicit rationality. It begins with the concluding moment of the earlier process, what Hegel comes to call the workings of an "immediate will" or "Personality." Here reason attempts to find itself embodied in an "immediate external *thing*." Eventually, reason will be dissatisfied with this projection. True reason can only satisfy itself with that which it creates,[17] and so reason withdraws its concern from the ob-

---

[10]PR, 22, par. 5A.   [11]PR, 22, par. 6.   [12]*Ibid.*
[13]PR, 23, par. 7.   [14]*Ibid.*
[15]PR, 25, par. 11.   [16]*Ibid.*
[17]PR, 46, par. 52A. Hegel also claims that, "It is my mind which of all things I can make most completely my own."

jects of the world. It searches for universal truth in "a reflection of the will into itself," in activity where the "will recognizes something and is something, only in so far as the thing is its own and as the will is present to itself there as something subjective."[18] This change is set in motion by reason's refusal to restrict its activity to the mere appropriation of an external world. Now it seeks truth in a world of self-propelling mental operations. Hegel calls this the sphere of Morality, and he certainly has in mind Kant's ethics as its prime exemplar.

Self-assertion and moral self-exploration are valuable and essential in their service as "moments." Yet they remain abstract while they are merely and separately external or internal demonstrations of the power of thought. They are realized in conjunction only in that hierarchy of in-stitutional relationships (Family, Civil Society, and State) that Hegel calls Ethical Life. This is the matrix in which reason finds both practical and theoretical coherence, and therefore is itself fully realized.

Property finds its particular significance in the first moment of this complex tri-partite accomplishment of Rational Truth. It is the object of work by the Personality, by an "inherently single will" first attempt-ing to locate its truth in things. For Hegel property is primarily this rela-tion of individual will to things. Its worth will be consistently measured in terms of the value and character of this relationship. It is crucial to explain in detail why Hegel makes this argument.

Personality, Hegel's "implicitly rational man," is more specifically defined as

a person . . . making decisions . . . related to a world of nature directly confronting him, and thus a personality of the will [standing] over against this world as something subjective. Personality is that which struggles to lift itself above . . . restriction and to give itself reality, or in other words to claim the ex-ternal world as its own.[19]

To claim the world as its own is, of course, also the broad imperative of Reason itself. And thus, the action of Personality is at least in its pur-poses always rational, in a very general sense of the word.

But Hegel has very particular notions of what rational activity en-tails. Regardless of the forms its activities take, Personality finds its meaning as a term to describe individuals conscious of their power over the immediate objects of the external world. The exercise of this power is a first and essentially important service of a higher truth. It is the ground for Hegel's claims that the very concept of Right, the organized social embodiment of reason, is "in the first place the immediate em-bodiment which freedom gives to itself in an immediate way."[20]

There are two major facets of this important embodiment, only the first of which will be of concern here. The first is "possession, which is property-ownership"; the other is Contract, the means by which "as

[18]PR, 76, par. 107.   [19]PR, 38, par. 39.   [20]PR, 38, par. 40.

owners . . . two persons really exist as persons for each other."[21] Intellectually, the achievement of Contract is a higher stage in the process of the will making the world its own. It is the relation of one will to another, not merely to a thing.[22] It also has to be said that both Property and Contract are ultimately to be taken as they are subsumed in the necessary movement to a full development of Right in the Hegelian State. Even though its appearance presupposes its surrender to higher concepts, property as Hegel conceives it is nonetheless an imperative whose tasks must be completed. Practically, this means that the attempt to establish property is absolutely necessary to the development of each individual as a conscious rational agent: "I as free will am an object to myself in what I possess and thereby also for the first time an actual will, and this is the aspect which constitutes the category of property, the true and right factor in possession."[23]

There is much that can be said about the particulars of Hegel's idea of property, but unless one grasps their philosophical origins they make little or incomplete sense. Two points need emphasis. First, Hegel's explanation of property can only be discovered in his description of the overall pattern of the growth of reason. The second point is new, but it is a direct outgrowth of the first. It is to be found in recognizing how Hegel's explanation rebuts and then encompasses theories of earlier political thinkers, most particularly those of various natural law philosophers. This point might be explained more fully in another essay, but a few useful observations can be offered here.

The thinking of natural law philosophy on property regularly begins with an attempt to answer this question: How may it have happened that when one man took a portion of that common stock originally available to all men in Nature, the rest of mankind permitted it and felt obliged to respect that portion as his private property? There are various answers to the question, and Hobbes and Locke established the two extremes between which the argument from natural law regularly fluctuates.[24]

---

[21]*Ibid.*   [22]PR, 57, par. 71.   [23]PR, 42, par. 45.

[24]Briefly, Hobbes's stance was that rights to private property could exist only because men had, for their own safety and benefit, agreed both to assume the rights and simultaneously to establish political institutions with force sufficient to guarantee them. Locke's view, on the other hand, was that an individual man's freedom to claim a part of nature as particularly his own was legitimated by a self-evident law entitling him to the fruits of his labor in working those resources. This almost instinctive law obliged each man to respect the property of other men long before any human institutions had been conceived or realized. The problem of determining the exact origins of property has crucial implications both in legitimating obligation to the state and in describing the extent to which the state can exercise its power. If, as Hobbes claims, property can exist *only* if men have the institutional means of securing it, then government holds absolute power over all individuals and their property. If, following Locke, property exists as the reward of the labor exercised or owned by individual men, then it is those men who can properly draw boundaries which the state should never cross. And if the state presumes to direct these men in the use of their property, they would be justified in rising against it.

The important thing for our purpose here, however, is not to examine how these answers may oppose that of Hegel. In fact, the most significant difference develops primarily as a result of the character of the original question about property. Remember Hegel's question: In observing the process of human intelligence developing in the material world and becoming explicit in a coherent, rational philosophy, how might one locate and evaluate property? In his less polemical moods, Hegel does not want to argue that this question is directly set against that asked by the natural law philosophers.[25] Admittedly there is an assertion like this one:

The point is that legal and political institutions are rational in principle and therefore absolutely necessary, and the question of the form in which they arose or were introduced is entirely irrelevant to a consideration of their rational basis.[26]

But when he is faithful to his own dialectical mode of thinking, Hegel claims that his question is rather one of a higher order. It includes that of the natural law thinkers, not denying its appropriateness but placing its relevance in perspective. This is the idea at work in the following statement:

The opposite to thinking of the state as something to be known and apprehended as explicitly rational is taking external appearances—i.e., contingencies such as distress, need for protection, force, riches, &c.—not as moments in the state's historical development, but as its substance.[27]

Hegel objected to the essentially contingent character of natural law philosophy—difficulties in the state of Nature alone automatically served to bring about the formation of social and political structures. He called this view the kind of thinking that was tied to "sense perception and the play of fancy," and hence he refused to admit that it could ever provide permanent, rational truths about anything. More important than these understandable objections to superficial philosophizing, however, was Hegel's more dramatic claim that he himself had finally grasped both the means of arriving at the truth about life and at least the external form of that truth itself. In regard to property, this means that Hegel finds himself justified in saying: "The rationale of property is to be found not in the satisfaction of needs but in the supersession of the pure subjectivity of personality. In his property a person exists for the first time as reason."[28] And typically of Hegel, this statement speaks less about particular truths of property as an empirical fact than it does

[25] It is the nature of Hegel's dialectical thought, writes J. N. Findlay, to criticize one's "mode of conceiving things, rather than the actual matter of fact that one has conceived." Findlay, "The Contemporary Relevance Of Hegel," *Hegel: A Collection of Critical Essays*, ed. Alasdair MacIntyre (Garden City, N.J., 1972), 5.

[26] PR, 141, par. 219.   [27] PR, 157, par. 258A.

[28] PR, 235–36, par. 41A.

of a larger philosophical truth which property is ultimately designed to serve.

3. *Some Particulars of Property's Moment.*—An important and intriguing aspect of Hegel's thinking about property is his insistence on its privacy. Philosophically, this claim has its basis in the relationship between the individual will and the emergence of its awareness of a capacity to reason. For Hegel, the first rational stirrings appear partly as a result of a confrontation between men and the external world. But for individuals in their relation to one another the confrontation itself is a self-contained, private process. Practically, this must mean that reason can first be served only by the separate workings of different personalities. A thinking person can begin to relate to the world properly only as a self-consciously distinct individual. And therefore one's relationships with things in the world must be individual, i.e., private.

Hegel is saying this: private property is the unavoidable first step in an individual's rudimentary realization that what he most desires is rational freedom. It is an initial, basic expression of an essential worldly purpose: the free mastery of external reality. Possession in common would dangerously check that freedom, because individuals would not be allowed to direct the use of their property as a full expression of their particular wills and purposes. Common possession, moreover, has "the character of an inherently dissoluble partnership in which the retention of my share is explicitly a matter of my arbitrary preference."[29]

It is important to note that for Hegel the individual will's relationship to property is not at all significant in terms of *how much* of the external world it actually comes to "master." Nor does it matter significantly how one might choose to express that mastery. At issue is the effort to possess, not actual possession. Insofar as Personality has a right to property, Hegel writes, "what and how much I possess . . . is a matter of indifference."[30] The "owner's will . . . is the primary substantive basis of property"; use, therefore, is only a "further modification of property, secondary to that universal basis."[31] Differences in the amount of property possessed, moreover, have no important social features; they merely express differences among personalities.[32]

Given the premise that reason appears to consciousness in individual strivings, Hegel concludes that each personality is obliged to attempt to embody itself in its own distinct possession of property. This is the only quest that men can share as equals. Hegel forcefully makes the point explicit: "Of course men are equal, but only *qua* persons, that is with

[29]PR, 42, par. 46.   [30]PR, 44, par. 49.   [31]PR, 49, par. 51A.
[32]PR, 44, par. 49A. Hegel also writes: "The demand sometimes made for an equal division of land, and other available resources too, is an intellectualism all the more empty and superficial in that at the heart of particular differences there lies not only the external contingency of nature but also the whole compass of mind, endlessly particularized and differentiated, and the rationality of mind developed into an organism."

respect only to the source from which possession springs; the inference from this is that everyone must have property."[33] This statement, however, is not a practical directive; it makes sense only when one keeps in mind that it is *the attempt to have* that really concerns Hegel here.

However, it has to be said next that Hegel is rather reluctant to confront the extreme variety in the results of this crucial attempt. Hegel's attitude toward the poor—those who have-not—and its implications present serious problems in evaluating Hegel's political thought as a whole, as well as in clarifying his attitude to property. Postponing a consideration of the poverty issue for the final section of this essay, I move now to an examination of Hegel's thinking on a related problem: the punishment of those who encroach on the property of others, a group which has always included a large number of the poor. Also, this is an appropriate place to begin formulation of a more critical perspective upon the idea of property in Hegel's overriding scheme of values.

There are two important points to be made: the first relates to empirically verifiable qualities of property and their effect on punishment; the other to the philosophical limits of Personality's relationship to property. In regard to the first, Hegel writes:

In becoming existent in something the will enters the sphere of quantitative extension and qualitative characteristics, and hence varies accordingly. For this reason, it makes a difference to the objective aspect of crime whether the will is so objectified and its specific quality is injured throughout its entire extent . . . or whether it is injured only in a single part or in one of its qualitative characteristics, and if so, in which of these.[34]

With some sifting, one finds that Hegel here is trying to dispel any inclination to make the objects of property sacrosanct in themselves. Crimes against property potentially have an infinite variety of "qualitative characteristics." Punishments to suit them must always attend with care to all the possible differences. This is what Hegel means when he says: "How any given crime is to be punished cannot be settled by mere thinking; positive laws are necessary."[35]

Beyond this practical directive, there is a more fundamental limitation in the Personality-Property symbiosis. Hegel points to the limitation when he first explains his concept of Personality: "For personality, however, as inherently infinite and universal, the restriction of being only subjective is a contradiction and a nullity."[36] Personality in its quest for property expresses only a subjective attempt to master external reality. This attempt, therefore, is only of transient value in the more ambitious creation of rational freedom. A personality in relation to its property is but "the freedom of a single person related to himself," only an "abstractly related actuality."[37]

---

[33] PR, 237, par. 49A.   [34] PR, 68, par. 96.
[35] PR, 246, par. 96A.   [36] PR, 38, par. 39.   [37] PR, 37, par. 34.

In regard to what property means and how punishments for its abuses are to be derived, this second point is crucial. The implication is that for Hegel there is no permanent philosophical value in the mere existence of certain objects one can call one's own. The truth is rather in the infinitely more complex need which the search for property first makes one aware of. There can be, therefore, no crimes against the rights of human nature in those crimes against the objects of property. At the level of property itself, in fact, there is no such thing as the rights of human nature, since property itself represents only a starting point in man's recognition that he has a need and a capacity to discover what his nature will be. This I take as a valid interpretation of what Hegel means when he says: "in personality particularity is not present as freedom, everything which depends on particularity is here a matter of indifference. To have no interest except in one's formal right may be pure obstinacy. . . ."[38]

One can hardly think of Hegel as being overly lenient in regard to punishment, but he does separate himself from the Draconian rationality of Kant's prescriptions in *The Metaphysical Elements of Justice*.[38a] And it is very important to remember that in spite of the large claims he makes for his philosophy, Hegel consistently attempts to avoid binding man in any sort of chains: either philosophically in proclaiming categories in which reason is bound to operate, or politically in setting severe punishments for men who are still only potentially rational and hence likely to continue to make mistakes. Hegel's thought—in its development at least—defends and embraces changes in an individual's thought and behavior. Those changes necessarily include crime and errors of judgment, and these mistakes Hegel can tolerantly include in expounding his system.

Property, then, will inevitably and understandably be trespassed upon; Hegel does not overlook obvious facts about the actual workings of private property. As Marcuse has pointed out, "The rights of property owners must of necessity clash since each stands against the other, the subject of his own particular will . . . the agreement of . . . private will with the general will is only an accident that bears the germs of new conflict."[39] However, this tension, observable in the real world, is in large part anticipated by the internal workings of Hegel's thought. His philosophy is held together by concepts specifically designed to trespass dialectically on those which precede them in thought. Hence, property is not expected to hold its ground against the intrusions of higher forms of rational behavior: most immediately, the securing of contractual relationships among men; and, ultimately, life in the State.

The individual personality itself, in fact, first expresses the limita-

[38] PR, 235, par. 37A.   [38a] John Ladd's translation (New York, 1965), 131–33.
[39] Herbert Marcuse, *Reason and Revolution* (Boston, 1960), 196–97

tions of property in the process of manipulating objects of possession.[40] In trading, in bartering, or even in being coerced to surrender property, a personality realizes that no one object or group of objects contains its essence. Hegel writes that the universal essence of individual self-consciousness is, in fact, inalienable: universal "freedom of will," "ethical life," and "religion" are retained regardless of the fate of one's property. Hence, as Raymond Plant has pointed out in his recent excellent book on Hegel, while personality "requires property in order to develop the powers of his mind . . . the mind does not require *this* property as opposed to *that*, for if it did the development of self-consciousness would depend upon and be tied to the particularity of nature. The possibility of alienation of property, thus inherent in the relationship between property and human personality, leads fairly naturally to the notion of contractual relationship."[41] Property has thus had its separate moment, and now will be an active, if less important, memory at work in all of those moments of the State's "becoming."

Admittedly there is more to be said about the details of Hegel's idea of property. Property itself has its three philosophical "moments": possession, use, and alienation.[42] The first two express aspects of an individual will's relation to a thing. The third expresses the will's return to self-reflection and hence the start of a movement to something higher concepts. But this part of my argument has been primarily an attempt to relate the idea of property to the movement and structure of Hegel's political philosophy as a whole. Any effort to describe Hegel's bold strokes in a brief space necessarily involves overlooking many details in the strokes themselves. And to wrestle here with at least part of the substance of Hegel's larger claims, it is best to move on to consider how his justification of each individual's right to property is related to the fact that for many men that right may be altogether meaningless.

4. *Poverty in the "World as Reason."*—An evaluation of Hegel's attitude toward poverty best begins by remembering his criticism of one of its regularly proposed solutions, the common ownership of property. The communism of Plato's *Republic*, Hegel charges, would prevent the movement of man's intelligence toward rational freedom:

The general principle that underlies Plato's ideal state violates the right of personality by forbidding the holding of private property. The idea of a pious or friendly and even a compulsory brotherhood of men holding their goods in common and rejecting the principle of private property may readily present itself to

[40] PR, 52, par. 65.

[41] Raymond Plant, *Hegel* (Bloomington, 1973), 155.

[42] It is almost common knowledge that these triads appear everywhere in Hegel's work. But George Lichtheim has correctly pointed out (and I have attempted to demonstrate his point here) that the "thesis-antithesis-synthesis is not essential to Hegel's system, whose motor is rather to be found in the dialectic of the whole and its parts." Lichtheim, *Marxism* (New York, 1964), 7.

the disposition which mistakes the true nature of freedom of mind and right. . . .[43]

In the most fundamental way, then, communism is philosophically unacceptable to Hegel: it eliminates that preliminary obligation of each individual to become aware of his rational power and potential. Hegel consistently holds to this objection, and the epistemological premise which supports it, in trying to find proper ways of dealing with poverty.

It may seem misleading to give too much attention to Hegel's remarks on poverty in the *Philosophy of Right*. His very concentrated consideration of it covers only three intriguing but inconclusive pages. One finds in the "Additions" only a few supplementary comments that expand in an important way on the original text.[44] The brevity here, however, does not matter. It is precisely the inconclusiveness of it all that is so significant.

Consider, for example, what Hegel says: "The important question of how poverty is to be abolished is one of the most disturbing problems which agitate modern society."[45] This is an accurate remark to be sure, but neither original nor memorable. It is a modest and resigned statement which one has trouble assimilating into the regularly challenging bravado of Hegel's thinking. "The great thing is to apprehend in the show of the temporal and transient the substance which is immanent and the eternal which is present."[46] Yet in the *Philosophy of Right* Hegel does not offer the poor any "rose in the cross" of their unhappy condition.[47] He does give some account of how poverty comes into being, but he cannot explain why it *has* to be.

What does this charge of incompleteness mean? Two less fundamental questions need to be answered beforehand. First, does Hegel admit that, philosophically, poverty is a serious problem? And if so, should Hegel have come to terms with the problem completely? In regard to the first question, the acknowledgment is explicit: "to be confined to mere physical needs as such and their direct satisfaction would simply be the condition in which the mental is plunged in the natural and so would be one of savagery and unfreedom. . . ."[48] Thinking men are not to be obsessed with securing material goods.

---

[43]PR, 42–43, par. 46A.

[44]The significant paragraphs in PR are 240–46, pp. 148–50. The most important additions (to paragraphs 240 and 244) concern the "rabble," pp. 277–78.

[45]PR, 278, par. 244A.

[46]PR, 10. This sentence is the best clarification of that famous line which precedes it—"What is rational is actual and what is actual is rational."

[47]There is some discussion of the hopes in colonization (cf. 278, par. 248A). But Hegel would ultimately come to disavow colonization. He recognized that it was inconsistent with his attempt to build a state which directly confronts and incorporates the varieties of human social life. See below my remarks of "The English Reform Bill" essay for more on this. [48]PR, 128, par. 194.

Hegel uses this argument in describing the condition of the wealthy as well as that of the property-less. And thus the link between great wealth and great poverty in modern economic life has for Hegel both a philosophical and a socio-economic basis. Both represent directly related conditions of intellectual and material bondage.[49]

In the structure of *Philosophy of Right,* poverty is to be found in the realm of Civil Society, which Hegel takes to be the equivalent of the developing commercial economy of nineteenth-century Europe. Hegel recognized (probably with the assistance of the Scottish moralists) that poverty was not simply the accidental by-product of the modern economic market. In a system that sanctioned universal economic self-seeking, there would inevitably be many who would not have the talent or the opportunity to succeed.

The important thing here, however, is to determine the extent to which Hegel actually wants this inherently inequitable economic individualism to survive. Hegel's stature as an economic thinker is at best uncertain. One senses some elegant and elevated paraphrasings in those early writings that Avineri has made so much of in his recent study of Hegel. And given the conspicuously slow growth of industry on the European continent at the time, there is certainly no need to take Hegel to task—as Avineri has done—for omitting the industrial workers as a necessary additional political Estate.[50] Economic modernity very likely existed for Hegel only between the covers of particular books: in this case, his volumes of Stewart, Ferguson, and Adam Smith. But regardless of where he found it, there can be no doubt that Hegel knew quite well that poverty was a stark fact of European life. Admittedly, he did not overlook some of the serious problems it presented; but it has to be said that he did not look into them as deeply as one would expect, given what he claimed for his philosophy. There is no need to ask here for specific and workable remedies. No one has ever had them; Hegel, perhaps correctly, did not see that he had a responsibility to offer such remedies. But one can very properly ask Hegel, on the basis of his own grand claims, to give us more than he does. He claims to have interpreted "the world as reason." Poverty either finds its place in that interpretation or the interpretation itself is revealed to have at least one gaping hole.

Hegel discusses and criticizes what are for him inadequate solutions to the problem. We know his reason why communism will not do. Private charity, on the other hand, is essentially "subjective," an operation unacceptably dependent on the contingencies of "private sympathy

[49]Cf. Hegel's remarks on wealth in his early essay, "The Spirit of Christianity and its Fate," *Early Theological Writings,* trans. T. M. Knox (Chicago, 1948), 221–22.

[50]Shlomo Avineri, *Hegel's Theory of the Modern State* (Cambridge, 1972), 109; also all of Ch. 5.

and the accidental occurrence of knowledge and a charitable disposition. . . ."[51] Dismissing these solutions, Hegel considers possibilities already existing within the individualistic Civil Society itself. The result is only a series of vague encouragements: the clear, if unusable, point being that the poor should not remain unattended. It is very important to note, however, that since in his system poverty is the product of Civil Society, Hegel ultimately and in spite of his statism assigns the responsibility for its remedy to the individualistic economic realm. There is a curious reasoning behind this, and it needs to be explored in detail.

There are two important and related features of Hegel's uncertain concern for the poor. First, there is a fairly bold, but again vague, proposal: "Public social conditions are . . . to be regarded as all the more perfect the less . . . is left for an individual to do by himself as his private inclination directs. . . ."[52] On the basis of such a remark, Avineri has found in Hegel the essentials of a modern welfare state. This finding, however, overlooks the second point, viz., Hegel's particular reliance on Civil Society in dealing with poverty. As Hegel describes it, the modern economic realm is so internally organized in its various corporations that these institutions are to be the ground for a restricted and harmless self-seeking. And these institutions are to be checked by the State only when the self-seeking is carried to extremes: "The individual must have a right to work for his bread, but the public also has the right to insist the essential tasks shall be properly done."[53]

Hegel does not consistently bring himself to consider poverty as one of the unacceptable extremes of economic individualism. First, and his economic thinking is altogether uncertain here, Hegel for practical reasons does not allow the State to provide for the poor by giving them work. Not believing that "public works" might stimulate or sustain production, Hegel feared that they would produce unwanted goods. He simply was not ready to tear down that much of the wall he imagined could properly exist between politics and economics. This last claim needs careful justification. A defense of it arises in a consideration of the three solutions of the problem of poverty which Hegel either accepts or seems to consider seriously in *Philosophy of Right*. Significantly, it can be shown that the first remedy does not really make consistent sense; the second Hegel later came to abandon; and the third is to be taken only as a temporary palliative.

The first plan is as follows: corporations, all of those institutions which form the economic structure of society, would be something like "second families" within Civil Society. They also are to be political units within the economic realm. In these two capacities they care for their

[51]PR, 149, par. 242.   [52]*Ibid.*
[53]Avineri, *op. cit.*, 101; also PR, 276, par. 236A.

particular members whatever their material condition. "Within the Corporation," writes Hegel, "the help which poverty receives loses its accidental character and the humiliation wrongfully associated with it. The wealthy perform their duties to their fellow associates and thus riches cease to inspire either pride or envy. . . ."[54] But there are problems here that Hegel overlooks. There is a clear possibility of bitter competition between corporations as politically self-interested units. And in championing the interests of separate segments of the Civil Society, corporations are themselves in political competition with that very structure which is intended to contain and control them: the State itself.[55] More serious than all of this, however, is the fact that Hegel's hopes for the work of corporations permit him to forget his own description of who the poor are: by definition they lack "all the advantages of society."[56]

But this does not mean that the State is bound to come to their rescue. Hegel's idea of the State has virtually nothing to do with a welfare state system, in the sense that this system does represent the direct dependence of many individuals upon the State for their survival. Welfarism, moreover, is not the cure for economic individualism; it is its crutch.

Hegel's State is clearly not a collection of individuals. It is a rational ordering of a variety of institutions composed of individuals. For Hegel's purposes, the meaning and danger of finding disorganized numbers of poor individuals dependent on the State for their material well-being surfaces in a statement like this:

. . . it is of the utmost importance that the masses should be organized, because only so do they become mighty and powerful. Otherwise they are nothing but a heap, an aggregate of atomic units.[57]

This "aggregate of atomic units" becomes what Hegel calls the "rabble." It is a collection of impoverished individuals without emotional attachments to society or state and, even worse, ultimately without the desire to be integrated into them. In a general way their situation may describe what a welfare state is today. And that only speaks defeat for Hegel's idea of the political state.

The first plan to deal with poverty, then, does not hold together on Hegel's own terms. And there is no justification for interpreting Hegel's State as a Corporation for the poor. The second plan seems to develop out of an implicit recognition of the inadequacies of the first and a read-

[54] PR, 154, par. 253.

[55] In his *Critique of Hegel's Philosophy of State* (1843), Marx describes the Hegelian corporation as "the attempt of civil society to become state." *Writings of Young Marx on Philosophy and Society,* eds. and trans. Loyd D. Easton and Kurt H. Guddat (Garden City, N.J., 1967), 185.

[56] PR, 149, par. 253.   [57] PR, 198, par. 303.

ing of Adam Smith. "The inner dialectic of civil society thus drives it . . . to push beyond its own limits and seek markets, and so its necessary means of subsistence, in other lands which are either deficient in the goods it has produced, or else generally backward in industry, etc."[58] On the surface, systematic economic colonization and the wealth that should accompany it make sense, given the unresolved problem which exists in Civil Society. Moreover, Hegel was certainly correct in anticipating that this would have to be the way modernizing European economies would behave later in the nineteenth century. But that expansion, not unlike Hegel's justification of it in *Philosophy of Right,* did nothing to resolve what clearly were to remain underlying fundamental tensions. Perhaps, as Smith had argued before Hegel, the poor were better off in an expanding capitalist market economy. The obvious and troubling fact remained, however, that they would always have to remain poor in relation to the rest of society. Mere quantitative expansion could not eliminate the persistent and more troubling differences in the quality of life.[59]

It should be said that Hegel appears to have recognized this in his last piece of writing, his essay on "The English Reform Bill." For Hegel, the Reform Bill of 1832 was simply an attempt to release tensions temporarily, not to resolve them. He recognized that economic prosperity at home had served to prevent the English from approaching their fundamental problems with the rational care they required. Hegel's complaint was: "Fame and wealth . . . make it superfluous to go back to the foundations of rights, a process to which external need, and the need of reason thereby aroused, has driven people who have felt the existing rights oppressive."[60] It is clear that Hegel recognizes here that hopes for the success of external economic expansion would only end in maintaining the existing lopsided socio-economic order. The unassimilated poor would still be there.

The third possible solution of the problem of poverty is to be found by extrapolating from Hegel's attitude toward war. Briefly, Hegel saw a state's organization and execution of a war as a temporary but crucial acknowledgement that the existence of the state actually expresses a transcendence of all material interests. It is proof that the values of

---

[58]PR, 151, par. 246.

[59]Remember that Adam Smith never says that free and full economic growth will eliminate poverty. It is rather that the condition of the laboring poor "seems to be the happiest and most comfortable" in this circumstance. *The Wealth of Nations* (New York, 1937), 81. More emphatically, the young Marx notes in his "Economic and Philosophical Manuscripts" that increased wages in a capitalist economy mean nothing for the poor but a *"better slave-salary* and would not achieve either for the worker or for human labor significance and dignity." *Writings of Young Marx, op. cit.,* 298.

[60]*Hegel's Political Writings,* trans. T. M. Knox, introd. Z. A. Pelczynski (Oxford, 1964), 312.

competitive individualism in Civil Society are relative; the successes and failures in that realm are subordinate to the unity of the state as a whole. It does not matter whether one is rich or poor; all will join hands in battle.

There are two important qualifications to be kept in mind here. First, Hegel insists (without any serious justification) that modern warfare is to be limited and humane. He refuses to acknowledge the horrible realities and the destructive possibilities (e.g., Napoleon's campaigns) of total warfare. For Hegel, war was to be the active resolution of a sort of philosophical identity crisis of separate collective wills. In the main body of opposed armies, hostility would be something "vague," giving "place to each side's respect for the duty of the other."[61] In addition to this, wars were never to be fought for territorial or material aggrandizement. They showed men that they could surmount the limits of material success and self-protecting fears.

The expression of unity in war is crucial, but also ephemeral; it too is supposedly only an "ethical moment." Hegel wants his wars to end quickly. This means then that within the State all hands are joined only temporarily. And recall that the joining is only for its own sake; the unity has no purpose aside from its own conscious expression. No one is to profit materially from Hegel's wars. There is, or ought to be, no accumulation of goods, no permanent conquests. ("Is" and "ought" are fused here as elsewhere in Hegel—"What is rational is actual and what is actual is rational.")

There is perhaps a question as to whether Hegel intends war to be used as a check on the unorganized rabble or as a stimulus for the self-interested bourgeoisie. The two purposes go hand-in-hand, however; as Hegel remarked: "As a result of war, nations are strengthened . . . peoples involved in civil strife also acquire peace at home through making wars abroad."[62] For the poor, the meaning of this passing exuberance in war, then, is quite clear. Relatively speaking, it is only for a moment that they are allowed to forget their condition. Once war is concluded, they quickly resume their identity as political and social outcasts.

There is no way out here but to charge that something is seriously wrong with the "architectonic of reason" which Hegel claims he has constructed in *Philosophy of Right*. And Avineri is thus quite wrong in claiming that Smith and his followers have been *aufgehoben;*[63] the problem of poverty remains—economic individualism, on this serious issue, survives Hegel's supposed challenge. If, as it seems fair to infer when reading Hegel as a political economist, there is a "cunning of reason" issuing commands to Smith's "hidden hand," it is now clear that this cunning shows no great wisdom in dealing with poverty. The implications of this comparison with Adam Smith, however, are

[61]PR, 210, par. 324A.   [62]PR, 295, par. 324A.   [63]Avineri, *op. cit.*, 147.

considerably more serious in judging Hegel than in judging Smith. Smith's "hidden hand" after all failed to do its work at times, and Smith specified a number of occasions when the more visible hand of a political state might be obliged to interfere. The "cunning of reason," on the other hand, always has to be at work behind anything of significance in the world. "Rationality," wrote Hegel, "consists of the thoroughgoing unity of the universal and the single."[64]

In regard to the unresolved discussion of poverty, then, it would be inappropriate on Hegel's own terms to praise, as Avineri has done, Hegel's "basic intellectual honesty"[65] in finally throwing up his hands with his conclusion that poverty is one of the "most disturbing problems which agitate modern society." Hegel's "honesty" is another serious problem in itself. Here we should recall that his world is the "world as reason" and his State the "actuality of concrete freedom." The poor clearly do not find a place in either one of these realms; and to see this is to see a basic part of the exaggerated character of Hegel's most characteristic claims.[66]

Brandeis University.*

[64] PR, 156, par. 258A.   [65] Avineri, *op. cit.*, 154.

[66] It may be needless to point out that Marx, as Hegel's most masterful student, does not repeat his teacher's failure. In his early *Critique,* Marx's recognition of it is in large part what first sets his radicalism in motion. But it is very important to note that Marx does not solve the problem of poverty in terms of Hegel's anthropological values. Marx charged that Hegel failed to see the "social power" at work in the relationship expressed in private property. But recall that Hegel's treatment of property in PR occurs in the discussion of Abstract Right, the realm of individual intellectual awakening. That placement, rightly or wrongly, shows the fundamental difference between Hegel's notion of man and that of Marx, and therefore also the very different meanings which property assumes in their writings. Marx, to his own advantage, described the difference in this way: "Labor is man's coming-to-be for himself within externalization or as externalized man. The only labor Hegel knows and recognizes is abstract, mental labor." There is no reason to believe that thought was the only labor which Hegel recognized, but it is certain that it was the labor that primarily concerned him. Hegel's man becomes aware of his highest self in thinking; Marx's man is to do the same, but rather through actual physical labor. For this reason it does not concern Hegel to look at the character of man's productive activities in society. Man could be satisfied with only the attempt to produce, to "own," since for Hegel the effort at ownership was a rudimentary way of knowing—of each man becoming aware of his power to share in constructing a rational world. For Hegel, man was ultimately obliged to move to a complex philosophical perspective on life. For Marx, man was obliged to perfect his imaginative and practical powers as a laborer. Private property was a spur to philosophizing for Hegel; it was *the* substantial practical hindrance for Marx.

*My thanks to George A. Kelly and Alasdair MacIntyre who provided useful comments on an earlier version of this essay.

XIX

BOURGEOIS AND PROLETARIANS

By Gerald A. Cohen

I. Bourgeois and Proletarians

In *The Holy Family* Marx draws an important distinction between the alienation endured by the worker and the alienation endured by the capitalist in bourgeois society:

> The possessing classes and the class of the proletariat present pictures of the same human self-estrangement. But the former class feels at home in and confirmed by this self-estrangement, recognizes its estrangement as its special power, and enjoys in it the semblance of a human existence; the latter feels annihilated in its estrangement, and glimpses in it the reality of an inhuman existence.[1]

My first task is to explain what Marx means in this difficult passage, and why he thinks it is true. It is impossible to fulfil this task without drawing upon material from works other than *The Holy Family*. This is because the passage is embedded in a section which throws little light on it, since it uses the distinction to argue that the proletariat is revolutionary and the bourgeoisie conservative, without elaborating the distinction itself. Furthermore, almost the entire text of *The Holy Family* is given over to polemic of an unusually minute, clownish, and altogether dated kind. Serious theoretical discussion occurs only in fragments. I shall therefore explore the meaning of the *Holy Family* passage by paying attention to a characterization of the human essence which is offered in *The German Ideology* and to the doctrine of alienation as it unfolds in the *Paris Manuscripts*. These materials do solve the puzzles in the text I have quoted.[2] I be-

---

[1] "Die besitzende Klasse und die Klasse des Proletariats stellen dieselbe menschliche Selbstentfremdung dar. Aber die erste Klasse fühlt sich in dieser Selbstentfremdung wohl und bestätigt, weiss die Entfremdung als ihre eigene Macht, und besitzt in ihr den Schein einer menschlichen Existenz; die Zweite fühlt sich in der Entfremdung vernichtet, erblickt in ihr ihre Ohnmacht und die Wirklichkeit einer unmenschlichen Existenz." *Karl Marx: Die Frühschriften*, ed. S. Landshut, (Stuttgart, 1953), 317. Translations alternative to the one offered above are given by T. B. Bottomore, in Bottomore and Rubel (eds.) *Karl Marx: Selected Writings in Sociology and Social Philosophy* (London, 1956), 231; and by R. Dixon in *The Holy Family* (Moscow, 1956), 51. They translate the text less literally, though without, I think, any gain in intelligibility.

[2] To illuminate one work by means of passages drawn from another is often, exegetically speaking, problematical. In the present case the problems are multiplied, for a number of reasons:

(1) There is the alleged division of Marx's writings into those which belong to his "young" period and those which belong to his "mature" period. And if there is

gin with *The German Ideology:*

Men can be distinguished from animals by consciousness, by religion, or anything else you like. They themselves begin to distinguish themselves from animals as soon as they begin to *produce* their means of subsistence.[3]

I shall treat this as a declaration about man's essence, because one way of fixing the essence of something is by allocating it to its genus and species, its species being determined by the differentia between it and other species of its genus; and it is man's differentia which Marx is providing. Men belong to the genus animal, or at any rate to a genus of which animals are the other species. To ask which species man is is to ask what distinguishes men from (other) animals. Marx's answer is that man himself does the distinguishing. Man makes that part of his essence in virtue of which he is not an animal. This means that it is man's nature to make his nature,[4] that he is by nature a

---

such a transition in Marx, it may reasonably be located within the time during which the three texts mentioned here were written. *The Manuscripts* were composed between April and August 1844; *The Holy Family* from September to November 1844; and *The German Ideology* in 1845–6. Their composition thus occupies a small number of months, but these were months of great ferment in Marx's thinking.

(2) Many of Marx's works were not published: the *Manuscripts* remained manuscripts, and *The German Ideology* was "left to the gnawing criticism of the mice." This fact reduced the pressure on Marx to signal shifts in his use of concepts or changes in his general orientation. Two other facts had the same consequence:

(3) The works which were published were often intended for a largely non-academic audience.

(4) Marx did not see his own writings, both published and unpublished, as the work of someone undergoing an exclusively intellectual development. He often wrote in response to (what he conceived to be) the changing of the social struggle.

Notwithstanding these reasons for caution, I regard my exegetical procedure as legitimate, since the other writings are used not to embellish a passage which already has a clear meaning, but to establish a meaning where Marx's intentions are somewhat dark. When a passage is very difficult the interpreter must be liberal in his choice of instruments; the main test of their validity will be their success in rendering the passage less puzzling. But it is also important that Marx wrote *The Holy Family* immediately after writing the *Manuscripts* so that they constitute, in a sense, a continuous *oeuvre*. And although *The German Ideology* (the other work which flanks *The Holy Family*) is very different in theme from the *Manuscripts*, it echoes the latter's stress on man as an essentially productive being. Finally, it may be conceded that there is a measure of artificiality in distributing so much additional material around the *Holy Family* passage. My main object is to depict a worker/capitalist contrast which runs inexplicitly through the *Manuscripts*, and I begin with *The Holy Family* because in that work the same contrast is explicitly, though obscurely, drawn.

[3] *The German Ideology* (Moscow, 1964), 31, (Marx's emphasis).

[4] Marx's view should not be overassimilated to Sartrean existentialism. It is not an originally featureless being, or Nothingness, which makes its nature, but a certain kind of animal. Animalhood rather than mere existence precedes essence for Marx.

maker, or producer, in the most general sense: he produces what he is. But Marx is also proposing that man is a producer in a more specific sense. For he performs the act of distinguishing himself from animals —the act which is productive in a general sense—by engaging in particular acts of production, in the making of things. Such acts are the concrete content of man's universal act of self-creation.

For Marx, a man is self-estranged if his existence is not in conformity with his essence. Since man is really a productive being, he should behave like one in his empirical life,[5] and his empirical life-conditions should support the possibility of such behavior. Productive activity must be each individual's purpose, his fundamental interest and aim, since essence is the proper end of existence. To be non-alienated, therefore, is to engage in productive activity as an end-in-itself, to use one's powers in order to exercise them, and to exult in manifesting them. The fact that neither capitalist nor worker does this explains the first sentence of the *Holy Family* passage, which asserts that they are both alienated. The capitalist does not produce at all: he is not a producer, but an owner. And the proletarian produces, not in order to realize his powers, but for an alien reason: to stay alive.

But why is the bourgeoisie *content* in its self-estrangement, and the proletariat not? The answer falls into two parts: (a) the bourgeoisie, unlike the proletariat, cannot *hope* to escape its alienation; and (b) the bourgeoisie, unlike the proletariat, has no *desire* to escape its alienation.

(a) Capitalists and workers are, respectively, owners and producers. It is possible to be a non-alienated producer, but it is not possible to be a non-alienated owner. It follows that a worker can *hope* to become disalienated: the transformation is no threat to his identity. He is identified as a producer, even though he produces for alien reasons, and, as we shall see, in an alien way.[6] But a capitalist can hope for no salvation from alienation, for "non-alienated owner" is a *contradictio in adjecto*. An owner cannot cease to be alienated without ceasing to be. The capitalist *must* cling to his alienated life, since there can be no non-alienated life for him.

It might be objected that though the capitalist, insofar as he is a capitalist, cannot wish to be disalienated, this need not be true of

[5] If he fails to behave in this way, he sometimes comes to resemble an animal, he slips back into animalhood, from which he is essentially distinguished. There are suggestions of this kind in the *Manuscripts*. See T. B. Bottomore, *Karl Marx: Early Writings* (London, 1963), 125. (Henceforth "Bottomore.")

[6] The worker's activity is a paradigm of the activity of mankind throughout history, which is also conceived as alienated production. Mankind has revealed its essence through the "history of industry" which is "an open book of the human faculties," though it shows us the essential human faculties in an alienated form. (Bottomore, 162–3.)

the man who *is* a capitalist; it appears true of the man only when we focus on one of his aspects: his ownership of capital. But (at least for some purpose) Marx did treat the capitalist abstractly. He developed a phenomenology of the abstract man who is purely an owner, and nothing besides. The lines of this phenomenology will be traced later in the paper. The justification of the abstract perspective will be provided elsewhere. (A brief version of it is given in IV-3, below.)

(b) The contrasting *desires* of capitalist and worker are explicable if the following maxim, to which Marx was committed, is accepted: If a person is aware that the conditions of his life are antagonistic to the realization of his essence, he will be dissatisfied with his life situation. To this must be added the general principle that a man can demand or desire only those states of affairs of which he has some conception. The conjunction of these propositions entails that a man will desire to be disalienated if and only if he is in some way aware that he is alienated. It remains to show that the worker is conscious of his alienation, while the capitalist is not. This will explain their discrepant desires.

I shall introduce the explanation by means of an analogy. Let us say that to be non-alienated is analogous to possessing a fine human body. To be alienated is to lack a fine human body. When the capitalist confronts himself in the mirror, he sees a finely clad body. He does not realize that he lacks a fine body, because he does not even see his body—it does not exist for him: he sees only his clothes. When the worker gazes in his mirror he sees a naked but bruised and misshapen human body. He sees his body, and he sees that it is not fine. And so he desires a fine body, while the capitalist does not.

To interpret the analogy. The worker is forced to labor, and in laboring he confronts his specifically human powers, but is frustrated through being unable to exercise them properly. The capitalist never engages with his powers, even in an alienated way. *His* powers are utterly dormant, because his money exerts power *for* him: it hides his powers from him as his clothes hide his body in the analogy. He experiences no frustrating exercise of his faculties, for he does not exercise them at all.

We are now close to what Marx meant when he said that the bourgeoisie had a semblance of a human existence. He did not mean that they are nearer to being really human than are the workers. He meant that their capital, their money, the machines they own, *are* human for them: their possessions take on human powers, in a manner which will be elaborated later. They feel no need to be truly human, for they have the full gamut of human powers in their capital.[7] They have a

---

[7] They therefore feel themselves to be active and productive: see Georg Lukács, *Geschichte und Klassenbewusstsein* (Berlin, 1923), 182: ". . . für den Kapitalisten

substitute or *ersatz* humanity. The proletariat lives a truly inhuman life, while the bourgeoisie lives a falsely human life. And this is why the proletariat desires to be truly human and the bourgeoisie does not.

It is because the capitalist has lost all perception of and contact with his essence that he tolerates his alienation. But the worker daily glimpses his essence at a distance from him and experiences his humanity in a distorted form,[8] so that he hopes and desires to live in a non-alienated world. The idea that the worker possesses his humanity in a warped form while the capitalist has lost it completely can be defended by reference to the well-known characterization of alienation as the circumstance in which man becomes a thing. For the thing which the worker is said to become is a thing very like man, namely a machine, a thing conceived and described in the vocabulary of human powers. But the thing which the capitalist becomes, as we shall see, is much more grotesque and quite lacking in human qualities, since it lacks all qualities. The capitalist, it will emerge, is a bearer of properties which he does not have.

I have been trying to illuminate the *Holy Family* passage by means of the notion that the worker is a productive, active being, while the capitalist is not. Additional light is cast in the same direction by Marx's suggestion that whereas the workers really suffer, the capitalists do not. While not systematizing his views on suffering, Marx does reveal an attitude to it in the *Manuscripts*. The topic enters into the first paragraph of the work, where Marx, following Adam Smith, speaks of the separation of capital, landed property, and labor, which bourgeois society has wrought. It has sundered factors of production which were more integrated at an earlier period of economic history. (The division of labor is a fragmentation of what is already a fragment.) And Marx points out that this loss of unity (which for him is a token of alienation, since he thinks any incidence of discrete spheres in society is such a token) is *harmful* only for the workers.[9]

Two pages later, he gives an ontological formulation of this thesis:

---

ist diese Verdoppelung der Persönlichkeit, dieses Zerreissen des Menschen in ein Element der Warenbewegung und in einen (objektiv-ohnmächtigen) Zuschauer dieser Bewegung vorhanden. Sie nimmt aber für sein Bewusstsein notwendig die Form einer—freilich objektiv scheinbaren—Tätigkeit, einer Auswirkung seines Subjekts auf."

[8] That the worker has his essence in a warped form is suggested in the *Manuscripts* (Bottomore, 126), where we read that his activity manifests itself as passivity, his strength as powerlessness, his creation as emasculation. (The capitalist lacks activity, strength, and creation in *any* form.)

[9] Bottomore, 69. Cf. *Capital*, Vol. III, Ch. LII. On what it is like for the three factors to be integrated, see the *Grundrisse* (*Pre-Capitalist Economic Formations*, ed. E. J. Hobsbawm (London, 1964), 67, 86–7, 97–9. For the most relevant passages in Smith, see *The Wealth of Nations* (Everyman's Library), 41–8, 57–60.

. . . it should be noted that where both worker and capitalist suffer, the worker suffers in his existence while the capitalist suffers in the profit on his dead Mammon.[10]

Earlier we found that the capitalist does not act on the world. Marx is now contending that he is, equally, not acted on *by* the world, it cannot make *him* suffer. His money insulates him against the impact of things in the world. It is only when his dead Mammon suffers, when his capital is depleted, that he has any relation to suffering, and that relation is completely external. To return to the mirror analogy: his clothes can be violated, but his body cannot be harmed. Sometimes, when he looks in the mirror, he notices that his garments are torn.

This is obviously meant to be true not of particular capitalists, but of an abstract being who is nothing but an owner of money. Yet empirical exemplification of the point is available. For three-dimensional capitalists worry when their fortunes decline, even when there is no chance that the decline will be great enough to disturb their mode of life in any way. In the Marxian contention, they are upset because they identify themselves with their capital, and they do so because, not being producers, they lack a human identity without it. They can possess human powers only derivatively, *through* their capital. The worker, by contrast, suffers directly. He suffers inhumanly, but he does suffer, just as he produces inhumanly, but does produce.

Marx's understanding of the significance of suffering confirms what was urged above: that the workers know that they are alienated, while the capitalists do not. For in Marx's early thought suffering is a mode of knowledge. In certain later writings he asserts that the workers' misery prevents them from entertaining illusions about their position and sharpens their insight into social processes in general. He appears to think that he who knows the Woe must know the Vale. But in the *Manuscripts* the relation between suffering and knowledge is more intimate and less situational: suffering is itself a *way* of knowing.[11] This result is attained through a series of conceptual assimilations. Suffering *from* something is associated with suffering or undergoing that thing, that is to say, *experiencing* it, which is in turn related to *perceiving* it, that is, gaining knowledge of it. It seems that the English word "suffer" has nuances which stimulate a development of this

---

[10] Bottomore, 71. What might be called the *empirical manifestation* of this is given on 76: "In the declining state of society, the worker suffers most. The particular severity of his hardship is due to his situation as a worker, but the hardship in general is due to the condition of society."

[11] Landshut (ed.), *op. cit.*, 275: "Sinnlich sein ist *leidend* sein." "Der Mensch als ein gegenständliches sinnliches Wesen ist daher ein *leidendes* und weil sein Leiden empfindendes Wesen ein *leidenschaftliches* Wesen. Die Leidenschaft, die Passion ist die nach seinem Gegenstand energisch strebende Wesenskraft des Menschen."

kind. We have only to think of the interchangeability of locutions like "I suffered many years of torment" and "I knew many years of torment." [12] And the German word *leiden,* which is the one Marx used in the present connection, has similar shadings. So it appears that Marx's idea of suffering helps to explain the vision of reality of which he speaks in the *Holy Family* passage. But I am committed to elucidating that passage by means of his account of the essence of man, and suffering, it seems, failed to enter into that account.

It does not enter explicitly, but it is a corollary of the stress on production. Man cannot produce without using his body, without bringing it to bear on things in the world, and in that contact the world acts on man, and must be borne by him. On the Marxian view, activity and passivity entail one another, since each entails and is entailed by commerce with the world: "As soon as I have an object, this object has me for its object." [13] Thus productivity has a passive dimension, and since Marx is prepared to treat any passive relation to the world as a form of suffering, we are able to conclude that suffering is part of man's natural estate.

In sum: the man who works for a living encounters the world both as agent and as patient, though in an alienated way; while the man who owns for a living is separated by what he owns from both active and passive contact with things outside him. In the rest of the paper I shall explore proletarian and bourgeois alienation in greater detail.

II. The Worker's Relation to his Machine

Capital is the link between the worker and the capitalist, since the former works at a machine, which is a physical form of capital, and the latter owns money, which is convertible into capital. I shall discuss the worker's alienation in his relation to the machine, and the capitalist's in his relation to money, since I wish to compare their situations, and capital provides a convenient meeting-point for the comparison.[14] This means that I shall neglect certain aspects of alienation, such as man's distance from his fellow man, and his incapacity for sensuous enjoyment of nature. In treating the capitalist, I shall

---

[12] We also say "I knew many years of happiness," which is replaceable not by "I suffered . . ." but by "I enjoyed many years of happiness." So knowledge has no special association with suffering, but only with passivity in general. The link with suffering is more obvious to Marx, since he is speaking of suffering and passivity as interchangeable.

[13] Bottomore, 208.

[14] See Hobsbawm (ed.), *op. cit.,* 108, where Marx asserts that money becomes convertible into capital just when labor becomes powerless, when workers cease to own their means of production. Hence the machine achieves its power over the worker just when it is an embodiment of money become omnipotent.

try simply to expound Marx, since exposition of his views on this subject is rarely offered. By contrast, many discussions of the worker's alienation are available. Indeed, often what is presented as an account of man's alienation is restricted to a consideration of the worker. I hope the present paper shows such a procedure to be mistaken. As to the worker, I shall confine myself to three possible criticisms of the relatively familiar Marxian description of his position. They concern (1) Product-alienation and Process-alienation; (2) Aspects of Process-alienation; and (3) The dictum that "Man becomes a machine."

(1) Product-alienation resides in the fact that what the worker makes is taken from him. The result of his labor does not benefit him: the more he produces, the more impoverished he becomes. In addition, there is alienation "in the process of *production,* within *productive activity* itself." [15] Marx thinks that there is an intimate connection between these two modes of alienation:

> How could the worker stand in an alien relationship to the product of his activity if he did not alienate himself in the act of production itself? The product is indeed only the *résumé* of activity, of production. Consequently, if the product of labour is alienation, production itself must be alienation—the alienation of activity and the activity of alienation. The alienation of the object of labour merely summarizes the alienation in the work activity itself.[16]

This seems unacceptable. "Active alienation" consists in the soul-destroying effects that laboring at the machine has on the worker. It seems that these cannot entail product-alienation, since a man can consistently be supposed to control the product he makes by inhuman toil. If the division of labor removes this possibility, since under its sway there can be no product on which any man has a special claim, the community of workers could still own the goods they slavishly produce: at the very least those goods need not be used, as product-alienation demands, to enslave them further. Isn't Marx just wrong in thinking that from what happens to the worker within the factory one can infer what happens to the product after it leaves the factory?

Marx is also committed to the converse implication, that product-alienation entails process-alienation. (A close reading of the text reveals that he thinks the entailment is mutual. His metaphor of summation alone suggests this, since in one sense series and sum entail one another.) And this proposition seems equally dubious. For we can imagine men who have some dignity in the labor-process, although their products are taken away. Indeed many Marxists concede this, when responding to liberal claims that work has been or can be made enjoyable and fulfilling by arguing that this only conceals alienation, since the product is still taken from the worker. These defenders

---

[15] Bottomore, 124 (Marx's emphasis).   [16] *Ibid.*

abandon Marx when they give this answer, for they are separating what he connected.

Notwithstanding these objections, I think the two modes of alienation can be seen to associate naturally with each other. This begins to be clear once we recognize how bizarre it is to suggest that the workers might control the products of the factory in which they slave. For they would have the power to do so only if they owned the factory, and if they owned it, they would not submit themselves to a debasing regimen. If they controlled the product, they would not let the process alienate them. But the man who in fact controls the product is willing to rob the worker of the fruits of his toil. Such a man will naturally make working conditions as exploitative as possible. He shows himself oblivious to the worker's needs in the way he treats his product. Consistency will lead him to shape the man to the needs of the machine in the process of production. One cannot reply that the capitalist would provide salubrious conditions for the worker if he thought it profitable to do so. For the capitalist with whom we are concerned is only the agent of the machine. *It is the machine that exploits the worker.* The capitalist exploits him only because he owns the machine. He does not exploit him by means of the machine. (These asseverations are defended in III-3.)

Finally, the worker brings to the factory a consciousness that he is not working for himself, and this affects him negatively when he is in the throes of the labor-process.

It might be thought that the filiation between product- and process-alienation traced here could be short-circuited, in the following way. Product-alienation meant that the product is used to enslave the worker, and that means that it is (or is used to build) a new machine, which facilitates further process-alienation. On this interpretation, the product stays within the factory, or within the whole factory-system, to increase the agony of industrial life. But this solution to the problem eliminates much of what Marx comprehended in the notion of product-alienation.[17]

(2) We have seen that Marx wishes to fuse product-alienation and process-alienation. He also thinks that a number of seemingly

[17] In this section alienation has been rooted in the fact that the worker does not receive the product he makes. Earlier alienated labor was identified as work not performed for its own sake. These formulations seem at best independent, at worst, inconsistent. But they can be reconciled. Producing is not the worker's freely chosen end, *because* he is bound by contract to work, and he enters this contract to satisfy needs other than the need to exercise his powers. That the product is not his is a sign that his activity is alienated, though it does not and need not follow that if the product were his, he would not be alienated. If he does not receive the product, there can be no joy in his work, yet true joy in work is not to be had from the prospect of receiving the product.

separable elements of process-alienation are inextricable from one another. These are listed in the *Manuscripts:* [18] (i) the worker denies himself rather than fulfils himself; (ii) he feels miserable; (iii) he does not develop his energies; (iv) he is exhausted; (v) he is debased; (vi) he works involuntarily; (vii) his work is not the satisfaction of a need but the means to the satisfaction of his needs; (viii) he works for another.

These indices of alienation do take on a certain coherence if we begin with (vii) and use the definition of and principles about human nature which were advanced earlier in the paper; (vii) is outlawed by the definition of man. It therefore entails (v), since "debased" means "dehumanized," and it entails (iii), since the negation of (iii) is activity in accord with man's essence. Again, we have seen that the worker knows that he is alienated in his work, and that a man will resent agencies which he knows alienate him. This allows us to infer (ii) and (vi); (viii) is licensed by the insistence that no one would impose alienating work conditions on himself. This leaves (i) and (iv). As far as I can see, (i) is simply a vague way of summarizing aspects already dealt with, and (iv) need not be true if physical exhaustion is intended, but it is certainly warranted by the picture I have tried to compose, if emotional exhaustion is allowed to count.

(3) In the *Manuscripts* Marx approvingly quotes Wilhelm Schulz, who, one year prior to the time at which Marx was writing, maintained that "the important distinction between how far men work *with* machines or *as* machines has not received attention." [19] Marx addresses himself to this question, and selects the second alternative: hence his dictum that *man becomes a machine.* It is perhaps worth registering that he does not mean this literally. He does not think that what is left of the human being is a robot. What he holds is that man is forcibly adapted to fit the machine, rebuilt to accommodate its demands on him.[20] He is accorded the treatment proper to a machine, and in the factory his behavior resembles that of a machine.

I do not think this famous dictum should be retained by Marxists. I think it should be replaced by a formulation which is critically different. It is better to say that man is transformed into a *tool,* or, in the words of Marx elsewhere, into an appendage of the machine.[21] Here is why the latter terminology is preferable. The craftsman *wields* a tool. The industrial worker cannot be said to wield a machine, for

[18] Bottomore, 125.

[19] Bottomore, 80. The quotation is from *Die Bewegung der Produktion. Eine geschichtlich-statistische Abhandlung* (Zurich, 1843), 69.

[20] For the empirical content of this idea in contemporary factory work, see Robert Blauner, *Alienation and Freedom* (Chicago, 1964), 19–22.

[21] *Manifesto of the Communist Party,* 40, *Marx-Engels Selected Works* (Moscow, 1962), Vol. I.

the machines of modern industry cannot be wielded. Marx wishes to say that the machine wields the worker, since he conceives him as placed at its disposal, to be pushed and pulled. A machine in operation is a system in motion and the man is what is moved. But this makes it impossible to characterize the worker as a machine. The same conceptual barrier which prevents us from thinking of the worker as wielding the machine blocks the thought that the worker has become a machine once it is asserted that the machine wields *him*. The machine relates to the worker as the craftsman relates to his tool, and not as the worker ought to relate to the machine, since machines cannot be wielded. If we turn from wielding to the more general concept of controlling, under which it falls, we can then say that the worker ought to control the machine although the machine controls the worker. But if we comprehend this control concretely, then we must allow that what the machine does to the worker is *not* something the worker can do to the machine.

My rejection of the machine dictum as a succinct label for alienation in the factory is supported by Alan White's enlightening remarks on the meaning of the word "mechanical":

"Mechanical" describes the manner in which we carry out some continuous train of action, such as knitting or playing the piano. It is typically used of routine or *skilled* performances which from practice we can go through without attention to the details and, hence, without showing or needing originality or liveliness; in short, like a smoothly functioning machine.[22]

Now this is perhaps not the noblest kind of work given to man. But it is difficult to see how it is possible or why it should be thought desirable to abolish it, for to do so would be to abridge our repertoire of skilled performances. So the machine dictum not only fails to sum up alienation in the factory; it fails to point unambiguously at a depressing idea. Anyone who insists that all mechanical activity is alienated or objectionable is being overdemanding and even silly. But if supreme value lies in realizing men's productive powers, then it *is* necessary to reject activities in which man resembles not a machine, but a tool.

I think Marx failed to consider productive work of the kind White mentions because of his wavering perception of the difference between human productivity and what appears to be productivity in animals. In one place [23] he cites advance planning as the distinguishing factor.

---

[22] *Attention* (Oxford, 1963), (my emphasis).

[23] *Capital*, I, 198 (Chicago edition). Elsewhere Marx offers other differentiae: (i) Men can produce when not compelled to by need; (ii) men produce a whole environment, not just consumables; (iii) men produce instruments of production. Bottomore, 126–8; *Capital* I (Chicago edition), 197–205, esp. 198; Hobsbawm (ed.), *op. cit.*, 91.

But certain *bona fide* skills are acquired just because they eliminate the need to apply a plan in the course of the work they enable.

Earlier in this paper I treated the idea that the worker becomes a machine as a mark of his superiority over the capitalist. That idea must be abandoned, but the point can still be made, in a different way. For the worker, though a tool, remains intimately involved in the productive process; [24] and he is a living tool, never utterly inert. He is still closer to the essence of man than the capitalist is.

III. The Capitalist's Relation to his Capital

(1) At least four images of the capitalist can be found in Marx's writings: (i) He who owns things instead of producing them, or the capitalist as *Owner;* (ii) He who accumulates and hoards things instead of enjoying them, or the capitalist as a *Miser;* [25] (iii) He who consumes things instead of producing them, or the capitalist as *Consumer;* (iv) He who is a most stupendously productive individual, as a member of a class under whose dominion man has changed the shape of nature.

The first of these conceptions must be treated as dominant and must be carefully explored if the quotation from *The Holy Family* is to be understood. I shall immediately grant that it is irreconcilable with the fourth conception, so boldly sketched in *The Communist Manifesto,*[26] of the capitalist as dynamic director of man's conquest of nature. In *The Holy Family* Marx is suppressing this aspect of the capitalist, and in the *Manuscripts* we see the result of making this abstraction: the capitalist becomes a mere appendage of his capital,[27] though he is not appended in the same way as the worker. The legitimacy of the abstraction cannot be considered here. It must suffice to point out that although capitalists are energetic and entrepreneurial in the first phases of capitalism, Marx thought that they would tend to become pure owners, divorced from the productive process, as capitalism developed its distinctive character, so that the first image is more revealing than the fourth.

While (i) excludes (iv), it is plainly compatible with (ii), though it does not entail it. As I expound (i) in detail it may come to seem incompatible with (iii), and (ii) and (iii) are apparently incompatible

---

[24] This becomes less true in those modern industrial settings in which workers do not engage with machines but merely "tend" them. See Daniel Bell, *The End of Ideology* (New York, 1962), 270.   [25] Bottomore, 171.

[26] *Op. cit.,* p. 35. For the values latent in capitalist production, see Hobsbawm (ed.), *op. cit.,* 84–5.

[27] See also *Capital,* Vol. I (Chicago edition), 365 (quoted in fn. 34 below) and 648–9.

as they stand. Yet I believe it is possible to entertain an idea of the capitalist which embraces all three elements, in which the profligate life of the self-indulgent bourgeois (iii) is represented as a mode of existence of the capitalist who is a Scrooge (i & ii). This synthesis is articulated in the *Manuscripts:*

Of course, the industrial capitalist also has his pleasures, . . . but his enjoyment is only a secondary matter . . . it is . . . a *calculated, economic* enjoyment, for he charges his pleasures as an expense of capital and what he squanders must not be more than can be replaced with profit by the reproduction of capital. Thus enjoyment is subordinated to capital and the pleasure-loving individual is subordinated to the capital-accumulating individual.[28]

The enjoyment of the capitalist as consumer is "calculated" and "economic" because he does not surrender himself to it. He cannot give himself up to it, because he remains tied to his money. We must now examine the nature of this tie, the nature of capitalist ownership. We must try to answer the question, what is it to be fundamentally an owner?

(2) For Marx, capital cannot exist without a capitalist who owns it. "The concept of capital implies the capitalist." [29] Property must have a human embodiment if it is to be allowed entry into economic equations. But although capital must be possessed by a capitalist, the relation of possession which binds them is most peculiar. For, as I shall try to show, it follows from the fact that the capitalist owns proper*ty* that he himself lacks proper*ties*.[30] Only someone who is in a certain sense qualityless can qualify for the rôle of Owner. In the terms of the mirror analogy, there is no body under the capitalist's clothes, but only empty space.

Now for Marx all truly human properties are powers, or propensities to have effects on the world. He forbids us to predicate a feature of a human being unless the standard effects of possessing that feature are realized. A capitalist may appear ugly, but if his money buys beautiful women for him, then, Marx says, he is not ugly, since the effect of ugliness, its power to repel, is annulled by money.[31] This restriction on what is to count as a human feature derives from Marx's view of man as an essentially productive being, through a generalization in which productivity covers *all* powers. It is in this sense of properties that the capitalist has none: his self is not manifested in the world. And the explanation of this is the fact that he owns prop-

---

[28] Bottomore, 179 (Marx's emphases). Cf. fn. 32(b) below.

[29] Hobsbawm (ed.), *op. cit.,* 118, *q.v.* See Schumpeter, *Capitalism, Socialism and Democracy* (New York, 1950), 45.

[30] Marx discusses the two senses of "property" in *The German Ideology, op. cit.,* 248–9.   [31] Bottomore, 191.

erty, which keeps the world at a distance from him. The workers do operate on the world, in an alienated way, so that they have a dehumanized humanity, but the capitalist's humanity is a void.

Let us turn to the *Manuscripts:*

The less you *are,* the less you express your life, the more you *have.* . . . Everything which the economist takes from you in the way of life and humanity, he restores to you in the form of *money* and *wealth.* And everything which you are unable to do your money can do for you; it can eat, drink, go to the ball and to the theatre. It can acquire art, learning, historical treasures, political power; and it can travel.[32]

We shall shortly [in (3)] consider how money performs for the capitalist, so that he does nothing himself, and therefore lacks a nature, just because he owns capital, which has such a rich nature ("it is the true opulence").[33] But first I want to indicate how Marx contrasts this form of ownership with the relation the feudal lord enjoys to his property:

. . . in feudal landownership . . . there is an appearance of a more intimate connexion between the owner and the land than is the case in the possession of mere *wealth.* Landed property assumes an individual character with its lord, is knightly or baronial with him, has his privileges, his jurisdiction, his political rights, etc. It appears as the inorganic body of its lord.[34]

It is crucial that the landowner does not see his property as something he can sell. Instead, he has entered into an "honorable marriage with his land." [35] If he comes to treat his property as alienable, he possesses it only contingently, since the very same thing could be possessed by another, and he is on the way to being a capitalist, whose ownership can be so abstract that in some instances neither he nor anyone else

[32] (a) Bottomore, 171 (Marx's emphases). It should be noted that Marx is speaking of anyone's money, not just the capitalist's. I take the liberty of applying what he says to the capitalist in particular, since while the worker's money latently possesses similar powers, there is never enough of it for these powers to spring into action. (b) The next sentence but one after this excerpt reads: "But although it can do all this, it only *desires* to create itself, and to buy itself, for everything else is subordinated to it." This confirms and extends what was argued above, that the Scrooge notion of the capitalist subjugates and limits the Consumer idea.

[33] Bottomore, 171.

[34] Bottomore, 114. (Marx's emphasis. I have corrected the translation.) Note that here property assumes the features of its owner, rather than vice-versa, as is the case in capitalism. The bond between a person and his property counts as personal if it depends on the person's characteristics. See *The German Ideology, op. cit.,* 93. In *Capital* Marx no longer offers special compliments to the feudal lord: "It is not because he is a leader of industry that a man is a capitalist; on the contrary he is a leader of industry because he is a capitalist. The leadership of industry is an attribute of capital, just as in feudal times the functions of general and judge were attributes of landed property." (Chicago edition, I, 365.)

[35] Bottomore, 115.

can say *what* he owns, but only how *much*. Manors maketh men, but factories maketh owners, and the capitalist merely owns his wealth. He engages in no intimate interaction with what he owns, he never really *has* it, where to have it is to hold it. (I intend that sense of "have" in which it is incorrect to say of an object that I have it when it is neither within my grasp nor under my control. In this sense, I do not *have* the spectacles which I have left at home.) With the advent of bourgeois society "all personal relationships between the property owner and his property . . . cease."[36] No one is firmly connected with the particular property he owns and the result is that

the medieval adage, *nulle terre sans seigneur*, is replaced with a new adage, *l'argent n'a pas de maître*, which expresses the complete domination of living men by dead matter.[37]

Let us examine the character of this domination.

(3) I have already cited a number of capacities which Marx ascribes to prodigious capital, in its money form. But what is it for my wealth to eat and drink and go to the ball or the theatre *for* me? Well, the ball and the theatre are essentially social occasions, where men and women get together. Marx means, I think, that money defines who comes, that I come *qua* money-owner, and that I am interested in going only *qua* money-owner. Money attracts me and brings me to these places. It is money which actually pays them a visit, and it drags me along. Where eating and drinking are also understood in their social aspects, similar interpretations could be offered.

Chief among the features of capital is its "*power of command* over labor and its products." And Marx tells us that "the capitalist possesses this power, not on account of his personal or human qualities, but as the *owner* of capital" and that "capital itself rules the capitalist."[38] Thus it would be a mistake to conceive the capitalist as a human being who forms the intention of controlling the worker and uses his capital to do so. On the contrary, it is capital, the machine, which controls the worker, and the capitalist does so only derivatively, and abstractly, as an extension of capital,[39] not because of any personal aspirations or through any individual virtues, such as were

[36] *Ibid.*

[37] *Ibid.* Similar to Marx's discussion is Hannah Arendt's distinction between property and wealth. See *The Human Condition* (New York, 1959), 56. The distinction between feudal lord and capitalist takes a radical turn in and is essential to the work of Schumpeter. See *Capitalism, Socialism and Democracy, op. cit.,* 137ff.

[38] Bottomore, 85 (Marx's emphases).

[39] Relevant here is Karl Löwith's excellent account of Marx's early article concerning the law about theft of lumber, in which Löwith makes plain how lumber acquires an autonomous status and its owner plays a subordinate rôle. See *Nature, History and Existentialism* (Evanston, 1966), 85–6.

needed by feudal lords, who exacted respect through their own breeding and bearing.

The way in which capital wreaks an alchemical transformation on its owner is most strikingly expressed in the following passage:

What I *am* and *can do* is . . . not at all determined by my individuality. . . . As an individual I am *lame*, but money provides me with twenty-four legs. Therefore, I am not lame.[40] I am a detestable, dishonorable, and stupid man, but money is honored and so also is its possessor. Money is the highest good, and so its possessor is good. Besides, money saves me the trouble of being dishonest; therefore I am presumed honest. I am *stupid*, but since money is *the real mind* of all things, how should its possessor be stupid?[41] . . . I who can have, through the power of money, everything for which the human heart longs, do I not possess all human abilities? Does not my money, therefore, transform all my incapacities into their opposites?[42]

As Bottomore translates the passage, the capitalist has these faculties *through* rather than *by means of* money. (The German preposition is *"durch,"* which can be translated either way.) I believe Bottomore's decision accords with Marx's intentions, for I do not think Marx meant that capital is an *instrument* I use to get what I want. Rather, my capital gets it and has it *for* me, and I have it only in a derived sense, *through* my capital. Money shines on my life and makes it bright, but the light in my life is always a reflection. Marx is not saying that a woman falls in love with me because I am rich, or that I entice her by means of my money. Rather, she is attracted *to* my money, she is seduced *by* my money, not *by means of it,* and it is even money which satisfies her. Again, when I am honored because of my money, it is my money which is honored, and I only as its keeper. I have neither love nor honor, but complete semblances of both, since my money has both, and my ownership of my money is only a semblance of real possession.[43]

These theses can be called philosophical: it is not easy to establish precise verification-conditions for them. Yet they correspond to some observable tendencies in capitalist society. Some capitalists do have abilities which decay because they have no need or occasion to use them. When a society tends to make a healthy body and a healthy mind mere means to survival or enrichment, these gifts tend not to be used when money can secure whatever they enable a man to get. Thus the ontological topsy-turvy is accompanied by psychobiological corruption.

[40] Therefore I cannot even suffer. See p. 216 above.
[41] "Stupid" and "mind" are translations of *geistlos* and *Geist*.
[42] Bottomore, 191 (Marx's emphases).
[43] For the meaning of real possession, see Bottomore, 193–4.

IV. Concluding Remarks

(1) The contrast between bourgeois and proletarian may now be restated. For Marx, human characteristics are powers, and powers are interpreted as capacities to produce. In bourgeois society property is what is produced, so that to have properties is to create property. The worker does create property, in an alienated way; therefore he has properties, of a deformed sort. The capitalist, as mere Owner of property, has no properties. He does not even *have* the property he *owns*, for to have a thing is to be in intimate active contact with it. The capitalist is more distant from being truly human than the worker is. He is not a creator and he is therefore not even a real possessor: he is a sham possessor. The worker is a degenerate creator, and this is thought to be better.

Each is a man who is dominated by a thing, namely capital, whose most immediate form for one is the machine, for the other, money. In the body of the paper I have tried to show the objective differences between the two relations of domination. Now I wish to bring into relief certain more psychological aspects. To this end I propose the following schedule of possibilities.

CHART OF PSYCHOLOGICAL POSSIBILITIES

Relation between Man and Thing
(worker and machine—i.e. capital; capitalist and money—i.e. capital)

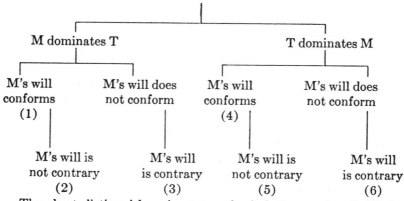

The chart distinguishes six states of mind. I am using "will" in a very general sense, comprehending any mode of desire or volition. My will conforms to my situation (1, 4) if I enjoy what I am doing, if I feel fulfilled in it. If my will fails to conform (2, 3, 5, 6), this may be because I am opposed to what I am doing and I find it oppressive (3, 6) or because I merely acquiesce in my position, without investigating my self in it (2, 5).

The images of capitalist and worker which we have examined both belong on the right-hand side of the schedule, for they are both alienated. Marx usually locates the worker under (6), portraying him as disposed to resent and react against his position. The worker never falls under (4): he never enjoys his alienated life. Some things Marx says about the worker warrant the application of (5). But (6) must be standard for the worker: he can satisfy (5) only temporarily, since otherwise his revolutionism would disappear.

In the *Holy Family* passage, the capitalist is allocated to category (4): he enjoys his alienated life. I have found confirmation and explanation of this in the *Manuscripts,* although some of the texts I have used might be construed so as to deposit the capitalist in category (5), making him a dull and passive agent of his capital. But no interpretation could make him satisfy (6).

What would satisfy the descriptions on the left-hand side of the table? It seems that (1) applies to the energetic capitalist presiding in the early phases of bourgeois society. Such a capitalist is as close as any can be to being non-alienated. I hesitate to say that he would be regarded as fully non-alienated, since Marx would perhaps consider him too removed from concrete productive processes to deserve this title. Items (2) and (3) could represent resourceful industrialists who, in different ways, get no satisfaction out of their activity. Such types do not occur in Marx's writings, at any rate not as central characters for the purpose of theory. A worker who fell under (1) would be a genuinely non-alienated man. There cannot be workers of types (2) and (3), for this would violate the principle that it is satisfying to live in accordance with the definition of one's essence. Nevertheless many contemporary alienation-hunters would be prepared to find cases of (2) and (3), and would declare that they instantiate alienation, since psychological phenomena are now often treated as sufficient for that designation. Again, much of what is now identified as alienation falls under (4), another category containing no workers for Marx. This is the worker as described by semi-Marxist radicals who make concessions, like those I referred to in II-1. C. Wright Mills' "cheerful robot" [44] probably belongs in this category.

(2) This paper can be read as a reply to a recent article by D. C. Hodges in which the author claims that the only party to alienation in the *Manuscripts* is the worker, and that the capitalist is free in the measure that the worker is alienated. I do not know what Hodges would say about the *Holy Family* passage, for he does not mention it. That his case with respect to the *Manuscripts* is weak has, I think, been demonstrated here.

[44] *The Sociological Imagination* (New York, 1959), 171.

Hodges [45] deals with the power of money by saying that "to the enlightened bourgeois it is a means and not an end." [46] But I can find no such enlightened bourgeois in the *Manuscripts*. Hodges exploits Marx's assertion that "if the worker's activity is a torment to him, to another it must be a *delight* and his life's joy." [47] But the *Holy Family* passage shows that Marx took this kind of delight to be compatible with the deepest alienation. I am in full agreement with one of Hodges' theses: Marx's doctrine of alienation does not refer to "the human situation as such." [48] He is not concerned with the alienation of man in general but with the alienation of particular kinds of men. But I deny that the worker is the only kind of man who is alienated.

Nor do I think, with Hodges, that embracing the capitalist within the alienated fold must have the consequence of reducing emphasis on the proletariat as the agency of revolutionary social change. I am, with Hodges, against those who wish to draw this inference, for I have sought (in I) to explain why the capitalists cannot be expected to revolt against their situation.

(3) I would like to suggest that, in proposing his concept of the capitalist who merely owns, Marx is adumbrating the idea of the separation of ownership and management, which has been so popular since Berle and Means.[49] It might be thought that in making this attribution I am trying to vault an unpassable gap between metaphysics and economics, but it is significant that Marx refers to an ownership/management cleavage in the third volume of *Capital*,[50] and assigns a crucial importance to it.

But why, it may be asked, do I suppose that there can be a connection between the phenomenological study of the abstract capitalist, considered in this paper, and the remarks Marx made on a purely empirical basis about the tendencies in capitalist development which lead to the atrophy of the capitalist, as far as the production process is concerned? To generalize the objection: why is it supposed that from the sort of analysis provided in this paper one can reach an understanding of real capitalists in the real world?

I believe I can answer these questions, but here I shall only outline the steps I would take: (1) It can be shown that the worker whose alienation Marx discusses is also a product of abstraction, and was known to be such by Marx. (2) The justification of treating both

[45] "The Young Marx—A Reappraisal," *Philosophy and Phenomenological Research*, 1966–7.   [46] *Ibid.*, 228.

[47] *Ibid.*, 227. Quoted from Martin Milligan's translation: *Economic and Philosophic Manuscripts of 1844* (Moscow, 1956), 79.   [48] *Ibid.*, 224.

[49] *The Modern Corporation and Private Property* (New York, 1932).

[50] See 449–59, 516–18 (Chicago edition).

worker and capitalist abstractly is that bourgeois political economy implicitly does so. (3) The justification of beginning with the abstractions of political economy in an enquiry which purports to be relevant to three-dimensional people is that, for Marx, that science sums up, anticipates, and even prepares the future development of capitalism, for the movement of modern history is a movement towards abstraction, and political economy is the ideal expression of that movement.[51] Complete abstraction can never be achieved because men cannot become completely dehumanized without ceasing to be human beings. What halts the increasing alienation is the socialist revolution,[52] to which bourgeois economists are blind. But Marx thought and said that they were sharp-sighted when they described the condition of man *under* capitalism.

University College, London.

[51] The passages most relevant for establishing the truth of these claims are in Bottomore, 76–7, 82, 137–9, 181.

[52] In which the proletariat brings human existence into harmony with the human essence: *The German Ideology, op. cit.*, 54–5.

XX

THE ECONOMIC PENETRATION OF POLITICAL THEORY: SOME HYPOTHESES

By C. B. Macpherson

I propose to look at the record, over the centuries, of the varying relation between political theory, on the one hand, and on the other, ideas or assumptions that we may properly call economic. Can we explain why economic ideas at some times seem to enter into political theories only slightly if at all, and at other times are there in such strength that they may be said to penetrate the political theory? This is the economic penetration referred to in my title. If there is also in the title an implication that the penetrating quality of a political theory, its ability to get to the root of the political problems it is concerned with, depends somewhat on its economic grasp, I shall not disavow that position. But the economic penetration I am directly concerned with is the penetration of political theory by economic ideas.

I do not say "by economic theory." That would narrow the enquiry too far. For the relation between formal economic theory and political theory is only a small part of the relation I want to look at. It is true that some of the outstanding political theorists have also written treatises or tracts or papers in economic theory—Bodin and Locke, for instance, in monetary theory; Hume and Burke on various problems of economic policy; Bentham on public finance especially; and of course both James and John Stuart Mill produced complete *Elements* or *Principles* of political economy. But it is not always clear whether, or how much, their political thinking was shaped by their formal economic theorizing. With Bentham at least, it seems to be the other way around. In any case, I am after something broader than the relation between formal economic theory and political theory. The economic penetration I want to look at is the entry into political theories, on the ground floor or perhaps one should say in the basement, of ideas or assumptions which may properly be called economic.

I take "economic ideas" to be ideas or assumptions about the necessary or possible relations between people in their capacity as producers of the material means of life. This is not, of course, recognizable as a description of the content of modern economics. In so describing "economic ideas," I am deliberately going back to the classical political economy tradition. There is good reason for doing that, rather than seeking a starting point in modern economics. For, since the late nine-

* Slightly revised version of paper presented at the 1974 meeting of the Conference for the Study of Political Thought, at York University, Toronto, April 19, 1974.

teenth century, economics has largely turned its attention away from that concern which had made earlier economic thought so congruous with political thought, namely, its concern with the relations of dependence and control in which people are placed by virtue of a given system of production. Modern economics has turned instead to treating people as undifferentiated demanders of utilities. Autonomous consumer demand has been taken as the motor of the whole economic system. People are economically related to each other as demanders and exchangers of things which have market values. The central concern has become the market values of the things. Economic relations between people have in effect been reduced to relations between things: the underlying economic relations of dependence and control between people have dropped out of sight.

Twentieth-century economics has thus rendered itself incapable of illuminating political theory. Economic ideas which are confined to relations between things, or to relations between disembodied persons who appear only as the holders of demand schedules, cannot enter into political theory at any fundamental level, since political theory is about relations of dependence and control between people.

We may notice here, incidentally, one unfortunate side-effect of this change in the focus of economic theory. In giving economics a new precision, it made economics an object of admiration and imitation on the part of mid-twentieth century political scientists (who saw that they were far behind in precision). This induced political scientists to carry over into their thinking, by a superficial analogy, the impersonal market model of the marginal-utility equilibrium economists. Hence we have had in recent decades many attempts to explain the democratic political process as a political analogue of the competitive market economy. These explanations do not go very deep.[1] They read back into the political process an economic relation which had already had the real relations of dependence and control taken out of it: they read back a consumers' sovereignty model of the economy without recognizing that the purchasing powers of various consumers are determined by their place in the relations of production.

The twentieth-century political scientists' application of economists' equilibrium models to the modern democratic process might seem to be an outstanding example of the penetration of political theory by economic ideas. But in my view, penetration is just what it is not. The equilibrium market model cannot penetrate political theory because it has abstracted from the power relations with which political theory is concerned. In what follows, therefore, I shall not treat this borrowing

---

[1] Cf. "Market Concepts in Political Theory," in my *Democratic Theory: Essays in Retrieval* (Oxford, 1973), and Ch. IV of my *Life and Times of Liberal Democracy* (Oxford and New York, 1977).

of an economic model by political scientists as a case of economic penetration of political theory.

To return, then, to the question what are to be counted as economic ideas for the purposes of this enquiry. Most broadly, for the reasons just given, I take them to be ideas about the necessary or possible relations between people as producers. And those relations may include, and at least from Aristotle on usually have been taken to include, relations between *classes,* distinguished by their function in the productive system or, more sloppily, by their share of the whole social product.

Moreover, since these relations between individuals and between classes require, and become congealed in, some institutions of *property,* we may take economic ideas to include ideas about the relation of property to other political rights and obligations. I say *other* political rights and obligations, because property is a right which has to be maintained politically. Property, as Bentham said, "is entirely the work of law."[2]

Finally, since observed relations between people as producers are apt to be read back, at a conceptual level, into assumptions about the necessary social relations between people as such, and even into assumptions about the very nature of man, we may include, under the head of economic penetration of political theory, any influence of this sort which we can see in the political theorists' models of society and of man.

How, then, are we to measure the extent of the economic penetration of political theory? As a first approximation we might say that the criterion is the extent to which actual or supposedly necessary or possible economic relations are seen as setting the *problem* of the best possible political order, or setting the problem of justice. As a closer approximation we might take the extent to which economic relations are thought to set not merely the problems, but the inescapable *requirements,* of the political system. Or, if you like, the extent to which it is thought that (to adapt Marx's much quoted statement), the anatomy of political society is to be sought in political economy.[3] And we may treat, as signals of such penetration, the amount of attention, or the centrality of the attention, given to property, or to class.

Another dimension that might be considered is the extent to which the economic assumptions are conscious and explicit, or more accurately, the extent to which there is a conscious and explicit assumption that economic relations set the political problem and set the inescapable requirements of a system of political obligation. But the consciousness and explicitness of this assumption cannot be used as a single measure

[2] *Principles of the Civil Code,* ed. C. K. Ogden (New York, 1931), Part 1, Chap. 8, paragr. 1.

[3] *Contribution to the Critique of Political Economy* (Chicago, 1904; Moscow, 1970), Preface.

of the economic penetration of political theories. For the economic assumptions may get into the political theory only indirectly (but none-theless powerfully) at the level of a generalized model of man or of society which then determines the political theory. Since these models are generally presented as models of man or society as such, their authors cannot be expected to be conscious that they reflect any particular set of economic relations.

In looking for explanations of the varying penetration of political theory by economic assumptions, we may look first for mere correlations between the changing penetration and some other factors, and then enquire if the correlations suggest causal relations.

Looking at the whole sweep of Western political theory—ancient, medieval and modern—one correlation suggests itself, and I shall make this my first hypothesis. I shall state it first in an oversimple form, which is irresistibly suggested by a famous formulation (about something else, namely, the division of labor) by the father of political economy. I shall accordingly offer as my first hypothesis: (1) *That the economic penetration of political theory varies with the extent of the market.* More accurately this should be, varies with the extent to which market relations have permeated the society, or, the extent to which the relations between people as producers are market relations.

This hypothesis is suggested by looking simply as the broad contrasts between ancient, medieval, and modern theory. The political theorists in all three eras paid some attention to property and class, and to economic relations more generally, but the extent of their interest in them was rather different, and they let them enter their political theories in different ways.

Plato and Aristotle lived in a somewhat market-oriented society, a society more market-oriented than the medieval, though nothing like as much so as the modern. Their society was still near enough to a household or simple peasant and artisan exchange economy, that standards appropriate to those could be thought natural. And the rest of the productive labor was mainly slave labor, not labor exchanged in a market between laborers and buyers of labor. So the market had not permeated society, although Aristotle's strictures on unnatural money-making show that he was dealing with a fairly commercialized society. Yet Plato and Aristotle neither created man in the image of market man nor allowed that economic relations between men set the main problems or the inescapable requirements of the polity. They saw the state as not at all *for* the economy, but as having a much higher purpose. The household and the village were for the material requirements of life, the *polis* was for the good life. They did not, that is to say, allow economic assumptions to penetrate their political thinking very far. They not only put other values higher than material ones—almost all political theorists have done that—but they tried to design a polity which would provide the good life by counteracting or limiting the play of economic motives which they thought deplorable, sometimes unnatural, and at any rate always less than fully human.

Medieval society was on the whole less market-oriented; and medieval theory, at least before the rediscovery of Aristotle, showed even less economic penetration. Until then, there was not much more economic content than the Augustinian explanation of private property as punishment for, and partial remedy for the effects of, original sin.

As we move into the modern period, in which society becomes more and more permeated with market relations, with labor itself soon becoming a market commodity, the penetration of economic assumptions into political theory becomes increasingly evident. From relatively small beginnings in Machiavelli, who saw at least a necessary correspondence between a political system and the class structure, and made the class structure depend not just on amounts of property but on the kind of property (feudal vs. mercantile), there is an increasingly full assumption that economic relations set the dominant requirements of the political system. Hobbes deduced his whole system of political obligation from a model of bourgeois man, and a model of society as a market in men's powers. Locke, seeing a man's labor as an alienable and generally alienated commodity, and consequently seeing society as naturally class-divided, was able from those assumptions to justify a class state from his initial postulate of equal natural rights. For Hume, the origin of justice, and the whole need for the state, lay in man's numberless material wants and the consequent need not only for joint labor but also for exchange and contracts. Burke and Bentham made capital accumulation through market operations the *sine qua non* of civilization, and made security for capital accumulation an essential, if not the essential, function of the state.

So one could go on. The overall pattern is fairly clear: the penetration of political theory by economic assumptions has varied roughly with the extent to which market relations have permeated society. As far as it goes, then, the pattern supports my first hypothesis.

But granting that there is historically such a correlation, is there any reason for it? Is there any causal relation? One such relation suggests itself at once. Market society requires a kind of individual freedom not found in non-market societies. It requires that men be owners of something, free to sell what they own, exempt from most of the constrictions that prevail in non-market societies. Market society encourages, even enforces, rational maximizing behavior by all individuals. In doing so, it makes man restless. So the emergence and development of market relations raises new problems for political stability, and for any other political goals; and it is only a matter of time until perceptive political theorists see the source of the new problems, and see that they require an economic perspective.

This suggests a second subsidiary hypothesis, which must however be treated with some caution and probably should be discarded. *Hypothesis 2* is: *That the economic penetration of political theory varies with the extent of recent or current change in actual economic relations.* The actual change could of course only be correlated with the theorists' awareness of the change, which is obviously the operative factor, if we assume a standard acuteness or standard time-lag in the theorists' perception. This is a risky assumption, but it might be allowed over a very long run.

The main support for the second hypothesis lies in the contrast between the medieval period and either the ancient or the modern. There was not, comparatively speaking, much economic change in medieval society; and the comparative lack of change does correspond to the comparative lack of economic penetration of political theory in the medieval era.

But when one looks within either the ancient or the modern period, the hypothesis seems rather shaky. For in many cases it is not clear whether the theorist saw the actual economic relations which he did admit into his political thinking, as something new, something recently changed, or currently changing.

Aristotle certainly saw and deplored an accumulative mercantile society. But did he see it as a recent change? One might conclude, by inference from the position he took about unnatural money-making and about limited property, that he did not, or at least that he did not see it as an irreversible change. For what he did was to apply standards appropriate to a household or simple exchange economy to what was, by his own account of it, an advanced exchange economy driven by desire to accumulate without limit.

And in the modern period, the towering figure of Hobbes presents similar doubts. Hobbes saw (and regretted) that market man and market society were here to stay, but he fell short of recognizing clearly that this was a recent change. Now he saw it, now he didn't. His analysis of the causes of the Civil War, in *Behemoth,* does recognize it. But in *Leviathan,* and his other two theoretical treatises, there is no such recognition: in them he presents his models of man and society, which we can see are bourgeois models, as models of man and society as such. Not until the eighteenth century, in Millar and Ferguson, Hume and Adam Smith, with their three or four stages, do we find a clear recognition that society *has* changed by virtue of changes in the productive relations; and not until Rousseau do we find both a recognition that man and society have so changed, and a belief that man may change, or be changed, again.

In view of these outstanding doubtful cases, I think we should discard the second hypothesis. We are back then with nothing but the extent of the market. But this does not take us far with the changes observable within the period of the modern market society, particularly the changes within the liberal tradition from, say, Locke to the present.

There I see one fairly clear pattern of economic penetration of political theory, but it is not at all clear, at first sight, to what other factors this corresponds. The pattern is one of increasing economic penetration of liberal political theory from Locke through to Bentham and James Mill, and decreasing economic penetration from John Stuart Mill to the present. In the first period it is increasingly fully and explicitly assumed that economic relations are what set the problem and the requirements of political obligation and rights, set the problem of justice and the purpose of the state. To see this one need only compare Locke's fudge with the clarity of Hume and Bentham about the centrality of economic relations. Parallel with this, there is the increasing explanatory depth of political economy, from Petty and Boisguille-bert, through the Physiocrats and Adam Smith, to Ricardo.

One is tempted to the simple hypothesis that, with the increase of the scale of the full market economy, political economy got an increasingly better grasp of the essentials of the economy, and that, correspondingly, political theorists were more influenced by political economy. Certainly the personal links became closer—Hume and Adam Smith, Adam Smith and Burke, Economistes and Encyclopédistes, James Mill and Ricardo.

Now the improvement in political economy was due to its increasing recognition of a class of industrial and agricultural (rather than mercantile) capitalists, whose share of the whole annual produce of the nation, i.e., profit, was seen to be not wages of superintendance, nor akin to rent or interest, nor merely from taking advantage of momentary terms of trade. Instead, it was seen to be the excess of the value added by the current labor which that capital employed over the wage paid. This amounts to a recognition that profit was due to the extractive or exploitive power of capital. One is therefore tempted to the further hypothesis that the economic penetration of liberal theory varies directly with the recognition, by the political and economic theorists, of the necessarily exploitive or extractive nature of market relations in a fully capitalist society.

Let us see if this is a feasible working hypothesis. An immediate objection that may be made to it is that the political economists, although they increasingly saw profit as a deduction from the value added by labor, did not see this as exploitive. It is true they did not. That is, in their formal economic theories of wages and profits there is no notion of exploitation. The reason for this is plain. *Given* the pattern of ownership which they assumed, everyone got a fair reward for what he put in. They assumed the necessary and permanent division of all modern and progressive societies into three classes: those whose income derived from (a) ownership of land, (b) ownership of capital, and (c) ownership only of their own capacity to labor. They assumed this without asking how these classes were formed. But they were well enough aware that that pattern of ownership itself was broadly exploitive. They saw that in any society in which there was a class without any material productive property (and this included the capitalist market society), that class was *used* by the others. Adam Smith made this point, and drew a political conclusion, in a well-known passage: "Whenever there is great property, there is great inequality. For one very rich man, there must be at least five hundred poor, and the affluence of the rich supposes the indigence of the many. The affluence of the rich excites the indignation of the poor, who are often both driven by want, and prompted by envy, to invade his possessions. It is only under the shelter of the civil magistrate that the owner of that valuable property, which is acquired by the labour of many years, or perhaps of many successive generations, can sleep a single night in security. . . . The acquisition of valuable and extensive property, therefore, necessarily requires the establishment of civil government. Where there is no property, or at least none that exceeds the value of two or three days' labour, civil government is not so necessary."[4] And again: "Civil government, so far as it is instituted for the security of property is in reality instituted for the defence of the rich against the poor, or of those who have some property against those who have none at all."[5]

The classical liberal political theorists, whether or not they also wrote economics, were similarly outspoken, and increasingly so from Locke to Bentham. And this went along with an increasing tendency to see the job of the state as set by economic relations: in other words it went along with an increasing economic peneration of political theory. So I shall put as *Hypothesis 3: That the economic penetration of political theory varies with the theorists' recognition of the necessarily exploitive or extractive nature of market relations in a society divided into owners and non-owners of productive material property.* A glance at some highlight of liberal theory from Locke to Bentham offers some support for this.

Locke, in making the protection of property the chief end for which men enter civil society and set up government, blurred the relation by including in "property" life, liberty, and estate. But he was explicit that it was *unequal* material property that was to be protected, and he took for granted a society in which some had nothing but their labor to sell. He combined this with a rudimentary labor theory of value, but he did not draw the conclusion that the laboring class was exploited.

Hume, more clearly than Locke, saw government as needed only when great and unequal property had been accumulated, and went

---

[4] *Wealth of Nations*, Bk. V, Ch. 1, part ii (Modern Library ed., 670).
[5] *Ibid.*, 674.

beyond Locke in relating this to the emergence of the market: government is needed when the market comes to include men totally unknown to us. Hume goes on from a utilitarian justification of individual property in land and goods to an explicit recognition that *market* relations are the fundamental relations of society. The right of private property, the right to exchange property, and the obligation of contracts are asserted to be the three fundamental natural laws because they are all necessary for a market society. He assumed that there would always be a class of laboring poor, but he was still some way from seeing this as exploitive. That is, he did not single this out as *the* exploitive relation, though he thought almost all social relations were determined by the avidity of conflicting individual material desires.

Diderot likewise made property the *raison d'être* of the state, but went further in seeing the exploitive nature of property. Not only did he see that wage-labor is employed only because it produces a profit for the employer: he also saw that it condemned many to an inhuman existence.

Les mines du Hartz recèlent dans leurs immenses profondeurs des milliers d'hommes qui connaissent à peine la lumière du soleil et qui atteignent rarement l'âge de trente ans. C'est là qu'on voit des femmes qui ont eu douze maris.
Si vous fermez ces vastes tombeaux, vous ruinez l'État et vous condamnez tous les sujets de la Saxe ou à mourir de faim ou à s'expatrier.
Combien d'ateliers dans la France même, moins nombreux, mais presque aussi funestes![6]

Diderot saw no alternative to the exploitive wage-relation, but hoped for some regulation of it. And he was a more consistent utilitarian than Bentham was to be, for he held that a smaller net product equally distributed is better than a larger net product so unequally distributed as to divide people into rich and poor classes.[7] Diderot saw no way out of the contradiction between the wage relation and human values, but at least he saw the contradiction.

Burke, who insisted that there was a natural functional order of subordination between laborers and capitalists, and wrote that "the laws of commerce . . . are the laws of nature, and consequently the laws of God,"[8] made capital accumulation the *sine qua non* of civilization. He recognized, in words very like Diderot's, the exploitation inseparable from it, but he would permit no interference with it. Referring to "the innumerable servile, degrading, unseemly, unmanly, and often most

---

[6] *Réfutation d'Helvétius, Oeuvres Complètes de Diderot, éd. Assezat* (Paris, 1875), II, 430-31.
[7] *Encyclopédie*, art. Homme (politique).
[8] *Thoughts and Details on Scarcity, Works* (Oxford World's Classics, 1907), VI, 22.

unwholesome and pestiferous occupations, to which by the social economy so many wretches are inevitably doomed," he insisted that it would be "pernicious to disturb the natural course of things, and to impede, in any degree, the great wheel of circulation which is turned by the strangely-directed labour of these unhappy people."[9]

Bentham similarly did not mince matters. "In the highest state of social prosperity," he wrote, "the great mass of citizens will have no resource except their daily industry; and consequently will be always near indigence. . . ."[10] It was the fate of those without property to be so used. This was the inevitable outcome of the fact that "human beings are the most powerful instruments of production, and therefore everyone becomes anxious to employ the services of his fellows in multiplying his own comforts. Hence the intense and universal thirst for power; the equally prevalent hatred of subjection."[11] And Bentham was clear that security of property must have priority over the claims of equality: "When security and equality are in conflict, it will not do to hesitate a moment. Equality must yield."[12] This was in spite of the fact that Bentham had shown that, by the principle of diminishing utility, aggregate utilities would be maximized by complete equality of property. But equality was incompatible with capital accumulation and hence with maximization of wealth.

If I might venture a slight digression, I should say that Bentham had done the same thing as the neo-classical economists were to do at the end of the nineteenth century. As Joan Robinson has pointed out about Marshall *et al.*: "The method by which the egalitarian element in the [marginal utility] doctrine was sterilized was mainly by slipping from *utility* to physical output as the object to be maximized. A small total of physical goods, equally distributed, admittedly may yield more *utility* than a much larger total unequally distributed, but if we keep our eye on the total of goods it is easy to forget about utility."[13] This is just what Bentham had done. Security of property, he argued, must be put ahead of equality because security is necessary to maximize physical output, not utility: he did not notice that he had slipped from one to the other.

With James Mill we touch the high point of recognition of the exploitive nature of market society, though he fetched it from a principle of human nature which he held to be universal. "The desire . . . of that power which is necessary to render the persons and properties of human beings subservient to our pleasures, is a grand governing law of human nature. . . . The grand instrument for attaining what a man

---

[9] *Reflections on the Revolution in France* (Pelican Classics ed. 1968, 271).
[10] *Principles of the Civil Code*, Part I, Chap. 14, Sect. 1.
[11] *Economic Writings* (ed. Stark), 1954, III, 430.
[12] *Principles of the Civil Code*, Part I, Chap. 11, para. 3.
[13] *Economic Philosophy* (London, 1962), 55.

likes is the actions of other men."[14] So everyone seeks exploitive power over others. This view is not carried into his formal economic analysis of wages and profits. But there is in his *Elements of Political Economy* a suggestive passage about slave labor and wage labor. "The only difference" between the manufacturer who operates with slaves and the manufacturer who operates with free laborers, "is, in the mode of purchasing. The owner of the slave purchases, at once, the whole of the labour which the man can ever perform: he, who pays wages, purchases only so much of a man's labour as he can perform in a day, or any other stipulated time. Being equally, however, the owner of the labour, so purchased, as the owner of the slave is of that of the slave, the produce, which is the result of this labour, combined with his capital, is all equally his own."[15] Mill's readers would assume that the slave relation was wholly exploitive. For Mill to say, then, that the only difference between it and the wage relation is in the mode of purchasing, is to leave a pretty plain implication that the wage relation is equally exploitive.

It may be noted that, in this catalogue of classical liberal theorists, those who held most strongly that society was necessarily contentious and hence exploitive—namely, Hume, Bentham, and James Mill— asserted this of society as such, not just of capitalist society. But they were able to assert it to be inherent in any society only because they had put into the very nature of man the motivations of bourgeois man. Hume deduced the necessary opposition of passions and consequent opposition of actions from a postulate of insatiable material desire: "This avidity alone, of acquiring goods and possessions for ourselves and our nearest friends, is insatiable, perpetual, universal. . . ."[16] James Mill's "grand governing law of human nature" takes this a step further, as does Bentham's self-evident proposition, already quoted, that because human beings are the most powerful instruments of production, everyone tries to use everyone else. And Bentham brought this to a finer point by making the pleasure of acquisition stronger than the pleasure of possession. "It is the pleasure of acquisition, not the satisfaction of possessing, which gives the greatest delights."[17] Possession is of course needed to consolidate acquisition, and is helpful as a means to further acquisition.

Thus all three theorists read back into human nature their observation of bourgeois man—man as infinite appropriator. Having done this,

---

[14] *Government,* Sect. IV, ed. Barker (Cambridge, 1937), 17.

[15] *Elements,* Chap. 1, Sect. 2 (in Winch, ed., *Selected Economic Writings* (1966), 219).

[16] *Treatise,* Bk. III, Part 2, Sect. 2, in F. Watkins, ed., *Hume, Theory of Politics* (1961), 41.

[17] *Principles of the Civil Code,* Part I, Chap. 6; in *Theory of Legislation,* ed. C. K. Ogden, 105.

and having made this the reason why government was necessary, they saw no need for further explanation nor any need to make excuses for the social relations it produced.

I find, then, in the classical liberal tradition from Locke to Bentham and James Mill, an increasing recognition of the exploitative nature of a society based on the capital/wage-labor relation, and a corresponding increase in the extent to which the job of the state was thought to be set by economic relations.

With John Stuart Mill and T. H. Green (and their twentieth-century liberal followers) there is a remarkable change. There is in them no recognition, indeed there is a denial, of the exploitative nature of capital; and there is correspondingly a decline in the extent to which the job of the state was thought to be set by economic relations.

It may seem strange to take John Stuart Mill as the watershed, as the beginning of a declining economic penetration of political theory. For in no other theorist is there such a massive relation between political theory and political economy: no one wrote more about both, or linked them so deliberately. But the link is not direct: both are linked to social philosophy. And it was a social philosophy which departed from the utilitarian tradition precisely in its denial that all human values could or should be furthered by or reduced to the market: that was the upshot of Mill's introduction of qualitative differences in pleasures. Mill was concerned to rescue human values from their then subordination to the market. The job of the state was not to facilitate an endless increase in the production of wealth but to fashion a society with higher ends. He was thus, we might say, opposed in principle to the economic penetration of political theory.

At the same time he failed to see that the wage/capital relation was by its nature extractive or exploitive. He saw indeed the exploitation in nineteenth-century society, and denounced it in the strongest terms. Nothing was more unjust than the prevailing relation between work and reward, by which the produce of labor is apportioned "almost in an inverse ratio to the labour—the largest portions to those who have never worked at all, the next largest to those whose work is almost nominal, and so in a decreasing scale, the remuneration dwindling as the work grows harder and more disagreeable, until the most fatiguing and exhausting bodily labour cannot count with certainty on being able to earn even the necessaries of life. . . ."[18] But he insisted, as did T. H. Green, that this was not inherent in the capital/labor relation, but was due to something else—the original (feudal) forcible seizure of the land, and the failure of subsequent governments to counteract its effects.

---

[18] *Principles of Political Economy* (Toronto and London, 1965), Bk. II, Chap. 1, Sect. 3. (*Collected Works*, II, 207).

He even argued that "industry" has for many centuries been modifying the work of force (*ibid.*).

Thus, where the earlier liberals had seen that capitalist profit was a deduction from labor's production, but had seen no need to reconcile this with a principle of equity because the system led to increased wealth all around, Mill rejected wealth as the criterion, insisted on a principle of equity, preferred a stationary economy to the rat-race of his contemporary society, but did not see that the prevailing inequity, and the trampling and elbowing, were inherent in the capitalist relation.

It is not just that he did not put exploitation into his economic theory of the determinants of wages and profits. No more, as we have noticed, did Adam Smith or James Mill. But in their cases it was because they made the wealth of the nation the grand criterion, and assumed the inevitability of existing classes, so did not see any need to justify or excuse the prevailing distribution. John Stuart Mill did see that that distribution was not automatically justified. He was the first of the liberals to see this, and to say it. He saw that there was a gap between his idea of maximized utility and the actual utilities that were produced by the class-divided society of his time. He saw that there was something to be explained. But he could not explain it except by denying that the exploitive relation was inherent in the capitalist relation.

Some would argue that Mill's well-known disjunction between the laws of production and the pattern of distribution[19] was his answer to, or his way of avoiding, the difficulty that a competitive market economy in which every bargain was entirely fair would result in a distribution which was utterly inequitable. If this disjunction was intended as such, it was a very poor logical resolution of the difficulty. For the disjunction he made was not between the social relations of production and the social distribution of the product, but merely between the physical laws (e.g. of the fertility of the soil, and hence diminishing returns on increasing applications of labor to the same land) which limit production in any system, whatever are the social relations of production, and any particular system of social distribution. His disjunction was perfectly valid, but it did not meet the difficulty. He simply did not see that capitalist production entailed capitalist distribution, or that the distribution was a co-requisite of the production. Instead, he attributed the inequity of the existing distribution to an historical factor extraneous to the system of production.

Accordingly, he did not see that men's economic relations set the requirements of the political system. In moving away from utility, by redefining it qualitatively, he moved his political theory away from political economy. And T. H. Green, starting from a different base,

---

[19] *Principles*, Bk. II, Chap. 1, Sect. 1 (*Works*, II, 199-200).

came full circle back to the Greek ideal of the good life as something apart from and even opposed to material maximization.

This retreat from economic assumptions was not, I think, simply coincidental with the failure to see the necessarily exploitive nature of capitalist productive relations. Both were perhaps due to a third factor: the increasingly evident incompatibility, in the nineteenth century, between the dehumanizing actual economic relations and any morally acceptable vision of a human society. All political theorists, not least those in the liberal tradition, have some vision of human needs and human excellence, and hence a vision of a humanly desirable society. Incompatibility between the exploitive nature of capitalist market relations and a humanistic ethic had not been a serious problem for the seventeenth- and eighteenth-century political theorists. They could, and did, square the massive inequality of the accumulative society based on free contract and wage-labor with a humanistic vision, by pointing out that the market society raised and could continue to raise the general level of material well-being. Since they saw this as a *necessary* condition of moral and cultural improvement, they did not look too closely at the question whether it was also a *sufficient* condition for that improvement.

But by the middle of the nineteenth century this would no longer suffice. The quality of life for the mass of the people in that unequal society had become so blatantly wretched that it could no longer be excused by the ability of the system to go on increasing the national wealth. Sensitive liberals such as Mill found the condition of the working class morally insupportable. Mill's way out, as we have seen, was to attribute the evil to something other than the capitalist relation.

But now we must notice another factor which contributed to the liberal change of position. Not only did sensitive liberals find the conditions of the working-class insupportable. So did some emerging working-class movements which were making their weight felt politically. There was thus an objective factor, a factor beyond the subjective humanistic perception of sensitive liberals, and it was the objective change that sparked the subjective one. Mill, writing in 1845 of the effects of the Chartist movement, which he described as "the revolt of nearly all the active talent, and a great part of the physical force, of the working classes, against their whole relation to society" said that "among the more fortunate classes . . . some by the physical and moral circumstances which they saw around them, were made to feel that the conditions of the labouring classes *ought* to be attended to, others were made to see that it *would* be attended to, whether they wished to be blind to it or not." He concluded: "It was no longer disputable that something must be done to render the multitude more content with the existing state of things."[20]

[20] *The Claims of Labour*, in *Dissertations and Discussions*, II, 188-90; and in *Collected Works* (1967), IV, 369-70.

This suggests that my third hypothesis can be taken one step further. Hypothesis 3 was that the penetration of political theory by economic ideas varies with the theorists' recognition of the necessarily exploitive or extractive nature of market relations in a society divided into owners and non-owners of productive material property. What may be thought a weakness of that hypothesis is that it merely relates one mental operation with another: the theorist's admission of economic assumptions with his *perception* of a certain inherent relation in society.

But now, if my point about Mill is right, we may substitute an external factor for that perception. Instead of a theorist's perception of the inherent exploitiveness of the capitalist relation, we may look to the *exploited class's* perception of its exploitation, and its consequent political action. Thus, for liberal theory, we would have the following proposition: the economic penetration of political theory varies *inversely* with the political strength of an exploited class. And, of course, for socialist theory, which speaks in the name of the exploited class, the economic penetration of the political theory would be expected to vary *directly* with the political strength of an exploited class.

We may frame this as *Hypothesis 4: That the economic penetration of political theory varies with the political strength of an exploited class; directly in socialist theory, inversely in liberal theory.* This hypothesis is borne out pretty well in both traditions.

In the socialist tradition, Marx may fairly be regarded as the high point of economic penetration of political theory, and his was the period of maximum political strength of class-conscious working-class action in the Western nations. Revisionist and Fabian theory, and subsequent democratic socialist theory, have corresponded with (and no doubt contributed to) declining class-conscious political action.

In the liberal tradition the inverse correspondence is fairly clear for the seventeenth to nineteenth centuries, in the line I have already sketched: the economic penetration increasing from Locke to Bentham, a period when the threat from below was at least quiescent if not decreasing—(it is true that Burke and Malthus saw a threat in the repercussions of the French Revolution, but Bentham and Ricardo and James Mill did not); then, from John Stuart Mill on through the rest of the nineteenth century, the economic penetration decreasing as the threat from below increased.

What about subsequent liberal tradition? I see, in the twentieth century, a continuation of that line. From Ernest Barker and A. D. Lindsay and John Dewey to, say, Maurice Cranston and John Rawls,[21] the economic penetration of liberal political theory has decreased. And its decrease is correlated with an increase in the apprehended threat

---

[21] Cf. my "Rawls's Models of Man and Society," *Philosophy of the Social Sciences* (Dec. 1973), 341-47.

to bourgeois liberal societies, not so much a threat by any *indigenous* class-conscious exploited class (for these have not amounted to much in the economically advanced Western nations in this century) but by the global threat of the socialist and Third World societies. It would be astonishing if liberal theorists in countries which, either directly, or indirectly as client states or nostalgic states, rely on global exploitation, did not respond, even if only subconsciously, to that threat. I see them as having done so, and hence as bearing out Hypothesis 4.

It may be objected that I have contradicted myself in referring the twentieth-century change in the Western *socialist* tradition to a *decline* in the political strength of the exploited, and the change in the *liberal* tradition to an *increase* in the threat from those presently or formerly transnationally exploited; it may be thought that the distinction I have made between indigenous and transnational threats is too artificial to hold my case together. But we may see a further unifying factor here, namely, the increasingly uncertain viability of capitalist society. The perception of this by liberal theorists makes them retreat from economic penetration to idealism. The same perception by socialist theorists in the affluent countries easily leads them to think that capitalism cannot keep going without submitting to steadily erosive reforms, and so leads them to press for concessions rather than confrontation, and to bend their theory towards reformism, with some lack of economic penetration.

I doubt if this explanation can be pressed very far, at least without a good deal of refinement and qualification. And since it concerns only the twentieth century (and only some developments within that time-span) it cannot serve as a general hypothesis. But it does suggest one further general hypothesis which is applicable to the whole rise and fall of the economic penetration of political theory from the seventeenth century on. If we look back over that stretch, which comprises the emergence and maturation and faltering of capitalism, we may entertain the idea, as *Hypothesis 5, That the economic penetration of political theory varies with the theorists' confidence in the ability of an emerging or established economic order to maximize human well-being and to achieve or maintain political dominance.* This may be said to hold both for the rise and decline of the economic penetration of liberal theory from the seventeenth century till now, and for its decline in Western socialist theory from Marx till now. It also appears to hold for the continuance and revival of Marxism in the non-Western world in this century.

The same weakness might be seen in this hypothesis as was seen in Hypothesis 3, namely, that it merely relates one mental operation to another—the theorists' use of economic assumptions with their confidence in some actual or possible economic relations. It would no doubt be tidier if we could reduce the latter to some external factor such as the actual performance of an economic system. We can do so in part, but not entirely.

An improving performance is indeed apt to bring increasing confidence in an existing system. And a faltering performance is apt to bring decreasing confidence in an existing system by its beneficiaries. But the faltering performance of an existing system also brings an *increasing* confidence, by its *non*-beneficiaries, in the possibilities of what they see as an emerging alternative system. This I take to have been as true of Adam Smith as of Marx.

To put the point most generally, confidence in an established or emergent economic system is not reducible to any external factor, because the possibility of an emergent one depends partly on people's perception of such new possibility. I do not see any determinate relation between actual performance and such perception. There are time-lags. There are variations induced by the operation of the system itself. There are different perceptions, by different sections of the community, of the relative value of aggregate affluence and general quality of life. Opinion in one nation may be compelled by changes outside to make a different valuation of the limits of the prevailing system and the possibility of alternatives.

All these things may be seen as happening in our own day. Even some economists have begun to count the cost of economic growth. An optimistic view is that quality of life will get the upper hand, and that we will move away from a society permeated by market behavior and material maximization. If my first hypothesis still governed then, the economic penetration of political theory would decline. But we should not expect a constant ratio to be maintained during such a move. At the theoretical end-point we might indeed expect it: with zero market there would presumably be zero economic penetration of political theory, if only because there would be zero political economy. Indeed, if, as I suppose, the full transcendence of market behavior requires an end of scarcity, might there not in that case be zero political theory? That is the logical conclusion that would follow from the postulates of classical liberal theory, which tied political obligation, rights and justice to scarcity; as Hume put it: "it is only from the selfishness and confined generosity of men, along with the scanty provision nature has made for his wants, that justice derives its origin . . . it is evident that the . . . extensive generosity of man, and the perfect abundance of everything, would destroy the very idea of justice . . . because they render it useless."[22]

However that may be—and it is surely not just one's professional bias as a political theorist that makes one resist the notion of the end

---

[22] *Treatise of Human Nature,* Bk. III, Part 2, Sect. 2 (in F. Watkins, ed.), 45-46.

of political theory—any move from a market-dominated society to a non-market-dominated society will clearly need the services both of political theory and political economy. And it will need a political theory that recognizes the determining role of necessary and possible relations between people as producers. If need always brought forth what is needed, we would be sure of a continued presence, indeed a revival from the present low point in Western political theory, of economic penetration. But if demand creates supply, we should still have to ask, whose demand? and the answer might not be very encouraging. Or if supply creates demand, we are no better off, for economic thought of the fundamental sort needed by political theory is now in rather short supply. The conclusion which seems inescapable is that we ourselves as political theorists will have to augment the supply, and take the lead in restoring to political theory the economic insight it once enjoyed.

University of Toronto.